MW01630977

Islamic Chinoiserie

Edinburgh Studies in Islamic Art

Series Editor: Professor Robert Hillenbrand

Advisory Editors: Bernard O'Kane and Jonathan M. Bloom

Titles include:

Isfahan and its Palaces: Statecraft, Shiʿism and the Architecture of Conviviality in Early Modern Iran
Sussan Babaie

Minaret: Symbol of Islam
Jonathan M. Bloom

Islamic Chinoiserie: The Art of Mongol Iran
Yuka Kadoi

Islamic Chinoiserie

The Art of Mongol Iran

Yuka Kadoi

Edinburgh University Press

Edinburgh University Press Ltd
22 George Square, Edinburgh
www.euppublishing.com

Typeset in 10/12 pt Trump Mediaeval by
Servis Filmsetting Ltd, Stockport, Cheshire, and
Printed in Spain at Graficas Santamaria S. A.
by arrangement with Associated Agencies Ltd, Oxford

A CIP record for this book is available from the British Library

ISBN 978 0 7486 3582 5 (hardback)

Published in association with al-Sabah Collection, Dar al-Athar
al-Islamiyyah, Kuwait.

Contents

Figures

Series Editor's Foreword

Edinburgh Studies in Islamic Art is a new venture that offers readers easy access to the most up-to-date research across the whole range of Islamic art. Building on the long and distinguished tradition of Edinburgh University Press in publishing books on the Islamic world, it is intended to be a forum for studies that, while closely focused, also open wide horizons. Books in the series will, for example, concentrate in an accessible way on the art of a single century, dynasty or geographical area; on the meaning of works of art; on a given medium in a restricted time frame; or on analyses of key works in their wider contexts. A balance will be maintained as far as possible between successive titles, so that various parts of the Islamic world and various media and approaches are represented.

Books in the series are academic monographs of intellectual distinction that mark a significant advance in the field. While they are naturally aimed at an advanced and graduate academic audience, a complementary target readership is the worldwide community of specialists in Islamic art – professionals who work in universities, research institutes, auction houses and museums – as well as that elusive character, the interested general reader.

Professor Robert Hillenbrand

Preface and Acknowledgements

This book is the result of my scholarly journey across the vast area of the Eurasian continent in search of the origin of chinoiserie. My love of chinoiserie stems from my obsession with the image of China, which has touched my heart since I chanced upon Chinese pagodas in Meissen wares some twenty years ago. This led me first to wander up and down Europe and the Middle East as a traveller to discover the essence of this artistic and cultural phenomenon, eventually to choose chinoiserie in Iranian art under the Mongols as the topic of my doctoral research and finally to turn my brainchild into a book. To challenge such a fascinating but laborious subject was not an easy task: it required perseverance, stamina and even courage. The topic did, however, gratify my research desire so strongly that I am convinced that I shall never lose my passion and enthusiasm to continue its further study.

It did not take me so long to find out that chinoiserie is not just an art-historical matter. The Meissen pagodas and other sinicising modes, such as Chinese dragons found in the art of Mongol Iran, are deeply rooted in a vital aspect of the human psyche – curiosity. Indeed, chinoiserie conveys positive signals of understanding other cultures, as well as of generating new ideas. While the term 'Islamic chinoiserie' in itself is somewhat contradictory, particularly for those who have a clichéd view of Islamicness in Islamic art and exoticism in chinoiserie, the outcome of this amalgamation was, which I hope that this book proves, a happy, eternal marriage.

My first debt of gratitude is to Professor Robert Hillenbrand for the advice, comments and humour that he offered me during my doctoral research in Edinburgh. It is therefore a distinct honour to publish this book in the Edinburgh Studies of Islamic Art under his editorship. I am also indebted to Edinburgh University Press, especially to Mrs Nicola Ramsey, who commissioned this book, and to Mr Eddie Clark, who guided the book through production with much patience.

My research was made a pleasure through the help and encouragement of numerous individuals, and my scholarly debts are found in the notes and the bibliography. Any mistakes are, needless to say, solely my responsibility. I am particularly grateful to Professor Bernard O'Kane for his invaluable comments on my doctoral dissertation, from which this book grew, and to three Chinese art lecturers in Edinburgh while I was undertaking this research, namely Dr Anita Chung, Dr Hongxing Zhang and Dr Hsueh-man Shen, for their help and wisdom. My special thanks also go to Professor Mayumi Tsuruoka for her continuous encouragement throughout the past fifteen years.

The writing of this book was made possible through research grants from the following organisations: the Barakat Trust, University of Oxford; the Gen Foundation, London; the Iran Heritage Foundation, London; the Kashima Art Foundation, Japan; the Overseas Research Students Scheme; and the School of Arts, Culture and Environment (formerly the Faculty of Arts), University of Edinburgh. My postdoctoral research at the Institute for Advanced Studies in the Humanities, University of Edinburgh, and the Warburg Institute, University of London, gave me wonderful opportunities to rethink the problem of chinoiserie from an inter disciplinary point of view. Equally valuable was my professional experience at the University of Edinburgh, the Museum of Islamic Art in Doha and the Art Institute of Chicago. I also wish to express my gratitude to the following institutions, which gave me permission to work on their collections: the Bibliothèque nationale de la France, Paris; the Freer and Sackler Gallery of Art, Washington, DC; the Special Collections, Edinburgh University Library; the Staatsbibliothek zu Berlin – Stiftung Preussischer Kulturbesitz, Orientabteilung, Berlin); and the Topkapı Saray Palace Library, Istanbul. The illustrations are acknowledged individually on the captions, with a special indebtedness to the al-Sabah Collection, Dar al-Athar al-Islamiyya, Kuwait, for its generous grant. Every effort has been made to trace copyright-holders, but if any have been inadvertently overlooked, the publisher will be pleased to make the necessary arrangements at the first opportunity.

I express my sincere thanks to my parents and sister for their long-term support, and the same debt goes to Mr Roy and Mrs Jean Faulkner, my 'Scottish parents'. Special thanks are also due to my friends from all over the world for their help and encouragement, and, above all, to Thorsten Hanke, who is behind the completion of this project.

Yuka Kadoi
South Queensferry, 2008

Note on Transliteration

For the sake of simplicity, I have eliminated most diacriticals of Persian and Arabic names and terms. For the romanisation of Chinese, I have used the *pinyin* system, except for widely recognised forms of spelling, such as Taipei (Taibei). For the Hijri date, I have followed Bosworth's *The New Islamic Dynasty* (1996), thus citing the Christian year in which the Hijri year begins.

Abbreviations

AA	*Artibus Asiae*
AB	*Art Bulletin*
AI	*Ars Islamica*
AO	*Ars Orientalis*
AP	R. Ettinghausen, *Arab Painting* (Geneva, 1962; repr. 1977)
BAI	*Bulletin of the Asia Institute*, NS
BL	British Library, London
BM	British Museum, London
BN	Bibliothèque nationale de la France, Paris
Bonn/Munich	*Dschingis Khan und seine Erben: Das Weltreich der Mongolen*, Kunst- und Ausstellungshalle der Bundesrepublik Deutschland, Bonn; Staatliches Museum für Völkerkunde, Munich (catalogue of exhibition, 2005)
BSOAS	*Bulletin of the School of Oriental and African Studies*
CAJ	*Central Asiatic Journal*
CHI	*Cambridge History of Iran*, 7 vols (Cambridge, 1986–91)
CP	J. Cahill, *Chinese Painting* (Geneva, 1960)
DA	*Dictionary of Art*, ed. J. Turner, 34 vols (London, 1996)
EI[1]	*Encyclopaedia of Islam* (1st edn)
EI[2]	*Encyclopaedia of Islam* (2nd edn)
EIr	*Encyclopaedia Iranica*
FGA	Freer Gallery of Art, Smithsonian Institution, Washington, DC
GH	M. B. Piotrovsky (ed.), *The Treasures of the Golden Horde* (St Petersburg, 2000)
Hayward	D. Jones and G. Michell (eds), *The Arts of Islam*, Hayward Gallery, London (London, 1976)
IA	*Islamic Art: An Annual Dedicated to the Art and Culture of the Muslim World*
KdO	*Kunst des Orients*

Legacy	L. Komaroff and S. Carboni (eds), *The Legacy of Genghis Khan: Courtly Art and Culture in Western Asia, 1256–1353* (New York, 2002)
MMA	Metropolitan Museum of Art, New York
OA	*Oriental Art*
PP	B. Gray, *Persian Painting* (Geneva, 1961; repr. 1995)
Sekai	*Sekai bijutsu daizenshu: Toyo-hen*, 18 vols (Tokyo, 1999–2000)
SI	*Studia Iranica*
SPA	A. U. Pope and P. Ackerman (eds), *A Survey of Persian Art from Prehistoric Times to the Present*, 3rd edn, 16 vols (Ashiya, 1981)
TOCS	*Transactions of the Oriental Ceramic Society*
TSM	Topkapı Sarayi Museum, Istanbul
Turks	D. J. Roxburgh (ed.), *Turks: A Journey of a Thousand Years, 600–1600* (London, 2005)
WSWG	J. C. Y. Watt and A. E. Wardwell, *When Silk Was Gold: Central Asian and Chinese Textiles* (New York, 1997)
ZMQ	*Zhongguo meishu quanji*, 60 vols (Beijing and Shanghai, 1985–96)

Introduction

Why chinoiserie in Iranian art needs re-examination

> Unlike China which accepted and then absorbed foreign influences, Iran has adapted them to her own genius with no premium on the blind retention of native features if something more interesting appeared on the scene.
>
> Richard N. Frye, *The Golden Age of Persia*[1]

No art movement can come into being without having contacts with other established arts; and few such movements flourish without having enough spontaneous enthusiasm to digest the essence of other art traditions and thereafter to eclipse them. This is the case with Iranian art. Iran has set a high value on foreign art and culture throughout the ages, and this has culminated in the occurrence of very curious mixtures of different artistic styles and of promiscuous unrelated iconography during the formative periods in which dynastic or regional conventions were being established. Such Iranian indebtedness to foreign art is particularly exemplified in the art of the late thirteenth and early fourteenth centuries, when Iranian taste was whetted by growing contacts with China. The dynamic encounter of two great civilisations – China and Iran – makes the time of Mongol domination a most exciting period of Iranian art to study.

The intention of this book is to retell the story of chinoiserie in Iranian art under the Mongols, reviewing the manifold problems of Chinese elements in Iranian art – a topic that has never previously been investigated in depth. In considering the stylistic and technical development of Iranian art, 'the Chinese element' is an inevitable issue. Any history of Iranian art under the aegis of the Mongols must include some accounts of the occurrence of these elements. Though Iran was affected by internal factors in earlier periods, it is indubitable that it experienced a shift in its aesthetic balance on a grand scale during the late thirteenth and early fourteenth centuries, as a result of the fruitful exchange of artistic ideas with China and, more broadly, East Asia.

Despite a wide acknowledgement of the role of China in the evolution of Iranian art traditions in the late thirteenth and early fourteenth centuries, chinoiserie in Iranian art under the Mongols remains one of the intangible matters in the study of Iranian art as a whole. One major problem of earlier scholarship is that most statements about Chinese themes found in late thirteenth- and early fourteenth-century Iranian pictorial and decorative arts have been made without presenting convincing visual and textual evidence; as a result, these have provided an indeterminate picture of the Chinese contribution to the artistic explosion in Mongol-ruled Iran and thus have made this subject somewhat murky. Such tendencies need reassessment.

In pursuing the whole question of chinoiserie in Iranian art under the Mongols, it is essential first to particularise each Chinese element and then to synthesise the evidence into a cohesive story. Thus I try to identify the key characteristics of each Chinese element and to track down its possible Chinese sources. How far did Iranian artists manipulate, half-understand or distort it? Is it a successful imitation, a product modified through Iranian reinterpretation or an element consisting of disparate sources? These are the main issues that the present book attempts to discuss on the basis of detailed comparison between Iranian and Chinese examples and through the extensive use of Chinese materials so as to provide a comprehensive view of chinoiserie in Iranian art under the Mongols in most of the major media. Indeed, the absence of incontrovertible archaeological evidence for the actual, physical availability of Chinese pictorial and decorative arts in Mongol-ruled Iran demands that this subject should be cogently argued with strong visual and textual evidence. Problems of 'Chinese influence' must therefore be thoroughly re-examined across a wide spectrum of Sino-Iranian studies, not only from the art-historical but also from the geopolitical and socio-religious points of view.

Above all, the term 'Chinese' must be treated with great caution. Some elements can safely be termed as Chinese, preferably in the context of one of the prototypical dynastic styles of Chinese art, but others are more likely to have originated in the Eurasian steppe, and thus beyond the traditional Chinese sphere, like the present Mongolia, the present Chinese province of Gansu, the Xinjiang Uighur Autonomous Region and the area formerly known as Turkestan.

Note on historiography

This is by no means the first attempt to tackle the occurrence of Chinese elements in Iranian art. On the contrary, the age-old artistic relationship between China and Iran, together with the socio-political interaction between the two civilisations, has been given much scholarly attention since the early twentieth century.[2]

Although both Iranian and Chinese artefacts had already entered museums and private collections in Europe and later in North America in increasing numbers from the late nineteenth century onwards, it was only in the early twentieth century that non-Western items began to be treated more generally as serious material for research. The emergence of scholarship in chinoiserie in Iranian art was particularly associated with the growth of interest in Iranian book painting in the Western world.[3] Chinese features in Iranian painting gradually came to the attention of collectors and scholars of the period, who formed their own collections of illustrated Oriental manuscripts. For example, the Chinese elements found in the illustrations of the *Jamiʿ al-Tawarikh* of Rashid al-Din (see Chapter 5) – which later became a benchmark of the artistic links between China and Iran during the Mongol period – had already been acknowledged at the time of the discovery of the London portion of the *Jamiʿ al-Tawarikh* manuscript.[4] A generation of scholars in the period before the Second World War, such as Martin,[5] Blochet[6] and Arnold,[7] embarked on the thematic and stylistic classification of Iranian manuscript painting, referring in the process to the presence of ambiguous 'Far Eastern' elements. One major problem for the scholarship of this period is a complete disregard for the detailed reading of each Chinese element. Most scholars confined themselves to allude to the availability of Chinese painting and artefacts or the involvement of Chinese artists in the production of book painting in medieval Iran, with little attention given to careful comparison between Chinese models and Iranian imitations. Thus, despite an awareness of the unusual features found in Iranian painting of the Mongol period, few attempts were made to incorporate the use of Chinese elements into the stylistic criteria used to define Iranian painting.

The turning points of scholarship in this subject came at three stages in the twentieth century – in the 1930s, the 1950s and the 1970s. The 1930s saw a rapid expansion of serious scholarship in both Iranian and Chinese art in the West, when the formations for properly extensive collections of Oriental art were laid in the private sphere, while public collections also grew apace.[8] As a result of the establishment of a field of academic studies focusing on Islamic art and more specifically on Iranian art as a scholarly discipline, as shown, for example, in the success of the *Exhibition of Persian Art* (London, 1931), the publication of journals devoted to Islamic art studies, such as *Ars Islamica* (1934–51) and *Athār-é Īrān* (1936–49), and the compilation of *A Survey of Persian Art from Prehistoric Times to the Present* (London, 1938–9), some scholars undertook the discussion of chinoiserie in Iranian painting, in the course of reassessing late thirteenth- and early fourteenth-century Iranian painting – one may think here of the work of Schroeder and de Lorey.[9] Such earlier scholarship in Iranian painting, despite the lack of scientific analyses of Chinese themes and the inadequate use of Chinese materials, still serves as a frame of reference for the scholarly investigation of the Sino-Iranian artistic relationship.

As publications on Iranian art and architecture, especially those from new centres of research in Iranian and Middle Eastern art in the United States, became voluminous in the 1950s,[10] the role of Chinese elements in Iranian painting gradually assumed increasing importance. Of particular note is the work of Richard Ettinghausen in this period – for example, his monograph *The Unicorn* (1950), which remains essential to the study of chinoiserie in Iranian art under the Mongols. His discussion of this subject remains valid in many respects: the detailed investigation of Chinese elements and his mastery of iconographic and stylistic features make his argument compelling. Iranian art exhibitions of this period are in general less ambitious than the grand-scale exhibitions held in the early twentieth century, yet Iranian art under the Mongols and its art-historical significance seem to have become topical.[11] The key to the scholarly development of chinoiserie in Iranian art in this period is the increasing number of archaeological research projects on Chinese ceramics in Iran and the Middle East – for example, those from the Ardabil Shrine.[12] This spurred ceramic experts to look more critically into the history of Sino-Iranian ceramic trading and to reappraise the role of China in the stylistic and technical development of Iranian ceramics.[13]

The 1970s witnessed the increase in the number of scholars who were involved in the study of Islamic art in the West, as well as the growth of scholarly interest in various media of the art of Islam, particularly in metalwork.[14] This was reflected in a wide-ranging presentation of Islamic art at the Hayward Gallery, London, in 1976.[15] Painting remained a major field of study, and a number of illustrated catalogues of Iranian manuscript painting were published in the 1970s,[16] though none of the catalogues addressed the problems of 'Chinese influences' specifically. There was, however, a renewed interest in Chinese art in the context of East–West cultural contacts, particularly Sino-European relations.[17] A colloquium of the Percival David Foundation entitled 'The Westward Influence of the Chinese Arts' (1972)[18] was, though the discussion extended into European chinoiserie, an important chapter in the establishment of the term chinoiserie in art history. This remained the case until the early 1980s, culminating in another London colloquium devoted to the Sino-Iranian artistic relationship in 1980.[19] Though much of the focus of this event was on the impact of Chinese art in Iran after 1400 – a time when Chinese fashions began to control certain aspects of Iranian art in a more drastic way – it is of particular importance as the first scholarly attempt to deal with Chinese elements in

Iranian art on an international scale. The papers delivered to this colloquium discussed various aspects of paintings in albums preserved in the Library of the Topkapı Saray Museum in Istanbul, known as the Saray Albums (see Chapters 5 and 6).

By the beginning of the 1980s it had become common practice among Islamic art historians to refer to Chinese elements in Iranian art, and some of these scholars had no hesitation in using the term 'Chinese influence' frequently in surveys and in major exhibition catalogues of Islamic art, in particular in the context of Ilkhanid (654/1256–754/1353; *il-khan* literally means a 'subservient khan') art.[20] This was also reflected in an increasing number of articles touching on this theme, ranging from those dealing with pictorial styles to those concerned with decorative motifs.[21] In the media of the decorative arts, the study of the mutual influence in ceramics between China and Iran made great advances thanks to the growth of archaeological finds and scholarly investigations.[22] Collaborative research in this field between Chinese and Islamic art historians will serve in future to provide a much richer picture of the artistic exchange between East and West Asia.

Since then, well-organised exhibitions, comprehensive catalogues of collections and archaeological discoveries of both Iranian and Chinese art have encouraged scholars to readdress the ill-defined relations between Iranian and Chinese art.[23] Among these, the Ilkhanid art exhibition in New York and Los Angeles in 2002–3 succeeded in presenting a comprehensive view of the taste of the Ilkhanids, though the role of China is still treated as a secondary theme.[24] An equally notable event for the theme of this book was a grand-scale exhibition of Genghis Khan held in Germany in 2005–6. Organised in conjunction with the 800th anniversary of his elevation to supreme khan, the exhibition brought together not only Ilkhanid artefacts but also recent archaeological finds from Mongolia.[25]

Above all, the scholarship of chinoiserie in Iranian art was conducted by Basil Gray, a pioneer of this subject.[26] By using his unrivalled knowledge of both Iranian and Chinese art, Gray made a significant contribution to the field of Sino-Iranian art studies. Having being involved in the study of Iranian painting and Chinese ceramics, he took pioneering steps in the study of chinoiserie in Iranian art,[27] and vice versa – namely, Persianisation in Chinese art.[28] Further efforts to solve the problem of Chinese elements in Iranian art, particularly in connection with ceramics, were made by the next generation of scholars, such as Rogers[29] and Crowe.[30] But Gray's precise use of Chinese comparative materials is a credit to his scholarship.

Yet, despite the advance of scholarship in Iranian art studies, the problems raised by the presence of Chinese elements in Iranian art under the Mongols are still open at the level of doctoral research. A number of dissertations have been devoted to the art and architecture of the Ilkhanid period since the 1970s.[31] However, compared with Timurid (771/1370–913/1507) chinoiserie, where 'China' has been more openly discussed,[32] none of the theses on Ilkhanid art and architecture has addressed specifically and at length the issue of Chinese elements.[33] Perhaps because of the difficulty in handling a large quantity of information about the Sino-Iranian artistic relationship during the late thirteenth and early fourteenth centuries, little effort has been made to bring miscellaneous facts together into a coherent story as well as to subsume the history of chinoiserie within the development of Iranian taste.

Thus it is now time – nearly 100 years after the discovery of Chinese elements in Iranian art at the turn of the twentieth century – to reassess earlier scholarship on Sino-Iranian art studies and to look more closely at sinicising fashions in Iranian art under the Mongols. Chinoiserie in Iranian art is by no means an intractable issue, if one discovers credible patterns in the process of adoption and adaptation of Chinese themes in the art of Iran.

A new approach to chinoiserie in Iranian art: the sources and methodology

In general, this subject is rich in source materials, and it can be studied on several different levels. This book, however, rather than deducing a theory of chinoiserie in Iranian art from the consideration of striking phenomena that manifested themselves in the major art forms, adopts a more discursive approach to this subject. The media that I have chosen in this book therefore comprise most types of pictorial and decorative art produced in late thirteenth- and early fourteenth-century Iran, though there are significant exceptions – namely, carpets,[34] calligraphy,[35] bookbinding,[36] coinage,[37] jewellery,[38] architecture and its decoration.[39] Such an extended field for discussion is likely to cause some digressions or to obscure the outlines of the argument in this book at times. Yet, on the other hand, such an interdisciplinary approach should be of great advantage in evaluating individual objects in the broader contexts of Iranian art traditions and, moreover, in considering the interdependence, interconnection and concurrence of Chinese elements in Iranian art as a whole.

The comparative material from China itself is also varied, ranging from *objets de luxe* – namely, artefacts that were exported to Iran initially as commodities and tributes through official trade routes – to objects that were brought from China incidentally as souvenirs or ritual utensils by travellers and monks. One of the central concerns of this study is to pursue the potential of Chinese printed materials, which have not yet been used to any great extent in the discussion of chinoiserie in Iranian art. The materials comprise woodblock prints, paper money, maps and Buddhist texts. Mural painting in China and Central Asia also offers promising material for comparison. Though intending to define the place of origin so far as information is available, I sometimes opt to use all-embracing terms such as 'Far East,' 'East Asia' or 'Central Asia' according to the context. Moreover, owing to the enormous geopolitical expansion of the Mongol Empire, the discussion encompasses several types of artefact spanning a vast geographical sphere in Eurasia during the late thirteenth and early fourteenth centuries.

In a study such as this, it is crucial to determine the scope of the discussion in order to keep a balance within each chapter and to avoid making it a mere summary. In particular, some limitation of scope is necessary for the discussion of manuscript painting of the late thirteenth and early fourteenth centuries, a period that witnessed great creativity in book painting in Iran. Hence, though this is regrettable, I have excluded some of the key pictorial examples of Ilkhanid Iran, including the Great Mongol *Shahnama* – which is without doubt the most important manuscript of all Ilkhanid painting and certainly merits a chapter or even a book to itself[40] – in the main discussion of manuscript painting and limited myself to quote them if necessary. A number of illustrated manuscripts that were produced at the workshops of provincial governors for the Ilkhanids – namely, some key examples of the Muzaffarid school (Fars, Kirman and Kurdistan; 713/1314–795/1393) and works of the Inju school (Fars; c. 725/1325–754/1353), as well as masterpieces of the Jalayirid school (Iraq, Azerbaijan; 740/1340–835/1432) – are equally worthy of close examination. But they cannot be dealt with in separate sections here for lack of space.[41]

By the same token, this book does not deal specifically with the historical background of Mongol-ruled Iran. This theme has been amply discussed and therefore needs little further consideration.[42]

Inevitably, this book touches on a foretaste of chinoiserie in pre-Mongol Iranian art. Although Iran consolidated its relations with East Asia during the Mongol period, it would be erroneous to assume that this is a phenomenon particular to this period. A trans-Eurasian artistic relationship did certainly exist before the end of the thirteenth century, thanks to both overland trade routes, widely known as the Silk Road, and sea routes through the Indian Ocean and the Persian Gulf, but it was rejuvenated in Iranian art and culture as a result of the far-flung impact of the Mongol invasion. An overall view of the role of China in the development of Iranian art up to the advent of Timurid supremacy should certainly reveal the uniqueness of chinoiserie in Ilkhanid art as well as the cycles of Chinese influence in Iranian art.

Lastly, the theory proposed in the following discussion depends on the availability of materials. It is particularly difficult to keep up to date with Chinese materials, because new information comes continuously from recent excavations, which have been conducted extensively throughout China. However, I have done my utmost to include the latest information in this book.

The definition of chinoiserie in Iranian art: the visions of al-Sin

> In the past, as at the present time, the Chinese have been famous for the skill of their hands and for their expertise in fashioning rare and beautiful objects.
>
> Thaʿalibi (d. 429/1038), *Lataʾif al-maʿarif*[43]

I begin this section with this famous passage because it represents the key to understanding the cult of Chinese art in medieval Iran and more broadly in the Middle East. The fascination with objects of 'rarity' and 'beauty' led to the occurrence of exoticism, a phenomenon that crystallised in Iranian art under the Mongols.

Throughout this book I use the term 'chinoiserie' to describe a sinicising mode particular to Iranian art, in distinction to a type of style that developed in late seventeenth- and eighteenth-century European art. While in Europe China remained a mythical land of fabulous riches and luxury – known as Cathay – until the arrival of reliable information about its civilisations in early modern times, Iranians already had a much clearer idea of the country and its art traditions before the expansion of horizons generated by the Mongols. Even at the time of Thaʿalibi, when exquisite vessels were, regardless of their real origin, generally called 'Chinese' in the Middle East, Iranians were in a better position to distinguish what were *objets d'art* and *objets de vertu* of China. The extent to which the mystique of Chinese pictorial and decorative arts was appreciated in the Iranian world before the Mongol period can be traced from several written sources, not only lexicographical works but also poetry.[44] The frequent allusion to Chinese textiles and painters in such written works could not have occurred without some degree of familiarity with Chinese art traditions. The visions of al-Sin thus contain to some extent the reality of China.

Yet the essential difference between European and Iranian chinoiserie lies not only in the availability of wide information about Chinese art, thanks to the geographical position of Iran, but also in the degree of acculturation. One should bear in mind that chinoiserie in European art is not the result of fruitful exchanges of artistic ideas with China. Genuine 'Chinese' elements have never been fused successfully with European artistic concepts, for European artists used their own traditions as a starting point and placed their own art in a position of centrality. They thus failed to recognise the major merits of Chinese art. Rather, they were interested in transfiguring the image of China to suit their own artistic requirements. On the other hand, the art of China operated more powerfully upon the imagination of Iranian artists, but in a different way. Iranian artists strove to imitate styles and techniques derived from Chinese pictorial and decorative arts and subsequently to incorporate many decorative elements of Chinese origin into their own repertoires. Despite incomplete and unsuccessful attempts at an earlier stage of adoption, which sometimes created fanciful and whimsical decoration, the Iranian motives for learning about Chinese art traditions were sincere and consistent. What is remarkable is that, along with the increased authentic knowledge of Chinese art, Iranian artists began to combine indigenous and Chinese elements. Such adjustment was perhaps necessary to make foreign conventions feasible for Iranian painters and artisans as well as to meet the tastes and requirements of new patrons and the cultural and religious circumstances. But this resulted in the creation of a magnificent synthesis of Sino-Iranian art.

It is for this reason that chinoiserie in European art ended in a temporary fashion, whereas in Iranian art chinoiserie became a long-lasting and influential tradition.

Subject of this book

This book has two principal goals: to furnish a sound art-historical analysis of Chinese elements in Iranian art under the Mongols, and to give a hitherto unknown insight into this phenomenon. The story of chinoiserie in Iranian art begins with textiles – a catalyst for the transmission of Chinese and Central Asian artistic ideas into West Asia. Ceramics further explain the artistic contacts between East and West over a period of more than 500 years. These two media offer a fascinating entreé into the complex history of chinoiserie in Iranian art. Another highlight of this book is the extended coverage of discussing chinoiserie in Iranian art by including hitherto neglected objects, namely metalwork and other types of the so-called minor arts – that is, lacquerware, glassware, woodwork and stonework – with the intention of using all of them to open up a fresh perspective of the subject of this book. But it remains true that half of the discussions in this book are devoted to manuscript painting, ranging from well-quoted examples in the discussion of 'Chinese influence' to relatively unknown material. Each chapter enquires into the issue of Chinese elements chronologically or thematically, following introductory remarks on the emergence of Chinese themes in each medium in pre-Mongol Iran.

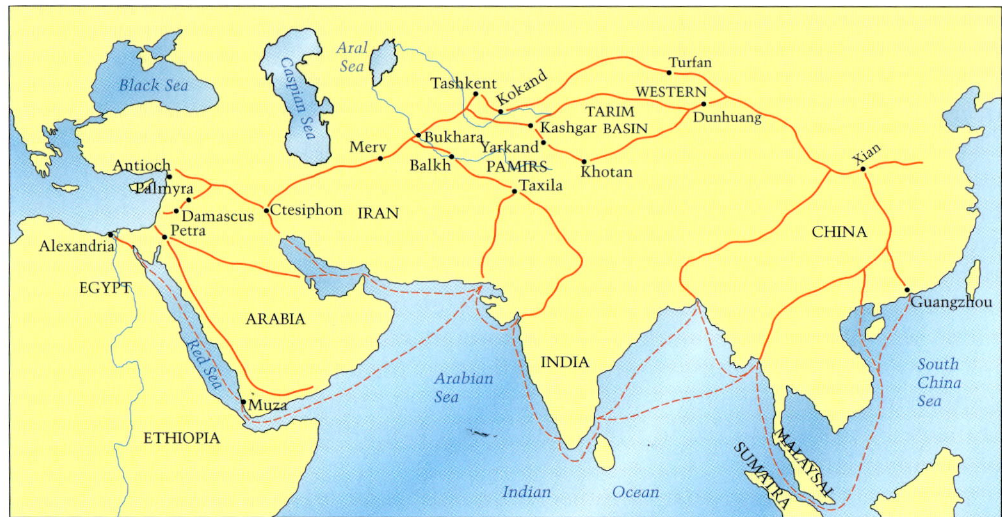

Figure 0.1 *East–West overland and maritime trade routes. The Silk Road (die Seidenstrasse), a term that was coined by the German geographer Ferdinand von Richthofen in the late nineteenth century, was a vital international trade network across the Eurasian continent in pre-modern times.*

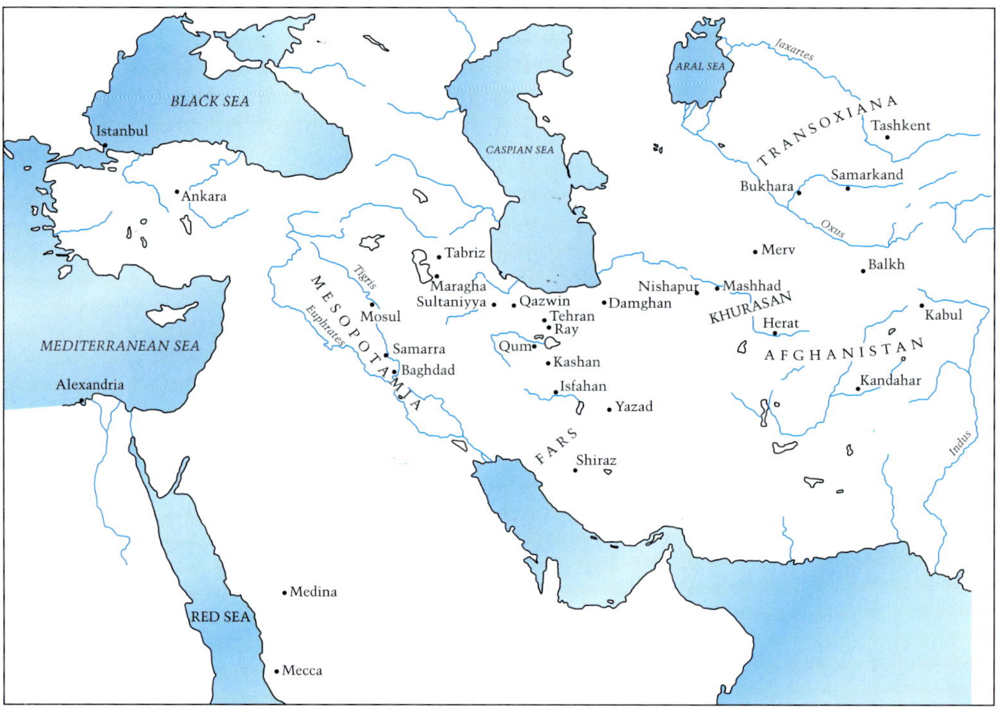

Figure 0.2 *Iran and its environs. The Persianate world was incorporated into the Mongol political and cultural domain during the Ilkhanid period (1256–1353).*

Notes

1. Frye 1975, 3.
2. See 'al-Sīn', in *EI*[2] (Bosworth et al. 1997), and 'Chinese–Iranian relations', in *EIr* (Chen 1992b; Khaleghi-Motlagh 1992; Liu and Jackson 1992; Rogers 1992a; 1992b; Sugimura 1992; Watson 1992). A classical work on this theme is Laufer 1919. For a recent study, see Allsen 2001a.
3. A good summary of the development of Iranian and broadly Islamic art collections in the West is to be found in Vernoit 2000. For the development of scholarship in Iranian painting in the West, see ibid. 35–7, 44–5. See also Blair and Bloom 2003 for a survey of Islamic art scholarship.
4. Morley 1854, 10.
5. Some of the remarks on Chinese elements in the London *Jami' al-Tawarikh* manuscript in Martin 1912 are tenuous. After commenting on the portraits of the Chinese emperors, he concludes without showing any concrete evidence: 'Chinese paintings were certainly used by the Mongols for decorating their tents and rooms . . .' (Martin 1912, 22). It seems more reasonable to consider that, as recent studies have suggested, textile fabrics – for example, in the form of hangings – were predominantly used for the interior decoration of Mongol royal tents (Figure 1.14). I shall discuss the portraits of the Chinese emperors in this manuscript (see Chapter 5).
6. See, e.g., Blochet 1929, 60–4. While he rightly points out Chinese elements in a double frontispiece of the Paris Juvaini (Figure 4.3) – for example, sinicising shades of colour (ibid. 88) – no attempts are made to specify possible Chinese sources.
7. Arnold (1928, 65–70) summarises chinoiserie in Iranian painting. While admitting that 'this problem has formed the subject of much violent controversy' (ibid. 65), he does not take a proper art-historical approach to Chinese elements in Iranian painting. He is one of the earliest scholars who invented misleading terms for describing Chinese themes in Islamic art. Chinese cloud patterns are termed, inappropriately or perhaps erroneously, as 'tai' (ibid. 70), while, according to the *pinyin* system, a Chinese character of clouds is pronounced as 'yun'.
8. Gray 1971–3; Vernoit 2000, 32–7.
9. Lorey 1935a; Schroeder 1939.
10. See major articles on Iranian art and architecture that appear in *AO* (1954–); *KdO* (1954–79).
11. e.g. *Art under the Mongol Dynasties of China and Persia* (BM, 1955; Gray 1955); *Persian Art before and after the Mongol Conquest* (University of Michigan Museum of Art, 1959; Ann Arbor 1959).
12. Pope 1956.
13. See, e.g., Pope 1952. Sino-Iranian relations in ceramic styles and techniques had already caught scholarly attention in the 1940s (see, e.g., Kahle 1940–1; Lane 1946–7).
14. See, e.g., Allan 1979; Melikian-Chirvani 1973; Fehérvári 1976.
15. See Hayward.
16. See, e.g., Grube 1972; Robinson 1976; Robinson (ed.) 1976.
17. The role of China in the development of European civilisation had been widely discussed from various angles since the 1950s (see, e.g., Needham 1954–; Dawson 1967; Lach 1970). For classic studies of

chinoiserie in European art and design, see Honour 1961 and Impey 1977. For further studies of this subject, see Arnold 1999 and Jacobson 1999.

18. Watson (ed.) 1972b.
19. See *IA*, 1, 1981; Grube and Sims (eds) 1985.
20. As in key exhibitions held in the 1970s, such as *Imperial Images in Persian Painting* (Scottish Arts Council Gallery, Edinburgh, 1977; Hillenbrand 1977).
21. See, e.g., İnal 1975; Rosenzweig 1978–9.
22. See Watson (ed.) 1970; Medley 1972b; 1975.
23. For example, the period between the late 1980s and early 1990s witnessed much development in the scholarship in Ilkhanid textiles, thanks to a conscientious series of studies by Wardwell (in particular, Wardwell 1988–9).
24. See *Legacy*; Komaroff (ed.) 2006.
25. See Bonn/Munich. This exhibition (with some changes of exhibits) travelled to Budapest in 2007, along with an exhibition on the Mongol Invasion of Hungary (Budapest 2007). I am grateful to Dr Iván Szántó for drawing my attention to this exhibition.
26. Gray's major articles are readily available in his collection of essays (Gray 1987).
27. For painting, see Gray 1948–9; 1972b; 1981. For ceramics, see Gray 1975–7.
28. See Gray 1940–1; 1963.
29. See Rogers 1970.
30. See Crowe 1976; 1991; 2002.
31. In particular, see Watson 1977; Blair 1986a; Carboni 1992; Masuya 1997; Fitzherbert 2001.
32. Whitman 1978; Sugimura 1981. I should also mention a dissertation by al-Gailani entitled 'The origins of Islamic art and the role of China' (University of Edinburgh, 1973). He tackled problems of Chinese influence on Islamic art in the first instance by analysing the decoration of Iraqi minarets.
33. See, however, the detail analysis of Chinese–Mongol elements in tile decoration at Takht-i Sulayman by Masuya 1997, 564–92.
34. Carpets: information about pre-Timurid Iranian carpets remains scattered. No securely dated Ilkhanid carpets have been identified, though some fragmentary rugs have tentatively been attributed to early fourteenth-century Iran (*Legacy*, cat. no. 78). Pictorial evidence shows that carpets were certainly in use in Ilkhanid Iran: the earliest representation of a prayer rug occurs in the Freer Balʿami (Ettinghausen et al. 1974, 12–13, fig. 2); a Central Asian-type kilim is depicted in the scene of the Kaʿba in the Edinburgh *Jami ʿal-Tawarikh* manuscript (Rice 1976, 100–1); and an illustration of the Great Mongol *Shahnama* contains the earliest known representation of an animal carpet, perhaps intending to depict a carpet of either Anatolian or Caucasian origin (Ettinghausen 1959a, 99–105). For further discussion, see an essay by E. Sims in 'Carpets' in *EIr*, 4, 864–6. Chinese links have been mentioned in the context of the design of the so-called dragon or Kuba carpets, yet most extant examples of this type of carpet are datable to no earlier than the late sixteenth century (see, e.g., Dimand 1973, 265–8; for a recent study of the provenance of the 'dragon' carpets, see Wertime and Wright 1995). For Chinese elements in Oriental carpet design in general, see Day 1989.

35. Calligraphy: apart from the introduction of paper, there is no definitive evidence for the role of China in the development of Iranian calligraphy. While the art of Chinese writing seems to have been recognised in Ilkhanid Iran by means of seals, its impact is not visibly reflected in the art of Mongol Iran. I shall address this issue in Chapter 3. For Iranian calligraphy in general, see Soucek 1979. For Ilkhanid calligraphy, see Blair 2006, 241–315. The issue of Iranian calligraphy and China raises yet another question as to the transmission of block-printing technology from China to the Islamic world. Perhaps because of the nature of Arabic script, which has joins between most letters, printing was not particularly developed in the medieval Islamic world (see an essay by G. Roper in 'Islamic art: printing' in *DA*, 16, 359–60). Importantly, however, Chinese woodblock prints offered a certain artistic inspiration to Ilkhanid painters (see Chapters 4–6).
36. Bookbinding: very few examples of bookbinding that can safely be attributed to Ilkhanid Iran are known to survive – e.g. the Morgan Bestiary (Maragha, c. 1300; M500, Pierpont Morgan Library, New York; Ettinghausen 1954); a Qur'an in Dublin (Maragha, 738/1338–739/1339; Is 1470, Chester Beatty Library; James 1980, no. 49). Their decoration is essentially devoid of Chinese traits. For a general survey of Iranian bookbinding, see Brend 1989.
37. Coinage: the design of Ilkhanid coinage is not particularly helpful in demonstrating the shifts in form and decoration that occurred under Chinese inspiration, except for the possible relationship between square Kufic and Chinese seals in *phagspa* script (see Chapter 3). For further information about Ilkhanid coinage, see Blair 1982; 1983; Album 1984; 1985. See also Kolbas 2006.
38. Jewellery: few examples of jewellery have been securely identified as Ilkhanid pieces, except for examples from the Golden Horde (see *GH*). For Islamic jewellery in general, see Jenkins and Keene 1982; Gladiss 1998.
39. Architecture and its decoration: in any study of Iranian art, it would be wholly inappropriate to omit the discussion of architecture and its decoration. The output of Ilkhanid monuments was immense: their decoration underwent a considerable development in terms of colour schemes and decorative programmes (for a survey of Ilkhanid architecture, see Wilber 1955; for the decoration of Mongol monuments in Iran, see Pickett 1997 in particular). Yet this book does not cover architecture as a separate chapter, for a full discussion of Chinese themes in Iranian architectural ornament of the late thirteenth and early fourteenth centuries would require a good deal of space. There is space here for no more than an indication of this topic in each chapter, especially in relation to tiles that are included in the chapter on ceramics (see Chapter 2).
40. The standard work on this manuscript is Grabar and Blair 1980.
41. The following works deserve special attention concerning chinoiserie in fourteenth-century Iranian painting: Muzaffarid painting – the Tehran Nizami (Fars, 718/1318, but later miniatures, possibly c. 1380; MS 5179, Tehran University Central Library; Titley 1972) and the Cairo *Shahnama* (Shiraz, 796/1393; MS Ta'rikh Farisi 73, Cairo National Library; O'Kane 2006); Inju painting – the Inju *Shahnama*s attributable to Shiraz, i.e. the 731/1330 manuscript (Hazine 1479, TSM; Rogers, Çağman and Tanındı 1986, 51, figs 32–42), the 733/1333 manuscript

(Dorn 329, Russia National Library, St Petersburg; Adamova and Giuzal'ian 1985), the dispersed 741/1341 manuscript (Simpson 2000) and the so-called Stephens *Shahnama* (753/1352; LTS 1998.1, on loan to the Arthur M. Sackler Gallery, Smithsonian Institution, Washington, DC; Sotheby's 1998, lot 41), and the *Kitab-i Samak 'Ayyar* (Shiraz, c. 1330–40; MS Ouseley 379–81, Bodleian Library, Oxford; Stockland 1993–5); Jalayirid painting – the London Nizami (Baghdad, 1386–8; Or. 13297, BL; Titley 1971), the Great *Kalila wa Dimna* (Tabriz, c. 1360–74; F. 1422, Istanbul University Library; Cowen 1989a), the *Mathnavis* of Khwaju Kirmani (Baghdad, 798/1396; Add. MS 18113, BL; Fitzherbert 1991) and the *Divan* of Sultan Ahmad (Baghdad, c. 1400; F1932.29–37, FGA; Klimburg-Salter 1976–7). Similarly, with regard to the selection of illustrations in this book, I was unable to reproduce some of the objects and paintings mentioned due to the shortage of space. Bibliographical references on such examples are provided in notes.

42. In particular, see Spuler 1955; *CHI*, 5, 1968; Morgan 1986; Allsen 1987.
43. Tha'alibi 1968, 141.
44. See Khaleghi-Motlagh 1992. As an additional note on this introduction, I use the adjectives 'Iranian' and 'Chinese' for artists, weavers, potters, metalmakers and painters in a generic sense but do not refer to their ethnic background.

CHAPTER ONE

Textiles

PERHAPS IT WAS through textiles that Iranians first encountered the art of China – their significance as a medium of the cultural exchange has been stressed not only in the discussion of chinoiserie in Iranian art but also in the whole issue of the East–West artistic relationship throughout the ages. Thanks to their portable nature – they are not as fragile as glass and ceramics and not as heavy as metalwork – Chinese textiles had already reached Iran and vice versa in large quantities before the Mongol period, and trans-Eurasian trade routes encouraged the mutual exchange of artistic ideas between East and West Asia. In particular, textiles produced during the thirteenth and fourteenth centuries have interesting but intricate characteristics, reflecting both the large-scale exchange of weaving products and the movement of weavers throughout Eurasia under the auspices of the *Pax Mongolica*.

The complex and dramatic history of the textile trade between East and West has aroused continuous scholarly interest. Studies of Chinese and Iranian textiles have become diversified in recent years, encouraged by the renewal of interest in textiles beyond the art-historical point of view. In addition to a scientific analysis of weaving techniques and materials, which is of great help in defining the provenance and date of textiles, another important development is an interdisciplinary approach to textiles in Eurasia. Their multifarious aspects, notably as commodities, tributes and items with religious function, have caught the attention of many scholars in the fields of social and cultural history: the role of textiles in the Sino-Iranian cultural exchange is, for instance, amply discussed in the study of the Mongol Empire by Allsen[1] and their socio-religious aspects in Eurasian history by Liu[2] and Foltz.[3] Yet a wide range of research potential of textiles remains open.

In order to understand chinoiserie in Iranian textiles under the Mongols, attention should also be paid to earlier stylistic changes of Chinese and Iranian textiles. The discussion of pre-Mongol Iranian textiles and their Chinese connections are indispensable for providing a clearer view of the process of adoption and adaptation of Chinese themes in late thirteenth- and early fourteenth-century Iranian textiles.

The beginning of the textile trade between China and Iran

Sericulture and silk production are among the most important Chinese inventions. In China – a country once called *Serica*, 'the Land of Silk', by the ancient Greeks and Romans – sericulture had already begun by around 3000 BC.[4] The Chinese dominance of the international silk trade continued even after the start of silk production outside China, where there was still continuous demand for high-quality Chinese silks.

The history of silk trading between China and Iran can be traced back to the early Han period (206 BC–AD 9; AD 25–220), when China embarked on the trans-Eurasian trade. Historically, this is attributed to Zhang Qian (d. 114 BC), a traveller whose expedition to the nomadic Xiongnu resulted in the expansion of Chinese political and military control into the Western Regions (*Xiyu*).[5] With the growth of trade routes throughout Eurasia, the silk trade eventually expanded into the Roman Orient, as testified by Chinese silk fragments found in Palmyra and Dura-Europos.[6] The Parthians, who ruled over Khurasan for almost 500 years until the middle of the third century (248 BC–AD 226), contributed to the development of the silk trade between China and the Roman Empire by acting as middlemen, and it was perhaps through them that the secret of sericulture first became known in Iran.[7] However, since virtually no complete examples of Parthian textiles have been found, the impact of Chinese textiles on Parthian textiles remains a matter of speculation.[8] Further archaeological excavations might yield answers to the problems of what contributed to the exact artistic relationship between China and Iran at that time.

The key to understanding the artistic links between China and Iran lies in textiles of the Tang (617–907) and Sasanian periods (224–642). A number of luxury goods from abroad arrived at the cosmopolitan Tang capital Changan (Xian), and the adaptation of foreign art was greatly encouraged by the sixth Emperor, Xuanzong (r. 712–56), who enthusiastically introduced Western culture to China.[9] Known as *bosi* in China, the Sasanian Empire had established full diplomatic relations with China as soon as China was reunited under the Sui dynasty (581–618),[10] and silk textiles of Sasanian Iran, called *bosijin*, were well known in Tang China.[11] Despite the lack of relevant Sasanian silk textiles discovered in China, the Chinese encounter with Iranian and more generally West Asian art traditions is discernible in the occurrence of a variety of new motifs of West Asian origin – for example, the grape and the camel.[12] The impact of Sasanian textiles is particularly reflected in the fashion for roundel motifs so deeply integrated into Tang textile design. Roundels of Tang textiles can largely be divided into the following two types: one consists of flower motifs forming the circular border, which seems to owe much to the indigenous development of decorative ideas in

China;[13] another type of roundel – widely known under the name of 'pearl roundels' – which encloses single or paired animals, such as birds, lions, elephants and rams, provides unmistakable visual evidence for artistic contacts between China and Iran.[14] The fashion for pearl roundels occurred in Chinese textiles as early as the late sixth century under Sui rule and did not die out even after the political upheaval following the collapse of the Sasanian Empire in 642.[15]

It is important to note that the stylistic development of Tang textile design ran parallel to the change in the role of textiles in China during the seventh and eighth centuries. Textiles first began to be incorporated into the codes of clothing in the bureaucratic system of the Sui and Tang courts, in which official status was shown by types of garment.[16] Furthermore, as the trade route served to propagate religious exchanges – Nestorian Christianity was brought to China from Iran by Western merchants and missionaries during the seventh century[17] – textiles became important media not only as commodities and general merchandise but also as essential items in religious contexts. In particular, the development of the silk trade was profoundly associated with the expansion of Buddhism, which brought an increased demand for silk textiles on ceremonial occasions as well as for the purpose of wrapping religious texts and bodies for burial.[18]

The continuous artistic communication between Tang China and post-Sasanian Iran owed much to the people of Transoxiana – the central figures in the trans-Eurasian trade from the seventh to the ninth century, a period in which the Sogdians played a major mediatory role between China and Iran. The silk-weaving industry already existed in Sogdiana before Islamic times, and Sogdian weavers produced high-quality textiles by using silk threads and weaving techniques imported from China. The collaboration between Sogdian and Chinese weavers was encouraged in China, perhaps in tandem with the increase of Sogdian populations in north-western China from the middle of the eighth century onwards.[19] From an artistic point of view, there are a number of decorative features of Sogdian textiles that indicate a close link with the art of Sasanian Iran. As has already been discussed at length by Shepherd and others, Sasanian elements in late seventh- to ninth-century Sogdian textiles are evident in the textiles categorised as the Zandaniji group, a term that was derived from the name of a village near Bukhara and was first identified by its inscriptions.[20] Typical features of Zandaniji textiles, such as paired-animal motifs, symmetrical arrangement and geometric composition, recall Sasanian conventions.[21]

Little is known about the Sino-Iranian artistic relationship in textiles during the Samanid (204/819–395/1005) and Buyid (320/932–454/1062) periods. It seems that the weaving industry in Iran and Transoxiana under Samanid rule flourished on the basis of Sogdian textiles, and the silk design ascribed to this period displays an artistic response to Sasanian textiles, adopting confronted animal patterns and roundels.[22] In the case of textiles of the Buyid dynasty, it remains difficult to grasp the whole stylistic development of Buyid textiles, owing to their dubious provenance, especially those allegedly found in medieval tombs at Rayy in 1925,[23] and to expand the argument to cover their East Asian connections.

Surviving textiles attributed to the thirteenth-century eastern Iranian world provide several interesting insights into the stylistic diversity of Iranian textiles before the full-scale introduction of Chinese artistic ideas into West Asia took place in the late thirteenth century. A silk fragment with felines and eagles in Cleveland (1990.2),[24] whose other section is now in the David Collection, Copenhagen (32/1989), for instance, contains hybrid motifs, exemplifying the decorative patterns available in Saljuq (c. 1050–1250) territory. Paired and addorsed felines arranged within lobed roundels recall Sogdian textile designs – for example, the Zandaniji textile – whereas double-headed eagle motifs, which are proudly present in the space between roundels, were originally developed in Byzantium.[25] Interestingly, the looped tails of each feline are often recognised in animal motifs used in contemporary decorative arts of the eastern Iranian world, especially those made in twelfth- and thirteenth-century Khurasan.[26] On the other hand, the design of eagles and felines whose tails terminate in dragons' heads is more likely to be a product of regional development in Anatolia and the Jazira, reflecting the fashion for dragon motifs in these regions at that time.[27] The pseudo-Kufic inscription, whose stems are interlacing, recalls examples from western Central Asia.[28] In terms of chinoiserie, the floral motifs that fill the background of this textile somewhat evoke lotus blossoms and can be viewed as one of the earliest Iranian reactions to Chinese themes found in textile design. However, because of a rudimentary modelling of lotus petals and a strong arabesque mode found in their stem parts, it is difficult to observe them as a pure Chinese derivation; they are more likely to be floral ornamentation based on conventional Islamic decorative schemes.

What is clear is that Chinese textiles were available in Iran before the Mongol invasion – silk textiles of the Northern Song period (960–1126) were found in Rayy, together with a number of twelfth- and thirteenth-century Chinese ceramics.[29] So far examples are insufficient to deduce to what extent such Chinese textiles stimulated Iranian artistic interest in imitating and adapting Chinese decorative themes and how they resulted in the fusion of Eastern and Western elements in tenth- to early twelfth-century Iranian textile design. Nevertheless, the availability of Chinese textiles in pre-Mongol Iran is of great significance when considering the diffusion of Chinese textiles into the Iranian world before the advent of the Mongols and their associations with later Iranian textiles.

Textiles in Ilkhanid and Yuan society

It has been observed that, despite a long history of the textile trade between China and Iran and apart from the introduction of sericulture and silk production from China to West Asia, few indications of chinoiserie can be detected in pre-Mongol Iranian textiles. Judging by surviving examples, Iranian textiles seem to have provided sources of stylistic inspiration more influentially than Chinese textiles, as reflected in the ubiquity of Sasanian pearl roundels in Tang and Sogdian textiles. The question then arises: when were Chinese themes first adopted and adapted in Iranian textiles?

As will be discussed at length through the observation of individual examples, it was during the Mongol period that textiles triggered the integration of Chinese themes into the Iranian world. This phenomenon was not only associated with the expansion of the trans-Eurasian trade under the *Pax Mongolica* or the intensification of both political and cultural contacts between China and Iran, especially under Khubilai (r. 1260–94) and Ghazan (r. 694/1295–703/1304),[30] but was essentially due to the significance of textiles in Mongol society and material culture: it is a common custom among nomads to travel together with their possessions, and therefore they give priority to the portability and practicality of products, as well as to the quality of their visual presentations as symbols of power and wealth. Despite the adoption of urban structures intended for the permanent settlement, Hulagu (d. 663/1265) and his immediate successors continued their steppe practices, whereby textiles well suited their sociocultural requirements.

The promotion of luxurious silk clothing and lavishly woven furnishings generated by the Mongols turned the Iranian world into a truly textile-conscious society. Not surprisingly, as the Mongols advanced westwards into West Asia with woven products of East and Central Asian origin, textiles propagated disparate artistic ideas throughout the Mongol Empire. The adoption of textile motifs from different parts of Mongol territory was perhaps initially caused by purely aesthetic reasons, but this in turn resulted in the visualisation of Mongol hegemony over Eurasia on a woven surface, almost like the map of their empire. This ultimately led to the occurrence of hitherto unknown modes in late thirteenth- and early fourteenth-century Iranian textile design.

The following two types of textile deserve special attention in an assessment of how Central Asian mediation affected Iranian appreciation of Chinese themes. One is silk tapestry, known as *kesi*. The technique of *kesi* was introduced into China from Central Asia through the mediation of the Uighurs during the Northern Song dynasty.[31] In China, *kesi* was mainly employed to cover or to wrap handscroll paintings. It was also used as a support for paintings, a technique that reached its high point in the Southern Song period

(1127–279); eventually, *kesi* itself came to be appreciated as a form of fine art.[32] In the non-Han regimes in northern China – namely, the Khitan Empire known as the Liao dynasty (907–1125) and the Tangut Empire known as the Xixia dynasty (1032–1227) – however, silk tapestry was used for items of clothing and furnishing.[33] Despite the difference in function, the exchange of decorative ideas was encouraged in both Central Asian and Chinese *kesi* woven from the eleventh to the thirteenth century. Chinese motifs, such as dragon-and-cloud patterns, were known in Central Asia in the context of conventional patterns used in Chinese silks, which were brought westwards from Song China as exports and, in the case of the Sino-Liao trade, as tributes,[34] and became fully integrated into the design concept of Central Asian *kesi* (Figure 1.1).

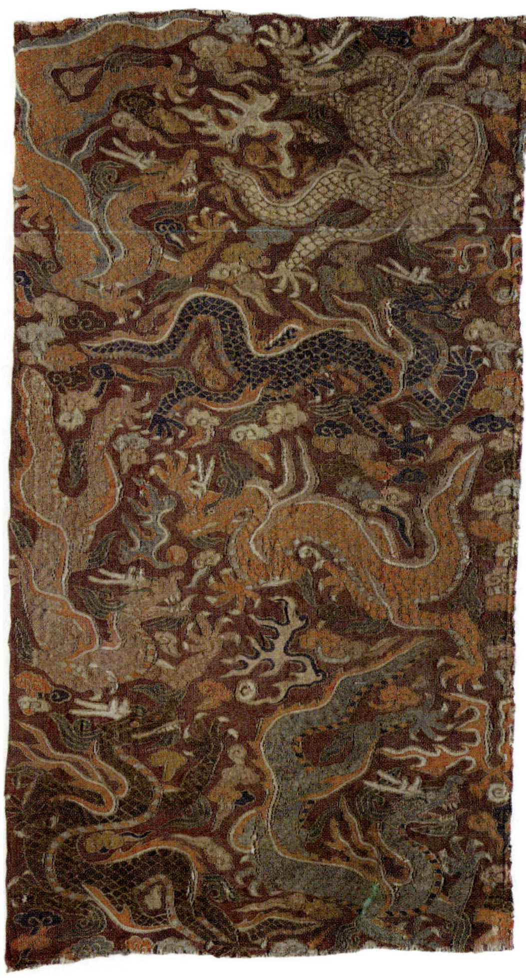

Figure 1.1 *Dragons chasing flaming pearls. Silk tapestry. Central Asia, c. 1200–1300.*

The other important type of textile is a cloth called *nasij* (*nasij al-dhahab al-harir*, literally 'cloth of gold and silk') or known as *panni tartarici*.[35] This particular textile can be viewed as the legacy of nomadism in ancient times – Central Asian nomads were dressed in garments with ornaments made of gold, and a similar golden effect was eventually applied to clothing.[36] Owing to its sumptuousness, cloth of gold was highly regarded throughout Eurasia during the Mongol period. As Ibn Battuta and Rashid al-Din mention, the luxurious weaving and extensive use of *nasij* caught the attention of contemporary travellers and historians from the West.[37] Most of the surviving *nasij* textiles, which found their way to the Middle East and Europe, have been preserved in religious and burial contexts.[38] A number of cloth-of-gold textiles datable to the late thirteenth and early fourteenth centuries, for instance, have been discovered in the tomb of Cangrande della Scala (d. 1329) in Verona (Figure 1.2),[39] demonstrating their immense commercial and artistic value at that time. The provenance and dating of the *nasij* textile can now be defined with some degree of certainty,[40] although the complexity of style and iconography found in this type of textile, as a result of cross-cultural relationships in Mongol Eurasia, makes it difficult to attribute the textile to a certain region.

Socially and economically, textiles played a vital role in both Mongol Iran and Yuan China (1271–1368). The production of *tiraz* – a textile with woven or embroidered Arabic and Persian inscriptions, carrying messages associated with power and authority[41] – continued at Baghdad, and the Ilkhanid capital Tabriz gradually became an important textile centre under royal patronage.[42] During the reign of the eighth Ilkhan, Uljaitu (r. 703/1304–716/1316), its manufacture was developed at the new capital of Sultaniyya under the control of the vizier Taj al-Din ʿAlishah.[43] A *tiraz* now in the Dom- und Diözesanmuseum in Vienna is particularly informative about the textile industry under the Ilkhanids.[44] Its careful execution suggests that this piece was woven at a royal workshop in Tabriz.[45] Judging by the inscriptions,[46] this textile is datable to the reign of Abu Saʿid, namely between 716/1316 and 736/1335. For various reasons, this fine piece travelled from Tabriz to Vienna, and was preserved as a burial garment for the Habsburg emperor Rudolf IV (d. 1365), perhaps through the mediation of Italian merchants.[47] Despite the lack of decisive Chinese elements, this is stylistically one of the most telling examples of Ilkhanid textiles. Its design consists of three types of bands – namely, running animals, medallions and Arabic inscriptions. Similar running animals can be found in the design of Central Asian *kesi*,[48] but they are more suggestive of conventional Islamic decoration.[49] A wide band contains polylobed and diamond medallions, a decorative device that is, as Wardwell has noted, associated with metalwork of the thirteenth century from Khurasan.[50] Importantly, this type of striped design, a feature of late

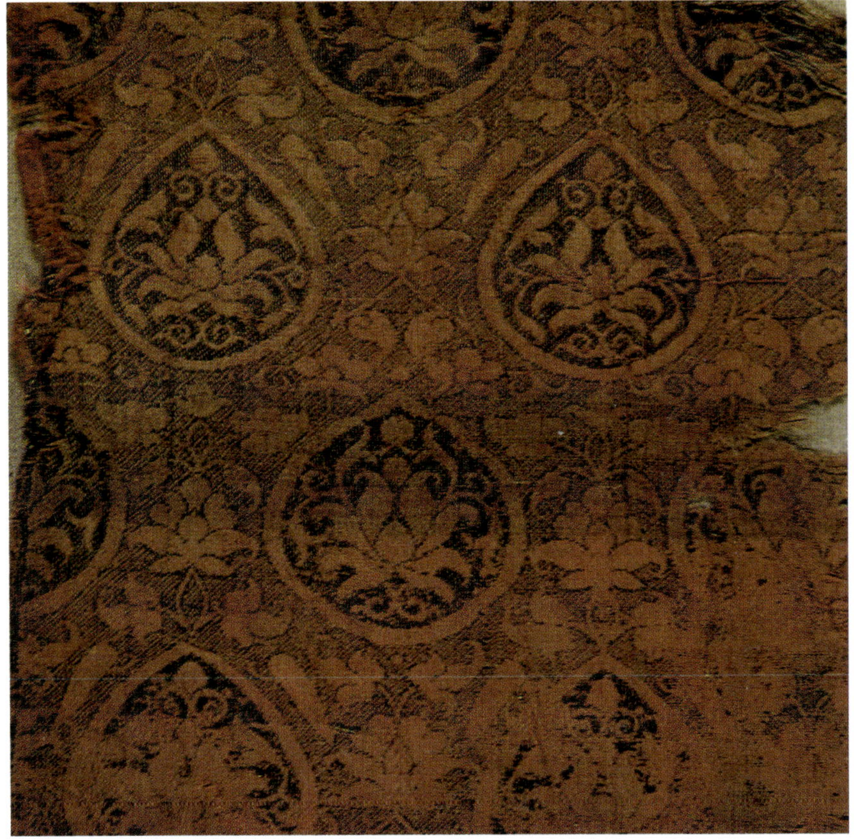

Figure 1.2 *Textile with lotus patterns. From the tomb of Cangrande della Scala (d. 1329). Lampas weave. Iran, c. 1300. This is a classic example of cloth of gold or the Tartar cloth, a group of textiles that have customarily been attributed to the eastern Iranian world during the Mongol period. The textile design in a sinicising mode, such as this lotus textile from Verona, provides visual evidence for chinoiserie in Ilkhanid art and material culture.*

thirteenth- and early fourteenth-century Iranian textiles,[51] recurs in early Ottoman textiles.[52]

With regard to Chinese textiles woven during the late thirteenth and early fourteenth centuries, the *Yuan shi*, a dynastic record of the Yuan period, provides useful information of how the Mongols made political and cultural use of textiles. According to the *Yuan shi*, the court restricted the use of the sun, moon, dragon and tiger on the decoration of silk and satin fabrics and that of the dragon and rhinoceros on horse saddles, as soon as the Yuan dynasty was officially established.[53] The use of the dragon was further controlled: the court first specified the use of five-clawed dragons for its imperial costumes in 1314.[54] This suggests that the Mongols intentionally adopted Chinese conventional motifs associated with imperial power for official clothing in the Yuan court.[55] The *Yuan shi* also refers to *nasij* textiles, which were produced on a large scale in China under Mongol patronage.[56] Because most *nasij* textiles were discovered outside China, the existence of domestic *nasij* production remains a matter of speculation; they were probably in the main exported to the West. Equally important is the role of foreign artisans in Yuan textile industry. As the number of weavers from the West began to increase from the 1220s onwards – for instance, more than a thousand artisans of the Western Regions arrived in China in 1223,[57] their cultural contribution to Yuan China became evident.[58] In 1275 Khubilai moved craftsmen from Besh Baliq to the Yuan capital Dadu, and an office was founded for the weaving of *nasij* textiles.[59] These craftsmen made a certain contribution to the development of the textile industry in Yuan China as government artisans.[60]

How chinoiserie occurred in the textiles of the Iranian world under the Mongols

Chinoiserie became a marked feature of Iranian textiles produced under Ilkhanid rule. Some textiles of this period bear striking Chinese elements, ranging from those typical of Chinese ornament, such as dragons and phoenixes, to those developed in the states of non-Han tribes in northern China. An examination of the Nuremberg textile (Figure 1.3)[61] is a good starting point for understanding the Iranian reaction to Chinese themes from the late thirteenth century onwards. The images – *qilin*-like animals and clouds surrounded by teardrop-shaped units – are visibly inspired by a specific Chinese textile design, whose basic decorative ideas can be traced back to the common motifs used in brocades of the Jin period (1115–1234),[62] a dynasty of the Jurchens that ruled some northern parts of China before the Mongols held supremacy over the area. In the case of the Nuremberg example, features of crouching deer, known as *djeiran* (a Central Asian antelope), surrounded by teardrop-shaped units, closely resemble those of the Cleveland Jin brocade (Figure 1.4), except for the absence of moon patterns.[63] The *djeiran* had a Sogdian ancestry. It became a popular motif in Tang decorative arts and was revived during the Jin dynasty.[64] Compared with the Jin brocade, however, each teardrop unit in the Nuremberg example is arranged in narrower spaces, which are filled with flower-like symbols. Such decorative adjustments are presumably associated with one of the guiding principles in Islamic ornament, namely the so-called 'horror vacui'[65] – a tendency to embellish a background with ornament.

Representations of clouds in the Nuremberg textile are bulky and simplified. Yet they still betray their stylistic indebtedness to the conventional cloud patterns used in Song textiles – for example, thirteenth-century silk textiles discovered in the tomb of

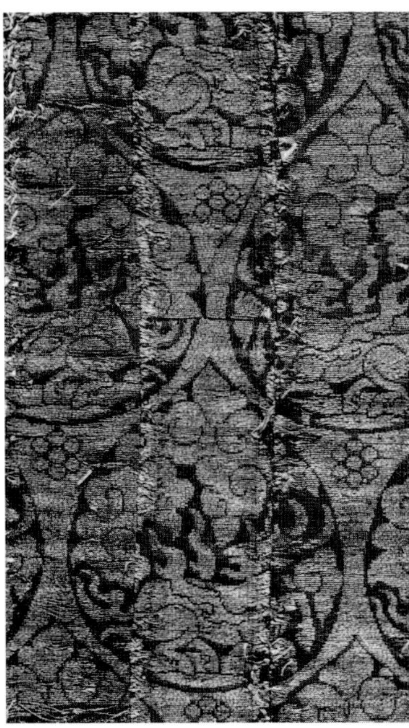

Figure 1.3 Djeiran *surrounded by teardrop units. Lampas weave. Eastern Iranian world, c. 1300.*

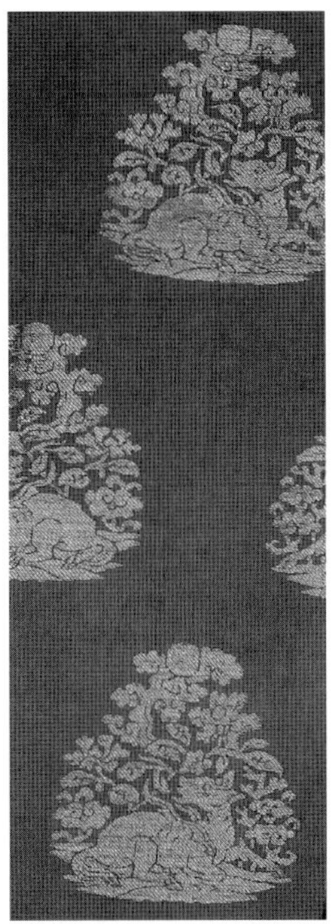

Figure 1.4 Djeiran *with floral branches and moon. Tabby brocade. China, Jin dynasty.*

Hang Sheng (Figure 1.5).[66] Clouds are one of the oldest artistic themes in Chinese art, and their basic designs were already established in the Shang and Zhou periods (c. 1500 BC–770 BC).[67] This motif essentially served to imply immortality and good fortune, but its significance often went beyond its use as an auspicious symbol; in Daoist thought the cloud was regarded as the accumulation of the cosmic breath, *qi*.[68] Its shapes were increasingly diversified during the Tang dynasty with the aid of images of creatures.[69] It seems that Chinese cloud patterns became familiar in northern China under Khitan rule in the context of conventional animal-and-cloud patterns and gradually moved westwards into Central Asia.[70] Iranian attachment to cloud patterns became obvious in the late thirteenth century, not only in textiles and other decorative objects, often together with animals, but also in painting, where they function as landscape elements.[71]

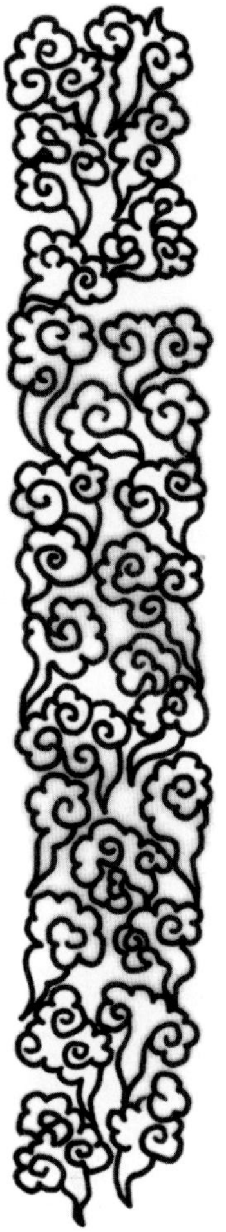

Figure 1.5 *Embroidery with cloud patterns. From the tomb of Hang Sheng. China, Southern Song dynasty.*

Another contemporary lampas found in Gdansk (Figure 1.6) is impressive by virtue of the subtle coexistence of Islamic and Chinese themes. Islamic features are evident in the confronted parrots with Arabic inscriptions on their wings and tails. As its inscriptions mention,[72] the textile was made for the Mamluk Sultan Nasir al-Din Muhammad (ruled intermittently from 693/1293 to 694/1294 and from 698/1299 to 741/1341), as one of the gifts offered by the last Ilkhan Abu Sa'id following the truce in 723/1323. It does not contradict an Arabic record mentioning that one of the Mongol rulers dispatched to him a present of 700 textiles woven with the sultan's titles,[73] and this textile might have been one of them. In the light of its political role, the design of the Gdansk textile must have been chosen with deliberation. In this respect, the inclusion of the ascending twisted dragons in the interstitial spaces of the polygonal roundels, a design that is evocative of early Yuan textiles,[74] invites discussion as to their iconographic function – how the Ilkhans viewed the dragon (*long*) – the symbol of longevity and the power of creation in China.[75] Perhaps the dragon was initially a mere fancy decorative motif for them. But, given the fashion for Chinese dragons not only in Iranian textiles of this period but also, as will be seen in the following chapters, in other media of Ilkhanid art, it must have gained a certain recognition in Ilkhanid contexts – for example, as a convenient device to underline a cultural affiliation with China. Interestingly, the dragon in the Gdansk example does not have five claws. This suggests that a model of the dragon used in this textile was unrelated to imperial production in Yuan China, or this may simply be due to the fact that the number of claws was modified, owing to the iconographic confusion that weavers with a non-Chinese cultural background must inevitably have faced.

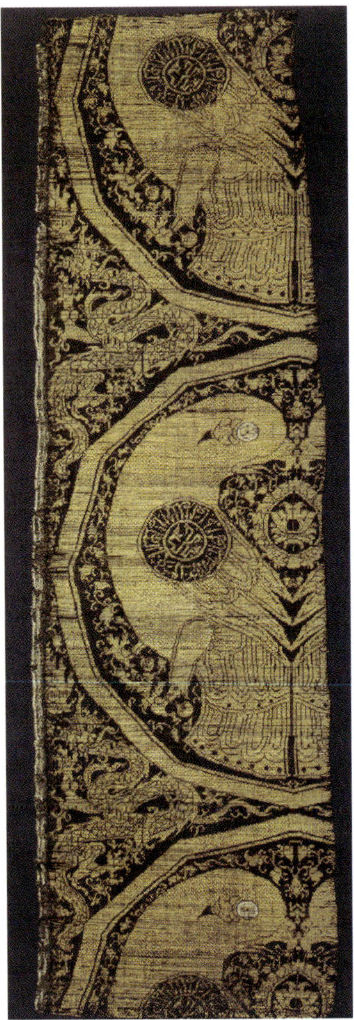

Figure 1.6 *Parrots and dragons. Silk and gold wrapped thread. Central Asia, c. 1300.*

In terms of chinoiserie, a lampas weave in the Kunstgewerbemuseum, Berlin (Figure 1.7),[76] is undoubtedly one of the key examples of eastern Iranian textiles under the Mongols. The artistic value of this textile lies in the presence of coiled dragons in roundels, small banks of clouds on the background and flying birds in the frieze decoration, all of which are distinctively of Chinese style. The coiled dragon motifs here are most reminiscent of those used in contemporary Yuan textiles,[77] or even resemble those of Jin brocades (Figure 1.8). The coiled dragon, often represented as chasing a pearl-like jewel[78] amid scattered clouds, was originally a literary creation of the Han period, and its image was developed in decorative contexts during the Tang dynasty.[79] The dragon patterns in the Berlin textile are slightly modified through Iranian interpretations – the pearl is absent from this example; the dragon tails here terminate in dragons' heads.

Another distinctive chinoiserie element in the Berlin example is a group of cloud patterns in the form of a pair of spectacles represented throughout the background, each of which is linked to long wisps of clouds. It shows a close stylistic affinity with contemporary Chinese textiles – for instance, similar cloud patterns are found in a Yuan blue silk textile fragment with cloud and longevity motifs (Figure 1.9).[80] This type of cloud motif was widely known as *lingzhi* (literally 'sacred fungus') in Chinese art.[81] This distinctive pattern was developed from the mushroom-like image of the top parts of clouds, whose decorative schemes were especially diversified in Tang art under the influence of Buddhism;[82] by the thirteenth century it had been associated with the image of the lobed head of the fungus of immortality.[83] The pattern soon became much more stylised into a peculiar motif called *ruyi* (literally 'as you wish'),[84] which was extensively adapted to various media of the decorative arts during the Yuan period.[85] Weavers of the Berlin textile seemingly intended to represent conventional Chinese dragon-and-cloud patterns called *yunlong*, which were closely associated with imperial power, serving as a symbol of the emperor.[86]

Yet another eye-catching element in this textile is the bird-and-flower design that appears against a background of pseudo-Kufic decoration in the frieze decoration between dragon roundels. The design, which consists of birds amid stylised foliage ornament,

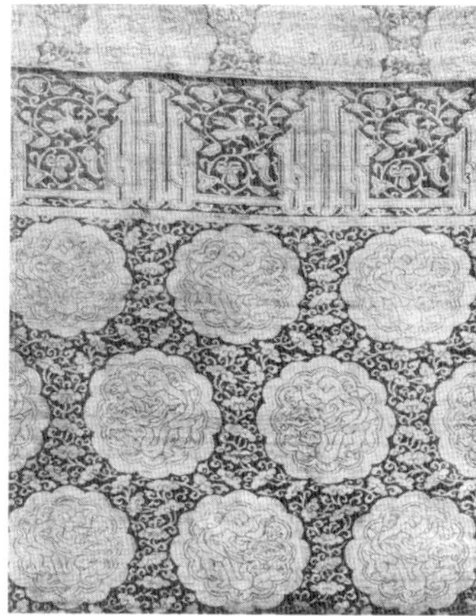

Figure 1.7 *Coiled dragons and clouds. Lampas weave. Eastern Iranian world, c. 1275–1350.*

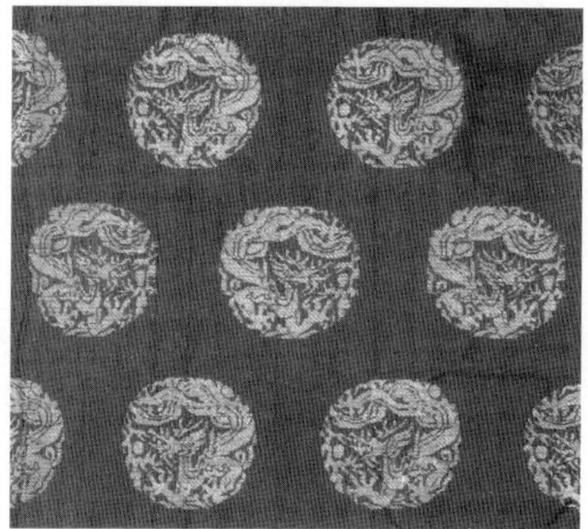

Figure 1.8 *Coiled dragons. Tabby brocade. China, Jin dynasty.*

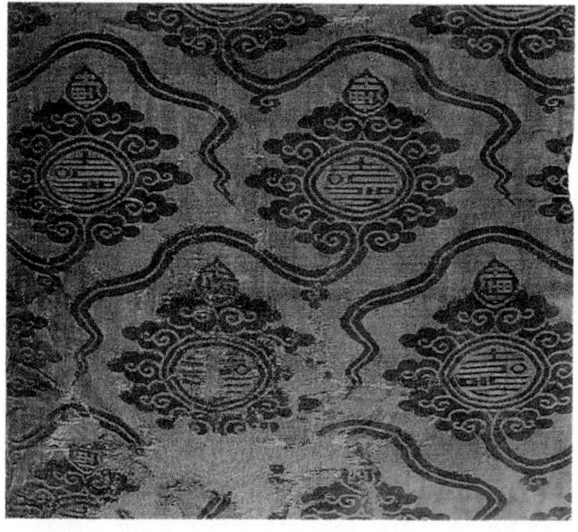

Figure 1.9 *Textile with cloud and longevity motifs. China, Yuan dynasty.*

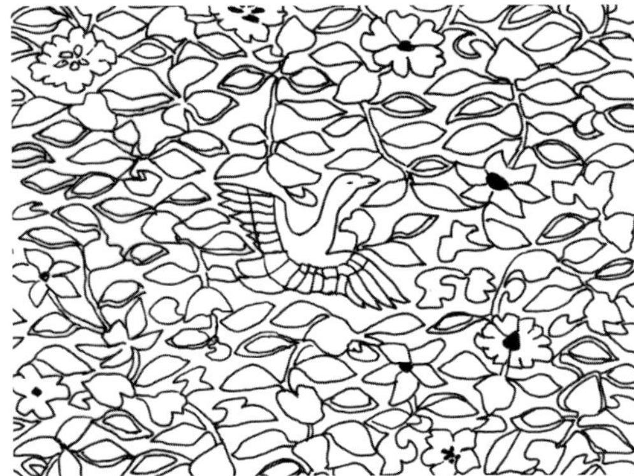

Figure 1.10 *Animals and birds amid flowers. Silk tapestry. China, Northern Song dynasty.*

Figure 1.11 *Birds and medallions. Lampas weave. Eastern Islamic world, c. 1250–1350.*

bears a certain resemblance to those of Song and Yuan *kesi* (Figure 1.10), though it is hard to identify the birds. More visible reaction to Chinese bird themes is observable in another textile that has been attributed to the late thirteenth- and early fourteenth-century eastern Islamic world (Figure 1.11).[87] Referring to traditional paired bird motifs in Islamic textiles, Chinese and Islamic themes are juxtaposed, so that Chinese phoenixes (*fenghuang*) resembling those used in Song and Yuan silk tapestries (Figure 1.12) replace Islamic birds and are joined to bulb palmettes. In spite of the symmetrical balance, suggestions of fluttering wings and rippling plumage help to create a sense of movement in the whole image. The *fenghuang* is, like the dragon, one of the most characteristic decorative patterns associated with Chinese culture.[88] The *fenghuang* was equated with the Red Bird of the South (*zhuniao*) in the Han period, but the image of the phoenix with beautiful plumage was developed in later Chinese art traditions. It was eventually incorporated into the imperial image as an emblem of the empress.[89]

Along with the introduction of Chinese animal themes, an artistic response to Chinese floral patterns manifested itself in Islamic textile design. Like one of the Cangrande textiles in Verona (Figure 1.2), Iranian textiles of the Mongol period display the imagery of lotuses with fidelity to Chinese conventions. The lotuses in the Verona textile, which contains eight-petalled lotus motifs enclosed in a teardrop-shaped frame, are merged deeply into the whole decorative schemes. They are present in an articulate form, and show an unmistakable stylistic indebtedness to conventional lotus motifs used in Song and Yuan decorative arts (e.g. Figures 1.12, 3.12).[90]

Thus the surviving Ilkhanid examples cited above reveal a close relation with Chinese artistic traditions; indeed, each Chinese theme is represented with such care that it is possible to track down its

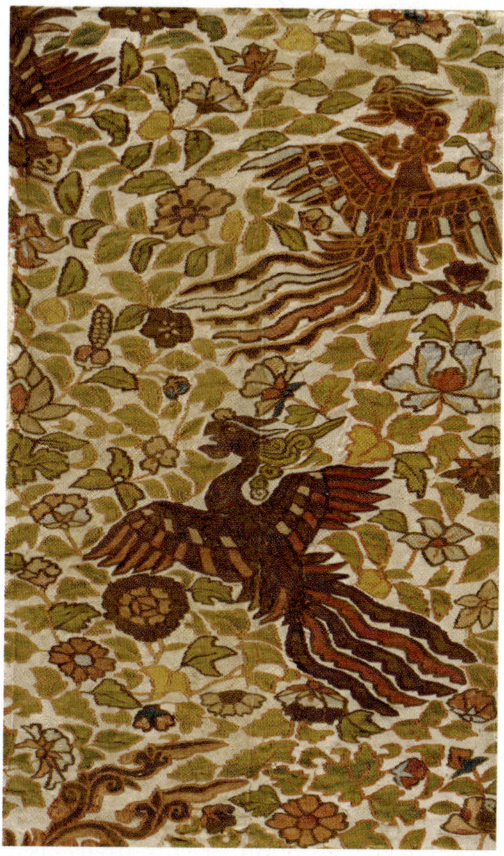

Figure 1.12 *Phoenixes amid flowers. Silk tapestry. China, Yuan dynasty.*

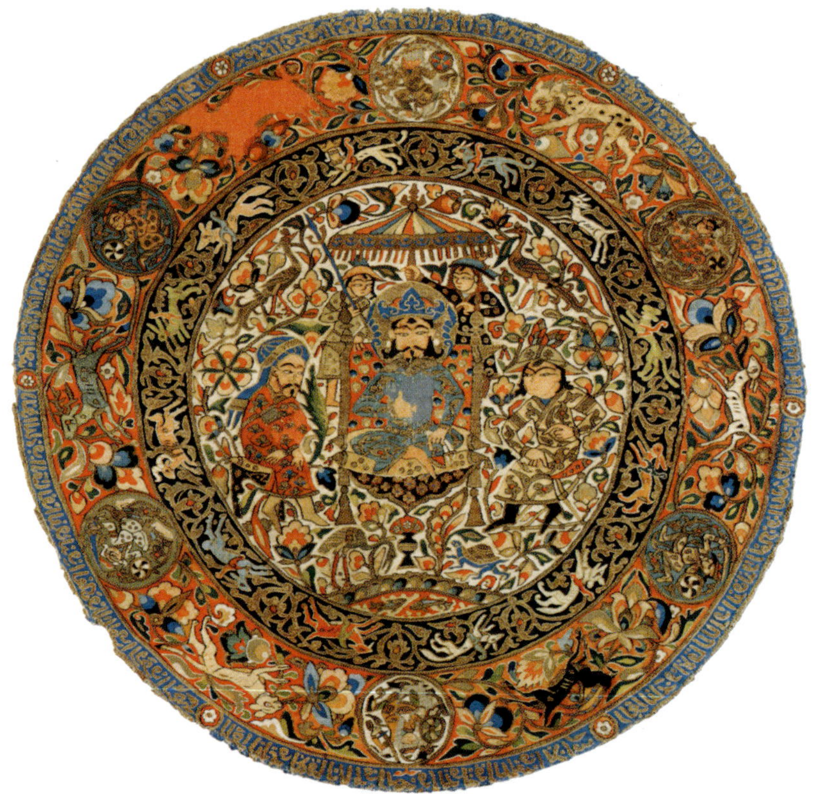

Figure 1.13 *Tapestry woven roundel. Iraq or Iran, c. 1325.*

Chinese sources. The important point to note is that the use of Chinese motifs in Iranian textiles was not merely employed to add exotic elegance. Reworking the new decorative ideas from East Asia suitable for indigenous cultural requirements, Iranian textiles of this period achieved unique, stylistic innovations.

Having looked in detail at Chinese elements in Ilkhanid textiles that have survived in fragmentary form, we can now extend the observation into how these elements were involved in the formation of the decorative programme as a whole. The following two examples from Copenhagen are particularly informative as to the overall impression of chinoiserie elements in large-size fabrics produced in Mongol-ruled Iran.

The coexistence of Islamic and Chinese themes in a silk tapestry in the David Collection (Figure 1.13) is worth consideration. The central image of this roundel – an enthroned prince surrounded by two attendants and two guards – is entirely Islamic, for a similar iconographical device is very common in contemporary Iranian manuscript painting and metalwork.[91] The background of this image is decorated with abundant floral patterns. Although they are supposedly intended to create naturalistic scenery, the flower motifs are merely employed to fill the space. On the other hand, Chinese themes are visibly incorporated into the animal scheme of the David Collection tapestry. Two flying birds with long plumage behind two guards evoke Chinese-inspired phoenixes of the type represented in the Cleveland bird textile (Figure 1.11). The crane and the tortoise that appear in front of the throne are novel accessions to chinoiserie repertoires in Iranian textiles. The crane symbolises longevity in Chinese art. It is a popular theme in Song art and can often be found in textiles and painting of the period.[92] The tortoise is generally regarded as an emblem of longevity, strength and endurance.[93] According to the *Liji* ('Book of Rites'), the unicorn (*qilin*), phoenix, tortoise and dragon are the four intelligent creatures.[94] The tortoise later became one of the animals symbolising the cardinal points, and was known as the Black Warrior of the North.[95] Since the tortoise does not occur frequently in Tang, Song and Yuan examples,[96] it is hard to track down Chinese models for the tortoise used in the David Collection *kesi*. In addition, the iconographic relationship between the crane and the tortoise remains unclear. The central motif is further encircled by two types of decorative bands: one depicts a running animal and the other comprises calligraphy. The first frieze consists of twelve animals running anticlockwise amid gold arabesques on a dark blue ground, and these colour and decorative schemes are, as Folsach has pointed out, akin to those found in thirteenth-century Central Asian *kesi*.[97] Chinese-inspired lotus motifs dominate the background of the second frieze, where six running animals and six roundels are represented alternately. Here their Chinese sources can be found in Central Asian or Chinese *kesi* – for example, in the elaborate *kesi* in Los Angeles (Figure 1.12).

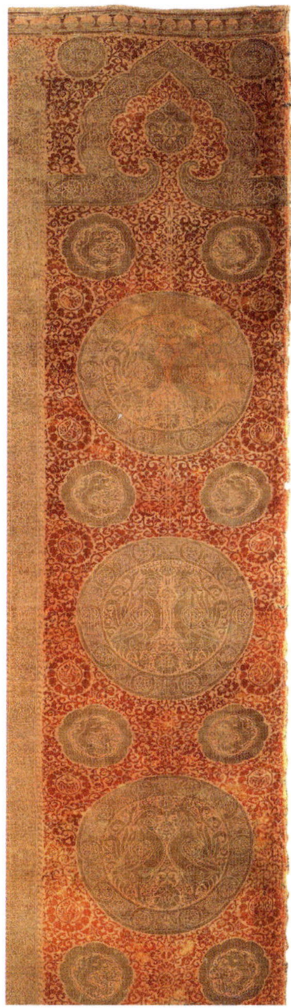

Figure 1.14 *Hanging with confronted roosters and coiled dragons. Lampas weave. Central Asia, c. 1300.*

A hanging in Copenhagen (Figure 1.14) is notable not only in its rich decorative schemes but also in its impressive size, namely more than 2 metres in height. The item, together with almost identical hangings in the Museum of Islamic Art in Doha (TE.40.2000),[98] was presumably commissioned for furnishing the interior of an extravagant tent and a royal palace. Such woven luxuries were well suited to Ilkhanid society and ideas of conspicuous consumption, for the Ilkhanid government remained mobile, travelling from one place to another according to the season, and the Mongol rulers and nobles in West Asia may have wallowed in nostalgia for their nomadic past in the steppes of north-east Asia, setting up large encampments with massive lavish tents or decorating their palaces with tent hangings.[99] The main motifs of the hanging are roundels of two different sizes: the large one, resembling Sasanian pearl roundels, contains paired roosters, a motif of Iranian origin.[100] In the interstices there are three different types of palmettes. The largest one, near the roosters' feet, is reminiscent of that often represented in thirteenth-century Central Asian textiles.[101] As for the coiled dragon used in the small medallions, as in the Berlin textile (Figure 1.7), Jin brocades and Yuan textiles (e.g. Figure 1.8) provide the best prototype of this design. Such motifs, beautifully highlighted against a red background, are further decorated with flower patterns and teardrop-shaped medallions with flying birds. Naturalism is absent in these floral patterns, which can more readily be described as arabesques of Islamic origin.

The most marked pattern in this piece is the four-lobed motif boldly used in the top section. This is the so-called cloud collar, *yunjian* (literally, 'cloud-shoulder'). The origin of the cloud collar remains uncertain.[102] The concept of cruciform motifs can be recognised in Han burial objects,[103] and similar patterns are found in Song textiles, which are composed of four *ruyi* patterns.[104] However, the cloud collar is not entirely of Chinese origin. It first became familiar to non-Han tribes on the northern fringes of China, such as the Jurchens and the Mongols, as a costume element during the twelfth and thirteenth centuries.[105] It is very likely that the cloud collar was introduced to China during the Mongol period and eventually became an important component in official costumes of the Yuan court.[106] This accessory, which is customarily woven into the robe[107] or attached to the shoulder (Figure 1.15),[108] must have been regarded as an important symbol to show class or wealth in Mongol society. By the middle of the thirteenth century, the cloud collar had reached Iran, as the adaptation of this design is recognised in the *tiraz* of Abu Bakr (r. c. 623/1226–658/1260), a Salghurid ruler of Fars, which is now in the David Collection (20/1994).[109] Although neither complete nor fragmentary cloud collars attributable to Mongol Iran are known to survive, the motif seems to have gained a certain recognition as a costume element in Ilkhanid territory, as reflected in representations of elaborate cloud-collar decoration attached to Mongol-type robes in contemporary manuscript painting.[110] This peculiar lobed design caught the fancy of both Iranian and Chinese artists as a potential framing device for other media of the pictorial and decorative arts during the Mongol period, ranging from Qur'an illumination (Figure 6.15) to ceramic decoration (Figure 2.17), and continued to be depicted in Iranian painting as an important decorative accessory for clothing until the sixteenth century.[111]

There had been continuous exchanges of artistic ideas between Chinese and Iranian textiles since the pre-Islamic period, yet clearly the Mongol invasions resulted in the encouragement of deeper Iranian contacts with Chinese art and fostered the full-scale

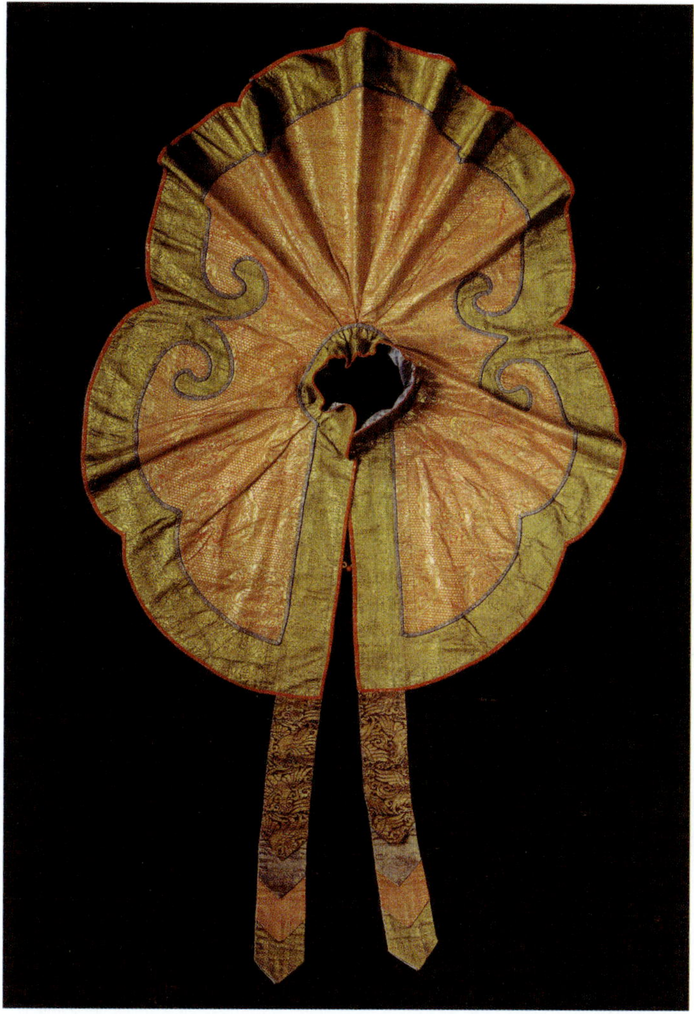

Figure 1.15 *Cloud collar. China, Yuan dynasty.*

introduction of Chinese themes into Iranian textile design. Chinese themes were not always conveyed directly to Iran; they often made their way there through the mediation of Central Asia. By the end of the Ilkhanid dynasty, however, Chinese decorative schemes had successfully been incorporated into the formation of the chinoiserie style in Iranian art.

The re-examination of Iranian textiles in this chapter has shown some basic patterns of the adoption and adaptation of Chinese themes in Iranian art. In the following discussion of chinoiserie in Iranian art, the interrelationship between Chinese themes used in Iranian textiles and those used in other media of Iranian art should always be kept in mind.

Notes

1. Allsen 1997.
2. Liu 1988; 1998.
3. Foltz 1999.
4. For further information about the early history of silk production in China, see Zhao 1999, 20–3, 38–43.
5. *Han shu* 1962, ch. 94, 3743–835 and ch. 96, 3871–932.
6. For a recent study of silk fragments found in Palmyra, see Stauffer 1996; Schmidt-Colinet, Stauffer and Al-Asʿad 2000, 58–81. For a Chinese textile found in Dura-Europos, see Mahler 1966, fig. 94. The main route between China and Roman Orient during the first two centuries ran through Central Asia to the Indus valley; going directly to the sea coast along the Indus or making a detour through Mathura, it connected with the Roman world by sea (Liu 1988, 19).
7. Harris (ed.) 1993, 68.
8. For Parthian textiles, see Kawami 1992.
9. For Tang exoticism, see Schafer 1963.
10. *Sui shu* 1973, ch. 83, 1856–7; *Jiu Tang shu* 1975, ch. 198, 5311–13; *Xin Tang shu* 1975, ch. 221b, 6258–60.
11. Sasanian textiles were also known in the Byzantine Empire. It is said that during the reign of the Emperor Justinian (r. 527–65) two Nestorian monks brought silk worm eggs to the West (for a summary of this issue, see Muthesius 1995, 120–2).
12. For further discussion of West Asian elements in Tang textiles, see Zhao 1999, 97–9.
13. For the development of roundels in Tang textiles, see ibid. 125–9.
14. For Iranian pearl roundels, see *SPA*, pls 197, 200, 201A, 202B and 203. It has been suggested that pearl roundels are of Chinese origin, because similar decorative ideas are found in Han textiles (Meister 1970). It is, however, generally agreed that this motif had already occurred at a very early time in the Middle East (McDowell 1989, 153).
15. See Zhao 1999, pls 03.04–03.08, 03.10 and 04.06.
16. See Liu 1995, 28–9.
17. See Saeki 1928.
18. Foltz 1999, 8–9.
19. Zhao 1999, 99. See also Sheng 1999a.
20. For Zandaniji textiles, see Shepherd and Henning 1959; Shepherd 1981a.
21. For further discussion about Sasanian elements in Zandaniji textiles, see Shepherd and Henning 1959, 34–5.
22. See Weibel 1972, 48, pls 99–101. See also a textile known as 'the shroud of St Josse', probably woven in northern Khurasan in the middle of the tenth century (7502, Louvre, Paris; Bernus et al. 1971). The design here is relatively simplified, stiff and repetitive.
23. See Shepherd 1974; 1981b; Blair, Bloom and Wardwell 1992.
24. *WSWG*, no. 43; Folsach 2001, no. 635. For a discussion of the provenance and dating of this textile, see Folsach and Bernsted 1993, 48–50; Wardwell 1992, 362–3. For a related example, see Schorta 2004.
25. For the discussion of double-headed eagle motifs in Saljuq textiles, see Wenzel 1990, 138–41. For Byzantine models of this design, see Weibel 1972, pls 60–60a.
26. Wardwell 1992, 363, figs 9–11.

27. See Öney 1969. See Chapter 4 for further discussion of Islamic dragons.
28. Wardwell 1992, 363. See also Blair 1992, 12–13, pl. 38.
29. See *WSWG*, no. 11.
30. For further discussion, see Allsen 2001a, 31–4.
31. On the origin of *kesi*, see Cammann 1948; Dubosc 1948. For a further discussion of the early development of *kesi*, see Sheng 1995.
32. Fong and Watt 1996, 249. See, e.g., *WSWG*, fig. 15.
33. For Liao and Xixia *kesi*, see *WSWG*, 59–60. Scholarly interest in Liao textiles has grown in recent years, thanks to the increase of archaeological discoveries in the last decade (see Zhao 2004; Schorta (ed.) 2007; Franses 2007). They are of great importance in filling the gaps in Chinese textile history from the ninth to the twelfth century, as well as in understanding how Chinese themes were conveyed into West Asia. The significance of the Tanghut Empire lies in its religious connections with the Tibetans and Mongols: Tibetan Buddhism, which was the state religion of the empire, was later adopted by Mongol rulers. For further information about this empire, see Franke and Twitchett (eds) 1994, 154–214.
34. The tributary exchange with the Liao Empire was necessary for Song China in order to stabilise frontier relations with nomadic neighbours (see Shiba 1983, 97–100; Jagchid and Symons 1989, 125–35). The westward transmission of Chinese art traditions presumably continued under the Kara-Khitay (1132–1211), a polity of the western Khitan tribes that was established by a descendant of the Liao dynasty. For the historical background of this realm, see Sinor 1998.
35. See, for the detailed discussion of the term *nasij*, Allsen 1997, 2–4. This term, derived from the Arabic verb, *nasaja* ('to weave'), was eventually adapted to Chinese as *nashishi* (*Yuan shi* 1976, ch. 78, 1931, 1938).
36. See Thompson 2004, 72.
37. See Juvaini 1958, 63; Ibn Battuta 1958–2000, 3, 558. Full information about contemporary sources is given by Allsen 1997, 1–10.
38. For further discussion, see Wardwell 1988–9. See also a cloth-of-gold textile found in Ukek, one of the Golden Horde cities (Nedashkovsky 2004, 152–60). In the case of a winged lion textile in the Cleveland Museum of Art (1989.50; *WSWG*, no. 35), datable to the mid-thirteenth century, the textile was found in Tibet; it was presumably woven as a part of the imperial donations from the Mongol Great Khans to Tibetan monasteries (ibid. 129; for further discussion about Mongol–Tibetan relations, see Petech 1983).
39. See Magagnato (ed.) 1983.
40. See Wardwell 1988–9, 133, app. 1. A number of accounts about textiles of the time are also useful for identifying weaving centres that existed in the Middle East and Central Asia in that period. Polo described Baghdad textiles as 'richly wrought with figures of beasts and birds', though he did not give any further information about their colours and decorative patterns (Polo 1993, 1, 63). Mosul, Tabriz, Sultaniyya, Shiraz, Yazd, Isfahan, Nishapur, Herat and Samarkand were all major weaving centres in the Iranian world in that period. For further information, see Wardwell 1988–9, 122, n. 1.
41. On the *tiraz*, see Grohmann 1934; Stillman et al. 2000.
42. Polo 1993, 1, 75; Serjeant 1972, 68–9.

43. Wardwell 1988–9, 109; Serjeant 1972, 25–7.
44. See Wardwell 1988–9, 108–9. A research project on this textile is currently being carried out under the directorship of Dr Markus Ritter.
45. Ibid. 109.
46. They read 'Glory to our lord the most great sultan, the exalted monarch ʿAlaʾ al-Dunya waʾl-Din [A]bu Saʿid Bahadur Khan, may God make his rule eternal' (ibid. 108).
47. Ibid.
48. See, e.g., *WSWG*, nos 14–15.
49. See Baer 1998, 34–6.
50. Wardwell 1988–9, 109; see, e.g., Melikian-Chirvani 1982, fig. 35, no. 41.
51. See, e.g., Wardwell 1988–9, figs 5, 13–14, 23–5 and 41–2; *Legacy*, cat. no. 75.
52. See Ettinghausen 1961.
53. *Yuan shi* 1976, ch. 7, 131 (quoted in Allsen 1997, 108).
54. *Yuan shi* 1976, ch. 78, 1942.
55. For further discussion, see Allsen 1997, 107–8.
56. In Yuan China, gold thread was produced under the control of the Gold Thread Office (*jinsiziju*) (*Yuan shi* 1976, ch. 88, 2226–7) and was used for the production of *nasij* at the Offices for Weaving and Dying (*ranzhi tijusi*), which were established in many locations under the control of the Ministry of Works (ibid., ch. 85, 2149–52).
57. *Yuan shi* 1976, ch. 153, 3609.
58. See, for further information, Chen 1966, 18–275. For a French goldsmith who worked at the Mongol court in China, see Olschki 1946.
59. *Yongle dadian* 1962, 92, ch. 19781, leaf 17 (quoted in *WSWG*, 130–1).
60. See Chü 1972; Oshima 1983. The involvement of weavers from Central and West Asia in Yuan textile production caused the revival of Occidentalism in the art of China during the Mongol period. Like Tang textile designs, Yuan textiles show multifarious stylistic features, derived from Central Asian and further west (see, e.g., Zhao 1999, pls 06.02, 06.03 and 06.06).
61. Similar pieces are found in Utrecht and Berlin (*SPA*, 2060, fig. 667; Wardwell 1988–9, fig. 54).
62. *WSWG*, 110, no. 28; Zhao 1999, pl. 05.09. The so-called swan hunt motif (*haidongqing*) was typical of Jin brocades and was famous for its use in royal robes designed for spring hunting (*Jin shi* 1975, ch. 43, 984; *WSWG*, 108). This design consists of teardrop units arranged in a horizontal row, each of which has an image of a falcon swooping down upon a recumbent swan. Other animals, such as dragons and phoenixes, were eventually adapted to this pattern, and these motifs survived until the Yuan dynasty (see Ogasawara 1989, fig. 10).
63. For the significance of the moon in *djeiran* patterns, see *WSWG*, 114.
64. Ibid.
65. For this principle, see Ettinghausen 1979b.
66. For this site, see Fujiansheng bowuguan (ed.) 1982.
67. See, for the development of Chinese cloud patterns, Wu 2000.
68. See Laing 1998, 32.
69. Rawson 1984, 139.
70. See, e.g., *WSWG*, no. 9.
71. This point will be addressed in the following chapters on manuscript painting. For further discussion, see Kadoi 2002.

72. They read, 'Glory to our lord the sultan, the king, the just, the wise Nasir' (Folsach and Bernsted 1993, 30).
73. Ibid. 29–30. For further discussion on Ilkhanid–Mamluk gift exchanges, see Little 2006.
74. See Zhao 1999, pl. 09.03.
75. For the dragon in Chinese art in general, see Rawson 1984, 93–9; Zhao 1991.
76. For a similar example in Leipzig, see Bonn/Munich, cat. no. 331. For the dating of this textile, see *WSWG*, 138; Folsach and Bernsted 1993, 54–5.
77. See, e.g., Brown 2000, 30–6; *WSWG*, no. 42.
78. A pearl-like jewel is more likely to be associated with Buddhist iconography. The jewel might have been derived from the Buddhist *ruyi baozhu* ('wish-granting jewel') that symbolises transcendent wisdom. It is, however, uncertain when the images of the dragon and the jewel combined (Brown 2000, 33).
79. *WSWG*, 116. Similar coiled dragon motifs are recognised in a portrait of a king of the Tangut Empire in Cave 409 at Dunhuang (Whitfield et al. 2000, 29).
80. This is one of the examples brought from Egypt to Russia in the late nineteench century, and this type of textile is thought to have been produced for the Mamluk market (Piotrovsky and Pritula (eds) 2006, 96–7). A similar piece from Durunka excavations is now in the Museum of Islamic Art in Cairo (MIA 2225; O'Kane (ed.) (2006), cat. no. 90).
81. Rawson 1984, 139.
82. e.g. ibid., figs 125b–d.
83. Ibid. 139.
84. See, for the development of *ruyi* patterns, Cort and Stuart 1993, 35–7.
85. See, e.g., *Sekai*, 7, no. 212.
86. The dragon is included in the twelve imperial symbols, which are thought to have been used for costumes of the rulers in pre-history. For further discussion, see Zhao 1999, 254–65.
87. For further discussion of the provenance of this textile, see Wardwell 1988–9, 107–8. See also a contemporary bird textile in Cleveland (1985.4; *WSWG*, no. 47). Here diving and standing phoenixes are alternately arranged in horizontal rows against a pale green background filled with floral vine motifs. The distinctive features of diving and standing phoenixes with elegant plumage seemingly originated in Central Asia and were introduced to China at least as early as the Song dynasty (Rawson 1984, 100–1; *WSWG*, 196).
88. For the development of the phoenix pattern in Chinese art, see Rawson 1984, 99–107.
89. See Williams 1974, 323–6.
90. See Chapter 3 for further discussion of lotus decoration in Ilkhanid art.
91. See, e.g., Simpson 1979, figs 12, 17, 22, 33, 49, 62–4 and 93–4. For a related image in contemporary metalwork, see Ward 1993, pl. 66.
92. See, e.g., Fong and Watt 1996, fig. 96. In a superb Northern Song *kesi* in the Palace Museum collection (*WSWG*, 56–9, fig. 14), for instance, the flight of cranes through clouds seems to have been associated with a Daoist cult of immortality. The crane is not common in Song ceramics (Wirgin 1979, 204).
93. Williams 1974, 404.
94. *Li ji*, ch. 7, 9 (quoted in Williams 1974, frontispiece).

95. Rawson 1984, 90–1. The other animals are: the Green Dragon of the East, the White Tiger of the West and the Red Bird (the Phoenix) of the South.
96. Wirgin 1979, 198–9.
97. Folsach 1996, 87. See, e.g., *WSWG*, no. 19.
98. Thompson 2004, cat. no. 19.
99. See ibid. 76.
100. See Daneshvari 1986, 56–67.
101. See, e.g., *WSWG*, no. 35.
102. On the origin of cloud collars, see Cammann 1951.
103. See, e.g., Watson 1995, fig. 171.
104. See Fujiansheng bowuguan (ed.) 1982, fig. 41.
105. The first literary evidence of cloud collars is found in the *Jin shi* 1975 (ch. 43, 980). For earlier visual evidence, see Gong Suran's *The Revered Concubine Crosses the Frontier* (c. 1127–62; Osaka Municipal Museum of Art, Osaka; Kessler 1993, fig. 39), where Wang Zhaojin is depicted as a Mongolian by her dress with an elaborate cloud collar.
106. *Yuan shi* 1976, ch. 78, 1940.
107. See, e.g., Zhao 1999, 202.
108. See also Hansen 1950, 6–11, fig. 4.
109. For this textile, see *WSWG*, 135, fig. 63; Folsach 2001, no. 639. It is highly probable that, judging by the occurrence of cloud collars in a group of early thirteenth-century Daghestan sculpture (Salmony 1943, figs 1–3), they may have been disseminated into the Caucasus region.
110. See Grabar and Blair 1980, pls 14, 28.
111. See, e.g., Lentz and Lowry 1989, 216–19.

CHAPTER TWO

Ceramics

A STUDY OF ceramics provides further clues to the artistic contact between Iran and China and a deeper understanding of how the Iranian desire to imitate the works of Chinese art was developed throughout the ages. Because of its continued significance during the long period of cultural interchanges between the two countries, chinoiserie in Iranian and broadly Middle Eastern ceramics has been widely discussed by both Islamic and Chinese art historians, especially since the increase in the number of archaeological discoveries and the flow of Chinese ceramics into Western art markets during the early twentieth century.[1]

There is little doubt that Chinese ceramics – which was referred to as *chini-i faghfur*[2] – continuously influenced Iranian pottery and played a decisive role in the development of all Middle Eastern ceramics. In particular, three periods, approximating to the ninth, twelfth and seventeenth centuries, have been emphasised as the periods in which Iranian ceramics underwent significant technical and stylistic changes through the greatest exposure to Chinese ceramics. The last period, equivalent to the Safavid dynasty (907/1501–1135/1722), is outside the scope of this book,[3] but it is necessary to reconsider the first two waves of chinoiserie in Iranian ceramics – even though the ninth and twelfth centuries are slightly inappropriate markers, since the end of each wave includes a part of the following century – in order to understand more clearly what happened in late thirteenth- and early fourteenth-century Iranian ceramics.

A complete overview of the impact of China on Iranian ceramics, however, has not yet been given; this is mainly due to the slow development of Iranian ceramic studies.[4] While studies in Chinese ceramics have been developing steadily along with the increase of archaeological discoveries, notably from Inner Mongolia, the chronology and dating of Iranian ceramics remain problematic. A major obstacle to the study of Iranian ceramics is the limited amount of information about kiln-sites and workshops during the Middle Ages. Archaeological discoveries, even though they have increased in number, remain too inadequate to ascertain reliably the dating and provenance of the finds.

The aim of this chapter is to construct a balanced picture of the development of chinoiserie in Iranian ceramics up to the late fourteenth century, by referring to newly acquired information from both Iranian and Chinese sources. The present argument is very likely to be modified by further archaeological discoveries, but it will be useful to collect and summarise the information currently available about Chinese elements in Iranian ceramics.

Before examining any actual examples, it would be useful to make a general observation about the Iranian reaction to the art of Chinese ceramics, by referring to the case of textiles, since both were key products during the prosperous period of the Sino-Iranian trade and were among the major channels through which Chinese art traditions were conveyed to Iranian artists. Both in China and Iran, ceramics were produced mainly for domestic use, whereas silk textiles were regarded as luxury items as well as having religious significance. As ceramics replaced metalwork as a major art form in Tang China, however, its functions developed accordingly. The manufacture of ceramics was divided into several functions – such as aesthetic appreciation, burial and simple utility – and by degrees the luxurious connotations of Chinese ceramics were echoed in Iranian potters' works.

A more fundamental difference between ceramics and textiles is that decorative concepts were not as influential as were techniques during the first stage of the Iranian encounter with Chinese ceramics. Motifs of Chinese origin, such as dragons and phoenixes, were not adopted immediately in Iranian ceramic decoration. Instead, certain unusual technical features of Chinese ceramics, namely translucence, whiteness and hardness – elements that had been difficult to create with materials available in Iran – made an immense impact on Iranian potters and inspired them to develop similar techniques and methods. In the course of copying Chinese examples, the coloured glazes so popular in early Middle Eastern ceramics – for example, those of dull green colour – were gradually replaced by more refined, visually appealing ones, some of Chinese inspiration. Moreover, the handsome shapes and thin bodies of imported Chinese ceramics had a great impact on the artistic concepts of Muslim potters, who modulated the shapes of their wares, which had hitherto rather clumsily copied metalwork, and transformed them into well-proportioned shapes more appropriate for ceramics. There is thus no doubt that the Iranian or broadly Middle Eastern imitation of Chinese ceramics resulted – in so far as this was technically possible – in refining the styles and techniques of their ceramic products. Iranian potters imitated Chinese ceramics primarily for artistic reasons, but the appearance of stereotyped copies and their wide distribution throughout the Middle East suggest that imitation was to some extent undertaken both intentionally and systematically to appeal to a wide range of clients in the Middle East for financial gain.

Early Sino-Iranian relations in ceramics: the first wave

The efflorescence of the Sino-Muslim ceramic trade first occurred under the Tang and ʿAbbasid Empires. Contemporary treatises by Arab geographers[5] and a number of Chinese sherds found at major Islamic sites of the period, notably Samarra in Iraq,[6] the capital of the ʿAbbasid court between 221/836 to 279/892, demonstrate that Chinese ceramics were extensively exported to the Middle East from the early ʿAbbasid period onwards, probably mainly by sea across the Indian Ocean.[7] The potters of the Islamic world were certainly aware of the fineness of imported Chinese wares, which must have been extremely valuable and expensive in the Muslim market, and very soon they began to copy Chinese pieces. The first encounter with fine Chinese ceramics greatly influenced them, and Muslim admiration for Chinese pieces did not diminish until Muslim relations with China became indirect in the seventeenth century,[8] though, as will be discussed later, the degree to which Chinese ceramics were received and imitated by Muslim potters differs from period to period.

The first phase of chinoiserie can be seen clearly in the pottery made in Iraq under the ʿAbbasid Empire, whose first capital, Baghdad, was a prosperous city of international importance from the eighth to the tenth century. One of the best examples of ʿAbbasid wares demonstrating striking Chinese elements as well as local development is a group of ninth-century earthenware bowls.[9] While this type of bowl had often been referred to as a 'Samarran' ware, it was most probably produced at Basra.[10] The so-called Samarran ware is particularly illustrative of Muslim attempts to imitate elegant shapes of Chinese wares, as reflected in the open shape with a rolled rim and narrow base of this type of bowl. It also shows their attempts to create a creamy-white appearance stimulated by the whiteness of imported Chinese porcellanous wares.[11] Their unrestrained impulse to imitate finally led them to create the impression of a white body and a smooth texture by using an opaque white glaze, which subtly hid local dull creamy-yellow clays. Interestingly enough, in spite of their great admiration for the whiteness of Chinese wares, pure white wares were rarely made by Muslim potters.[12] Perhaps because of a tendency in the art of the Islamic world to fill a given surface with ornament or in order to disguise a poor technique of glazing with decoration, they added their decorative vocabulary onto the quasi-white surface. The decorative repertoire of the 'Samarran' ware owes much to Islamic traditions, notably the epigraphy – which is one of the most important innovations in Islamic ceramic design.[13] The epigraphy here is devoid of any Chinese traits and bears little resemblance to contemporary Chinese ceramics;[14] it is more likely to have been indebted to local development, recalling later Umayyad and early ʿAbbasid coinage.[15] The other Islamic element of this type of bowl is found in the semi-naturalistic foliate decoration, which appears to be associated with arabesque decoration rather than Chinese-origin flower motifs, such as peonies and lotuses. In considering the cobalt blue glazes, it is important to note that, while the use of blue glazing was brought back into popularity in the Middle East in the ninth and tenth centuries under ʿAbbasid rule and was introduced eastwards into China,[16] Chinese potters refined blue glaze decoration and later created the world-famous blue-and-white porcelain; thereafter, blue-and-white porcelain was, as will be discussed later at length, imported from China into the Middle East during the fourteenth century.

It was during the late ninth century that, along with the rise of local dynasties ruled by governors in north-east Iran and Transoxiana during the ʿAbbasid period, such as the Samanids, the Iranian world first experienced a great innovative period in the production of ceramics, in both styles and techniques. Among Chinese ceramics, white stonewares and later white porcelain, which reached these areas through major ports and riparian cities in the Gulf during the ninth and tenth centuries – for example, Siraf[17] and Susa[18] – contributed to the development of Iranian pottery during its formative period and stimulated Iranian potters to imitate such elegant pieces. However, the potters seem more likely to have been inspired by the copies of Chinese pieces made in Iraq rather than by actual imported Chinese pieces.[19]

The so-called splashed or lead-glazed wares found in major Islamic sites, such as Samarra,[20] Nishapur[21] and Siraf,[22] have posed the question of Chinese connections.[23] The belief that such wares unearthed in the Middle East, especially the pieces excavated in Samarra, were derived from imported Tang *sancai* (literally 'three-colour') wares is no longer tenable.[24] Yet, even though it is now possible clearly to distinguish Chinese imports from local Islamic products, thanks to detailed scientific examination,[25] the origin of lead-glazed pottery in the Middle East, in particular whether it was indigenously invented or whether it was influenced by imported Chinese wares, remains unclear. It has been suggested, chiefly by historians of Islamic art, that the use of similar colour schemes or moulded decoration can be seen in earlier glazed relief wares produced in the Middle East, whose production can be traced back to the Roman period; this type of ware was certainly manufactured in Egypt and Mesopotamia, and its production seems to have continued up to the Umayyad and early Islamic periods.[26] The similarity between Chinese *sancai* and Islamic lead-glazed wares is thus coincidental. In the case of examples attributed to Nishapur,[27] which are thought to have been produced in the ninth and tenth centuries, it is assumed that the use of lead-glaze techniques was inspired by imported Iraqi wares;[28] apart from the splashed effect, there is little connection with imported Chinese *sancai*.

In China *sancai* production had already begun during the Han period, but *sancai* wares became popular only around the third quarter of the seventh century.[29] They were manufactured mainly for burial use, and the fashion reached its apogee in the first half of the eighth century.[30] *Sancai* production then declined, perhaps because of the political upheavals that happened in the middle of the eighth century in northern China,[31] but the fashion for *sancai* revived in northern China under the Liao dynasty.[32] As has been demonstrated by Rawson, Tite and Hughes, Chinese *sancai* sherds found in Mantai in Sri Lanka[33] and those discovered in Japan[34] suggest that the use of *sancai* wares was by no means limited to domestic burial objects. A variety of shapes and glazed decoration, as well as slight regional differences, can be observed in exported Chinese *sancai* wares, suggesting that each category of *sancai* ware was designed for a specific market. Lead-glazed wares with articulated forms and everted lips, reminiscent of metalwork, were perhaps made for Middle Eastern markets,[35] because Chinese potters must already have been aware of Middle Eastern taste through imported metalwork. Middle Eastern metalwork had widely been known in China through the Sino-Sasanian trade by the seventh century, and such metalwork had a considerable impact on Tang ceramic design.[36] Yet there is still little evidence to demonstrate that Chinese *sancai* wares were exported to the Middle East in sufficient quantities to provide a definitive source of inspiration for Islamic splashed wares. Future excavations on Chinese *sancai*, in particular those of the Liao period,[37] and scientific research on Islamic lead-glazed wares will perhaps provide more clues to understanding the nature of the Chinese contribution to the development of lead-glazed wares in the Middle East.

Early Sino-Iranian relations in ceramics: the second wave

The second wave of chinoiserie occurred in Iranian pottery from 1150 to 1250, equivalent to the time between the end of Saljuq rule and the end of the Mongol invasions of Iran. This is one of the most intriguing periods in the history of both Iranian and Chinese ceramics. It saw unprecedented technical transformations and drastic changes in terms of styles and decorative schemes. Several explanations can account for the revolution of Iranian ceramics in this period. But it is generally assumed that, after the decline of the Egyptian ceramic industry following the collapse of Fatimid rule in 909/1171, the centre of ceramic production in the Middle East shifted from Egypt to eastern Islamic lands.[38] Iranian ceramics reached a very high standard, thanks to skilful potters who are believed to have immigrated from Egypt via Syria.[39] Although the exact date and provenance of many categories of Iranian pottery produced during the pre-Mongol period are still ill defined, what is clear is that ceramics began to be treated by wealthy and art-conscious locals as a major art form and eventually acquired a sense of luxury. The striking evidence for this is the sudden appearance of rich overglaze ceramics attributed to Kashan. This city became the principal site of ceramic production in Iran in the late twelfth century, and, apart from some forty years during the Mongol invasions of Iran (few dated pieces are known to survive from this time, and it is thus difficult to trace the development of ceramic production), it dominated the Iranian ceramic industry until well after 1300.[40]

The development of Song ceramics is even more remarkable: the economic prosperity of Song China resulted in ceramics reaching a high point of productivity and degree of sophistication.[41] The demand for fine ceramics from imperial offices encouraged the establishment of Guan ('official') wares,[42] and the patronage for such pieces spread into the ranks of scholar-officers and wealthy merchants. The bulk of the more renowned pieces was produced in northern pottery centres, such as Ru, Jun and Ding. But, as soon as the capital had been relocated from Kaifeng to Hangzhou after the occupation of northern China by the Jins in 1127, southern pottery centres flourished around the new capital. The ceramic trade was greatly promoted by maritime commerce under the control of the Southern Song court:[43] the Southern Song government set up offices in charge of foreign trading, known as *shiposi*, at the coastal seaports of Guangzhou, Hangzhou and Ningbo, each of which had a living quarter for Iranian, Arab and other foreign merchants.[44] In due course, ceramics displaced silks as China's primary export.

The interest of Iranian potters in the whiteness and the shapes of Chinese ceramics did not languish even after the first wave of chinoiserie. Quasi-white wares continued to be produced in Iran in the areas of Khurasan and Transoxiana under Samanid rule, though chinoiserie is less distinguishable in their shapes and decoration.[45] However, as a result of the inspiration provided by the new type of translucent Chinese ceramics of the Song period, known as *qingbai* ('blue-white') wares,[46] which were presumably already known to eastern Islamic lands by the first half of the eleventh century according to some literary sources,[47] and possibly because of the increasing numbers of potters from Egypt who may have already been familiar with Song-type wares,[48] Iranian potters began to approach white wares in a different way. The whiteness was no longer created by the opaque white tin-glaze coating used over poor local clays. This was due to the unavailability of kaolin – a pure white clay derived from the decomposition of feldspar, which is essential for the production of porcelain through the process of firing at a high temperature. Instead, Iranian potters found a way to create an artificial body made of a mix of powdered quartz with a little clay and potash, known as frit, which may have been derived from the technique first developed in Egypt.[49] This new body material enabled the potters to imitate Chinese white wares more satisfactorily. Moreover, it led to the development of new shapes and methods of decoration in the Iranian world; for instance, it permitted painting under a translucent glaze. An excellent example in the Freer Gallery of Art (Figure 2.1),[50] datable to the late twelfth century, can be compared with an exquisite Ding ware or a Southern Song imitation of Ding wares (Figure 2.2).[51] In order to highlight the translucency, the holes of the two scroll bands in the Freer example are filled with transparent glaze. The shape of the Iranian pottery was visibly improved: it became thinner and sharper than Samarran wares and approached Ding wares in lightness. Iranian potters, however, as happened in Iraq three centuries earlier, did not forget to insert their own decorative vocabulary onto the white surface. The decoration of this bowl comprises a series of circles and palmettes in the outer parts and scrolls in the inner areas, recalling those often used in Samanid wares.[52]

While there is little stylistic indebtedness to contemporary Chinese ceramics in fine lustre ceramics produced in Kashan, Chinese inspiration seems to lie behind the black-and-white appearance of stone-paste pottery made in the Iranian world during the twelfth century (Figure 2.3).[53] The use of a strong black-and-white contrast here is particularly comparable to that in a popular type of stoneware, known as Cizhou wares, which were manufactured at many kilns throughout the northern provinces of Hebei, Henan and Shaanxi and were copied at southern kilns during the Southern Song, Jin and Yuan periods (Figure 2.4).[54] They are renowned for their versatile decorative techniques, colour schemes and variety of shapes, reflecting practical everyday use. Chinoiserie is reflected in the Paris example with a probable technical inspiration from Cizhou wares, such as the sgraffito technique – in which one layer of slip in one colour was applied on top of another and then cut away to create a contrast – and the painting technique that uses a black slip on the white slip ground.[55] Though, perhaps, merely coincidental, the simultaneous occurrence of similar colour schemes in Iranian black-and-white silhouetted wares and Cizhou wares is, like the splashed wares and *sancai* wares, worthy of note as a pattern of concurrence that appeared on several occasions in the history of Iranian and Chinese ceramics in medieval times. Yet, once again, Iranian potters adhered to their own decorative preference, showing a tendency towards the tenacity of prototypical epigraphy and palmette-derived motifs. Cizhou wares are, on the other hand, famous for their rich decorative schemes, including the full range of floral motifs, animals, fish, landscapes and figures.[56]

Another elusive question concerning chinoiserie in Iranian ceramics of the Saljuq period is a type of ceramic in animal or human shapes that was widely produced in twelfth- and thirteenth-century Iran.[57] Some sculptures have tentatively been attributed to Rayy[58] or

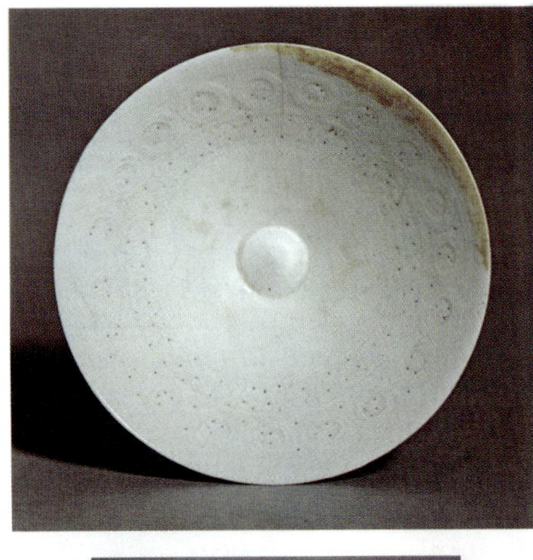

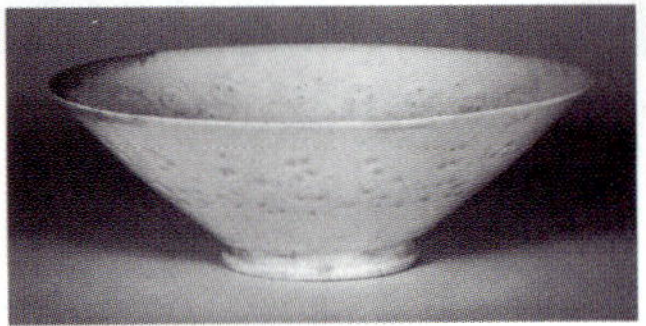

Figure 2.1 *Bowl with flaring sides, straight rim and low foot. Iran, twelfth century. This Iranian copy of Chinese white porcelain has a certain quality as a piece of artwork.*

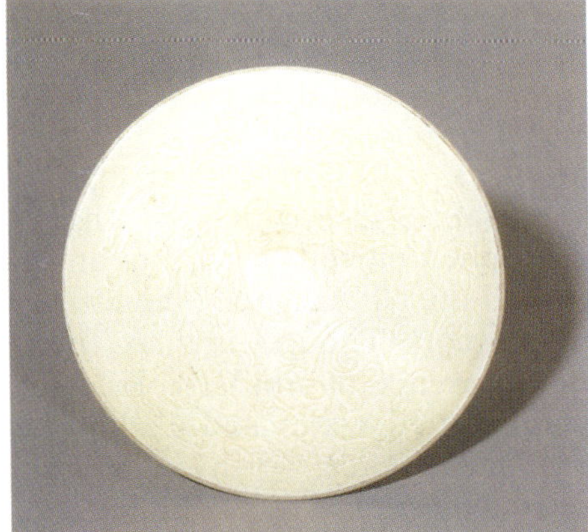

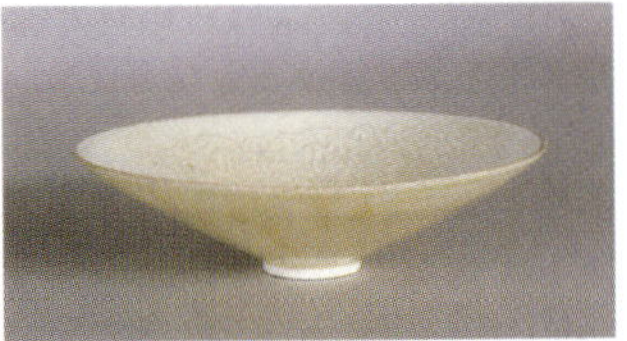

Figure 2.2 *Bowl with moulded floral decoration. Ding ware. China, eleventh–twelfth centuries, This Chinese prototype of the Ding ware surpasses the Iranian copy (Figure 2.1) in terms of modelling skills.*

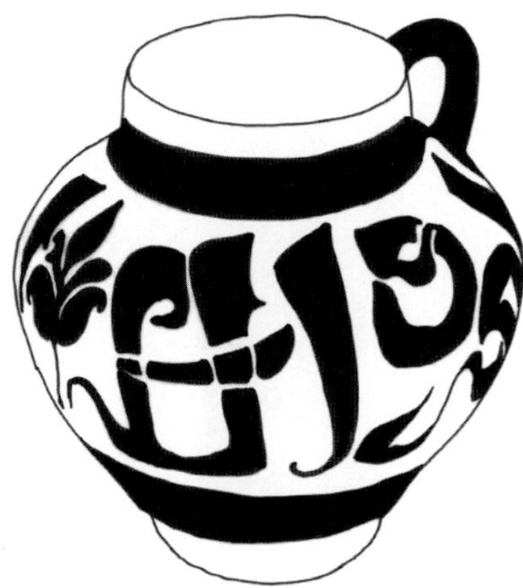

Figure 2.3 *Jar with inscriptions. Iran, twelfth century.*

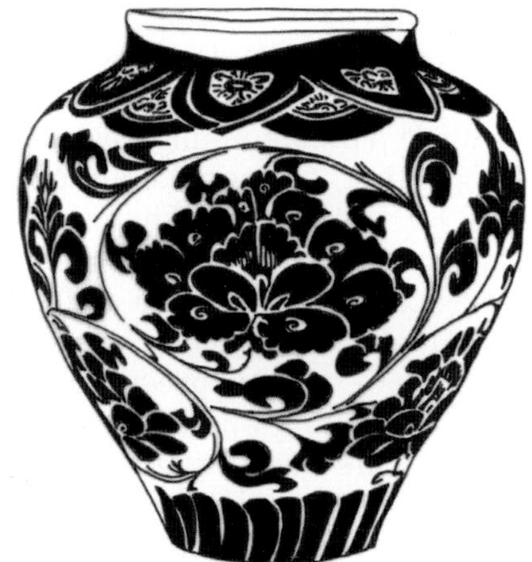

Figure 2.4 *Jar with peony scroll patterns. Cizhou ware. China, c. 1100–50.*

Kashan[59] on the basis of their stylistic associations with contemporary glazed wares from these sites, while others are thought to have been produced in Wasit in Iraq[60] and Raqqa in Syria.[61] In addition to their uncertain provenance, the most difficult problem posed by ceramic sculptures lies in their function and meaning. Some scholars have suggested that ceramic figurines with openings or handles were designed as utilitarian implements, such as aquamaniles, perfume containers, flower vases and toys. There are, however, a number of animal and human figurines that seem to have been appreciated as true sculptures. They were perhaps intended for display, forming an entire orchestra;[62] as for the Khalili chessman (Figure 2.5), this example is thought to have been made as one of a set of pieces used in a board game.[63]

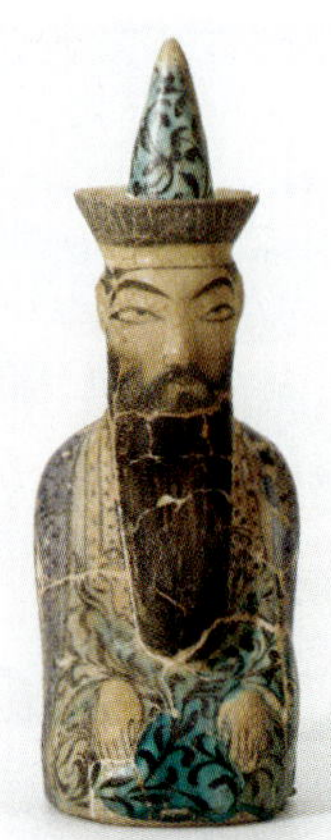

Figure 2.5 *Figurine of a seated man, identified as Sultan Tughril. Fritware. Iran, thirteenth century.*

Discussion can be made on the relationship between such figurines and Chinese ceramic sculptures, alluding to the availability and familiarity of imported Chinese ceramic figurines in the Iranian world under Saljuq rule.[64] Three possible objections may, however, be raised to this theory: first, Chinese ceramic figurines were predominantly intended for burial use. Their intrinsic associations with Chinese beliefs concerning the afterlife are clearly reflected in a number of archaeological finds from Qin and Han imperial tombs – for example, the well-known terracotta army from the Tomb of Qing Shihuang (259–210 BC).[65] Their production reached its apogee in the Tang period, as proved by a large number of funerary sculptures of various forms.[66] This tradition lingered on in China during successive dynasties, but the significance of ceramic figurines as tomb furnishings was gradually threatened by the replacement of paper figurines and later the fashion for using murals for tomb decoration.[67] Some archaeological finds have attested the continued production of ceramic figurines in China during the Song,[68] Jin[69] and Yuan[70] periods. A type of human figure datable to these periods can be comparable to the Khalili chessman in terms of their size and form. Yet, owing to the scarcity of relevant Chinese models, it would be unwise to postulate a direct interdependence between Song and Iranian ceramic figurines without further archaeological evidence for the inflow of Chinese ceramic sculptures into Iran.

Secondly, there is a clear time lag between the high point of the popularity of ceramic figurines in China and the occurrence of ceramic sculptures in the Iranian world. Despite a similar choice of subjects in Iranian and Chinese ceramic sculptures – for example, a Saljuq vase in the form of a camel[71] and a Tang *sancai* camel sculpture[72] – the exact chronological relationship between them remains disputable.[73] Thaʿalibi's reference to Chinese sculptures has been quoted as evidence for the availability of Chinese figurines in the Middle East,[74] but this is insufficient to explain satisfactorily the circulation of Chinese ceramic figurines in Saljuq Iran.

The third and the most crucial point is that no Chinese ceramic figurines have yet been found in the Middle East. Hence, unless the question of the distribution, function and manufacture of both Iranian and Chinese ceramic figurines is solved, it is hazardous to assume that the role of China in the development of Iranian ceramic sculptures was important. A more plausible explanation for the occurrence of ceramic sculptures in the twelfth- and thirteenth-century Iranian world is, as it stands, the inspiration drawn from a zoomorphic tendency in Islamic metalwork of the eleventh and twelfth centuries, as shown in bronze figurines of water-pouring vessels of lion and griffin form.[75]

Some remarks on Ilkhanid and Yuan ceramics

Until recently, studies in late thirteenth- and early fourteenth-century Iranian ceramics have lagged behind those focusing on other periods.[76] In particular, there is a gap between the end of the Mongol period and the advent of the Safavid period in the history of Iranian ceramics, in which, except for Timurid ceramics, little is known about the development of the art of ceramics during the Muzaffarid and Jalayirid periods and their Chinese relations. It is in fact not easy to locate the key kiln sites of the Ilkhanid period from limited examples, but the importance of Kashan in ceramic production during the late thirteenth and early fourteenth centuries is undeniable. Most Ilkhanid ceramics are generally attributed to Kashan, which continued to produce both lustre-painted and underglazed wares, while the Mongol invasions caused the degeneration of ceramic production in other major Iranian sites.[77] Kirman also appeared on the scene as a new centre of ceramic production.[78] The artistic activities of Kirman province were spared from Mongol devastation by the intervention of Buraq Hajib, a later governor of the province during the Mongol period; Kirman began to have a strong royal connection with the Ilkhanid capital Tabriz after the marriage of Buraq Hajib's daughter with Abaqa Khan (r. 663/1265–681/1282).[79] The finds from Tall-i Iblis and Ghubayra in Kirman province, which yielded Ilkhanid and Muzaffarid ceramics, provide useful sources for this field of study.[80] One of the striking aspects of the Ilkhanid period is, as will be discussed, the development of tile production, whose decoration in particular reveals an openness to contemporary Chinese art traditions.

Despite the fact that the Mongol invasions drove local potters out of production in northern China, much innovation took place in Chinese ceramics during the late thirteenth and early fourteenth centuries under Yuan rule.[81] Jingdezhen in Jiangxi province became a major porcelain production centre, especially after the establishment of the Fuliang Porcelain Bureau in 1278, which dominated both local and overseas markets until the Ming period (1368–1644).[82] The continuance of the Southern Song style can be seen in Yuan wares, but the taste in ceramics gradually changed from monochrome celadons with carved and incised decoration into more colourful and decorative polychrome wares, chiefly as a consequence of the re-encounter with foreign art traditions.

Mongol attitudes towards ceramics were not utterly negative, but the Mongols appear to have been more interested in the revenues that steadily increased through their overseas trade. Direct political links between East and West Asia under the *Pax Mongolica* made the international trade easier and more viable along both maritime and land routes and facilitated Chinese ceramic trading, which involved a vast area of Eurasia, including Kharakhoto[83] and Samarkand,[84] and stretched still further west. Both literary and archaeological evidence testifies that a variety of Chinese ceramics was brought into Ilkhanid territory during the Mongol period:[85] in addition to celadon wares, which were found in Old Hormuz[86] and Kirman,[87] wares identifiable as Cizhou pieces were discovered at Kharakhorum[88] and the island of Kish.[89] Chinese celadon sherds found in the Julfar sites at the lower end of the Gulf, which date from the fourteenth century, also demonstrate the importance of sea routes in the East–West ceramic trade.[90] Of equal significance is that both celadons and Cizhou wares of the thirteenth and fourteenth centuries were retrieved from Saray Berke in southern Russia, a capital of the Golden Horde (624/1227–907/1502).[91] As will be seen, there are a number of examples to prove the impact of Chinese celadon wares on late thirteenth- and early fourteenth-century Iranian ceramics, although Ilkhanid copies of Cizhou wares have not yet been discovered. The most famous finds of fourteenth-century Chinese ceramics in the Middle East are blue-and-white wares, which are among the key products in the context of chinoiserie.

How Chinese artistic ideas were incorporated into Iranian ceramics

What China chiefly provided from the end of the thirteenth century onwards were styles rather than techniques. The gradual absorption of Chinese decorative themes is reflected in almost all types of Iranian ceramics of the period. In particular, the impact of Chinese-origin designs is evident in lustre tiles intended for decorating the walls of both secular and religious buildings, such as palaces and mausoleums (Figure 2.6). A vigorous dragon is superbly depicted against *lingzhi* clouds and lotuses, and the prototype of this design can be found in contemporary or earlier Chinese and Central Asian textiles (Figure 1.1). A number of similar lustre tiles displaying Chinese-inspired dragons and phoenixes are now dispersed in major

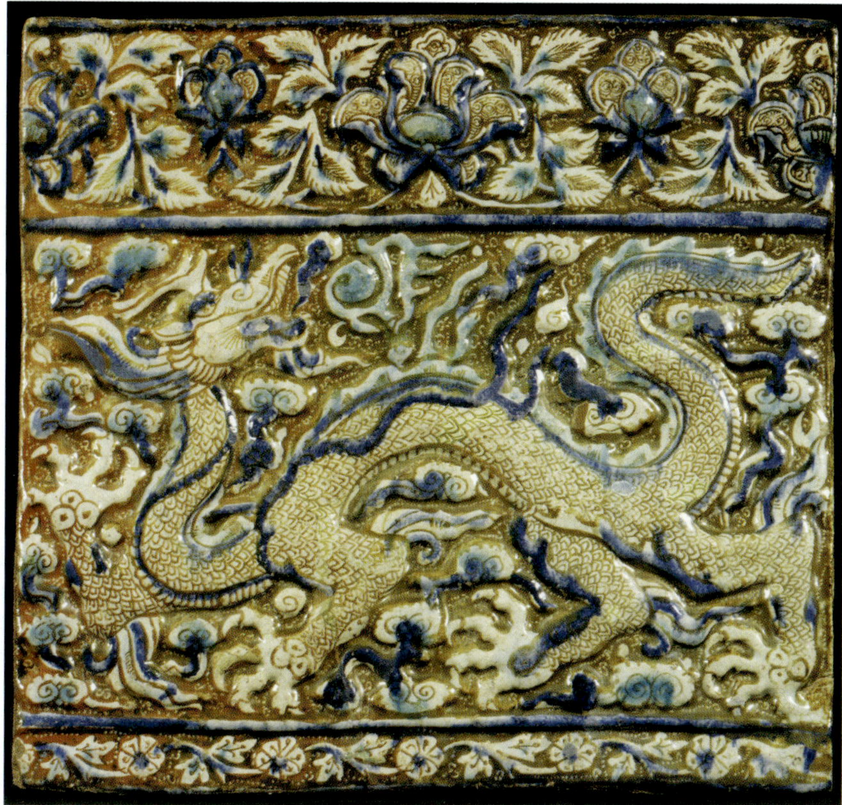

Figure 2.6 *Lustre tile with a dragon and lotuses. Iran, c. 1270–5.*

museums across the world, and most – if not all – of them probably originated in Abaqa Khan's palace at Takht-i Sulayman, which can be dated from 670/1271 to 674/1275.[92]

A group of tiles associated with Takht-i Sulayman suggest that chinoiserie motifs gained a certain acceptance among Mongol rulers and nobles in the context of secular buildings; such motifs were probably viewed, once again, as a symbol of their cultural association with China, or, as has been stressed in the importance of Takht-i Sulayman examples, they were part of the decorative ensemble of *Shahnama* images in this complex so as to suggest a link of Ilkhanid rulers to the ancient kingship in Iran.[93] What is more significant is that Chinese elements are assimilated into lustre tiles used in religious buildings, such as Chinese-inspired lotuses found in the background decoration of lustre tiles that originated in the Shrine of the Footprint of ʿAli at Kashan (711/1311)[94] and lustre phoenix tiles used in the Imamzada of ʿAli ibn Jaʿfar in Qumm.[95] Although it remains uncertain whether such tiles were specially ordered for this building or whether they came from secular buildings – for example, from Takht-i Sulayman[96] – the fact that Chinese themes were accepted for the decoration of religious buildings in Ilkhanid Iran is worth remembering.

Chinese themes are equally recognisable in the star-shaped and hexagonal tiles with either moulded relief or lustre-painted decoration, sometimes surrounded by an inscription border – for example, the eight-pointed lustre star tiles with bird motifs amid flowers and inscriptions (Figure 2.7).[97] Chinese prototypes of the bird motif used in this tile panel possibly came from various sources: while the bird's body is comparable to that found in Liao decorative repertoires (Figure 2.8), the overall decorative treatment here is evocative of a more generic bird-and-flower design used in Chinese textiles (Figure 1.10). Such tile revetments, subtly combined with turquoise cross tiles with vegetal patterns, serve to create a smooth, lustrous surface of the building, a visual impression that is almost equivalent to that generated by richly woven silk textiles – for example, a thirteenth- or fourteenth-century textile with birds in an alternating arrangement (Figure 2.9). In addition to dragons, phoenixes and lotuses, Ilkhanid lustre tiles contain figural imagery, often clad in typical Mongol garb,[98] and these are of great use in reconstructing the Mongol costumes that were coming into vogue in Ilkhanid Iran.

Chinoiserie is also discernible in *lajvardina* tiles (*lajvard* means 'lapis lazuli' in Persian), a new technique that had gradually replaced the overglaze painted *mina'i* technique by the end of the thirteenth century.[99] The luxury of this type of tile is enhanced by the lavish use of dark-blue glazes with overglaze painting in white, red and gold. Significantly, Chinese phoenixes coexist with Qur'anic inscriptions on some square *lajvardina* tiles (Figure 2.10),[100] which presumably originated in religious buildings, though it is unclear whether the phoenix borders have a precise symbolic meaning in Islamic contexts. A certain stylistic similarity is observable between the features of Chinese-inspired motifs in *lajvardina* tiles and those found in lustre tiles, both of which appear to have had the same Chinese sources – in the case of the David tile, contemporary Chinese textiles (Figure 1.12) are at best a tentative source.

The fine underglaze-painted wares of the Ilkhanid period, the so-called Sultanabad wares,[101] also serve to illustrate a close link to contemporary Chinese decorative arts. This distinctive type of ceramic became widespread in Ilkhanid Iran on a large scale from the early fourteenth century onwards, and it was found in several sites in the Iranian world.[102] The combination of phoenix-like birds and Chinese-inspired flower motifs is often taken as clear evidence for chinoiserie in Sultanabad wares (Figure 2.11). Such a vivid depiction of circling birds with long tails, which are stylistically different from the birds found in both the Victoria and Albert tile panel (Figure 2.7) and the David tile (Figure 2.9), appear

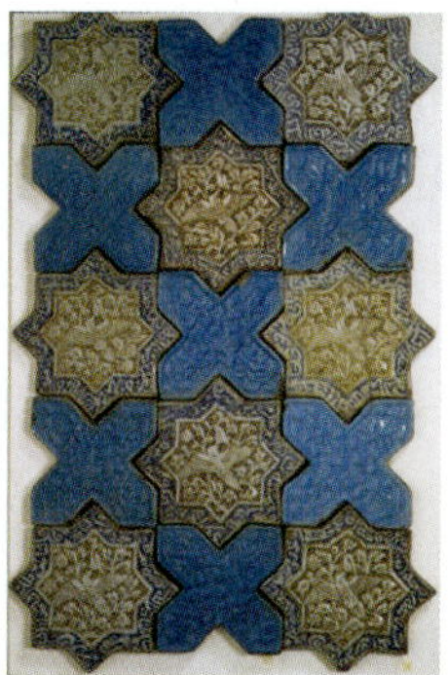

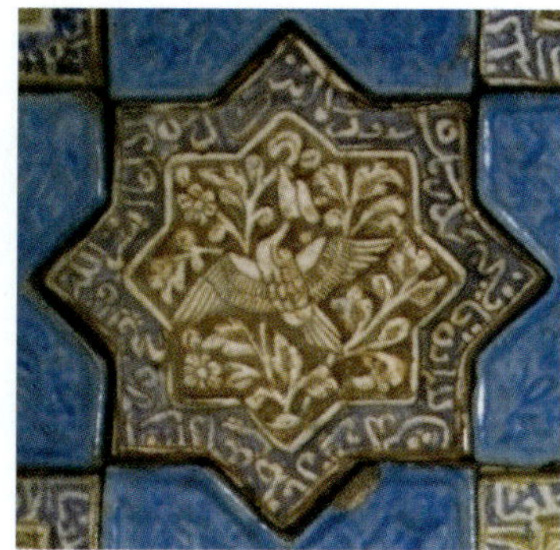

Figure 2.7 *Star tiles with phoenixes and cross tiles. Iran, late thirteenth–early fourteenth centuries.*

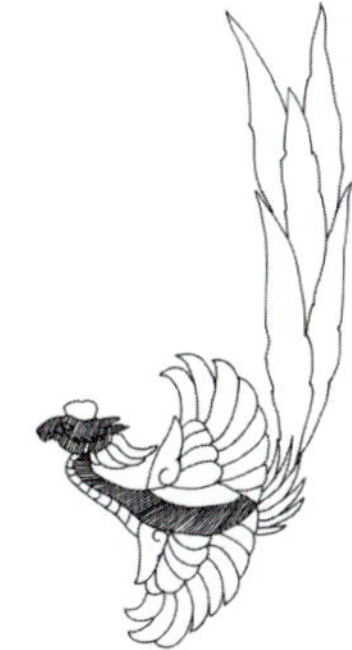

Figure 2.8 *Painted decoration of silver saddle flaps (detail). From the tomb of the Prince of Chen and Xiao Shaoju at Qinglongshan Town in Naiman Banner, 1018 or earlier.*

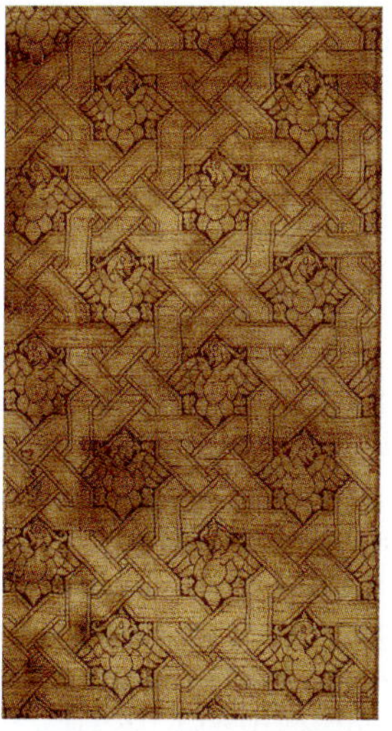

Figure 2.9 *Textile fragment. Islamic world, thirteenth–fourteenth centuries.*

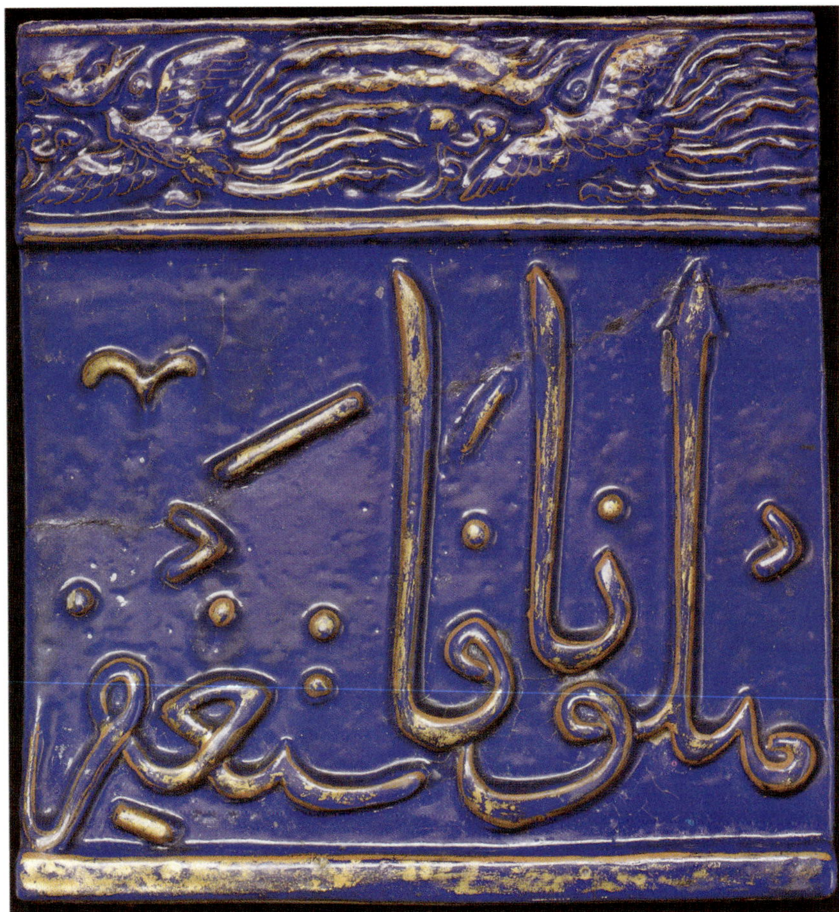

Figure 2.10 *Tile decorated with leaf gilding and red over a blue glaze (*lajvardina *ware). Iran (Kashan), c. 1300.*

to have been indebted to a type of flying phoenix motif widely used in Southern Song and Yuan decorative arts, including lacquer wares (Figure 2.12).[103] Apart from lacquer wares, ceramics is also a plausible source of inspiration for the two-bird design, since Chinese ceramics with similar motifs were in fact discovered on the site of Old Hormuz.[104] The birds in the Ashmolean bowl are, in the strict sense, not purely Chinese in style – the movement of their tails is rather stiff – but their faces and plumage retain their Chinese features. The role of the phoenix in this bowl is interpreted in multiple ways: the fondness for this type of bird design in Sultanabad wares is not a mere reflection of the impact of conventional Chinese phoenix-and-flower motifs, but the design may have gained some symbolic meaning in Ilkhanid contexts – for example, the idea of hunting, a theme that was suitable in the contexts of

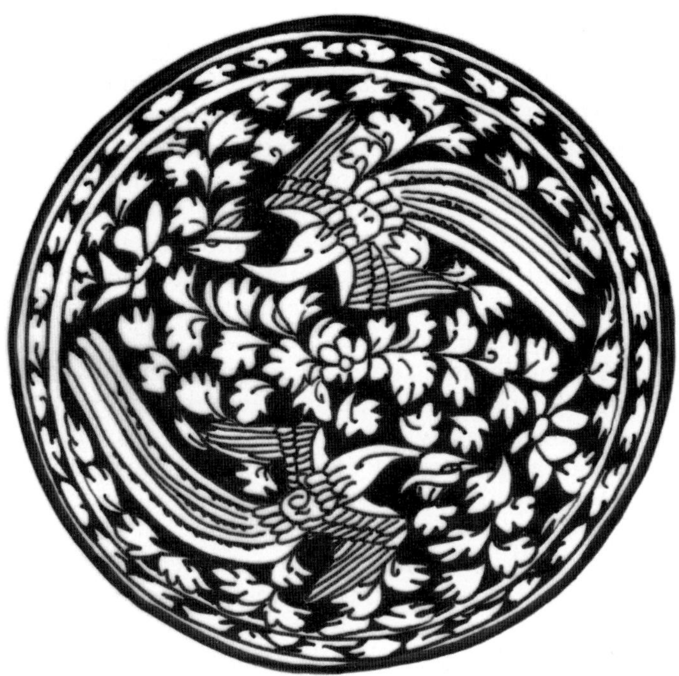

Figure 2.11 *Sultanabad bowl with birds. North-west Iran, fourteenth century.*

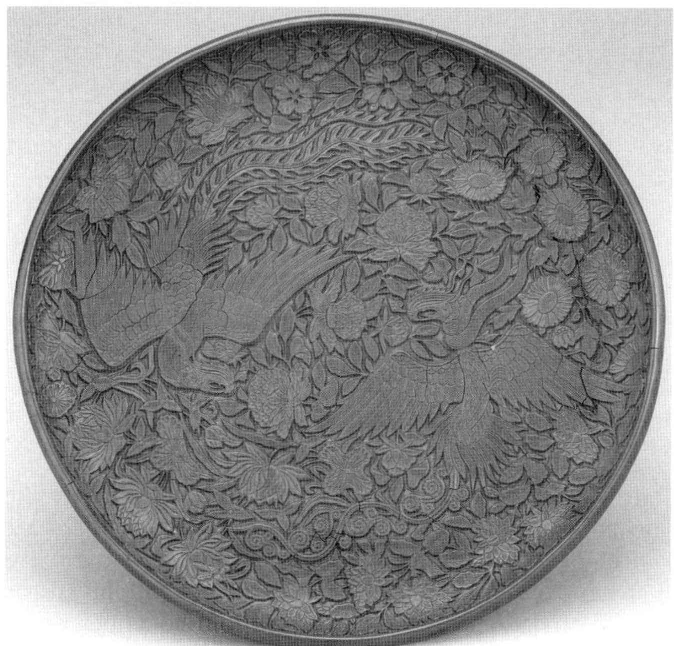

Figure 2.12 *Lacquer tray with flowers and birds. China, late Southern Song to early Yuan dynasty.*

both Mongol nomadism and Iranian kingship.[105] The lotuses here are also strongly inspired by those conventionally used in Chinese decorative objects, whose impact was already evident in Ilkhanid lustre tile design (Figure 2.6). The use of tiny petal patterns filling the background is atypical in contemporary Chinese ceramics and seems to have been developed indigenously in Ilkhanid Iran. Yet conventional flower motifs used in Chinese decorative arts must have encouraged Iranian potters to create more naturalistic features in the background decoration by using non-geometrical patterns. On the other hand, the rare occurrence of the dragon in Sultanabad wares remains a puzzle,[106] for Chinese-type dragons were widely known in Mongol Eurasia and were in vogue in Ilkhanid textiles and lustre tiles (Figures 1.6–1.7, 2.6), together with metalwork and manuscript painting, as will be seen in the following chapters. Perhaps it is just that very few examples of Sutanabad wares with dragon motifs have survived, or perhaps they still await discovery on Iranian sites.

Having observed the close decorative relationship between ceramics and other objects produced in late thirteenth- and early fourteenth-century-Iran, we should note that the transmission of decorative ideas from one medium to another in Mongol Iran was to a certain extent associated with the increasing use of paper in the process of design making at Ilkhanid workshops.[107] Paper became widely available and affordable in Iran under the Mongols, thanks to its close commercial links with China. This coincides with the introduction of architectural plans, in either paper or plaster, in the Iranian world,[108] not only for practical reasons but also with the intention of forming a distinctive, dynastic style. If this was also the case with the decorative arts, the intensive use of chinoiserie motifs, instead of authentic Chinese or Iranian designs, in portable objects would have been an ideal means for unifying decorative ideas throughout Eurasia so as to symbolise Mongol control over Chinese and Iranian cultural spheres in a visually compelling way.

Along with the increased import of Chinese celadons for the Islamic market,[109] the focus of Iranian admiration for Chinese ceramics shifted from white wares to grey-green wares, namely Longquan wares,[110] whose jade-like colour and texture fascinated Iranian potters. Despite a number of local imitations found in the major sites of the period, such as Tall-i Iblis[111] and Old Hormuz,[112] reliable information as to the exact provenance and date of production of Iranian celadon imitations is still unavailable. They are attributed vaguely either to the fourteenth or to the fifteenth century, but it seems that by the end of the fourteenth century at the latest Iranian potters had acquired the ability to imitate Chinese celadons (Figure 2.13).[113] The impact of Chinese celadons is particularly reflected in the use of the appliqué fish typical of Southern Song wares (Figure 2.14), although the original significance of the two-fish motif,

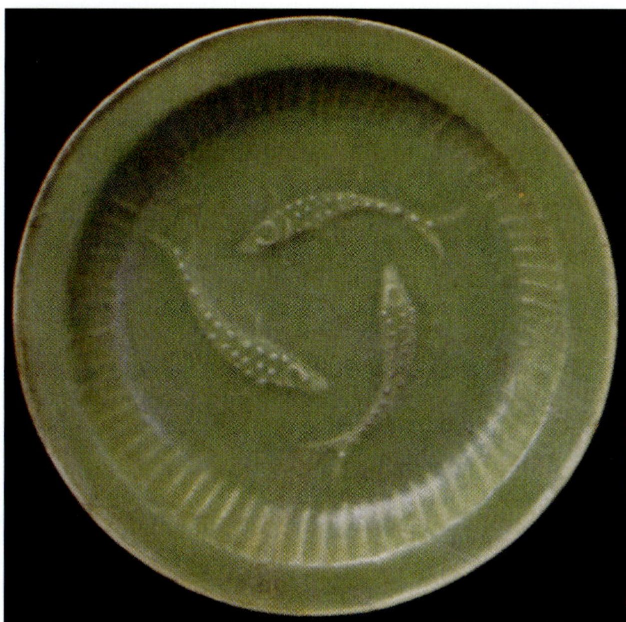

Figure 2.13 *Dish covered in a green glaze (celadon imitation). Iran, fourteenth century. This large apple-green dish is an almost perfect copy of Chinese celadon made by Iranian potters, apart from the three-fish motif.*

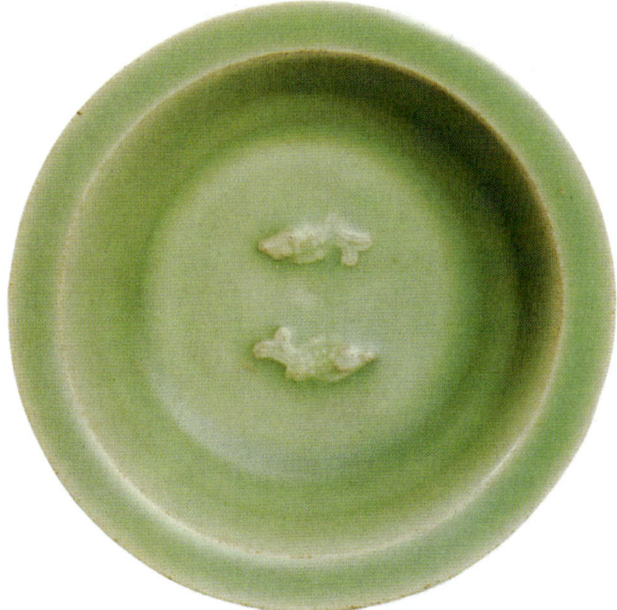

Figure 2.14 *Longquan dish with spring-moulded decoration. China, thirteenth century. In China, the two-fish motif is considered as a symbol of happy marriages.*

which symbolises good fortune and, in pairs, successful marriage,[114] was not properly understood by Ilkhanid potters. Iranian celadons show a marked preference for three or four fish swimming in a circular movement with radianting patterns near the rim, a design that seems to have been associated with the sun or with solar symbolism as in other media of Ilkhanid decorative arts[115] or simply intended to make the surface of this dish more ornamental. The other striking impact exerted by Longquan wares is, as has been widely remarked,[116] found in the lotus petals that often appear on the outside of lustre, *lajvardina* and Sutanabad wares (Figure 2.15). These were most probably derived from those seen in contemporary Longquan wares (Figure 2.16),[117] but Ilkhanid potters tend to paint such decorative devices on the exterior surface rather than to model them skilfully by hand.

The origins and evolution of Chinese and Iranian blue and white

In studying the Sino-Iranian artistic relationship, it is crucial to ponder the significance of blue-and-white porcelain, called *qinghua* ('blue flower') in Chinese, which has long interested both Chinese and Islamic ceramic experts.[118] In spite of the increase of archaeological discoveries around the world, blue-and-white porcelain poses continuous questions as to its origin, manufacture and distribution both inside and outside China. The difficulty here is that preconceived notions about the dating, provenance and function of Chinese blue-and-white porcelain – namely, 'the fourteenth century,' 'Jingdezhen' and 'export' – have been an obstacle to a clear understanding of its chronological development. Such views need to be reassessed.

The most perplexing problem is the origin of the technique of underglaze painting with cobalt-bearing minerals, in which there is still little agreement as to whether it was introduced to China from the Middle East after the first half of the fourteenth century or whether it was entirely a Chinese innovation.[119] Some archaeological discoveries of blue-and-white pieces in China suggest that the use of blue-and-white colouring in Chinese pottery can now be traced back to the Tang period, when Chinese potters coped well with cobalt imported from Iran as a decorative medium.[120] Fragments of small Tang stonewares with underglaze cobalt blue decoration excavated from the ruins of the ninth-century Tang city in Yangzhou in 1975 and 1983[121] and small yet complete examples of Tang blue-and-white dishes discovered in the Belitung shipwreck in Indonesia in 1998 and 1999[122] betray a simple and geometric treatment in the decoration atypical both of contemporary Tang ceramics and of later blue-and-white porcelain. Such pieces, which show a stylistic resemblance to early Middle Eastern pottery – for example, 'Abbasid blue-and-white wares[123] – were

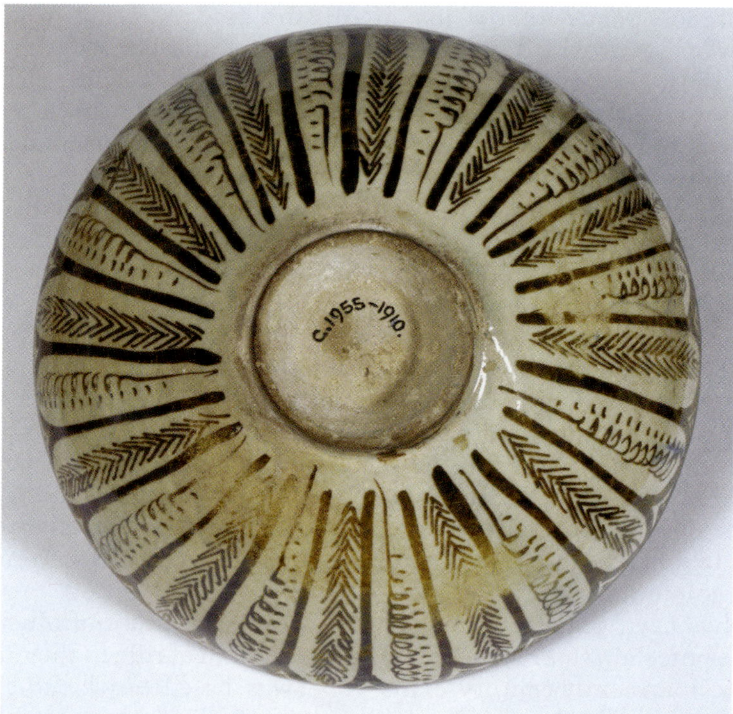

Figure 2.15 *Bowl. Iran, Ilkhanid dynasty.*

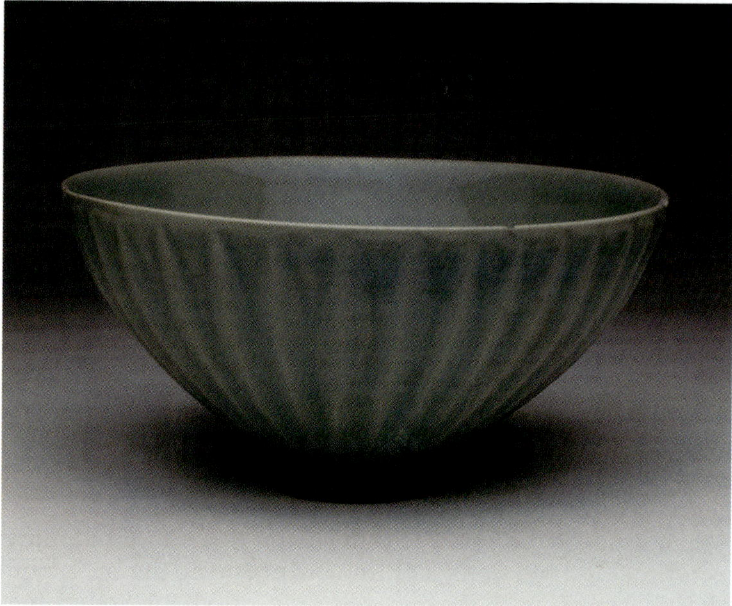

Figure 2.16 *Celadon bowl with lotus petals carved on the outside. China, c. 1300–1400.*

presumably made for the use of Muslim traders living in China or probably intended for the international market.[124] Although fourteenth-century Chinese potters were the ones to achieve colour schemes that contrasted light and dark areas by the subtle use of brilliant blue and clear white colours, the idea of blue-and-white colouring – as distinct from monochrome or three colours – must have owed something to the ceramic tradition of the Middle East during its formative period. The abrupt change of ceramic style in China during the fourteenth century – from the elegant forms of the preceding Song wares into massive forms recalling those of metalwork – was perhaps due to the impact of Middle Eastern metal products[125] – even if the quantity of such foreign imported work was small – as well as to requests for Chinese wares from Middle Eastern customers and from Muslims in posts of authority under the Yuan dynasty.[126] In due course, Islamic artistic concepts mingled with Chinese ceramic shapes and motifs; by the middle of the fourteenth century the design of Chinese blue-and-white porcelain had begun to display subtle decorative effects, in terms of both colour and design.

It has been generally thought that the manufacture of blue-and-white porcelain flourished in China under Mongol rule in the middle of the fourteenth century. This view was based on the so-called David Vases dated 1351,[127] which have served as a benchmark for the chronology of Chinese blue-and-white porcelain. However, since high-quality blue-and-white porcelain was found in the Jinsha pagoda in Longquan county, Zhejiang province, datable to the Northern Song period,[128] a simple attribution of blue-and-white porcelain to the late Yuan period has been questioned. Among examples of early fourteenth-century blue-and-white porcelain discovered in China in the 1970s, a pagoda-shaped urn excavated from a tomb dated 1319 at Jiujiang in Jiangxi province[129] has cast new light on the chronology of Chinese blue-and-while porcelain. Despite the lack of brightness in its blue colour and its unrefined drawing techniques, it displays a full range of the decorative repertoire, such as lotuses, peonies and cloud collars, and bears a similarity with well-known pieces attributed to the mid-fourteenth century (Figure 2.17). This suggests that the early fourteenth century was not a Dark Age in the history of Chinese blue-and-white porcelain but that it should more correctly be placed within the experimental period of this technique. The late twentieth-century finds retrieved in Inner Mongolia,[130] formerly in Jin territory, are also noteworthy as the earliest known examples of thirteenth-century blue-and-white porcelain. According to Kessler, they were presumably of the kind intended for diplomatic use between the Southern Song and Jin courts during the period of their strained relationship.[131] Further information about Song blue-and-white porcelain is still unavailable, yet there must have been a long pre-history of the manufacture of blue-and-white porcelain in China

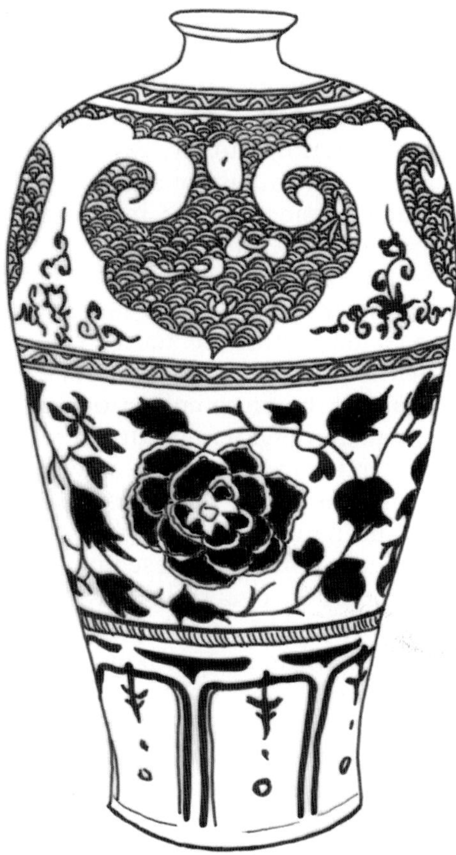

Figure 2.17 *White vase decorated in underglaze blue. China, Yuan dynasty.*

until it reached a period of maturity during the mid-fourteenth century.

What is fascinating is that Chinese blue-and-white porcelain gained a higher popularity in the Middle East than any other types of Chinese ceramic art. Both literary and archaeological sources for the history of Chinese blue-and-white porcelain from the fourteenth century help to reconstruct the expansion of its export routes to the Middle East and its subsequent impact on local ceramics.[132] Chinese blue-and-white porcelain was exported mainly via maritime routes: it travelled to the West through India[133] across the Maldive Islands,[134] and reached the Gulf ports,[135] the Red Sea area[136] and even East Africa.[137] A number of the sherds of Chinese blue-and-white porcelain, as well as local copies, were found in Fustat in Egypt, revealing that a taste for Chinese blue-and-white porcelain had stimulated local potters to imitate Chinese pieces as early as the fourteenth century.[138] Syria appears to have been an even more important destination for Chinese blue-and-white porcelain. In particular, the bulk of Chinese blue-and-white porcelain ranging from the Yuan to the Ming period was discovered in Damascus, and these wares must have exerted a great impact on local potters.[139] The so-called Hama dish in the Damascus National Museum (C917), datable to the late fourteenth century, reveals the clear intention of Syrian potters to imitate Chinese pieces as closely as possible.[140] Iran was also a popular destination of Chinese blue-and-white porcelain, most of which was taken to inland towns via the Gulf ports, notably Hormuz Island (New Hormuz).[141] The most famous examples of Chinese blue-and-white porcelain in Iran are those found in the Ardabil Shrine.[142] Finally, some fourteenth-century pieces of Chinese blue-and-white porcelain are stored in the Topkapı Saray, Istanbul, which has one of the finest collections of Chinese ceramics in the world, both in quality and in quantity.[143]

Although the overland trade routes became safer under the *Pax Mongolica* and remained active in the time when close contact was maintained between the Timurid and Ming courts,[144] it is reasonable to assume that the greater part of Chinese blue-and-white porcelain was exported to the Middle East via the maritime routes for practical reasons – namely, quantity, time and fragility. The eastward expansion of Chinese blue-and-white porcelain over the sea routes during the fourteenth century has been confirmed by finds from Japan,[145] Korea[146] and South-East Asia.[147]

The identity of the recipients of blue-and-white porcelain in the Chinese domestic market remains controversial. Blue-and-white porcelain was of great significance as an export product, yet it cannot be denied that the Mongols encouraged the manufacture of blue-and-white porcelain to some extent for domestic use: large-sized dishes, which have often been regarded as export products, seem also to have been made on demand for the Mongols, whose cuisine was eventually influenced by Central and Western Asian recipes and dishes.[148] The most distinctive shapes of Yuan ceramics are to be found in small-sized wares, such as pouring bowls and stem-cups.[149] Such pieces are likely to have been produced for Mongol customers, who were familiar with such unusual forms, reminiscent of the shapes of their own metal products.[150] Commercial and practical functions aside, however, there is little evidence to demonstrate that there was strong Mongol patronage of ceramics as a form of fine art. While it could be argued that the intensive use of cobalt blue in Jingdezhen ceramics was a Mongol initiative, because of the importance of blue in Mongol society,[151] the chief clients for blue-and-white porcelain in the domestic market were, it seems, Muslim merchants residing in the port town of Quanzhou in Fujian province, who controlled the marketing of porcelain.[152] Some types of blue-and-white porcelain – for example, the David Vases, dated 1351, which contain Chinese inscriptions and a full range of Chinese decorative repertoires, such as dragons, phoenixes, clouds and peonies, were produced in Jindezhen for internal consumption and were intended for certain Chinese recipients.[153] It is, however, assumed that, as an early Ming text has noted, blue-and-white porcelain was generally unpopular among Chinese clients, who regarded it as being very vulgar;[154] such a negative view perhaps predominated among them until the revival of Chinese taste for blue-and-white porcelain in the middle of the Ming period.[155] This does not contradict the fact that, although a considerable amount of Yuan blue-and-white porcelain has been found inside China, it is not comparable, either in quantity or in quality, to that discovered outside China.

The production of blue-and-white wares in Iran poses yet another question. Its production can possibly be traced back to the middle of the fourteenth century, but there is not much likeness between fourteenth-century Chinese blue-and-white porcelain, which is characterised by its harmonious ensemble of conventional Chinese motifs, ranging from rich floral decoration to fabulous animals,[156] and the earliest examples of Iranian-style blue-and-white wares, probably made in eastern Iran, whose decoration is confined to geometric motifs and symmetrical arrangement (Figure 2.18).[157] Even though Chinese pieces inspired Iranian potters to create ceramics with underglaze cobalt blue decoration, such heavily Islamised decoration makes it hard to trace their actual Chinese models. Compared with exquisite colour schemes created by intense blue colour against a lustrous white background in Chinese blue-and-white porcelain, the use of a cobalt blue glaze is less effective in the surface of Iranian blue-and-white wares, which was made of poor white clay. Another point to be noted is that most surviving examples of Iranian blue-and-white wares are bowls with narrow foot-rings, and some distinctive shapes of Chinese blue-and-white wares – for example, a high-shouldered vase (Figure 2.17), known as *meiping* in China, which had been one of the most popular forms in Chinese ceramics since the Song period – seem to have been less influential in Iranian ceramics of the Mongol period.

It was during the late fourteenth and early fifteenth centuries that widespread imitations of Chinese blue-and-white porcelain occurred in Iran, mostly under Timurid rule.[158] Timurid blue-and-white ceramics are more comparable to blue-and-white porcelain of the Yuan period than earlier blue-and-white wares made in Iran, though Chinese taste does not fully permeate Timurid pieces.[159] Timurid potters, for instance, adapted the so-called lotus-petal design, a stylised framing device typical of Yuan blue-and-white porcelain (e.g. Figure 2.17), which often includes auspicious emblems associated with Buddhism,[160] for their blue-and-white pieces. But the elements inside the framing devices in Timurid examples were sometimes simplified or replaced by arabesque scrolls.[161] The production of this type of blue-and-white ware in Iran coincides with the occurrence of depictions of blue-and-white wares in late fourteenth-century

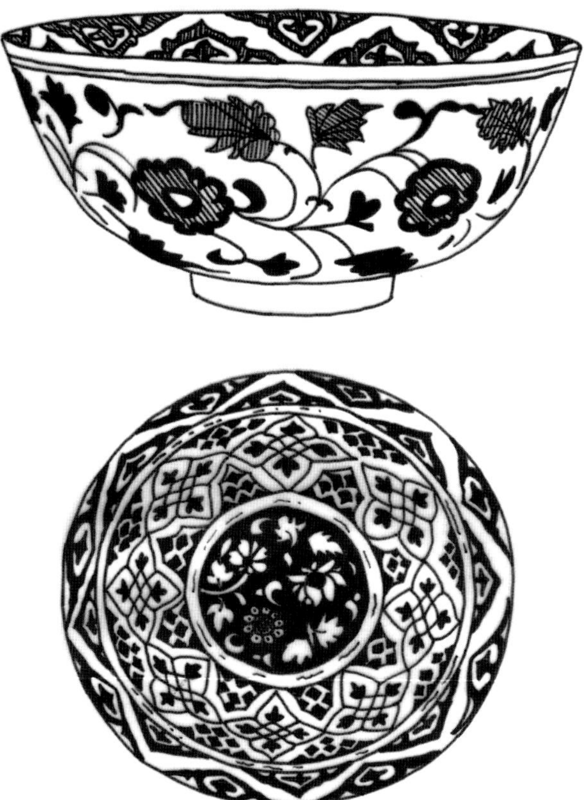

Figure 2.18 *Blue-and-white bowl in 'Persian' style. Iran, mid-fourteenth century.*

Iranian painting.[162] This is not a definite indication of the domination of Chinese blue-and-white porcelain in Iran, but possibly reflects the development of locally produced blue-and-white wares. The provenance of these Iranian blue-and-white wares remains uncertain. As some related examples were found in Tall-i Iblis,[163] Kirman is likely to have been a centre of manufacture of this type of blue-and-white ware during the late fourteenth and early fifteenth centuries.[164] Perhaps, blue-and-white porcelain reached Kirman from China via Hormuz and stimulated Iranian potters there to copy Chinese pieces.

This chapter has attempted to establish an overall view of the Chinese impact on Iranian ceramics up to the advent of Timur, focusing on its late thirteenth- and early fourteenth-century development. Iranian admiration for the translucency, thinness and resonance of Chinese ceramics was clearly reflected in the styles of three different periods of Iranian ceramics, and Chinese pieces had a far-reaching effect on the technical development of Iranian ceramics. Through the comparison of three pertinent Chinese wares – namely, white wares, celadons and blue-and-white porcelain, and Iranian copies of them – it has become clear how the Iranian impulse to imitate was apparent from the ninth to the early fourteenth century. Yet only after more discoveries and substantial arguments are made will it be possible to trace in appropriate detail the Iranian imitation of these three types of Chinese ware, especially blue-and-white porcelain, and their impact on other media of Iranian decorative and pictorial arts. In the meantime, one should admit that it is through lustre tiles, *lajvardina* tiles and Sutlanabad wares that the impact of Chinese modes on Ilkhanid ceramics can best be judged.

Notes

1. A full bibliography about this subject before 1976 is found in Grube 1976, 335–7. The scholarly development of chinoiserie can be traced in a series of articles in the *Transactions of the Oriental Ceramic Society* (see, e.g., Crowe 1975–7; Gray 1975–7; Carswell 1976–7). For recent research on this subject, see Watson 1992 and a series of articles by Carswell, Crowe, Morgan and Rougeulle. I am grateful to Mrs Rosalind Wade-Haddon for her valuable comments on this chapter. All errors do, however, remain mine.
2. *Faghfuri* is the Arabicised version of *Baghpur*, literally meaning Son of God in Middle Persian, and equivalent to Son of Heaven that the Chinese use for their emperors ('faghfūr', in *EI*[2]). Thus *chini-i faghfuri* means Chinese porcelain from imperial kilns (Soudavar 1998, 125).
3. For Chinese elements in Safavid ceramics, see Crowe 2002.
4. For a summary of the development of the study of Islamic ceramics and its problems, see Fehérvári 2000, 15–19.
5. Accounts of Chinese ceramics by Islamic writers of the ninth and tenth centuries are summarised by Kahle 1940–1, 32–3. It is said that 20 imperial Chinese wares (*chini-i faghfuri*) and 2,000 ordinary pieces were given to the Caliph Harun al-Rashid (r. 170/786–193/809) by ʿAli ibn ʿIsa, a governor of Khurasan (Lane 1947, 10).
6. Sarre 1925, 56–64. However, the Samarra finds are now ascribed to the tenth and eleventh centuries rather than the ninth century.
7. For example, a variety of Chinese ceramics ranging from the ninth to the nineteenth century was excavated in the Maldive Islands (Carswell 1976–7). The import of Chinese ceramics in the Middle East during the ʿAbbasid period has been studied in detail by Rougeulle 1991a.
8. The fall of chinoiserie in Iranian ceramics was presumably due to the obstruction of the Uzbeks in the land routes to China through Transoxiana, as well as to the rise of European power in the maritime trade between East and West (Rogers 1992b, 436).
9. See, e.g., Grube (ed.) 1994, nos 24, 29–32; Fehérvári 2000, 37–40; Watson 2004, 172–3.
10. For further discussion, see Mason and Keall 1991.
11. See, e.g., Scott 1989, 37, pl. 19; Vainker 1991, pl. 68. This type of white

ware was made in northern China, such as Hebei and Henan provinces.

12. For a rare example of Iranian white wares without decoration, see Grube (ed.) 1994, no. 18.
13. For the development of epigraphic decoration in Islamic ceramics, see Blair 1998, 148–63.
14. A comparison can be made between Islamic epigraphy and Chinese calligraphy in ceramic design (Grube 1976, 38), though a direct interdependence between them is difficult to demonstrate. The fact is that the use of calligraphy for decoration is not so common in Chinese ceramics. Calligraphy is employed in the exterior decoration of Cizhou-type bottles and pillows, but this fashion occurred from the eleventh to the fourteenth century (see Hasebe (ed.) 1996, pls 20, 21, figs 35, 47).
15. Hillenbrand 1982, 123.
16. FitzHugh and Floor 1992, 874. For ʿAbbasid blue-and-white wares, see Tamari 1995.
17. For Siraf finds, see Whitehouse 1970; 1972, 74, pl. Xa; 1973; Rougeulle 1991b.
18. For Susa finds, see Koechlin 1928; Rosen-Ayalon 1974. See also Chinese ceramics found in Ras al-Khaimah (Kennet 2004, 46–7).
19. This has been widely pointed out (Allan 1971, 15–16; Wilkinson 1973, 180, 254).
20. Watson 1970, 45–6.
21. Wilkinson 1973, 54–89.
22. Whitehouse 1972, pl. XI.
23. For this subject, see Rawson, Tite and Hughes 1987–8. This problem is summed up by Grube (ed.) 1994, 13, n. 28, 34.
24. Watson 1970, 45–6. For a summary of the so-called Samarra problem, see Grube 1976, 86, n. 1; Watson 1984, 242–6.
25. Rawson, Tite and Hughes 1987–8, 43–51.
26. Lane 1939, 57. For glazed relief wares, see Philon 1980, 5–34.
27. Wilkinson 1973, 69, no. 66, pl. 4.
28. Ibid. 54.
29. For the early history of *sancai* production, see Watson 1970, 41–2; Rawson, Tite and Hughes 1987–8, 39–40.
30. Vainker 1991, 75–81.
31. Rawson, Tite and Hughes 1987–8, 41. The rebellion of Anlushan happened in 755.
32. For Liao *sancai* wares, see Watson 1984, 218–19, pls 265, 279–80; Beijing 2002, 280–306.
33. Archaeological evidence has shown that a large number of Chinese wares were exported to the Middle East via Mantai in Sri Lanka (Carswell 1996). It has been suggested that Yangzhou in eastern China was one of the major centres for the export of *sancai* (Rawson, Tite and Hughes 1987–8, 41–2).
34. For lead-glazed pottery found in Japan and its Chinese connections, see Watson 1970, 44–5; Rawson, Tite and Hughes 1987–8, 41–2.
35. For example, a dish with a wide flat rim found at Samarra is not a Chinese prototype. For further discussion, see Rawson, Tite and Hughes 1987–8, 54–6, pl. 21.
36. The impact of Sasanian metalwork on Tang ceramics and metalwork has been widely pointed out, and this topic will be addressed in the

following chapter on metalwork. For a good survey of the relationship between Chinese ceramics and metalwork, see Medley 1972a.

37. Gray (1975–7, 232–3) has emphasised the importance of Liao *sancai* wares found in the Middle East, including a Nishapur find (Wilkinson 1973, 256, no. 9). Although there seem to have been diplomatic relations and commercial exchanges between the Liao state and Iran under the Ghaznavids (Rogers 1992a, 432), the extent to which Liao *sancai* was transported to West Asia remains uncertain.
38. See Lane 1947, 24, 37–8.
39. For the so-called migration theory, see Watson 1977, 33–5.
40. For Kashan wares, see Watson 1985.
41. See Gray 1984 for an overview of Song ceramics. For the socioeconomic development of Song China, see Gernet 1996, 298–329.
42. For Guan wares, see Kotz (ed.) 1989, 40–5.
43. For Song ceramic export, see Vainker 1991, 128–33. For the Song control of the foreign sea trade, see Deng 1997, 113–15.
44. Feng 1976, 47. See also Hirth and Rockhill 1911. For the history of Iranian settlements in south-east China, see Chen 1992b. Although not found in abundance, sherds of Iranian ceramics of the twelfth and thirteenth centuries were discovered in Yangzhou, suggesting that the city was also a centre of trading activity for Iranian merchants. For Iranian ceramics found in China, see Feng 1976, 47–9.
45. Samanid ceramics are characterised by their creamy-white engobes with innovative decorative schemes, such as elegant inscriptions, stylised human and animal figures and vegetal patterns. These motifs are predominantly painted in brown and red. For Samanid wares, see Volov 1966; Ghouchani 1364/1986; Pancaroğlu 2002.
46. *Qingbai* wares were produced at southern kilns in Jiangxi province, particularly at Jingdezhen. For *qingbai* wares, see Pierson (ed.) 2002. Fragments of this type of Chinese ware were found at Ghubayra in Kirman province (Bivar 2000, 193–4, pls 107b–c).
47. The statements about Chinese ceramics by Thaʿalibi and al-Biruni (d. c. 442/1050) are summarised by Kahle 1940–1, 33–6.
48. A number of Northern Song products, including ceramics and textiles, reached Egypt during the tenth and eleventh centuries. A sherd of Guangdong wares was found at Fustat (Scanlon 1970, 85, pls XIIa–b; Mikami 1980–1, 72, pls 8–9; Vainker 1991, 129–30, pl. 96). Fustat also yielded *qingbai* sherds (Mikami 1980–1, 73, pls 10–11).
49. For frit wares, see Grube 1992, 313–18; Watson 2004, 302–25. This technique was recorded in Abu'l-Qasim's treatise on ceramics written in 700/1301 (Allan 1973, 112, 115).
50. White wares of the period were discovered at Ghubayra in Kirman province (Bivar 2000, 140–1, pl. 87) and at Tall-i Iblis (Fehérvári and Caldwell 1967, 47). White wares were also produced in Afghanistan at that time (Fehérvári 2000, 165–8). While the role of China has often been emphasised in the occurrence of white wares in Saljuq-ruled Iran, Schnyder (1994) has discussed the internal development of white wares in Iran in relation to the growth of Islamic mysticism in the area of Kashan.
51. Although the Ding kiln was occupied by the Jins after the end of the Northern Song period, Ding wares were extensively copied in southern kilns. For Ding wares, see Taipei 1987; Qin 2000–1a.
52. Blair and Bloom 1997b, 265, pl. 133. Ding wares are often embellished

with metal rims on the mouth or foot-ring, a tradition that was developed in the late tenth century (Taipei 1987, 42). This device was, however, scarcely imitated by Iranian potters.

53. Pointed out by some scholars – e.g. Grube (ed.) 1994, 52. For other examples, see ibid., nos 198–9.
54. For Cizhou wares, see Hasebe (ed.) 1996; Qin 2000–1b.
55. For these techniques, see Medley 1989, 125–9. However, Allan has questioned Chinese associations with the development of the sgraffiato technique in Iranian pottery; he has suggested that the main source of inspiration of this decorative technique was probably metalwork (Allan 1971, 18).
56. See Hasebe (ed.) 1996, 93–104.
57. The standard works on this subject are still Grube 1966b; Rogers 1969. For a full bibliography about this subject before 1976, see Grube 1976, 373–4. Sculpture was made in a variety of media, e.g., stucco, in Saljuq Iran (see Riefstahl 1931).
58. See, e.g., Grube 1966b, fig. 2.
59. See ibid., figs 8–9.
60. A number of ceramic figurines have been excavated in Wasit (ibid. 173, n. 24).
61. For figurines attributable to Raqqa, see a horseman sculpture in the Damascus Museum (ibid., fig. 4); and figurines in the shape of a cock and a sphinx in the David Collection (Folsach 2001, nos 186–7). For a recent study of Raqqa wares, see Jenkins-Madina 2006.
62. Grube 1966b, 174.
63. Amsterdam 1999, no. 148. At 40.5 cm in height, however, it could not readily serve as a chess-piece.
64. See Rogers 1970, 161–74.
65. Los Angeles 1987, 41–4, figs 3–4.
66. Ibid. 127–43, nos 58–86.
67. Ibid. 61.
68. For Northern Song ceramic sculptures, see *ZMQ*: Sculpture, 5, 1988, nos 116–19, 121–3 and 127–33; for those datable to the Southern Song period, see ibid. 166–7, 170, 173 and 197–8. Buddhist statues of modest size (20–30 cm) were also produced in pottery during the Song period (see *ZMQ*: Decorative Arts, 2, 1988, nos 137–8, 170 and174).
69. Los Angeles 1987, nos 92–4; Paludan 1994, fig. 5.1.
70. Los Angeles 1987, nos 95–104.
71. See, e.g., Amsterdam 1999, no. 220.
72. Chinese camel sculptures have been examined at length by Knauer 1998. For Tang camel sculptures, see ibid. 70–97.
73. Song subjects were predominantly confined to human figures (Paludan 1994, 55). Few animal figurines of the Song period are known to survive (see a rare camel sculpture found in Jingdezhen, reproduced in *ZMQ*: Decorative Arts, 2, 1988, no. 173). The production of animal figurines, including camel ceramic sculptures, seems to have recurred in Yuan China (Los Angeles 1987, nos 96, 98–9, 103–4). In relation to the issue of ceramic sculptures, one may consider a possible Chinese association with the house model, a type of ceramic object that was popularly made in Saljuq territory (see Abu Dhabi 2008, no. 126). Yet again, its Chinese relations remain questionable.
74. Rogers 1970, 73–8. Thaʿalibi (1968, 141) says, 'they [the Chinese] are extraordinarily skilled at shaping statues'.

75. For further information about Islamic metal statues, see Dodd 1969.
76. For a recent study of Ilkhanid ceramics, see *Legacy*, cat. nos 79–135; Watson 2004, 327–93. See also P. Morgan's D.Phil. dissertation ('Change and continuity in Il-Khanid Iran: the ceramic evidence', University of Oxford, 2005; personally unconsulted).
77. For example, Rayy, a city that has been considered one of the major production sites of ceramics, was sacked by the Mongols in the 1220s. For further discussion, see Watson 1985, 40–1.
78. For Kirman wares, see Fehérvári 1973, 125–6.
79. Fehérvári 2000, 223.
80. For the finds from Tall-i Iblis, see Fehérvári and Caldwell 1967. For those from Ghubayra, see Bivar 2000, 127–96.
81. For a standard work of Yuan ceramics, see Medley 1974.
82. See Lovell (ed.) 1984 for an overview of Jingdezhen wares.
83. Carswell 1999–2000.
84. Kalter and Pavaloi (eds) 1997, 156–63.
85. It is said that 1,000 Chinese porcelain jars were included in a list of the holdings of the celebrated vizier Rashid al-Din (Soudavar 1998, 126).
86. Morgan 1991, 70–1, figs 7–11.
87. For the finds of Chinese celadons from Tall-i Iblis, see Fehérvári and Caldwell 1967, 58; Fehérvári 1973, 125.
88. P. Morgan 1995, 35–6.
89. Morgan 1991, 71, pl. VId.C. For the maritime trade of Kish during the Mongol period, see Kauz 2006.
90. Hansman 1985, 25–7.
91. Lane 1957, 15; Rogers 1989, 265; Fyodorov-Davydov 1984, 127. While Chinese celadons were indeed copied by Golden Horde potters (Fyodorov-Davydov 1991, 48–9, pls 91, 94), the extent to which Cizhou wares were influential in ceramics produced in the Golden Horde remains unclear. A bowl found in Solkhat, Crimea, which bears a festival scene painted in black and white (Kramarovsky 2004, figs 3–5), can be discussed in the context of Cizhou inspiration, yet no other relevant examples are known to survive.
92. For Takht-i Sulayman specimens, see Naumann and Naumann 1969; Masuya 1997. For a recent study of this site, see Huff 2006. For phoenix lustre tiles from this site, see *Legacy*, cat. nos 99 and 112–13.
93. See Melikian-Chirvani 1984; 1991.
94. Musée National de Céramique, Sèvres (MNC 26903, MNC 22688; Adle 1982b; its site is now lost). The tiles are often discussed in the context of the prevalence of Shiʿism in the region of Kashan (*Legacy*, 269). According to Watson (1977, 172–205), lustre tiles were used primarily by a minority sect, namely the Twelver Shiʿites, to decorate funerary monuments.
95. Godard 1937, fig. 145.
96. P. Morgan 1995, 30.
97. The star tiles contain inscriptions from the Qurʾan (*Legacy*, cat. nos 112–13; see the following discussion of the *lajvardina* phoenix tile). For similar examples, see Bonn/Munich, cat. no. 320.
98. e.g. *Legacy*, cat. nos 111, 126.
99. Abuʾl-Qasim mentions this new technique (Allan 1973, 112, 116–17). On the other hand, chinoiserie is less pronounced in the design of bowls and jars in the *lajvardina* type, which usually consists of

abstract floral and geometric patterns (e.g. Hayward, 252, nos 369–71). Carboni has pointed out the impact of Chinese ceramics in the shape of a *lajvardina* pilgrim flask in the Metropolitan Museum of Art (57.164; Carboni 1997, no. 15). Contemporary Chinese models of the flask are available (e.g. *Sekai*, 5, cat. no. 143, 396), yet their shapes are ultimately of West Asian origin (Medley 1989, 83, fig. 54).

100. See also Grube 1976, 254, no. 196; *Legacy*, cat. no. 93.
101. For Sultanabad wares, see Reitlinger 1944–5 and recently Fehérvári 2000, 121–4. The exact location of Sultanabad wares is problematic. It seems that, despite their name, most Sultanabad wares are the products of Kashan (Watson 1985, 42). Chinese themes in Sultanabad wares have been examined by P. Morgan 1995.
102. For Ghubayra examples, see Bivar 2000, 151–3, pls 99, 103. Also Saray Berke examples, for which see Rogers 1989, 265, pl. 22. Surviving examples of tiles in the Sultanabad style are few. This type of tile is still *in situ* in the *iwan* hall of the shrine of Pir-i Bakran, near Isfahan, datable to between 698/1299 and 712/1312 (Wilber 1955, 121–4; P. Morgan 1995, 19). Owing to the lack of relevant examples of Sultanabad tiles, it remains unclear to what extent Chinese themes permeated Sultanabad tiles as distinct from Sultanabad wares in general.
103. Pointed out in *Legacy*, 178. For the development of flying phoenix patterns, see Rawson 1984, 99–107, figs 81–4. The occurrence of a similar phoenix motif in various media of Chinese art – e.g. those used in woodblock illustrations of the Jin period (Chen and Ma 2002, 62) and those found in Yuan textiles (*WSWG*, no. 60) – is due to the fact that by the fourteenth century woodblock prints had become a major medium for the dissemination of decorative patterns in China (Fong and Watt 1996, 433).
104. P. Morgan 1995, 31, n. 43. For related bird motifs used in Southern Song ceramics, see Medley 1989, fig. 73.
105. P. Morgan (1995, 35) has argued that Sultanabad wares were probably intended for Mongol customers.
106. Pointed out by P. Morgan (ibid. 22).
107. Bloom 2001, 178–95.
108. See a stucco plate showing the plan for a *muqarnas* vault that was discovered at Takht-i Sulayman (Harb 1978, Tafel 1-1; recently Dold-Samplonius and Harmsen 2005). For architectural drawings in paper, see the so-called Topkapı Scroll (c. 1450–1500, Iran or Central Asia; Hazine 1956; *Turks*, cat. no. 223), whose format is evocatively of Chinese derivation.
109. For Chinese celadons in the Middle Eastern market, see Carswell 2000, 107–17. For the Topkapı collection of Chinese celadons, see Krahl and Ayers 1986, 1, 233–40, pls 1–546. For the Ardabil collection of Chinese celadons, see Pope 1956, 153–8, pls 121–30.
110. For Longquan wares, see Medley 1974, 63–81.
111. See Fehérvári and Caldwell 1967, 63.
112. Morgan 1991, 70.
113. For other examples, see Grube 1976, 278–81, nos 223–4 (attributed to the Timurid period); *Legacy*, cat. no. 132 (attributed to the first half of the fourteenth century). Fehérvári suggests that Kirman is the possible place of production. For Kirman imitations of celadons, see Fehérvári 1973, 125, no. 163, pl. 68.

114. Pierson 2001, 19.
115. For the fish design in Islamic art, see Baer 1968.
116. Watson 1985, 110.
117. This decorative device, originally developed from a metalwork design (Scott 1989, 36), had already occurred in ninth-century Chinese ceramics, as seen in Yue wares (Kotz (ed.) 1989, no. 3; Scott 1989, pl. 17). It is also found in Cizhou wares (Hasebe (ed.) 1996, nos 3, 4, 15–16, 18, 20, 43 and 53).
118. See, e.g., Pope 1952; Carswell 1985; 2000; Feng 1981; Li 2001.
119. For a survey of this controversy, see Krahl 1989, 2, 482–3.
120. It was only in the fifteenth century that the Chinese succeeded in mining their own cobalt (Carswell 1985, 24).
121. Tung and Leidy 1989, 98, figs 6–7.
122. Guy 2001–2.
123. See, e.g., Tamari 1995, figs 3a, 4, 8, 13 and 19.
124. Feng 1981, 266; Tung and Leidy 1989, 98. Importantly, the ship (dhow) found near the island of Belitung off the Indonesia coast was of Arab or Indian origin (Guy, 2001–2, 15).
125. The impact of Middle Eastern metal shapes became more apparent in early Ming blue-and-white porcelain (Gray 1940–1; Pope 1959; Carswell 1966), though its decoration was inclined to be more conventional, following Song traditions in ceramic design. For the change in style of blue-and-white porcelain from the end of the Yuan dynasty to the early Ming dynasty, see Carswell 2000, 79–105.
126. For the Muslims in Yuan China, see Rossabi 1981.
127. Formerly in the Percival David Collection of Chinese Art, London (PDF B613–B614; Scott 1989, pl. 55).
128. Feng 1981, 265, figs 175–6.
129. Ibid. 262, figs 170–1; Tung and Leidy 1989, 99, fig. 10; Li 2001, 46, pl. 7.
130. See Kessler 1993, 134–40.
131. Ibid. 138. After the Longxing Peace Accord in 1165, trade relations between the Song and Jin flourished. For the Sino-Jin trade, see Shiba 1983, 102–3. Kessler's attribution of early blue-and-white porcelain to the Song dynasty has, however, been questioned (Valenstein 1994).
132. This issue has been examined at length by Carswell (1985, 2000).
133. Gray (1964–6) first cast light on Chinese blue-and-white porcelain found in India. For Chinese blue-and-white porcelain found in the Tughlaq Palace in Delhi, see Smart 1975–7.
134. Carswell 1976–7.
135. Hansman 1985, 28–32.
136. For the sherds of Chinese blue-and-white porcelain discovered on a shipwreck in the Red Sea, see Carswell 2000, 175–82, 189–91, pls 203a–u.
137. For the finds from East Africa, see Carswell 2000, 64–5.
138. For Fustat finds and local copies, see Mikami 1980–1, 87, pls 48–9; Carswell 2000, 65–7, pls 34a–b, 61.
139. For the Damascus finds, see a series of articles by Carswell (1966, 1967, 1972a, 1972b, 1979).
140. For a recent reference of the Hama dish, see Gibbs 1998–9, 33–4, fig. 18. This dish must have been made earlier than 1401, when Hama was destroyed by Timur (Carswell 1985, 69).
141. For Hormuz finds, see Morgan 1991, 70, n. 39. At the beginning of the fourteenth century, the ruler of Hormuz abandoned the city on the

mainland and founded New Hormuz on the island of Jirun. For the trade between Ming China and New Hormuz, see Chen 1992a. Chinese blue-and-white porcelain was also found in Tall-i Iblis (Fehérvári and Caldwell 1967, 58).

142. Bahrami 1949–50; Pope 1956, 59–142, pls 7–199; Medley 1975.
143. Pope 1952; Ayers 1982–3; Krahl and Ayers 1986.
144. Perhaps, though to a lesser extent, Timurid–Ming relations led to the distribution of Chinese blue-and-white porcelain throughout Central Asia along the Silk Road in the fifteenth century, which passed through Kharakhoto (Pope 1956, 72–7, pls 133–4; Carswell 1999–2000), Xinjiang (Carswell 2000, 73–4) and Samarkand (ibid. 74). For the overland trade between the two empires, see Golombek, Mason and Bailey 1996, 10–12. A fifteenth-century illustration from one of the Saray Albums (fo. 130, Hazine 2153, TSM) reflects a romantic idea of the Silk Road and the transportation of Chinese blue-and-white porcelain to West Asia. For further discussion, see Carswell 2000, 74–6, pl. 71.
145. For Chinese blue-and-white porcelain found in Japan and local copies, see Carswell 2000, 156–64.
146. Chinese blue-and-white porcelain was found in the cargo of a ship wrecked off the Sinan coast and an excavation of the wreck was carried out in 1976. For further information, see Ayers 1978.
147. Beamish 1995.
148. Carswell 2000, 23–4.
149. See ibid. 30–3, pls 28, 30; Taipei 2001, cat. nos IV-59-62.
150. Carswell 2000, 30.
151. Soucek 1999, 128. For the significance of this colour in Ilkhanid material culture, see my study of blue in Ilkhanid textiles ('Blue in medieval Iranian textiles: the cycle of *chinoiserie*', paper given to the First Biennale Symposium of the Historians of Islamic Art Association (HIAA), Univesity of Pennsylvania, 17 October 2008).
152. Vainker 1991, 138.
153. The David Vases were made for the Buddhist Jingtang Society, according to the inscriptions (Scott 1989, 68).
154. According to the *Gegu yaolun* (1387) (quoted in Pope 1956, 44).
155. The stylistic change in ceramics from the end of the Yuan period to the early Ming period has been pointed out by Carswell 2000, 79.
156. For further information about the decoration of Chinese blue-and-white porcelain, see Pope 1956, 65–9; Nakano 1981, 283–94. Although most pieces are undated, it is to some extent possible to classify Chinese blue-and-white porcelain according to its decoration.
157. Grube 1992, 322. See also a rare example of blue-and-white tilework with Persian inscriptions discovered in the Golden Horde capital of New Saray (GE SAR-1491, State Hermitage Museum, St Petersburg; *Legacy*, cat. no. 127).
158. See, e.g., a blue-and-white bowl with an inscribed date equivalent to 779/1377 (1970.28, MMA; Golombek, Mason and Bailey 1996, pl. 14). One could also compare an Iranian blue-and-white jar with a dragon handle datable to the late fourteenth and early fifteenth centuries (Grube 1992, 322–5, pl. XXXVII) with a contemporary Chinese example (Vainker 1991, 104, pl. 104).
159. For instance, cloud-collar decoration (Figure 1.15), which was initially derived from nomadic costumes and became one of the key elements in Chinese blue-and-white wares (Figure 2.17; for further discussion,

see Gray 1975–7, 238–40), was by no means generally adapted for Iranian ceramic design throughout the centuries, nor even for Iranian blue-and-white wares.

160. For further discussion about this device in Chinese blue-and-white porcelain, see Pope 1952, 46–7; Nakano 1981, figs 83–112. For Buddhist elements in Chinese ceramic design, see Hitchman 1962–3.

161. See Golombek, Mason and Bailey 1996, pls 15, 28.

162. For this subject, see Ashton 1934–5; Gray 1948–9. For example, see fo. 42^{v} of the *Mathnavis* of Khwaju Kirmani (Baghdad, 798/1396; Add. 18113, BL; Barrett 1952, pl. 8).Though few in number, the works of the Shiraz school contain the earliest known representations of blue-and-white wares – e.g., as Fitzherbert has pointed out, one in the Istanbul Inju *Shahnama* (731/1330; fo. 59, Hazine 1479, TSM; Fitzherbert 2001, 331, fig. 112); similar devices are found in the legs of thrones depicted in the *Kitab-i Samak ʿAyyar* (e.g. fo. 47^{v}, MS Ouseley 379, Bodleian Library, Oxford; unpublished).

163. Fehérvári and Caldwell 1967, 47, 58 and 63, pl. 11.

164. Fehérvári 1973, 129. Mashhad became one of the major centres of manufacture of blue-and-white ceramics during the middle of the fifteenth century. A few dated examples of Mashhad blue-and-white wares have been known: a spittoon (848/1444) in the National Museums of Scotland, Edinburgh (no. 1888.570; Grube 1976, 235, figs 1–2) and a dish (878/1473) in St Petersburg (VG-2650, State Hermitage Museum, St Petersburg; Lentz and Lowry 1989, 227, fig. 84). The latter bears a strong resemblance to Ming blue-and-white porcelain. For Mashhad blue-and-white ceramics, see Fehérvári 2000, 236, no. 303.

CHAPTER THREE

Metalwork and Other Miscellaneous Objects

THIS CHAPTER AIMS to appraise metalwork as a significant medium for demonstrating important aspects of the artistic relationship between China and Iran. Except for some comments on the appearance of Chinese motifs, metalwork has been inadequately taken into account when assessing Chinese elements in the art of Iran. Above all, no studies have been devoted to the development of Iranian metalwork in a broader context of chinoiserie in Iranian art. Yet this does not mean that Iranian metalmakers were indifferent to the art of China – their reaction to Chinese metalwork in particular and to Chinese works of art in general merits detailed consideration, and bold interpretations are required to make sense of its characteristics.

The first section of this chapter discusses the artistic and technical interaction between Chinese and Iranian metalwork in the pre-Mongol period, focusing on three key materials. It then looks carefully at the occurrence of Chinese elements in Iranian metalwork under the Mongols. Special attention is paid to the use of lotus decoration in Iranian metalwork, because it is not only one of the finest and most inventive patterns in Islamic metalwork but also one of the key chinoiserie motifs in the whole of Islamic art. The discussion will also touch on Chinese features in other hitherto neglected media, namely glass, wood, lacquer and stone.

Early Sino-Iranian contacts: silver vessels, incense-burners and bronze mirrors

To present a detailed survey of pre-Mongol Iranian metalwork is beyond the scope of this book, but it is appropriate to look back to the early Islamic period and to comment briefly on silver vessels of the Tang period and their Iranian connections. There seems to be general agreement about the Iranian or Sogdian contribution to the stylistic development of Tang metalware.[1] West Asian metal objects exercised a great influence on Tang silverware in terms of shapes and decorative motifs – for example, stem-cups and lion motifs in relief.[2] Chinese admiration for the art of Iranian or

Sogdian metalware is also reflected in the adoption of metal shapes of West Asian origin to Tang ceramics, as seen in phoenix-headed ewers.[3] Such ceramics of exotic shapes and decoration may have been in the main produced as substitutes for metalware for burial use, yet as commodities they must have appealed to a wider clientele in cosmopolitan Tang society. Iranian or Sogdian influences have therefore been stressed in the study of Tang silver. But some indigenous Chinese elements can also be found in the decoration used in Tang silver vessels. While the animal patterns used in this context are mostly of West Asian derivation, Tang silver objects contain a number of decorative schemes native to China, particularly those initially used in architectural contexts, such as lotus or peony scrolls.[4]

Similarly, the extensive use of lobed outlines is one of the characteristics of silver vessels of the Tang period. Perhaps generated from lotus petals, whose distinctive shapes were most widely adapted for Tang mirrors,[5] lobed framing devices began to be applied to the decoration of metalware and architecture in this period.[6] It has been suggested that these made their way westwards and provided Iran with the idea of bracket-shaped lobed frames that first occurred in metalware in Khurasan during the twelfth century and subsequently spread throughout Iran and the Islamic world.[7] It is, however, reasonable to suppose that, if they were not local inventions, lobed frames were gradually incorporated into Iranian decorative concepts not specifically under the inspiration of Tang decorative devices but more broadly under the spell of Buddhist art, such as the haloes used for Buddhist figures[8] and the outline niches used for Buddhist architecture in Central Asia.[9] The fact is that Buddhism had already been introduced into the Iranian world during the Sasanian period as a consequence of maritime trading with India, and it coexisted with Zoroastrianism until the arrival of Islam.[10] In particular, the eastern provinces of Iran were strongly influenced by Buddhism during the early Islamic period.[11] A number of Buddhist sites have been discovered in Khurasan – for example, at Merv, now in Turkmenistan.[12] In addition to the chronological gap, the obvious difference between the lobed panels used in the outer decoration of Tang silver bowls and those found in Iranian architectural decoration in later medieval times is that the former hold to their intrinsic role as decorative frames designed for objects and never function as architectural decoration, while in the latter such devices are more easily understood in architectural contexts, not only in the form of isolated medallions but also as part of continuous bands in the interior decoration of buildings.[13] More elaborate multi-lobed panels were developed as architectural decoration in the eastern Iranian world under the Ghaznavids (336/977–582/1186) and Ghurids (early fifth/eleventh century–612/1215) – for example, trefoil arches with points on the top, as found in tombstones and cenotaphs.[14] Thus, although the simultaneous occurrence of formally related lobed frames or arches in both Chinese and Iranian art is of interest as a reflection of the versatility of the motif, little direct connection can be construed between the framing devices used in Tang metalware and those found in Iranian metalware and architecture of the pre-Mongol period.

One could also argue that Buddhist architectural idioms are pronounced on a type of incense-burner that has been attributed to Khurasan, including what is now in Afghanistan, under the Samanids and Ghaznavids. Fehérvárri has recently readdressed the stylistic impact of the Buddhist stupa in the use of a distinctive canopy structure, consisting of a hemispherical dome and a square base sometimes with zoomorphic appendices, in pre-Mongol Khurasani incense-burners.[15] Given the spread of Buddhist culture over Central Asia, Afghanistan and broadly the eastern Iranian world before and even after the advent of Islam, it would not be surprising if Iranians were already aware of the style of Buddhist temples (*bot-khana*) by the time of the Mongol conquest. As in the case of lobed framing devices, however, it is difficult to observe the use of the domed structure under a single source of inspiration. It is more likely to have been indebted to indigenous architectural ideas of this region, for this type of incense-burner is almost a miniature of domed mausolea, a type of which evolved in Transoxiana in early Islamic times,[16] such as the Tomb of the Samanids in Bukhara (datable before 331/943).

As a prelude to discussing the topic of chinoiserie in Ilkhanid metalwork, this section deals in more detail with the problems raised by a type of mirror that can be attributable to the Iranian world in the period between the twelfth and fourteenth centuries (Figure 3.1).[17] In Iran the production of a type of circular disc with a reflective surface, which can be interpreted as a mirror, can be traced back to at least the Achamenid period.[18] It is presumed that handled mirrors, which depended largely on Graeco-Roman models, continued to be produced in the Islamic world in early medieval times;[19] they were probably the standard type before the introduction of Chinese-type mirrors – namely, unhandled mirrors with knobs in the centre.[20] Mirrors were manufactured and distributed throughout Iran, judging by the mirrors unearthed at Nishapur,[21] Susa,[22] Siraf[23] and Ray.[24] Most surviving examples have tentatively been attributed to the eleventh, twelfth or thirteenth century, on the basis of a few dated pieces,[25] and have been ascribed vaguely to Iran, Anatolia or Mesopotamia.[26] This looser dating and uncertain provenance is due in part to the nature of mirrors – transportable and easy to copy.

It could be argued that Chinese mirrors reached West Asia in the course of the spread of Chinese mirrors into Central Asia in the pre-Islamic period, where Chinese mirrors had already circulated from the Han period onwards and were imitated at local workshops.[27] However, no positive evidence for this has so far been detected. A few Chinese bronze mirrors have been found in Iran – for example, those excavated at Susa[28] and Siraf[29] – but most of these lack any information as to dating and provenance. Literary evidence shows that Chinese mirrors had become famous in the Middle East at least by the tenth century,[30] which coincides with the introduction of the sand-casting technique from China to West Asia.[31] The impact of Chinese mirror design – for example, the use of knobs in the centre – is visible in the Cairo mirror dated 548/1153,[32] indicating the increased availability and popularity of Chinese mirrors in West Asia at that time.

Song or broadly tenth- to fourteenth-century Chinese mirrors following Tang prototypes are relevant examples to be compared with Chinese-inspired Iranian mirrors.[33] The design of a Song mirror (Figure 3.2) is evocatively of Tang style, consisting of animals symbolising the four quarters encircled by a band of the twelve animals of the Chinese zodiac, by grape vines and by additional epigraphic bands.[34] The arrangement of decorative bands shows a resemblance to that seen in a type of Iranian mirror (Figure 3.1),[35] though alterations are made to the detail of decoration and epigraphy in order to make the mirror more acceptable to Iranian taste. Instead of the four quarters and the twelve animals, two friezes in the Iranian mirror are decorated with six running animals in a clockwise direction and with reciprocating patterns. The three epigraphic bands used in the Chinese mirror – namely, the Eight Trigrams (*bagua*),[36] star constellations and Chinese inscriptions[37] – are reduced to one and are replaced by Kufic inscriptions on an arabesque ground. From a stylistic point of view, however, this mirror is a textbook example of how the appearance of Chinese mirrors was influential in the formation of mirrors in medieval Iran. Like typical Chinese mirrors, the Iranian mirror is round in shape. Iranian metalmakers also deliberately imitate the knob in the centre, though it remains unclear whether this device was added to the Iranian mirror for practical reasons – in Chinese mirrors, the knob was customarily used either for suspending by a ribbon or a ring, or for fixing on a mirror stand[38] – or merely for decorative purposes.[39]

In terms of function, there is an essential difference between Iranian and Chinese mirrors. While in China mirrors came to be used mainly for ritual purposes – for instance, mirrors were buried in association with the belief in the afterlife and ancestral worship or were presented as part of a dowry – Iranian or more generally Islamic mirrors functioned mainly as cosmetic accessories and perhaps as spiritual tools.[40] It seems that by the mid-twelfth century Middle Eastern metalmakers had established their own styles in accordance with the widespread interest in astrology,[41] such as a mirror decorated with astrological images, in the form either of the twelve

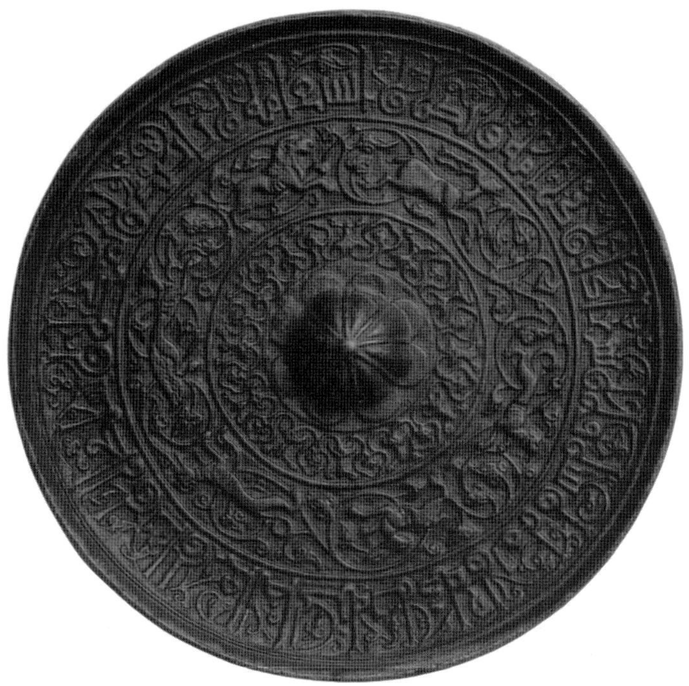

Figure 3.1 *Mirror. Iran (probably Khurasan), twelfth–thirteenth centuries.*

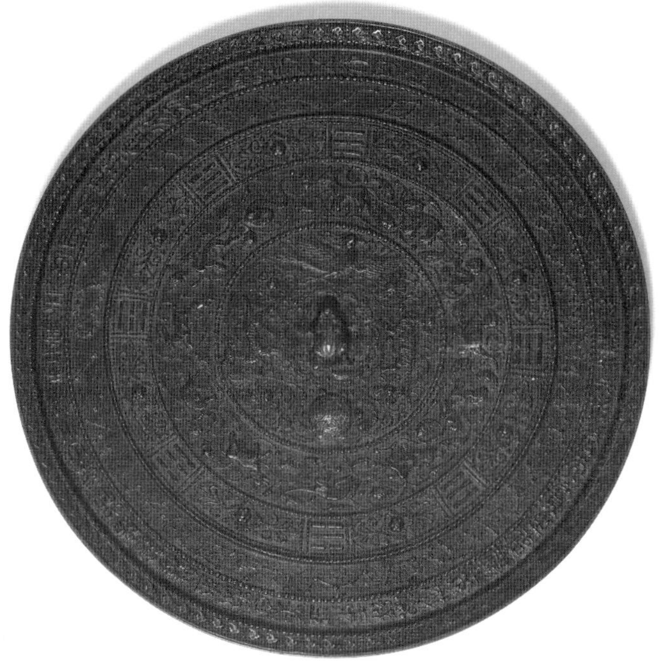

Figure 3.2 *Mirror. China, Song dynasty.*

medallions of the zodiac or of the image of the sun surrounded by representations of the planets.[42] Such is not the case with Chinese mirrors, where the twelve zodiacal signs were conventionally represented as animals. This type of astrological mirror, sometimes together with inscriptions expressing good wishes for the owner, may have borne a talismanic function of preventing sickness and bad luck.[43]

There are several possible explanations for the popularity of Chinese mirrors in twelfth-century Iran. Mirrors were certainly cheaper than silk textiles; they were less fragile than ceramics and were easy to transport. The political and cultural unification of the northern parts of China and Mongolia under Khitan and Jurchen rule from the tenth to the thirteenth century may also have facilitated the westward transport of Chinese mirrors. Chinese mirrors may have attracted a wider clientele, regardless of social class, ranging from merchants and aristocrats, as fashionable yet practical objects. It is also assumed that, because of their portability, Chinese mirrors were brought into West Asia by Muslim merchants as souvenirs, or they were perhaps carried as charms to bring a safe return journey. An increase in the import of bronze mirrors from China in this period was to some extent associated with the growth of the bronze industry in twelfth-century Iran, mainly owing to the shortage of silver.[44] As for the route, it is highly probable that, along with the northern overland route through Central Asia, Chinese mirrors were brought to the southern provinces of Iran on their way to the Red Sea via the southern maritime route, thanks to the increased importance of metals and metal objects, perhaps including bronzes, in foreign trading with Song China.[45]

Renaissance in Iranian metalwork: from the eve of the Mongol invasion to the end of Mongol rule

As happened in other media of Iranian decorative and pictorial arts, the Mongol conquest provided a catalyst for the technical and stylistic development of Iranian metalwork. This was in part due to the large-scale movement of metalmakers from eastern Islamic lands westwards in the 1220s.[46] The inlay workshops that flourished in Khurasan were forced to cease by the Mongol invasion, and their workmen dispersed to Egypt, Syria, western Iran, Anatolia or the Jazira. As a result of the migration of Khurasani artisans, however, the first half of the thirteenth century witnessed the renewal of large-scale metalworking in these places, particularly in Mosul under the patronage of Badr al-Din Lu'lu' (r. 629/1232–657/1259).[47] Brass workers and inlayers, who took an active part in the evolution of the Mosul school, were, in turn, transferred to Iran after the Mongols had overpowered the city in 659/1261 and were taken to new workshops located in north-west Iran and Fars. The Mosul style, and especially its emphasis on inlay, was thus influential at a developmental stage of Ilkhanid metalwork, as several surviving works indicate.[48] While Arabic inscriptions and geometric patterns still form part of the design in the works of the Ilkhanid school, decorative preference is given to figural representations. The decoration features friezes of hunters or medallions of an enthroned ruler, and these owe much to the figural imagery of Jaziran metalwork.[49] There are, however, some key examples of Ilkhanid metalware that yield an interesting insight into the patterns of adoption and adaptation of Chinese themes to Iranian decorative ideas under Mongol rule.

In comparison with ceramics, the impact of China, in terms of both design and form, is less discernible in Iranian metalwork of the Mongol period. Islamic metalwork seems to have continued to wield some influence over both the shape and design of Chinese metalware and ceramics of the thirteenth and fourteenth centuries.[50] This is suggestive of the fact that metal objects were not major exports from China to West Asia during the Mongol period; or, even if they circulated in Iran, they were insufficient in number and quality to provide new thoughts and inspiration for Iranian artisans. In general, the quality of Chinese metalwork, especially bronze and steel and to a lesser extent silver, had been in decline since the Song period and never again reached the level of Han and Tang times.[51] The design of later Chinese bronze objects was less revolutionised than the case of Han or Tang models.

How Chinese themes were reworked in Ilkhanid metalwork

A large-sized brass basin in the Victoria and Albert Museum, London (Figure 3.3a), is, though it has now lost most of its gold and silver inlay, undoubtedly one of the most spectacular examples of Ilkhanid metalwork. The decoration of the bottom surface consists of a single large roundel surrounded by an elaborate decorative band. The central roundel, perhaps symbolising the sun, is emphasised by the use of the so-called fish-pond ornament, an element that characterises fourteenth-century metalwork produced in the Ilkhanid and Mamluk realms.[52] The decorative band contains six small roundels and intervals, and they are particularly illustrative of the harmonisation of disparate Chinese and Iranian elements. Identifiable scenes from the *Shahnama* – namely, those related to the life of Bahram Gur – appear in two of the small roundels, while the rest are decorated with images of birds and dragons (Figure 3.3b).[53] Both the phoenix-looking *simurgh*s and the dragons amid *lingzhi* clouds are apparently derived from Chinese prototypes or from Chinese-inspired motifs that were already conventionalised at Ilkhanid workshops. Yet, unlike other Ilkhanid artists who used the chinoiserie motifs in textiles and ceramics, the artisans involved in making this basin seem to have been conversant with a particular type of animal

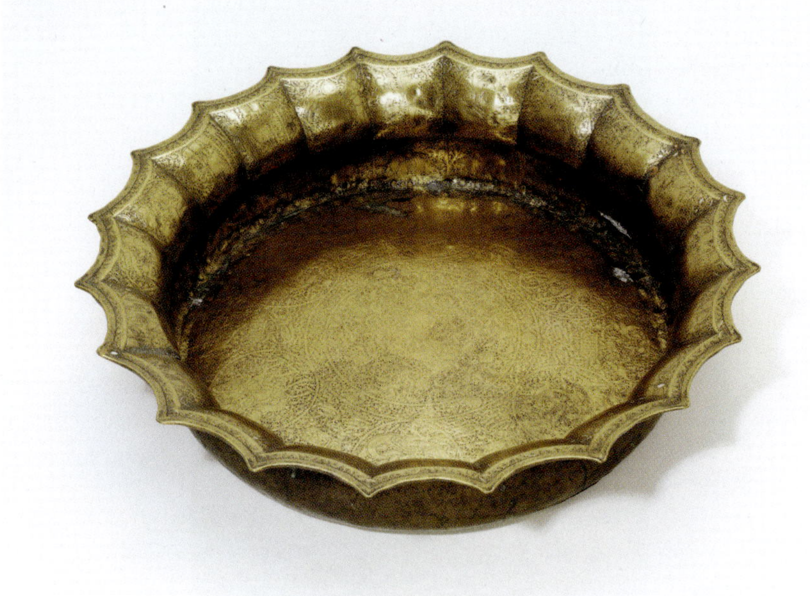

Figure 3.3a *Basin. Western Iran, early fourteenth century.*

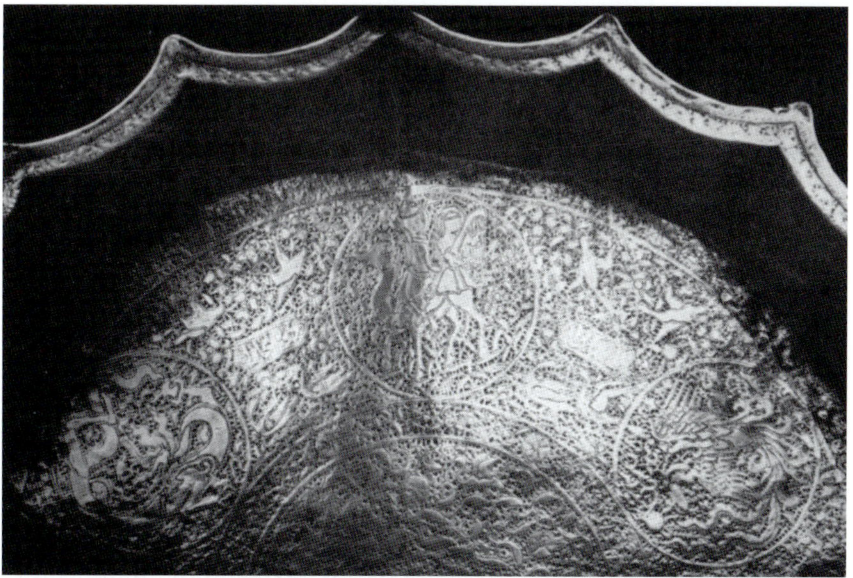

Figure 3.3b *Detail of the basin.*

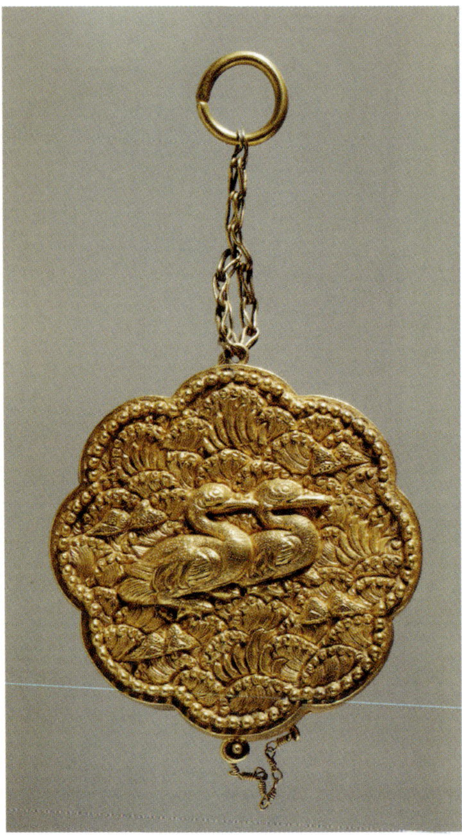

Figure 3.4 *Octagonal gold box. China, Liao dynasty, 1018.*

design in Chinese art: as Rawson has convincingly discussed, the *simurgh*s and the dragons depicted here bear a striking resemblance to phoenix and dragon motifs conventionally used in Liao objects.[54] Some distinctive features of the two animals, such as their twisted bodies, diving posture and graceful outstretched wings, can easily be found in the gold and silver ware as well as in the textiles of the Liao period.[55] There is further striking evidence for the association with Liao objects in the swimming ducks or geese, and the flying birds in pairs flanking floral patterns, which fill the intervals between each roundel. Images of swimming waterfowl are not original conceptions of Iranian metalworkers but are more likely to have been indebted to Chinese prototypes – for example, again, one of the Liao decorative repertoires (Figure 3.4).[56] This reinforces the importance of the period of the Khitan empires – namely, the Liao and the Kara-Khitay states, whose territories stretched over a vast area of Central Asia – as an introductory stage in the spread of Chinese themes into West Asia. It is likely that precious metal objects produced in the northern parts of China and Mongolia under Khitan rule, whose technical and artistic achievements have been attested by recent archaeological finds,[57] came to be known in the Iranian world by their unique hybrid styles, partly adopted from Tang China and partly developed independently.

Closely related to the Victoria and Albert piece is a basin now in Berlin. The decoration of the bottom surface in this example also contains a Chinese-inspired bird-and-dragon motif. Even though the London and Berlin basins are almost identical in shape – a type of Iranian basin called *lagan* – each work shows great individuality in decoration. The Chinese themes in the two basins are interpreted differently. While in the Victoria and Albert example the motifs are involved in the whole decorative programme, collaborating with Iranian themes in creating a drama rather than a pattern, in which Chinese-looking *simurgh*s and dragons are incorporated into images associated with the life of Bahram Gur, the Berlin example stresses a single image of the dragon-and-phoenix as decoration (Figure 3.5). The motif that mingles a dragon and a phoenix encompassing clouds and floral motifs in its background is rather overwhelmingly present in the central roundel and is disproportionate to the friezes of riders, which are of modest size.[58] As distinct from the Victoria and Albert basin, however, the connection with a specific dynastic style in Chinese art cannot be explicitly stated in the case of the chinoiserie motif used in the Berlin basin, for the amalgamation of a dragon and a phoenix is seemingly atypical in Chinese design of the pre-Qing period.[59] The motif is thus present in a traditional Chinese guise but

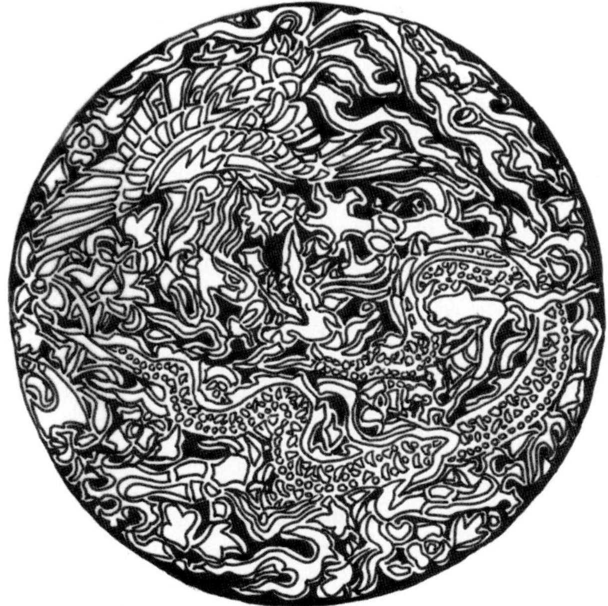

Figure 3.5 *Basin. Mosul, thirteenth–fourteenth centuries.*

is more likely to have been a local variation, with the probable intention of making the central image more original.

The dragon and phoenix used in the Berlin example may have been derived from separate Chinese sources – in this case the most immediate Chinese sources are those used in Chinese textile design[60] – or the image appears to have been a compound of the models for dragons and phoenixes respectively that were in current use at Ilkhanid workshops. The occurrence of the dragon-and-phoenix motif in this basin was presumably due to an iconographical confusion on the part of the Iranian metalworkers, who were not fully aware of Chinese art traditions, or it was indeed due to Iranian inventiveness in the adaptation of Chinese elements. It could also be argued that the Mongols did not make a clear distinction between a dragon and a phoenix and regarded both animals equally as a symbol of absolute power.[61]

The use of Chinese elements is also recognisable in the small medallions on the bottom surface of the Berlin basin, together with figural images perhaps associated with the life of Bahram Gur.[62] This decorative programme, then, recalls that used in the Victoria and Albert basin, but the Berlin example shows a different response to Chinese animal themes. Two of the medallions exhibit another interesting fusion of Chinese conventional animal motifs – a phoenix and a *qilin*.[63] Although both these mythical creatures have been used to decorate artefacts since ancient times, the combination of a phoenix and a *qilin* is not typically Chinese. Like the dragon-and-phoenix motif used in the decoration of the bottom surface, these iconographically unrelated animals are inaccurately combined by Ilkhanid artists, perhaps owing to their lack of knowledge about Chinese conventions. Or it can be assumed that the artists intended to represent a bird and deer in a phoenix or a *qilin* guise in order to enliven the image of the hunting exploits of Bahram Gur.

Chinese themes are equally recognisable in large candlesticks, a type of which is particular to Ilkhanid metalware. One of the most telling examples is a drum-shaped candlestick in the collection of the National Museums of Scotland, Edinburgh (Figure 3.6). The main decorative theme is the hunt amid lively animals, both real and imaginary, which is expressed in various manners in four poly-lobed medallions. This long-lived subject in Iranian art began to be applied for metalwork design from the thirteenth century onwards,[64] but a striking analogy to the hunting scenes depicted in the Edinburgh piece occurs in manuscript painting of the Ilkhanid period, especially in *Shahnama* illustrations datable to the early fourteenth century[65] – for instance, Mongol-clad hunters on horseback are evocative of those depicted in some illustrations of the Great Mongol *Shahnama*.[66] Besides figural representations, a certain stylistic association with contemporary book painting, especially in reaction to the occurrence of Chinese themes, can be found in

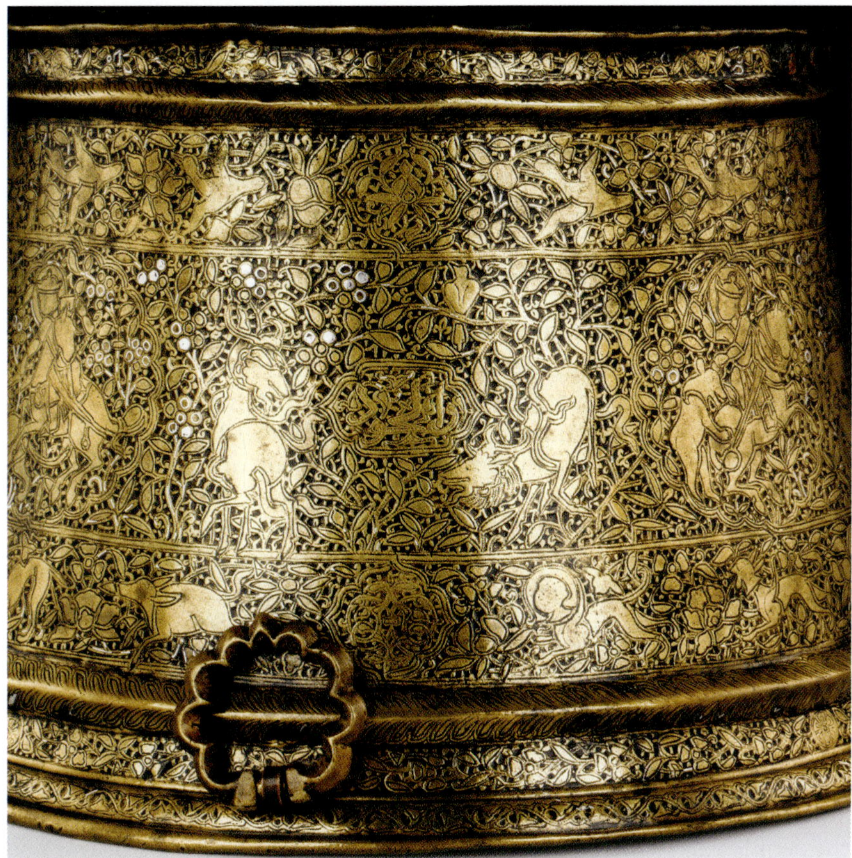

Figure 3.6 *Candlestick base (detail). Iran, early fourteenth century.*

the rendering of animals. In particular, the images of flame-bearing *kargs* are comparable to those depicted in Ilkhanid *Shahnamas*.[67] Such a close relationship between metalwork and book painting is, as mentioned in the cross-media relationship between Ilkhanid textiles and ceramics, suggestive of the pivotal role of drawings in the process of designing and painting, a practice that came into wider use in fourteenth-century Iran.[68] Emphasis is also laid on the infusion of naturalism into the background, which is suffused with various kinds of foliage and floral motifs. The shrubs and tiny flowers, recalling the intricate floral background often used in Song textiles (e.g. Figure 1.10), are not merely employed in filling the background. Rather, the layers of vegetal motifs serve to soften a geometrical rigidity, which predominates in earlier metalwork, and to create a fluency of pattern, giving this piece a great deal of decorative charm. Thus the close association of the Edinburgh candlestick with early fourteenth-century manuscript painting made in Ilkhanid territory, as well as its stylistic maturity – for instance, its attempt to integrate into a harmonious ensemble figural, animal and vegetal motifs of both Iranian and Chinese origin – are evidence for the Ilkhanid dating of the Edinburgh candlestick.[69]

In addition to the manufacture of brasses or bronzes inlaid with silver, Iran also provided a home for silversmiths' work from the thirteenth century onwards.[70] Surviving Iranian silver objects datable to the Ilkhanid period are relatively scarce, and thus they are not particularly helpful for the subject of this book.[71] However, a certain artistic relationship can be detected between surviving silver objects attributable to thirteenth-century Iran and those found in the territory of the Golden Horde[72] – a Mongol state of thirteenth- to fifteenth-century Eurasia, whose centre was located in the Volga Basin in the Kipchak Steppe. The importance of silver objects of the Golden Horde lies in their multiple roles, not only in bridging the gap in the history of Iranian silver but also as an intermediary in the introduction of the mastery of toreutic work of Central Asia as well as of East Asian elements into the Middle East.[73] Metalwork designated as Golden Horde shows a close link to artefacts produced in the northern parts of China and Mongolia under Liao, Jin and Yuan rule for both forms and patterns, while their stylistic affinities with Song decorative arts are less prominent. A type of silver goblet manufactured in the Golden Horde (Figure 3.7), for example, was equally popular in other Mongol states in Eurasia, perhaps including Ilkhanid Iran.[74] In China, such footed cups, which made their first appearance in Tang China,[75] recurred in both metalwork and porcelain from the Yuan period onwards.[76] A stylistic association between this goblet and Chinese decorative arts can also be found in the use

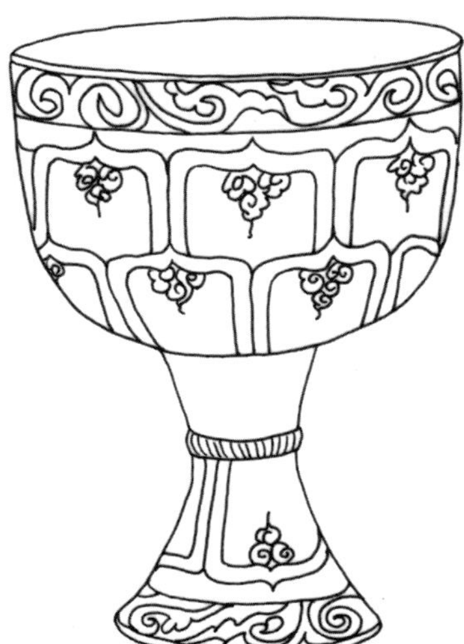

Figure 3.7 *Silver goblet. Golden Horde (southern Russia), late thirteenth–early fourteenth centuries.*

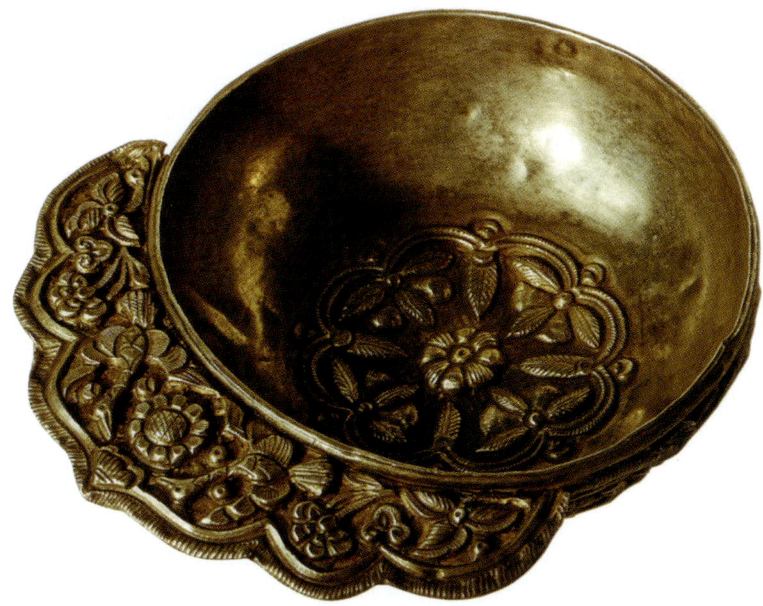

Figure 3.8 *Silver-handled cup. Golden Horde (southern Russia), late thirteenth–early fourteenth centuries.*

of patterns derived from lotus petals, recalling those often seen in Yuan blue-and-white porcelain (Figure 2.17).

Particularly notable kinds of metalware made in silver in southern Russia under Mongol rule are handled vessels – one is a cup whose rim is decorated with an elaborate multi-lobed flange (Figure 3.8),[77] and the other is a shallow bowl with a dragon-head handle.[78] Both seem to have been designed for travellers as a portable container either to be carried in a bag attached to the belt or to be suspended from the belt by the loop in the dragon's mouth as a portable container.[79] The production of drinking cups similar to the former example can be traced back to the Tang period,[80] but this type was initially developed in the northern parts of China and Mongolia from the eleventh to the thirteenth century, as exemplified in cups with side handles of the Liao and Jin dynasties.[81] Early fourteenth-century Iranian painting – for example, Arabic copies of the *Jamiʿ al-Tawarikh* of Rashid al-Din (Tabriz, 714/1314)[82] – provides pictorial evidence for the availability of a ladle closely akin to the Hermitage bowl in Ilkhanid territory. Prototypes for the bowl with a dragon-head handle can equally be found in those made in northern China under foreign rule.[83] Except for some features of the dragon, the bowl is not redolent of Chinese taste but rather evokes nomadic life in the steppes. Importantly, the two types of drinking bowl, together with the goblet discussed above, were also manufactured in gold on a large scale in southern Russia during the thirteenth and fourteenth centuries.[84] This indicates that the bowls and the goblets made in gold – a key material that was highly regarded in Mongol society – were in a certain demand – for instance, they performed burial and ritual functions in the territory of the Golden Horde and probably in the whole Mongol Empire.[85]

From consideration of artefacts of the Golden Horde, despite the fragmentary information, it is clear that artistic concepts that evolved in northern China made great inroads into southern Russia during the thirteenth and fourteenth centuries. This can provide supportive evidence to intensify the role of Liao and Jin objects in the formation of chinoiserie elements in Iranian art.

Lastly, it is worth considering the issue of the mirror industry in Iran during the late thirteenth and early fourteenth centuries. There are some Iranian bronze mirrors that seem to postdate the Mongol invasions.[86] Attempts have been made to reconsider the dating of some individual pieces, mostly those that are handled or used to have handles, such as a mirror portraying Bahram Gur and Azada on the hunt[87] and a mirror with the so-called fish-pound patterns,[88] though its remains difficult to establish a reliable identification of Ilkhanid mirrors and to trace their associations with Chinese mirrors. A variety of decorative schemes used in the proposed Ilkhanid mirrors may suggest that Iranian mirrors of the late thirteenth and early fourteenth centuries were in a developmental stage in the formation of Iranian styles in mirror decoration.[89] Additional evidence for the circulation of mirrors in Ilkhanid Iran is found in contemporary manuscript painting – for example, the London *Jamiʿ al-Tawarikh* and the Great Mongol *Shahnama*.[90]

Of equal note is a type of Iranian mirror whose reflective side is engraved with talismanic designs, consisting of magical letters, numerals and symbols.[91] Although the bodies of some of the mirrors may have been produced during the twelfth and thirteenth centuries, they were later remodelled as talismanic plaques, perhaps mainly ordered by the Shiʿite and Sufi communities.[92] The exact date of remodelling remains uncertain, though some scholars have associated it with the evolution of mysticism in Iran during the Mongol and Timurid periods.[93] What is clear is that such magic mirrors continued to be popular in both Iran and India until the nineteenth century.[94] Interestingly, a type of Chinese mirror also came to be known as a magic mirror, or literally a 'light-penetrating mirror' (*tou guang jian*).[95] As the Chinese characters indicate, when such a mirror is exposed to the light, the characters and images on the back are reflected on the wall, as if the light passes through the mirror.[96] This type of mirror was already in wide use in eleventh-century China and attracted scholarly interest in its technique.[97] Unlike Iranian magic mirrors, however, Chinese magic mirrors seem to have been intended as optical instruments rather than as talismans.

In relation to magic mirrors, there is a type of bronze seal or plaque that seems to have been made in Iran during the Mongol period. A small square seal in the David Collection, Copenhagen (Figure 3.9), is a case in point, not only to establish the development of seals in Ilkhanid Iran but also to enquire into how writing of East Asian origin entered Iranian decorative schemes. This square plaque, which comes from the sanctuary of the Sufi Shaykh Abu Ishaq at Kazarun in Fars, was used to stamp pledges or other kinds of documents or manuscripts issued by the shrine.[98] The use of square Kufic inscriptions distinguishes the David seal clearly from contemporary Islamic seals used in official documents, which are in the main carved in intaglio and are engraved in flowing cursive script.[99] It is tempting to relate this unique form of lettering to the impact of Chinese seals engraved in the seal script known as *zhuanshu*, which highlights the angularity of lettering.[100] Chinese seals might have already been known in Iran before the Mongol period through Chinese painting, in which seals were used to authenticate works of art (e.g. Figure 4.5), or through coinage of China, both silver and bronze, which flowed out of the country in parallel with the growth of the foreign trade during the Song period.[101] It has been suggested that Chinese rectangular script provided a source of inspiration for the use of the so-called square Kufic in architectural decoration in the eastern Islamic world,[102] although it is more likely that the square Kufic, whose earliest occurrence can be traced back to the early twelfth century,[103] was an indigenous development of Iran; in fact, the use of Kufic ornament became a marked phenomenon in Ilkhanid architecture.[104]

It was during the Mongol period that Chinese seals seem to have become more familiar in Iran, as seen, for instance, in the occurrence of Chinese style seals in official documents among the Ilkhans.[105] In Yuan China, seals were customarily used to validate official documents among Mongol rulers and officials, who were unable to write Chinese characters correctly or to sign documents with brush and ink.[106] However, the likeness between the David plaque and a Yuan seal carved in *phagspa* characters (Figure 3.10) – distinctive characters that were invented by a Tibetan monk during the reign of Khubilai[107] – is much stronger than that of Chinese seals, in that both the David piece and the *phagspa* seal use enigmatic and maze-like lettering. The *phagspa* characters began to be recognised in Iran perhaps not only through actual *phagspa* seals and some documents stamped with *phagspa* seals, but also through the *paiza* with the inscription of *phagspa* script[108] as well as through paper bills brought from Yuan China.[109] A *firman* (decree) of the Ilkhan Gaykhatu (r. 690/1291–694/1295) (Figure 3.11), one of the exquisite examples of Ilkhanid official documents on paper, is stamped in red with a type of imperial seal known as *al-tamgha*[110] – in this case a seal engraved in *phagspa* characters.

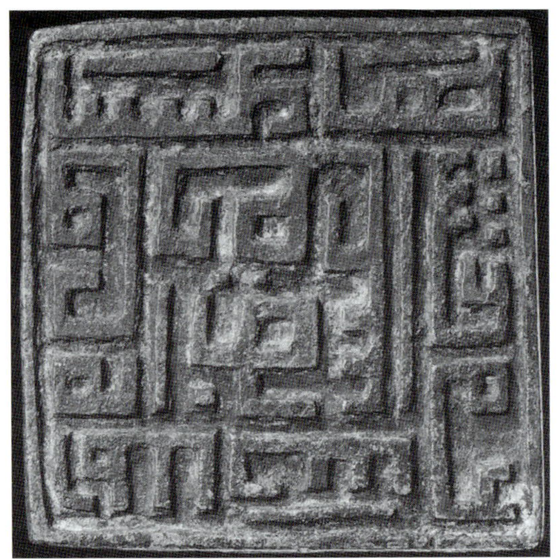

Figure 3.9 *Seal. Iran, fourteenth century.*

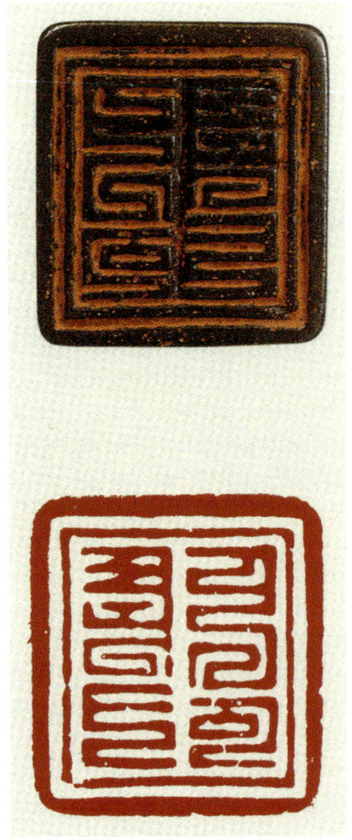

Figure 3.10 *Bronze seal with* phagspa *script. China, Yuan dynasty.*

Problems of the lotus in Iranian metalwork

The history of lotus decoration in Iranian metalwork is more complex than that of other chinoiserie motifs in Iranian art. In addition to its dual origin – ancient Egypt and India[111] – the motif was diffused over a wide geographical area and was to a large extent transformed by absorbing indigenous elements. In this section, however, the focus is given to a specific type of lotus decoration of Indian origin, as well as to the role of China in the assimilation of this intriguing motif into Iranian decorative concepts. The following discussion includes a brief history of the development of Chinese lotus decoration; the evolution of Iranian lotus decoration under Mongol rule and its Chinese associations; the use of this motif in Iranian metalware; and the significance of the lotus in Ilkhanid contexts.

Figure 3.11 Firman *of the Ilkhan Gaykhatu. Ink on paper. North-west Iran, 692/1293.*

The lotus is an important component of Buddhist iconography, as a symbol of rebirth, purity and the Buddha.[112] On the Indian subcontinent, the lotus occurs in earlier Buddhist monuments and statues predominantly as a highly stylised rosette or medallion, perhaps derived from the form of pointed oval petals, rather than as a floral motif of naturalistic traits.[113] It is highly probable that the significance of this sacred plant had already become known in Iran before the Mongol period in the course of the spread of Buddhism from India to Afghanistan and Central Asia.[114] Yet the real point of departure of the lotus as ornamentation is not India or Central Asia but China. Lotus seeds were imported from India, and the plant had taken physical root in China by the time of the Six Dynasties, as Buddhism moved eastwards into China. Although the adaptation of lotuses for decorative motifs was not undertaken at an early stage, it was during the Tang period – when the lotus was still exotic to the Chinese[115] – that lotus scrolls were by degrees developed as decorative devices for Buddhist statues[116] and monuments[117] and later as motifs for decorative objects, particularly for metalware.[118] This was perhaps inspired by contacts with intricate foliage patterns of Central Asian origin, such as the acanthus and vine scrolls.[119] By the tenth century, this foreign motif had become truly Chinese: while scrolls became less complicated, lotus blossoms began to appear prominently in stylised forms in major decorative objects of China.[120] This versatile motif was used either to form a single image (e.g. Figure 3.12) or to enrich background patterns (e.g. Figure 1.12). Unlike Indian lotus decoration, which is predominantly shaped like medallions, the lotus in these Chinese examples is shown to be a distinctive floral motif based on a realistic rendering of a type of water lily with rounded petals. But the symmetrical arrangement of each petal recalls that often seen in the lotus motifs evolved in ancient Greece, though calyxes are often omitted in Chinese lotus motifs.[121] The lotus flower, however, had gradually lost its Buddhist significance by the end of the Song dynasty; instead, its symbolic meanings associated with purity and integrity began to be highlighted under the influence of Confucianism.[122] Under these circumstances, the convention of lotus decoration entered on a large scale into the repertoire of decoration in West Asia following the Mongol invasion in the thirteenth century.

The date of the first appearance of the lotus in Iranian art cannot be fixed with certainty. It is, however, generally agreed that the occurrence of Chinese-related lotus ornament did not predate the Mongol conquest.[123] Although vernacular motifs of a lotus-looking form – namely, those used in association with the palmette and arabesque of ancient Egyptian and Mesopotamian origin – were already built into Iranian design prior to the Mongol period,[124] lotus decoration marked by fidelity to Chinese prototypes – a distinctive motif derived from lotus blossoms, consisting of a teardrop-shaped stamen and six or eight petals – began to be incorporated into Iranian decorative repertoires no later than the second half of the thirteenth century. According to Morgan, the earliest dated example of an Iranian version of this type of lotus decoration is to be found in lustre tiles from the Imamzada Jaʿfar at Qumm dated 665/1267.[125] The lotus here shows some degree of decorative appeal, but its depiction remains rudimentary and is not easily distinguishable from other flowery patterns. Increasing Iranian interest in naturalism can also be seen in tile decoration found in other religious monuments of this period.[126] Indeed, as will be discussed later at length, the lotus may have been regarded by degrees as an appropriate motif for Ilkhanid religious monuments.

Among the examples of Ilkhanid tiles that display the clearest manifestation of the lotus motif are those used in the decoration of Abaqa Khan's palace at Takht-i Sulayman. The design and arrangement of the lotus found in the Takht-i Sulayman specimens are more diversified than earlier examples: the motif appears in various shapes of tile, ranging from squares to stars to crosses; it is also found on the upper part of tiles, making an effective ensemble with dragon (Figure 2.6) or phoenix motifs below. Apart from animal themes, Chinese-inspired lotus patterns began to appear as primary decorative elements in Ilkhanid tiles. A type of lotus decoration, which is composed of small pointed petals and long stalks, is found in *lajvardine* tiles,[127] though the use of gold for lotus flowers is not effective in recreating a naturalistic atmosphere. On the other hand, another

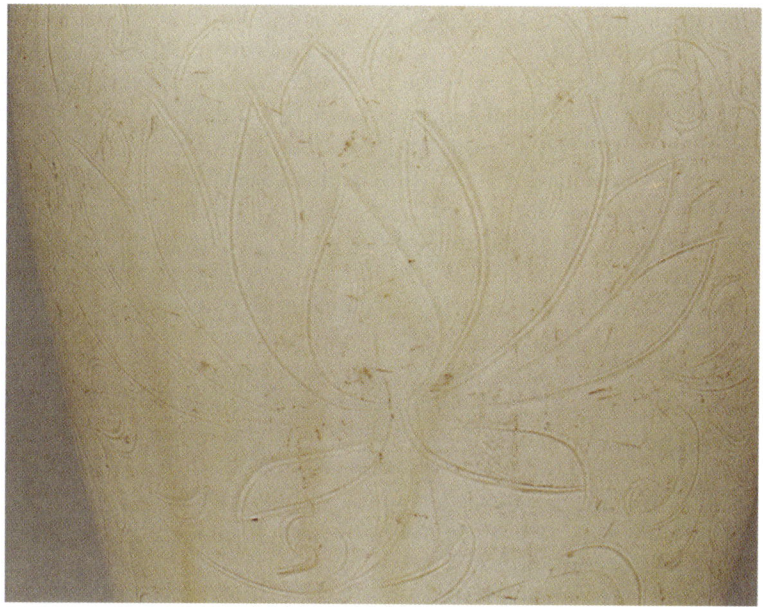

Figure 3.12 *Vase with incised lotus patterns. Ding ware. China, Northern Song dynasty.*

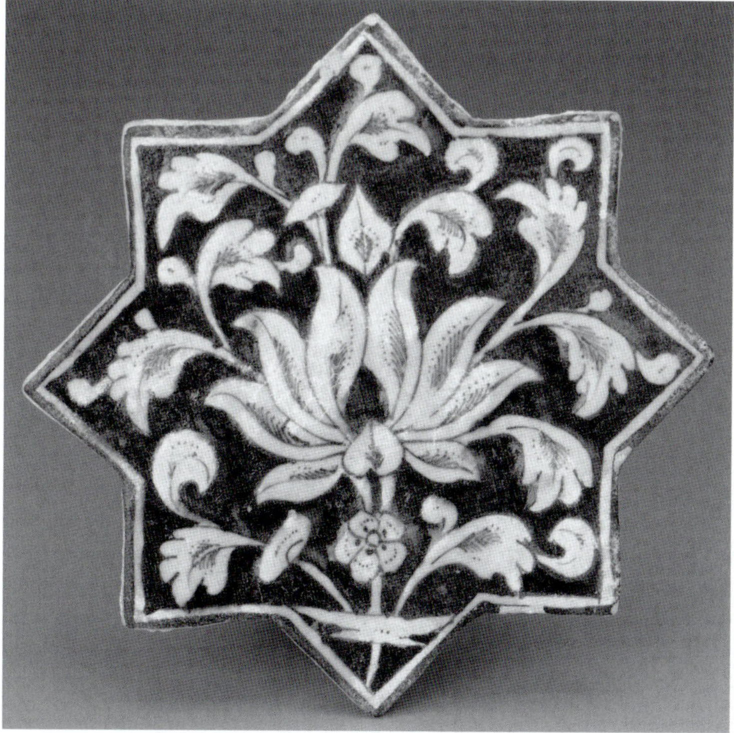

Figure 3.13 *Star-shaped tile with lotuses. Iran, c. 1300.*

type of lotus flower used in an eight-pointed star tile (Figure 3.13) is more reminiscent of Chinese prototypes (Figure 3.12). In addition to its graceful outlines and the organic rhythm of the design, the use of white for the patterns and its contrast with a cobalt blue background serves to enhance the sense of purification, which is one of the symbolic meanings of lotuses according to Buddhist thought. Iranian fascination with lotus decoration became more obvious in some dated pieces that were produced during the reign of Uljaitu,[128] particularly those used in his mausoleum at Sultaniyya (Figure 6.14).[129] Along with the fashion of the lotus for tile design, the motif seems to have increased its popularity in other media of architectural decoration. Among the most exquisite examples is a band of lotus decoration found in the top frieze of Uljaitu's *mihrab* made of stucco in the Masjid-i Jamiᶜ of Isfahan and dated 710/1310 (Figure 3.14).[130] The decoration is itself a curious repetition of the lotus surrounded by a lobed frame, yet the frieze as a whole is successfully interwoven with intricate arabesque motifs and several types of calligraphy below in a forceful Islamic setting.[131]

The trends of lotus decoration became increasingly apparent in other decorative objects of Iran, such as pottery (Figure 2.11) and textiles (Figure 1.13), from the early fourteenth century onwards, perhaps largely inspired by the use of this motif in contemporary architectural decoration. The evidence of painting also illustrates how pervasive a motif the lotus was in Ilkhanid territory. Importantly, while the lotus in its first phase of introduction to Iranian pictorial concepts seems to have functioned as a landscape element, judging by its naturalistic appearance in the early stages of Ilkhanid painting – for example, in the *Marzubannama* (Baghdad, 698/1299; MS 216, Archaeology Museum Library, Istanbul)[132] – it tended later to be confined to the adornment of costumes and interior settings. In manuscript paintings datable to the first and second decades of the fourteenth century, such as the Small *Shahnama*s (probably north-west Iran or Baghdad, c. 1300),[133] the Freer Balᶜami (probably the Jazira, c. 1300)[134] and the Edinburgh al-Biruni (probably north-west Iran or Mosul, 707/1307),[135] the motif is essentially employed in textile design, throne decoration and patterns on

Figure 3.14 Mihrab *to celebrate Uljaitu's conversion to Shiᶜism. Stucco. Iran, 710/1310.*

curtains, and in most cases serves as a mere pictorial device. Equally, in Arabic copies of the *Jamiʿ al-Tawarikh* of Rashid al-Din, the motif is ubiquitous throughout the illustrations of the manuscripts – for example, in the decoration of furnishing in enthronement scenes and even as part of armour design in battle scenes.[136] In the case of the Great Mongol *Shahnama*, the use of lotus decoration remains frequent, but a balance with the other motifs is somehow maintained.[137] The lotus depicted in the decoration of buildings in this manuscript has a highly articulate form,[138] evoking that of the lotus in Uljaitu's *mihrab* (Figure 3.14). The convention of Iranian lotus decoration, which was first developed in architectural contexts, was thus certainly passed on to Ilkhanid craftsmen and painters. As in the cross-media occurrence of chinoiserie motifs in Ilkhanid art, the use of drawings in the design process at Ilkhanid workshops could have resulted in the interchange of this motif between several media of the pictorial and decorative arts.

It is a thorny problem to determine which medium of Chinese art was influential in the introduction of lotus decoration to Iran. Since the lotus is one of the most popular motifs in Chinese art from the tenth century onwards, any types of lotus motif used in various media of the decorative arts can best be considered within the context of chinoiserie in Iranian lotus decoration. In addition to major decorative objects – for example, textiles produced in China and Central Asia during the thirteenth century (Figure 1.12), lacquer ware of the Song period (Figure 2.12), jade carvings,[139] bronze mirrors,[140] as well as scroll painting[141] – the potential of Chinese printed materials for the transmission of this motif into Iran is utterly undeniable. Moreover, the difficulty is to determine the particular Chinese sources of Ilkhanid lotus blossom motifs, since the Song and Yuan periods were a transitional period for flower motifs in Chinese decorative arts.[142] Between these two dynasties flower motifs were diversified by the introduction of bird images;[143] the peony gradually replaced the lotus as a popular decorative theme.[144]

Nevertheless, there are two key types of object that can help to pin down the immediate Chinese sources for Iranian lotus decoration. One is ceramics. The frequent occurrence of stylised lotus motifs can be seen in pottery made in twelfth- and thirteenth-century China, a trend that became more evident in ceramics produced in northern kilns during the Jin and Song periods (Figure 3.12).[145] Though the visual impression of the lotus created by the delicate linear movement of the potter's hand in Chinese ceramics is different from that engraved in monuments by a chisel or woven into textiles of Ilkhanid Iran, some original features of Chinese lotuses, such as elegant pointed petals, remain intact in Iranian versions of lotus decoration, thanks to the successful adjustments made by Ilkhanid artists. The other type of object is the horse trappings of

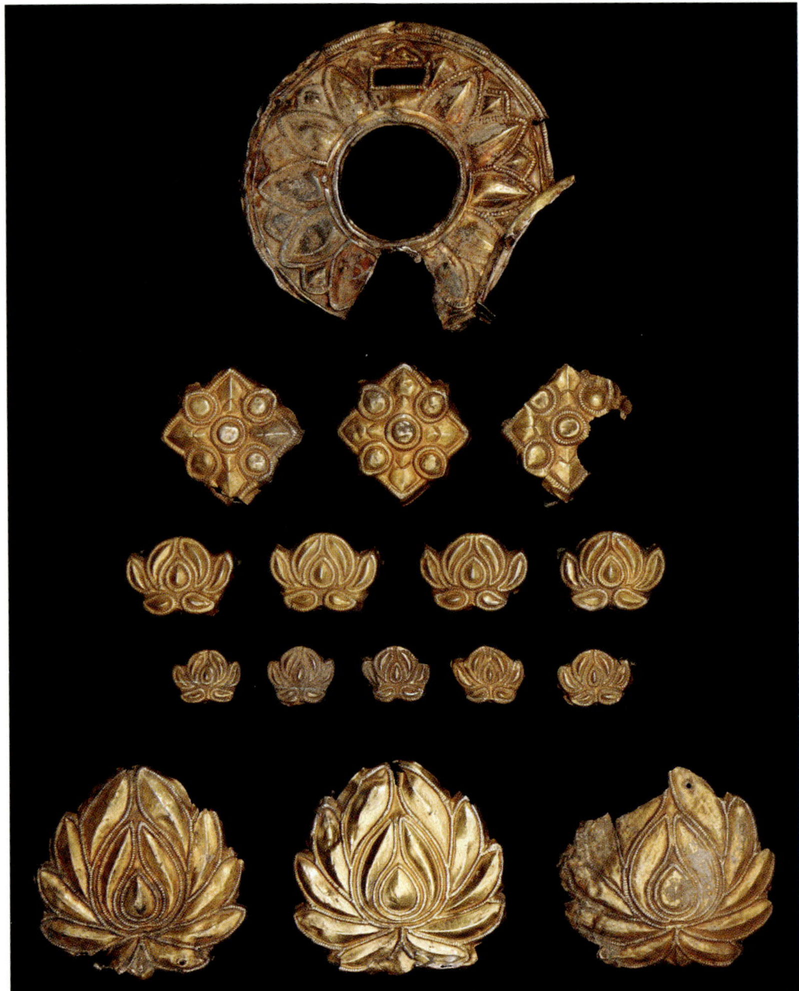

Figure 3.15 *Horse trappings. Probably Iran, thirteenth–fourteenth centuries. In Mongol Eurasia, luxurious connotations were given to the decoration of the horse, the most important form of property in nomadic society.*

lotus form – for example, those in the Khalili collection, London (Figure 3.15).[146] The underlying concept of design in the lotus-shaped harness is similar to that found in Ilkhanid examples, but it creates a vigorous impression when it covers horse's bodies. It is conceivable that this type of harness inspired Iranian artists to apply their distinctive shapes to the decoration of other types of artefact.

In addition to the overland route, another possible course of the spread of Chinese lotus decoration into Iran is through the artefacts brought from China via the sea route, in which Hormuz – a main centre for the commercial activities between East Asia

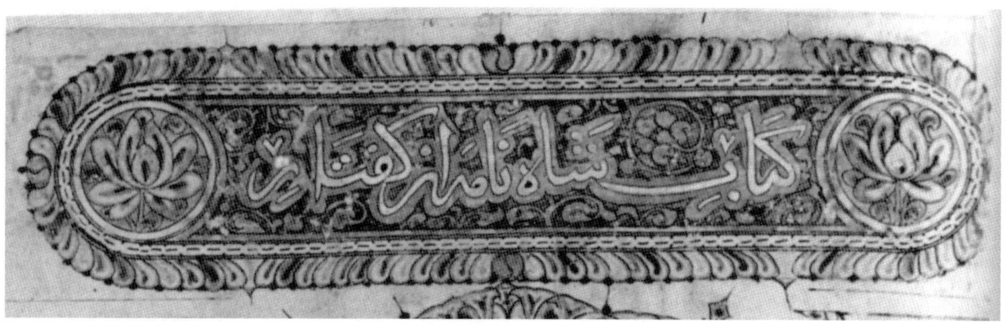

Figure 3.16 *Frontispiece from the* Shahnama *of Firdausi. Shiraz, 731/1330.*

and Iran via India – was an important entrepôt that served to distribute imported goods throughout Iran.[147] This hypothesis seems especially applicable to lotus patterns that occur in the book painting of the Inju dynasty, suggesting that the artists possibly came into contact with Chinese objects with lotus decoration as soon as these were circulated in southern Iran. In one of the Inju *Shahnamas*, the lotus appears with greater frequency not only as part of textile design and landscape elements[148] but also in its frontispiece as the principal decorative motif of the illumination (Hazine 1479, fo. 1, TSM; Figure 3.16).[149] Yet the lotus depicted in this manuscript is still at the embryo stage, betraying the simple mechanism of adopting lotus motifs derived from Chinese prototypes. The painters were presumably unaware of the potential for modifying lotus motifs into pure landscape elements or new decorative concepts.

The insets of lotus decoration into Ilkhanid metalwork correspond closely to this technique in other media of Iranian art of the period, but the motif carries a different aesthetic message. In general, there are two artistic intentions in the use of lotus decoration in Ilkhanid metalwork: to enrich other decorative schemes, or to function as a secondary motif in hunting or animal themes. A candlestick given to the shrine of Bayazid Bastami by a vizier of Uljaitu in 708/1308 (Figure 3.17), one of the earliest surviving dated pieces of Ilkanid metalwork, belongs to the first category. Perhaps incited by the fashion in architectural decoration, the medallions of this candlestick are studded with six-petalled lotus blossoms. The detail of their petals is more delicately rendered than that in other contemporary examples,[150] but the lotus group still tends to form a geometric and rigid composition.

On the other hand, the lotus often appears in a more refined form in the hunting or animal scenes in various types of Ilkhanid metalware.[151] In the cases of the Victoria and Albert Museum basin (Figure 3.3) and the Edinburgh candlestick (Figure 3.6), the lotus is deeply involved in creating naturalism in the background, together

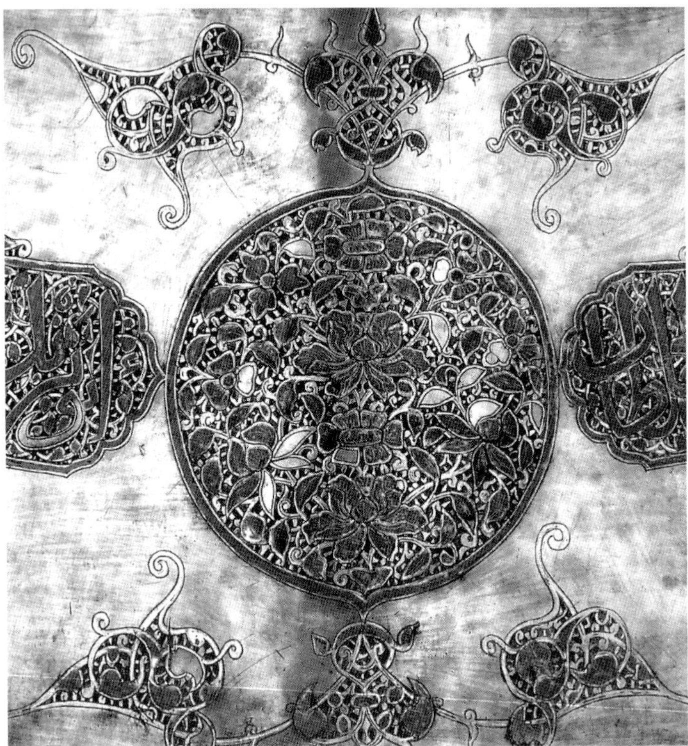

Figure 3.17 *Candlestick (detail). Iran, 708/1308.*

with other vegetal and flowery motifs. Another interesting example of this group is a vessel in the treasury of the Tekke of Jalal al-Din Rumi at Konya, known as the Nisan Tasi.[152] This vessel is also garnished with lotus motifs around the rim of its lid. The inscription mentions the name of Abu Saʿid,[153] so it is not surprising that some features of the lotus used in this vessel – for example, the decorative band of lotus blossoms enclosed by cloud collars – betray a stylistic indebtedness to the lotus motifs that had already been popularised in Iran during the reign of Uljaitu, as seen in the border decoration found in the *mihrab* of Uljaitu (Figure 3.14) and the decoration of the tile used in his mausoleum.[154]

Several comments on the popularity of the lotus motif in Ilkhanid art are called for. For artistic reasons, the lotus must have been a great addition to the decorative repertoire for Iranian artists. They seem to have found something congenial in the shapes of lotus petals, as well as the potential for using this motif widely in both painting and the decorative arts. The extensive use of this motif for architectural decoration, ceramics, textiles and metalwork is indicative of its pivotal role in the development of Ilkhanid decorative ideas, whereas in manuscript painting the lotus serves to enliven enthronement scenes or to spotlight rulers' luxurious garments.

Yet the ubiquity of lotus decoration in Ilkhanid monuments can perhaps be explained more intriguingly from three religious or funerary aspects of Ilkhanid Iranian society. First, in view of the multi-faith trends in Ilkhanid Iran during the late thirteenth century, the rise of Buddhism could have helped to familiarise Iranian artisans with lotus motifs.[155] The Ilkhanids, especially Arghun (r. 683/1284–690/1291), patronised Buddhist monks, mainly those from Tibetan Lamaist sects.[156] In addition, some Buddhist concepts introduced by Indian ascetics seem to have affected the development of Islamic mysticism in the Mongol period.[157] Quite a number of Buddhist temples were built in north-west Iran in the late thirteenth century, such as the Rasatkhaneh Caves at Maragha[158] and Buddhist cave-temples at Qonqor-olong near Sultaniya.[159] Despite the official conversion of Ghazan to Islam in 694/1295,[160] this motif, with its reminders of Buddhism, did not fall completely out of use in Ilkhanid Iran; on the contrary, builders and artisans who were involved in constructing Buddhist temples seem to have remained in Ilkhanid territory and continued to be actively employed in artistic production.[161]

Secondly, since most architectural examples showing the integration of the lotus into their decorative schemes were constructed in relation to Shiʿism,[162] it is tempting to assume that some of the symbolic meanings of this Buddhist motif – for example, purity – began to be associated with Shiʿite doctrines or practice.[163] The occurrence of the lotus in Ilkhanid art and architecture associated with Uljaitu, who converted to Shiʿism in 710/1310, may perhaps suggest the significance of this motif in Shiʿite contexts.[164] Given the frequent use of lotus decoration in Ilkhanid pictorial and decorative arts in non-Shiʿite contexts, this is not a particularly persuasive explanation for Shiʿite reinterpretations of this Buddhist motif. But what is certain is that the lotus was regarded as a motif that was acceptable for Shiʿite monuments in Iran at that time.

The third aspect of this motif is its association with death. Lotus decoration appears with frequency in funerary contexts, such as the tiles used in mausolea, where the motif can be seen as a symbol rather than as a mere decorative pattern, perhaps evoking peaceful, eternal rest or the flowering garden of paradise. Such a symbolic aspect of the lotus is likely to have been inspired by Mongol funerary customs, for the lotus is symbolically depicted in murals found in Yuan tombs[165] and in some leaves of the Diez Albums depicting Mongol funerals, which were presumably part of the first volume of the *Jamiʿ al-Tawarikh*.[166] In the case of metalware, too, the lotus seems to have served not only to enrich decoration but also to evoke sumptuous religious and burial rites. Lotus-bearing candlesticks akin to the Boston example (Figure 3.17) are depicted in the scene of Iskandar's bier in the Demotte *Shahnama*,[167] an image that reflects the use of this type of metal object in royal funerary arrangements in Ilkhanid Iran. Such symbolic aspects of lotus motifs are indeed unique to Ilkhanid art.[168]

As the lotus motif travelled westwards, this Buddhist element took on a new significance in a new cultural setting. In Iran, the lotus perhaps began to appear in architectural decoration in the 1270s, but subsequently entered both painting and the decorative arts. By the middle of the fourteenth century, this foreign-born motif had blossomed into a quintessentially Iranian motif. What is significant is that the lotus brought Ilkhanid artistic concepts into a wider spectrum of religious and ritual concerns. Perhaps more than any other chinoiserie motifs, the dynamism of the cultural and artistic interaction between East and West in the Mongol period is reflected in this enchanting motif, as a reminder of the past of Iran and China in the sphere of Buddhist culture as well as of the geopolitical unification of Eurasia under the Mongols.

Chinoiserie in miscellaneous objects

Having carefully examined Chinese elements in Ilkhanid textiles, ceramics and metalwork, we are now in a better position to expand the discussion into what happened in other media of the decorative arts and to look for some internal coherence between the major art forms of Iran in the Mongol period. Presented below are not detailed analyses but rather introductory notes on Chinese themes in Iranian glass, woodwork, lacquer and stonework, since relevant examples prior to the Timurid period are insufficient to make a comprehensive survey of chinoiserie in these four media. The main point of this section is, therefore, not to seek Chinese elements nor to make up a story of chinoiserie from limited sources but rather to look for reasons why Chinese themes are rather less discernible in glass, woodwork, lacquer and stonework.

Glass

The recent increase in the archaeological finds of imported West Asian glass in China serves to reinforce the theory that the traffic of influences between China and Iran in this art form was essentially from the West, but not the East.[169] Finds of Roman and Sasanian glassware, for example, have often been taken as convincing evidence for their vital role in the progress of glass-making in China as early as the first century; through them, it is argued, Chinese artisans learned to copy foreign examples, to melt imported glassware and to reuse it for decorating bronzes or for making replicas of jade and lacquer objects.[170] This did not, however, lead to any considerable growth of the glass industry nor to the exploitation of indigenous materials and techniques in China.[171] Chinese appreciation of West Asian glass reached its peak in the Tang period, not only in its association with exoticism,[172] but probably also because of its increasing religious connotations in Buddhist contexts.[173] Among the sherds or vessels of Islamic glass discovered in tombs and archaeological sites throughout China,[174] Islamic glassware retrieved from the Famen Temple sites in Shaanxi Province, which were active from the eastern Han to the late Tang period,[175] is remarkable for its good state of preservation and quality. Most of the finds are closely related to those excavated in Nishapur,[176] suggesting the importance of this region in the manufacture of glass as well as the interchange point of the glassware trade from Mesopotamia towards the Silk Road. Yet the inflow of glass artefacts from the Islamic world did not affect the Chinese glass industry in its own right. China seems to have relied on imported glass in succeeding dynasties, when glass artefacts continued to be imported from West Asia both by land and by sea.[177] While the fashion for imported glass in the northern part of China is evident from archaeological finds, particularly those datable to the Liao period,[178] the demand for glass must also have increased in the south, helped perhaps by frequent contacts with the Middle East through Muslim merchants who settled in the coastal towns of southern China from the ninth century until Yuan times.[179] Owing to the absence of undisputedly Song and Yuan examples of glassware, however, there is no way to trace the development of the art of glass in China from the twelfth to the fourteenth century and to expand the discussion into its relationship with contemporary Iranian glassware.

In addition to insufficient documentation and research on Song and Yuan glassware, the discussion of chinoiserie in Iranian glass is hampered by the lack of decisive evidence for glass production in Iran between the Ilkhanid and late Safavid periods. Even though the stylistic and technical development of Islamic glass as well as the historical and cultural circumstances of the glass industry in the Middle East have been studied in more detail in recent years, thanks to the growth of scholarly interest in Islamic glass,[180] Iranian glass of the Mongol period tends to be eliminated from the main argument, owing to the scarcity of reliable examples. The finds retrieved from Takht-i Sulayman, now in Berlin (I.19/69, Staatliche Museen zu Berlin, Stiftung Preußischer Kulturbesitz), may be considered as potential material for a future study of Ilkhanid glassware.[181] But, so far as published examples are concerned – typically greenish colourless glass with moulded decoration – their value as evidence for the impact of China is negligible.

These uncertainties about the art of glass in the Ilkhanid period suggest a decline in the glass industry in Iran at that time. Perhaps, while pottery and metalwork blossomed into established art forms under Mongol patronage, glass production was unable to regain its place in Iranian decorative arts after the devastation caused by the Mongol invasion. The hope for further studies of the art of glass of

Mongol Iran and its Chinese connections perhaps lies in the archaeological finds from the territory of the Golden Horde – though the study of the Golden Horde finds is still in its infancy, and the inaccessibility of the Golden Horde material remains an obstacle to the clearer understanding of the whole picture of glass making in the wider Mongol empire.[182]

While no clues to provide a conspectus of the glass industry in Ilkhanid Iran are available at present, glassware was certainly in use in Iran at that time for both utilitarian and liturgical purposes, and imported glassware of Syrian and Egyptian provenance may have met most of the demand for glass vessels and furnishings in Ilkhanid Iran. Evidence to substantiate this assumption is the fact that glass objects, such as goblets and lamps, are depicted in Ilkhanid painting,[183] and some of these are identifiable in actual surviving Mamluk enamelled and gilded glassware.[184]

There is room to argue about the difficulties in tracing a residue of the impact of China in Iranian glass. This can be associated with one principle of chinoiserie – Chinese themes spread westwards, thanks to the rarity of certain materials. Despite the rise of the glass industry, glass seems to have never been regarded as the highest art form in China, unlike jade, lacquer and porcelain. The art of glass in China did not come fully into its own, for the supply of glassware was invariably dependent on Islamic and Western glass – namely, glass of Mesopotamian and Iranian origin in medieval times and later that of Europe. Perhaps the potential of this material was not fully realised in China until early modern times. It seems that, unlike silk and porcelain, the westward export of glassware was not particularly promoted in China. Even if some Chinese glassware reached West Asia, Iranian familiarity with glass as a material and perhaps the Iranian sense of superiority to Chinese glass products may have reduced an appreciation of shapes and motifs of Chinese glassware, so that there was less incentive to adopt them in other media of the decorative arts. Rather, Chinese ceramics seem to have encouraged Iranian glassmakers to some extent to look for artistic inspiration for a well-proportioned shape.[185] Thus, in these circumstances, no dramatic encounter or fruitful exchange of artistic ideas between Chinese and Iranian glass could be expected.

Woodwork

The perishable nature of wood is one of the reasons for the lack of archaeological evidence for the availability of Chinese wooden products in West Asia as well as for their impact on Iranian woodwork.[186] Yet there seem to be more fundamental reasons for the Iranian unawareness or disregard for the art of Chinese woodwork: to give one simple yet persuasive answer, wooden products were not a major export from China to Iran and were intended mainly for domestic use, as indicated by the difficulties in tracing the foreign trade of Chinese wooden products.[187] Wood has been in great demand in China since ancient times as a chief material for architecture and furniture as well as for objects for burial and religious use, such as vessels and sculptures.[188] Even though more easily obtainable wooden products – for example, stationery – began to be made on a large scale in accordance with the development of Chinese material culture and the growth of scholarly tradition, particularly in the Ming and Qing periods,[189] very few indications of the impact of Chinese woodwork can be found in Iranian woodwork or other media. What is more probable is that, although Iranians may have encountered Chinese wooden objects at some point in the course of the Sino-Iranian trade and have even been aware of their fine quality, they did not appreciate them as much as their own; rather, the art of Chinese wood carving could have been recognised by Iranians mainly in association with lacquer, a topic that will be dealt with in the following section. In a more general context, the lack of specific Chinese models in wood for Ilkhanid woodwork is not an insuperable problem, because the ability of motifs to travel from one medium to another was already well established at this time.

Though small in number, some Ilkhanid examples of certain types of furnishing that were incorporated into mosques, such as *minbar*s, *maqsura*s, *sanduq*s and doors, have survived in a good state of preservation. Curatola has cast light on a group of cenotaphs as a proof of the evolution of wood carving in the region of Sultaniyya during the reign of Uljaitu.[190] The materials discussed in this study are sufficient to demonstrate the continuation of superb craftsmanship, both technically and artistically, in Iranian wood carving in the Mongol period. Yet little evidence for the use of distinctive Chinese-inspired motifs has been found in these examples. The ornamentation found here is essentially geometric.[191]

Surviving examples from central Iran – for example, the *minbar* in the Masjid-i Jamiʿ at Na'in (711/1311)[192] – are distinct from those found in northern Iran in the way in which the carvers explored the design potential of floral patterns. Yet it is difficult to construct a theory of chinoiserie merely from this phenomenon, for the patterns cannot be identified with confidence as typical Chinese-inspired floral motifs, such as lotuses or peonies. Even though the insertions of non-geometric elements into the ornamentation of the Na'in *minbar* are effective in reducing the rigidity of the traditional star-and-polygon decoration, this is inadequate drastically to deconstruct the prevailing sense of geometry. The decoration of the *minbar* keeps rich floriated arabesques in the control of star or polygonal frames.

Thus, surviving examples of Ilkhanid wooden furnishings illustrate aspects of the conservativeness of ornamentation in Iranian woodwork at that time. As for wooden fittings in general, the wooden doors depicted in the illustrations of the Great Mongol *Shahnama* give useful evidence.[193] While most of the doors in the Great Mongol *Shahnama* are undecorated or decorated with stale geometric or arabesque patterns, the doors represented in the scenes of Ardashir contain chinoiserie motifs – namely, elaborate cloud-collar and lotus patterns.[194] Since no actual examples of wooden doors with such motifs are known to survive, doubts may remain as to whether these are mere pictorial devices invented by the painters. Yet, judging from the authenticity of the depiction of costumes, textiles, carpets and metal objects in this manuscript,[195] it may safely be assumed that the doors depicted in this manuscript also reflect to some extent the current fashion of Ilkhanid woodwork and its use of Chinese-inspired motifs.

The period following the disintegration of the Ilkhanid Empire is a turning point in the history of wood carving in Iran and Central Asia, for at this time woodwork underwent several stylistic revolutions. While a sense of geometry is still retained in decoration, as seen in a large Qur'an box in the al-Sabah Collection in Kuwait (745/1344; LNS 35 W),[196] a rare survival that was made under the Chobanids (736/1335–758/1357), Chinese themes emerge in both fixed and portable wooden furnishings produced in Iran and Central Asia in the middle of the fourteenth century, perhaps owing to the increase in fresh information about the art of East Asia. The use of lotus patterns became more intensified in post-Ilkhanid woodwork produced in central Iran, as exemplified in the *minbar* in the Suryan Mosque, Fars, datable to the Muzaffarid period.[197] Instead of the familiar geometric patterns, the surfaces of both sides of the *minbar* are densely patterned with elaborate lotus motifs. Compared with the lotus forms found in other media of fourteenth-century Iranian art, the motifs modelled by chisels are more impressive for their third dimensionality. Though still framed by star- or polygonal-shaped units, this floral ornament shows a sense of fluidity and the desire to create organic rhythms.

A Qur'an stand in the Metropolitan Museum of Art, New York (Figure 3.18), dated 761/1360, and therefore in fact post-Ikhanid, is more illustrative of the influx of Chinese elements. The advance represented by this lectern lies not only in its masterly carving techniques but also in its well-constructed decorative schemes, a point that is made more evident by comparing this piece with earlier Qur'an stands – for example, those made in Saljuq Anatolia.[198] Floral motifs with Chinese traits, evoking peonies used in blue-and-white porcelain (e.g. Figure 2.17), are delicately fitted into the background, accompanying tendrils with an emphasis on their elastic movement. They are depicted in harmony with a cypress tree, which is flamboyantly framed by a cloud collar-shaped arch and elaborately carved inscriptions. Despite the uncertainty of its provenance,[199] this is

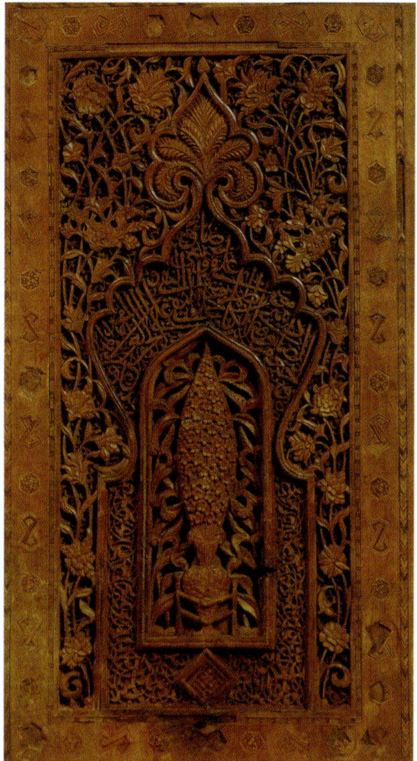

Figure 3.18 *Wooden Qur'an stand (detail). Iran or Central Asia, 761/1360.*

undoubtedly a key example that proves the existence of a highly sophisticated wood-carving tradition in Iran and Central Asia prior to Timur's rise to power.

Although the use of Chinese floral decoration was slow to appear, it clearly resulted in the advent of more naturalism into the repertoire of Iranian woodwork. By the middle of the fourteenth century, Iranian wood carving seems to have laid the foundations for the full-scale adaptation of Chinese themes, including animals, that occurred in the subsequent century under Timurid rule.[200]

Lacquer

It seems that Iranian artists gradually familiarised themselves with the use of the lacquer technique – the application of a series of layers of resin-like substance known as lac – as early as the twelfth century.[201] However, the active development of this varnishing technique can be safely traced back only to the late Timurid period,[202] and it was only under subsequent dynasties that Iranian appreciation of lacquerwork as an art form became self-evident. Iranian 'lacquer' is fundamentally different from the technique exploited in China, which is based on the properties of the sap from a tree native to China, called the *Rhus vernicifera*, which was subsequently distributed throughout East and South-East Asia. In China, and broadly in East Asia, lacquer is traditionally used for the final treatment of painted wooden surfaces, whereas in Iran the design is painted on the base of the object, which is then coated with lacquer.[203] Therefore Chinese associations with the development of lacquer techniques in Iran remain tenuous; there has been no definitive evidence that Chinese lacquer techniques were familiar to Iranian artists.[204] Rather, it does seem that the full-scale production of lacquered objects occurred in Iran only in recent centuries, and European fashion dictated many aspects of later Iranian lacquerware.[205] Yet much can be said about the availability of Chinese lacquerware in Mongol-ruled Iran and its importance as a major source for the influx of chinoiserie motifs across various media of Iranian art.

Lacquer has been venerated in China since early times, and, like bronzes and jade, it was initially designed for ritual and burial use.[206] Both literary and archaeological evidence for the import of Chinese lacquerware into Iran remains unsubstantial, yet Iranian awareness of the art of Chinese lacquer can be verified by the occurrence of motifs that evoke those found in Chinese lacquer objects in Ilkhanid decorative arts. For instance, as mentioned in the discussion on ceramics, Sultanabad wares often contain bird-and-flower motifs that bear a close resemblance to those found in Chinese decorative objects of the thirteenth and fourteenth centuries, particularly lacquerware of the Southern Song period (Figure 2.12). The motifs carved in lacquer, whose details are silhouetted against a radiant glow of vermilion red, may well have become embedded in the minds of Iranian artists. The visual impression and texture created by Chinese lacquerware, which differ from that of other media more commonly associated with Iran, such as pottery and glass, were certainly new to Iranian artists. This suggests that, of the two types of Chinese lacquerwork – painted and carved – carved lacquerware was more influential in late thirteenth- and fourteenth-century Iran, which corresponds to the period of change in Chinese lacquerwork from monochrome to more intricate carved ware.[207] The uniqueness and unfamiliarity of lacquered objects brought from China may thus have stimulated Iranian interest in adapting motifs often used in Chinese lacquerware for a wide range of the pictorial and decorative arts, perhaps including their own lacquer objects.[208]

Additionally, despite the lack of archaeological evidence, the availability of Chinese lacquered furniture in fourteenth-century Iran can be attested by pictorial evidence, especially manuscript painting produced in the early fourteenth century. Examples are readily to be found in the enthronement scenes of the *Jamiʿ al-Tawarikh*, where thrones and footstools are depicted as heavily or partly lacquered in red (e.g. Figures 5.12, 5.16–5.17).[209] These are evocative of those found in Song imperial portraits (Figure 5.15). The catalyst for introducing Chinese lacquered furniture into West Asia remains, however, speculative. There are many gaps in the history of Chinese lacquered furniture from the Han to the Ming period.[210] Yet the frequent occurrence of Chinese-related lacquered furnishings in Iranian painting is sufficient to deduce that Chinese lacquer somehow made its way westwards in the form of furniture. Fine pieces of lacquered furniture were presumably transported westwards from China by land or by sea, or perhaps Chinese experts in lacquer techniques were employed at Ilkhanid workshops.

Stonework

Despite the rarity of stone as a building material on the Iranian plateau, some important Mongol monuments with elaborate stone-carving decoration are known from Azerbaijan, such as the dressed stone façade of the Masjid-i Jamiʿ at Asnaq,[211] and stonework can thus be included in the discussion of chinoiserie in Iranian art under Mongol rule. An unequivocal proof for this is the so-called Viar dragon (Figure 3.19),[212] a remarkable fragment of sculpture that was incorporated into a Buddhist monument built into a rocky complex in the region of Sultaniyya during the Ilkhanid period. This dragon is visibly derived from some East Asian prototype: though it is surrounded by an oblong frame, a sense of liveliness in the dragon is created by the sinuous movement of its well-proportioned serpentine body, exhaling flames or clouds. Such a lifelike dragon is distinct from Islamic-type dragons, which are characterised by their stillness and symmetrical arrangement.[213] The religious context of this monument suggests that Chinese dragon conventions, including those brought by Buddhist monks, were certainly available in north-west Iran. As in the case of the tiles found at Takht-i Sulayman, the dragon motifs used in Chinese or Central Asian textiles (Figure 1.1) are most likely to have provided a model for the Viar dragon. The accuracy of the depiction of the dragon's body and the detail of its face also points to the involvement of artists who were conversant with the iconography of the dragon in the Chinese tradition – for example, the dragons carved in relief that were often incorporated into imperial buildings.[214]

Some additional information about the Sino-Iranian artistic relationship can be gleaned from tombstones or cenotaphs in China and Inner Mongolia. The incorporation of Chinese elements was already visible in the relief carving on Muslim tombstones found in mosques of the Song dynasty, particularly those that were built in Quanzhou.[215] This demonstrates that Muslims resident in southern China of the period were not hesitant about the use of Chinese-inspired motifs, such as clouds and lotuses, on their tombstones,

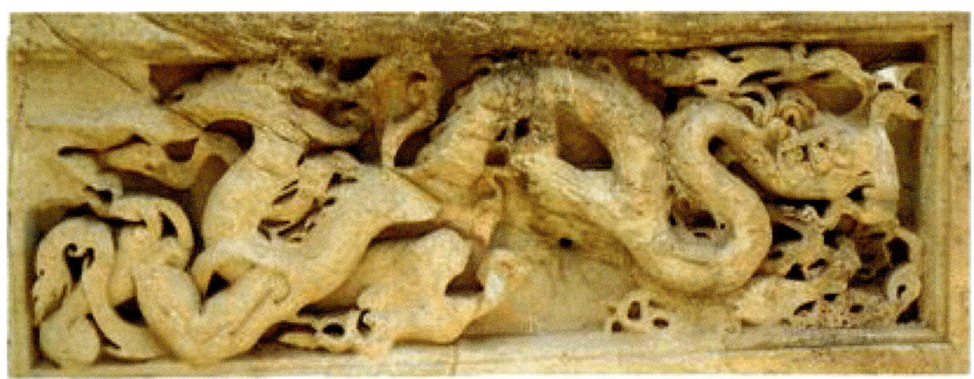

Figure 3.19 *Rock-carved dragon. From a Buddhist site near Viar. Multiculturalism is reflected not only in Ilkhanid pictorial and decorative arts but also in Iranian architecture of the Mongol period. The Viar dragon, a remarkable sculptural work in Ilkhanid Iran, coexists with the* mihrab *in a mosque-converted Buddhist site near Sultaniyya.*

together with Arabic or Persian inscriptions; they were at least familiar with such motifs.[216] This tempts one to speculate about the introduction of Chinese stone-carving traditions to West Asia through Muslim merchants, yet there has so far been no decisive evidence to prove the actual diffusion and acceptance of such tombstones in Iran before the fifteenth century. A Muslim cenotaph relevant to the present discussion has recently been discovered in Inner Mongolia,[217] suggesting that the tradition was taken over by Muslims in Yuan China in the fourteenth century. This type of cenotaph – with its emphasis on profuse ornamentation and basic motifs developed from those seen on Song tombstones – may well have prevailed in northern China under Mongol rule, although it remains unclear whether the specific decoration of Chinese relief carving ever made its way to Mongol Iran. It was finally during the Timurid period that the increased availability of information about East Asian artistic traditions saw the assimilation of Chinese decorative repertoires into the tombstones of Iran and Central Asia.[218]

On the other hand, the extent to which Chinese stone-carving objects proper served to disseminate East Asian themes into Iranian decorative arts before the Timurid period remains uncertain. In this respect, a special question arises as to the connection between Iranian and Chinese jade. Jade – which is readily associated with China – has been highly prized in China as a most precious material since earliest times and was initially developed for ritual use.[219] In the medieval Middle East, however, as al-Biruni mentions in his treatise on mineralogy, jade seems to have been linked with the land of the Central Asian Turks rather than with China.[220] The fact is that one of the chief sources for earlier Chinese jade was the Khotan

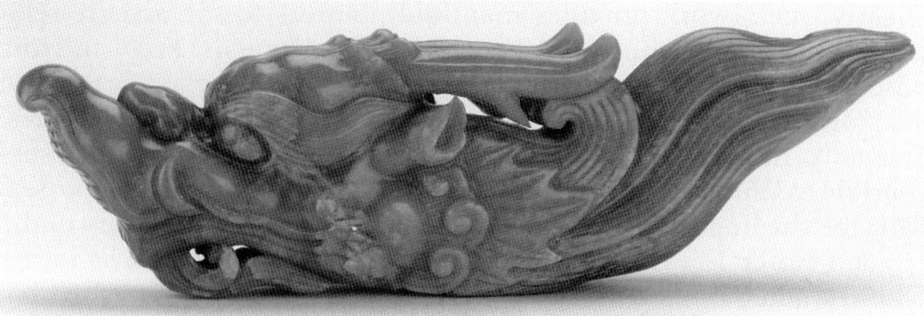

Figure 3.20 *Jade dragon-head finial. China, Yuan dynasty.*

area, and carved jade objects from this region were also sent to China as tribute until the end of the Tang period.[221]

One can only assume that, even though jade objects were brought from China in the period before and after the Mongol invasion – a continuous tradition of jade carving in the Song and Yuan periods can be proved by surviving examples intended for ritual use and display, such as sculpture and jewellery[222] – Iranian interest in Chinese jade was insufficient to result in the development of its own tradition of jade carving during the late thirteenth and early fourteenth centuries.[223] Perhaps this was because of the lack of nephrite in Mongol Iran, or simply because Iranian artists were incapable of copying Chinese models in this intractable medium. What Chinese jade may have provided for Iranian artists in pre-Timurid times was not an impulse to imitate Chinese jade itself but an inspiration to re-create the appearance of jade in pottery, as exemplified in types of Saljuq and Ilkhanid ceramics with a special emphasis on translucency (Figures 2.1, 2.13).

A jade dragon-head finial (Figure 3.20) is an intriguing example that illustrates the richness of the jade-carving tradition in Yuan China. The actual impact of such jade dragon decoration on the architecture of Ilkhanid Iran is difficult to certify from extant Mongol monuments in Iran.[224] This piece was, however, judging by its relatively small size, installed as part of the edges used for decorating a throne or a chair rather than the roof of a building, and this kind of jade object may have served at the Ilkhanid court mainly in the context of decoration for furniture. There is ample visual evidence for the prevalence of this type of decorative element in the thrones depicted in Ilkhanid painting (Figure 5.16).[225]

Once again, the real point of departure for the discussion of chinoiserie in Iranian jade is the Timurid period, when Iranian appreciation of Chinese jade reached its highest point.[226] In this era, thanks to the background of indigenous Central Asian traditions of jade carving, the art of jade carving became an established genre in decorative arts of the Iranian world and played a key role in the evolution of Timurid taste.

Clearly, metalwork provides manifold pointers to the artistic relationship between China and Iran under the Mongols. First, mirrors pose a number of problems concerning the process of adoption and adaptation of Chinese elements in Iranian art over several centuries. Secondly, Ilkhanid metalworkers were, like weavers and potters, susceptible to Chinese themes, including dragons, phoenixes and lotuses. Thirdly, the importance of artefacts retrieved from the territory of the Golden Horde as evidence for the interaction of artistic ideas in the Chinese and Iranian cultural spheres needs fresh emphasis.

The lotus – that simple yet artistically expressive motif – is a good example of how a motif of Buddhist origin evolved during its passage westwards and of how it was revolutionalised through Iranian interpretations during the Mongol period. Of particular interest is that the decorative potential of this motif was quickly digested by Ilkhanid artists.

Other media of the decorative arts, such as glass, wood, lacquer and stone, reflect a variable history of chinoiserie in Iranian art, demonstrating the fact that Iranian artists extended their field of adoption of Chinese themes beyond textiles, ceramics and metalware. Indeed, these four media provide an alternative theory of chinoiserie in Iranian art. They serve to enrich the decorative vocabulary of Iran under the Mongols, sometimes in a unique way.

Notes

1. For further discussion, see Melikian-Chirvani 1970a; Medley 1970.
2. See Rawson 1982, 2, figs 1–3, 10.
3. See Juliano and Lerner 2001, cat. no. 111.
4. For further discussion, see Rawson 1982, 10–15.
5. Rawson 1984, 125.
6. For further discussion, see ibid. 125–32.
7. Baer 1998, 73–4.
8. See Rhie 2002, figs 2.42–3.
9. Rawson 1984, 159. For relevant examples found in Buddhist monuments in ancient Gandhara, see Behrendt 2004, figs 18, 28, 63, 96 and 99.
10. For example, the Chehel-Khaneh caves at Zir Rah were known as a Buddhist cave in Sasanian Iran (Ball 1976, 104–27). For Buddhism in pre-Islamic Iran, see Emmerick 1990.
11. This issue has been widely discussed: Melikian-Chirvani 1972, 56–9; Bulliet 1976; Emmerick 1983, 957.
12. Frumkin 1970, 146–9; Pugačenkova and Usmanova 1995.
13. See, e.g., the main wall decoration in the Masjid-i Jamiʿ at Qazwin (509/1116; Baer 1998, fig. 93).
14. See Hillenbrand 2000b, pls 11–12 and 20.
15. Fehérvári 2005. See also Melikian-Chirvani 1975, 55–8.
16. Another possible source for the domed mausoleum in the Islamic Iranian world is the Zoroastrian fire temple (see Hillenbrand 1994a, 275–6).

17. For Iranian mirrors, see Rice 1961 and recently Carboni 2006. The issue of chinoiserie in Iranian mirrors has been discussed in much greater detail in my paper given to the Iranian metalwork conference in Dublin in 2004 (Kadoi forthcoming b).
18. See, e.g., Soudavar 1992, 16–17.
19. For Iranian handled mirrors, see *SPA*, pls 1302d, h. A mirror of this type is depicted in one medallion of the so-called Blacas ewer (Mosul, 629/1232, BM, OA 1866.12–29.61; *SPA*, pl. 1330e). For Greek and Roman prototypes of handled mirrors, see Rouen 2000, 18–99.
20. Unhandled bronze mirrors were produced in China on a large scale in the period between the late Eastern Zhou (771–256 BC) and early Han dynasties (206 BC–AD 220), and again in Tang times (see Watson 1962, 89–108). The use of a handle seems to have occurred first in Tang mirrors (Rupert and Todd 1935, nos 83, 124), but gained a certain popularity during the Song (Taipei 2000, 448; Kerr 1990, figs 81 right, 88) and Yuan periods (Kong 1992, 889, 895). The popularity of handled mirrors in China in these periods can be attested by surviving mirror stands, one of which is in the Victoria and Albert Museum, London (Kerr 1990, fig. 87). In terms of the interaction between China and Iran, it would be significant if the use of a handle in post-Tang mirrors stemmed from the inspiration of mirrors brought from West Asia.
21. Allan 1982, nos 76–7.
22. Ibid. 33.
23. Allan 1979, 145, no. 44.
24. Allan 1982, 33.
25. For example, a mirror in the David Collection, Copenhagen (4/1996), is datable to the period between 600/1203 and 660/1261, judging by the inscription mentioning an Artuqid ruler's name (Folsach 2001, pl. 503).
26. Two of the popular types of mirror are: (1) a mirror with human heads in four or five medallions (e.g. *SPA*, pls 1302d–h) – this type of mirror excavated from Qasr al-Hayr al-Sharqi, Syria, datable to the Mamluk period (Grabar et al. 1978, pl. 282, no. 33), suggesting its wider circulation throughout the Islamic world; (2) a mirror decorated with addorsed sphinxes (e.g. Melikian-Chirvani 1982, cat. nos 58–9).
27. A large number of Chinese mirrors have been discovered in the Minusink Basin (Loubo-Lesnitchenko 1973). Some scholars have suggested an interaction between the so-called pearl roundels, a feature of Sasanian textiles, and Han mirror design (see Meister 1970, 255–6), although pearl-roundel motifs seem more likely to have been indigenously developed in the Iranian world (see Chapter 1).
28. Ghirshman 1956.
29. Allan 1979, 50.
30. Thaʿalibi 1968, 141. He says: 'Chinese make iron into steel, and from this, mirrors, talismanic amulets, etc. are made.'
31. Allan 1979, 62.
32. Now in the Museum of Islamic Art in Cairo (inv. no. is unknown: Rice 1961, 289, fig. 1). It would be interesting to speculate on the relationship between the knob in Chinese mirrors and the frequent occurrence of a dot in the centre of Samanid pottery, which appears to be rather inharmonious with epigraphic decoration around the surface of the dishes (see Volov 1966, figs 1, 3, 4, 7 and 9).

33. The Song era was a transitional period in the history of bronze mirror making, when the position of bronzes as popular utensils began to be threatened by the wider use of porcelain (Kerr 1990, 9) and the shortage of copper – the chief raw material of bronze (for a decline in the metal industry and the production of bronze artefacts during the Southern Song period, see Chʿen 1965). This, however, did not cause the complete collapse of bronze manufacture in China: on the contrary, there was a growing interest in collecting ancient bronzes, initially in order to satisfy the demand for copper to mint coins; this later led to the growth of archaism as well as the copying of antique objects, including mirrors (for the production of archaistic bronzes during the Song period, see Watson 1973). A reasonable number of excavated bronze mirrors datable to the Liao (Liu 1997), Song (Cheuk 1986), Jin and Yuan periods (Kong and Liu 1991, 216–30) have been discovered since the 1980s, suggesting that bronze mirrors continued to be made in China from the tenth to the mid-fourteenth century. Most Song mirrors are undated. It seems more likely, however, that most surviving mirrors were produced in the thirteenth century, when the copper supply became increasingly more plentiful than in the twelfth century, thanks to the introduction of paper money (Kerr 1986, 163).
34. For Tang examples of this type, see Thompson 1967; Taipei 1986, pls 77–92.
35. It should be noted that there are striking analogies in the decoration between Chinese mirrors and metal dishes of the later Khurasan school – for example, an early thirteenth-century tray in the Victoria and Albert Museum, London (M.31–1954; Melikian-Chirvani 1982, no. 27). This indicates the impact of Chinese mirror design on various types of metal object produced in the eastern Iranian world at that time.
36. The Eight Trigrams are represented by an arrangement of signs consisting of various combinations of straight lines. They are used to interpret the future. See Williams 1974, 148–51.
37. Judging by its inscriptions, this mirror was perhaps intended for ritual use by Taoist monks (see Kerr 1990, 98).
38. For pictorial evidence for this custom, see Rawson (ed.) 1992, fig. 148.
39. For instance, the knob found in one of the Victoria and Albert Museum sphinx mirrors (442–1887; Melikian-Chirvani 1982, no. 59) is not pierced.
40. Pellat 1993.
41. Carboni 1997, 6.
42. See *SPA*, pls 1301a–b.
43. Carboni 1997, 6.
44. Allan 1976–7, 21.
45. For further discussion of this subject, see Schottenhammer 2001, 97–118. For the development of the maritime trade in Song China, see Lo 1955. For the Song foreign trade, see Shiba 1983.
46. Ward 1993, 87.
47. Works of the Mosul school have been widely discussed (e.g. Rice 1957).
48. A penbox inlaid with silver and gold (western Iran, 680/1281, OA 1891.6–23.5, BM; Ward 1993, no. 69) has often been taken as an

example showing the impact of the Mosul tradition in late thirteenth-century Iranian metalwork.

49. See, e.g., *Legacy*, cat. no. 171.
50. For further discussion, see Gray 1940–1; 1963; Taipei 2001, cat. nos IV–1, 2.
51. For post-Song metalwork, see Watson 2000, 239–44.
52. For 'fish-pond' ornament, see Baer 1968.
53. See also Melikian-Chirvani 1982, 203–4, pl. 93A; the figure in a howdah carried by a dromedary shown in this image can be interpreted as Sapinud, the Indian bride of Bahram Gur, while the image found in Figure 3.3b can be identified as Bahram Gur hunting with Azada.
54. Rawson (1984, 148–9) has compared Chinese-inspired motifs of the Victoria and Albert basin with the decoration of the Liao tomb discovered at the Qingling. For this tomb, see Tamura and Kobayashi 1953.
55. See Zhu 1998, figs 4, 23, 26, 33, 54, 61, 67 and 89; Beijing 2002, 36–7, 176–7, 191, 202–3, 215 and 310.
56. See also an Ilkhanid incense-burner with medallions of waterfowl in the David Collection, Copenhagen (47/1967; Folsach 2001, no. 514).
57. See Louis 2003 and New York 2006 for a recent study of Liao metalwork.
58. Enderlein 1973, Abb. 1–5.
59. To the best of my knowledge, no Chinese counterparts to this motif have as yet been identified.
60. Crowe 1991, 159.
61. Allsen 1997, 107.
62. Enderlein 1973, Abb. 12–17.
63. Ibid., Abb. 12, 15.
64. See Baer 1983, 229–35.
65. *Legacy*, 279. For further discussion of the stylistic relationship between manuscript painting and metalwork of the fourteenth century, see Simpson 1985; Komaroff 1994.
66. *Legacy*, 279. In particular, see Grabar and Blair 1980, nos 16, 33, 41, 51 and 53.
67. See Simpson 1979, figs 37–8 and 59–61. See Chapter 6 for further discussion on this animal in the Small *Shahnama*s.
68. *Legacy*, 184–94.
69. North-west Iran thus seems to be the likeliest location of this piece, though a Shirazi provenance has been suggested by Baer (1983, 231). The Fars school, presumably based in Shiraz, was another active workshop of metalmaking in Iran during the fourteenth century under the Injus and the Muzaffarids. A round-bottomed bowl decorated with cartouches and medallions containing figures of hunters or rulers typifies Shirazi metalwork of the period (see, e.g., Melikian-Chirvani 1982, nos 102–4). In comparison with Ilkhanid metalware, the impact of China is less apparent in the metalware of the Fars school. For further discussion of metalwork in Fars during the fourteenth century, see Melikian-Chirvani 1982, 147–52; Blair 1985.
70. For silver in Islamic Iran, see Allan 1976–7; Melikian-Chirvani 1986.
71. It is interesting to comment on a silver vase sold at Christie's in 2000 (Christie's 2000, lot 272), which has been attributed to Ilkhanid Iran. The high-shouldered body of the vase evokes that of the so-called *mei-ping* shape (Figure 2.17), whereas the decoration of medallions

contains Chinese-inspired lotus motifs. If its Ilkhanid date is the case, this indicates that chinoiserie made inroads into the art of silverwork in Mongol Iran. See also other arguably fourteenth-century Iranian silver objects sold at Christie's (1995, lot 254; 1997, lot 267).

72. Marshak and Kramarovsky 1993. They have compared a thirteenth-century Iranian silver bowl of the Walters Art Gallery, Baltimore, with a Golden Horde example in the Hermitage Museum. See also a related bowl in the Keir Collection (127; Ward 1993, pl. 65).
73. For the metalwork of the Golden Horde, see *GH*.
74. For a related silver goblet ascribed to Iran, see *Legacy*, cat. no. 153. The prevalence of such footed cups in Mongol-ruled Iran can also be attested by pictorial evidence – e.g., a leaf of the Diez Albums (Diez A. Fol. 70.S.11; Rührdanz 1997, Abb. 3). For gold goblets from the Golden Horde, see *GH*, cat. nos 43–5.
75. See Rawson 1982, pls 1–3, 8.
76. For Yuan examples, see *ZMQ*: Decorative Arts, 3, nos 7, 9, 23, 32–3; Shanghai 2000, 251, 253; Taipei 2001, cat. nos IV–33, 48; *Legacy*, cat. no. 196.
77. For other examples, see *GH*, cat. nos 58, 60 and 136.
78. See ibid., cat. nos 14 and 21.
79. *Legacy*, 276.
80. See Vickers, Impey and Allan 1986, pl. 35.
81. See Zhu 1998, figs 22, 59 and 60; Beijing 2002, 188–9.
82. See Rice 1976, E68 (NB: for the sake of convenience, I shall use E and K, instead of reconstructed folio numbers, for quoting pages from the London and Edinburgh manuscripts; see Chapter 5). See also some leaves of the Diez Albums (Diez A. Fol. 70.S.10 (*Legacy*, cat. no. 18); Fol. 70.S.23 (Bonn/Munich, cat. no. 290); Fol. 71.S.52 (Rührdanz 1997, Abb. 2)).
83. See Gyllensvärd 1971, no. 22; *ZMQ*: Decorative Arts, 2, no. 229.
84. See, e.g., *GH*, cat. nos 12–13, 40–1 and 43–5.
85. See Allsen 1997, 67–9.
86. For example, one talismanic mirror in the Art and History Trust Collection (probably Isfahan, 777/1375) seems to have been produced in commemoration of Shah Shuja''s capture of Tabriz (Soudavar 1992, cat. no. 17).
87. This mirror (*SPA*, pl. 1300; formerly on loan to the Harvard University Art Museums, MA), which had previously been ascribed to the twelfth century (*SPA*, 2484), was reattributed as an early Ilkhanid product in 1976 (Hayward, no. 201). In the light of Iranian partiality for this subject in various media of the decorative arts up to the mid-fourteenth century (Ettinghausen 1979a), the use of this theme does not help to pin down its precise dating.
88. AA 273, Louvre, Paris (Paris 2001, cat. no. 154). This piece is decorated with clearly defined fish-pond patterns, suggesting that this piece was in all likelihood contemporary with other Ilkhanid and Mamluk metal objects with fish-pond ornament of the fourteenth century.
89. It was in Mamluk Egypt that identifiable Islamic-style mirrors seem first to have occurred (see Hayward, no. 228). See also Islamic-style steel mirrors attributable to late fifteenth-century Iran (Allan 2000, cat. nos 34–5).
90. Blair 1995, K29; Grabar and Blair 1980, no. 56. Tang-type mirrors have been excavated from the territory of the Golden Horde (Fyodorov-

Davydov 1984, fig. 108; Nedashkovsky 2004, figs 37–40), suggesting the continuous impact of Chinese mirrors in West Asia during the Mongol period.

91. See Maddison and Savage-Smith 1997, nos 52, 79.
92. Ibid. 125. See, e.g., a mirror in the Khalili collection (MTW897), whose inscriptions refer to the five members of the holy family as recognised by the Shiʿite (ibid., no. 52). This is suggestive of the close association of mirrors with Shiʿites, who associate the mirror with a manifestation of God, considering that the image appears in a mirror but does not have substance (Pellat 1993, 106), and with the Sufi, who regards the mirror as a tool for polishing his heart until the radiance of God shines from it. The Sufi associations of mirrors are fully dealt with by Soucek (1972, 14) in her discussion on the idea of 'polishing' in Sufism, in an examination of a fifteenth-century illustration of the competition between painters from China and from Greece that occurs in the *Iskandarnama* of Nizami (Shiraz, 853/1449; 13.228.3, fo. 322, MMA). The conclusion of this competition is that, since the Chinese had polished his wall, while the Greek had painted his one, the Chinese reflected the Greek painting like a mirror. This episode is itself indicative of the close associations between China and mirrors in medieval Iran, an idea that perhaps evolved in parallel with the inflow of Chinese bronze mirrors into the Iranian world during the late twelfth and early thirteenth centuries.
93. Maddison and Savage-Smith 1997, 125.
94. See ibid., nos 53–7.
95. For Chinese magic mirrors, see Turner 1966; Murray and Cahill 1987.
96. Turner 1966, 94.
97. Needham 1954–, 4, pt. 1 1962, 95.
98. *Legacy*, cat. no. 167. The text reads 'Abu Ishaq, the shaykh, the spiritual guide, may God sanctify his soul' (Blair and Bloom 2006, 100).
99. See Allan and Sourdel 1978; Kalus 1986, 12. A bronze seal with foliated Kufic scripts sold at Sotheby's in 1997 (lot 7; Sotheby's 1997), which was used for the bales of silk, is a rare surviving example of the seals in the context of commercial enterprises in medieval Iran.
100. For Chinese seals, see Luo 1981.
101. See Peng 1988, 417–28; Schottenhammer 2001, 134–5. For Song coinage, see Guojia wenwu ju (ed.) 1989, 177–297.
102. *SPA*, 1748. For a summary of this controversy, see Majeed 2006, 56–8.
103. Blair 1998, 82–5. For example, Ghazna (the minaret of Masʿud III, c. 1100) and Gar (the minaret, 515/1121), reproduced in ibid., figs 7.35–7.
104. For example, Bistam (the shrine of Bayazid, 713/1313), Linjan (the Pir-i Bakran, 698/1299–703/1303), Natanz (the Kkanaqah, 716/1316–717/1317) and Varamin (the Masjid-i Jamiʿ, 722/1322), reproduced in Seherr-Thoss 1968, 110–11, 114–15, 120–1, 128–9. For further discussion on this issue, see Majeed 2006.
105. See Pelliot 1936, figs 28–31; Mostaert and Cleaves 1952, 482–5, pls 6–7.
106. Franke 1953, 28.
107. See Taipei 2001, 297–8.
108. See, e.g., *Legacy*, cat. no. 197.

109. Ibid., cat. no. 198. Under the inspiration of Chinese paper money (*chao*), paper currency was introduced into Iran in 693/1294 during the reign of Gaykhatu, but this resulted in economic chaos in Ilkhanid Iran. For paper currency in Ilkhanid Iran, see *CHI*, 5, 374–7; Jahn 1970b; Allsen 2001a, 177–80.
110. An imperial seal (*al-tamgha*) was sent by the Yuan emperor to mark the investiture of the *il-khan* in Iran and entrusted there to the minister of finance, who authorised to stamp fiscal decrees (Blair 2006, 272). See also Soudavar 1992, 35; Leiser 2000.
111. For a brief history of Egyptian and Indian lotus motifs, see Wilson 1994, 101–3, 143–51.
112. See Ward 1952.
113. For further discussion of the development of lotus medallions in early Buddhist art, see Hayashi 1992, 80–102.
114. Ibid. 104. See, e.g., the lotus-shaped pedestal found under the legs of Mithra in the relief of Investiture of Ardashir II at Taq-i Bustan (Fukai et al. 1969–84, 2, pl. XCII).
115. Schafer 1963, 127–9.
116. See Hayashi 1992, 108–15, 132–7.
117. See Rawson 1984, 64–75.
118. See Rawson 1982, 14–15.
119. For further discussion, see Hayashi 1992, 166–92, 238–42 and 274–371.
120. See Rawson 1984, 81–8.
121. For the relationship between Greek and Chinese lotus patterns, see Kadoi (2008).
122. For instance, a famous Confucian scholar Zhou Dunyi (1017–73) highly praised the lotus as 'the flower of purity and integrity' in his essay (Wirgin 1979, 170).
123. For a brief discussion of Chinese-inspired lotus decoration in Iranian art, see P. Morgan 1995, 32–5. For the lotus in Islamic ornament, see Shafiʿi 1957, 7–69; Rawson 1984, 173–93; Baer 1998, 20–7.
124. See Baer 1998, 7–20.
125. P. Morgan 1995, 32.
126. See, e.g., the tile decoration of the Imamzada Jaʿfar at Damghan dated 664/1266 and that of the Imamzada Yahya at Varamin produced around 660/1262 (Watson 1985, pl. 110, colour pl. K; Porter 1995, pl. 19).
127. e.g. Porter 1995, pl. 27.
128. See, e.g., tiles that originated in the Shrine of the Footprint of ʿAli at Kashan (711/1311; *Legacy*, cat. nos 119–20); a star tile dated 710/1310 in the Museum of Fine Art, Boston (31.729; *Legacy*, cat. no. 117). See also tiles found in the Masjid-i ʿAli at Quhrud (1300–54; Watson 1975, pls I–V) and tile decoration at the base of the minaret in the tomb of Abd al-Samad at Natanz (707/1307; Blair 1986a, pl. 64).
129. e.g. a quadrangular tile from Sultaniyya (*Legacy*, cat. no. 122). Lotus flowers in another tile from the same site (Pickett 1997, pl. 45) are inlaid in a continuous band of cloud-collar arches, a unique combination that was invented through an Iranian reinterpretation of patterns of Buddhist and Mongol origins.
130. Unfortunately, later restoration destroyed this evidence (I am most grateful to Professor Bernard O'Kane for this information).
131. The *mihrab*, whose inscriptions praise the virtues of Shiʿism and the traditions of ʿAli, may have caused increased hostility from the conservative Sunni population of Isfahan (see *Legacy*, 120).

132. See Simpson 1982a, fig. 51 See also a leaf depicting a rule enthroned in the Istanbul Saray Albums (c. 1300; Hazine 2152, fo. 60v, TSM; İpşiroğlu 1967, pl. 11); a painting of the lion and jackal in the Paris *Kalila wa Dimna* (Baghdad or southern Iran?, c. 1300; suppl. pers. 1965, fo. 16 v, BN; *SPA*, pl. 817 A; see Chapter 6).
133. See Simpson 1979, figs 3, 5, 8, 12, 15, 18, 20, 22, 32, 41, 43, 47, 49, 51, 63–4, 66, 70, 75, 77–8, 82–4, 89–90, 93 and 101. For the Small *Shahnamas*, see Chapter 6.
134. See, e.g., Fitzherbert 2001, pl. 7.
135. See Soucek 1975, figs 5, 7, 12 and 13. For this manuscript, see Chapter 4.
136. See Rice 1976, E16, E18, E51, E53–E54, E56 and E58; Blair 1995, K21.
137. See Grabar and Blair 1980, nos 1, 10, 11, 12, 14–15, 17, 37, 39–40, 42–4 and 55–6. See also the lotus in the Gutman *Shahnama* (probably Isfahan, c. 1335; Swietochowski 1994, pls 15, 17, 27, 28, 34, 38 and 44–5; see Chapter 6).
138. See, e.g., Grabar and Blair 1980, nos 10, 15 and 44.
139. A number of flower-shaped jade plaques are known to survive (see Cheng 1969; Rawson 1995, nos 25:16–25:17). The *yutian* ('jade floral ornaments') seems to have been a popular type of accessory in Jin and Yuan China.
140. See Kong 1992, 670–1.
141. e.g. Weidner (ed.) 1994, cat. no. 2.
142. Rawson 1984, 173.
143. For the development of flower-and-bird motifs during the Song dynasty, see Chen 2000, 40–8.
144. Rawson 1984, 173.
145. See also Wirgin 1979, 170–3, figs 8–10.
146. For Mongol horse trappings, see Kramarovsky 1996.
147. For the importance of Hormuz, see Morgan 1991. Titley (1983, 229) has stated that the lotus motif of Iranian art was mainly derived from textile designs imported from India. This suggestion is reasonable, taking account of the fact that Indian textiles, in particular block-printed textiles, were taken westwards into Egypt in the Ayyubid and Mamluk periods and had a wide distribution (see Barnes 1997). Yet no relevant examples of lotus decoration are found in surviving thirteenth- and fourteenth-century Indian textiles.
148. Rogers, Çağman and Tanındı 1986, pls 38, 42. For the lotus depicted in the 741/1341 *Shahnama*, see Simpson 2000, pls 2, 6–7 and 12. The use of lotus motifs is less apparent in the 733/1333 *Shahnama* (Adamova and Giuzal'ian 1985, pls 1–2).
149. See Titley 1983, 229–33.
150. See, e.g., Melikian-Chirvani 1982, no. 87.
151. See, e.g., the Keir window grill (132, Keir Collection, England; *Legacy*, cat. no. 171) and the David incense-burner (47/1967, David Collection, Copenhagen; ibid., cat. no. 170).
152. Baer 1973–4, 15–16, figs 11a–b.
153. Ibid. 3–8.
154. Pickett 1997, pl. 45.
155. For Buddhism in Ilkhanid Iran, see *CHI*, 5, 540–1.
156. Petech 1983, 183; Morgan 1986, 158.
157. Soucek 1975, 141.
158. Ball 1976, 127–43. Ball has also identified the Imamzade Maʿsum at

Varjovi near Maragha as a Buddhist cave complex of the Mongol period (Ball 1979).

159. Scarcia 1975. See the following discussion of stone-carving and the Viar dragon.

160. For the conversion of Ghazan, see Melville 1990; Amitai-Preiss 1996.

161. P. Morgan 1995, 35. For further discussion of Buddhist elements in Ilkhanid art, see Kadoi (forthcoming c).

162. For additional information on the use of the lotus in buildings with Shiʿite associations, see P. Morgan 1995, 33–4.

163. P. Morgan (1995, 34) has pointed out the association of lotus decoration with asceticism. For Shiʿism and dervish orders in the fourteenth century, see Halm 1991, 71–7.

164. For the conversion of Uljaitu and its impact on art, see *Legacy*, 117–20.

165. Pointed out in P. Morgan 1995, 34. See, e.g., *ZMQ*: Painting, 12, no. 184.

166. See *Legacy*, cat. nos 27–8. In the Istanbul copy of the *Jamiʿ al-Tawarikh*, a large lotus blossom is symbolically present on the coffin of Nuh ibn Mansur (Hazine 1653, fo. 208, TSM; İnal 1975, fig. 27).

167. Melikian-Chirvani 1987, 122, pl. VI.

168. The lotus was also disseminated northwards into the Transcaucasus under the rule of the Golden Horde (see, e.g., Fyodorov-Davydov 1984, figs 63, 64 (3), 65 (2–3), 68 (1, 3) and 78 (1)). The motif then spread to Transoxiana, perhaps first into Khwarazm under Mongol rule (e.g. the Mausoleum of Najm al-Din Kubra at Kunya Urgench (c. 1321–36; Degeorge and Porter 2002, 105–7)), and further east towards Central Asia after the reunification of vast tracts of Eurasia under Timurid rule. Among Timurid monuments, the use of lotus decoration in the shrine complex of the Shah-i Zinda, Samarkand, is unrivalled (for a recent study of this monument, see Soustiel and Porter 2003). More noteworthy is the westward transmission of lotus decoration into the Mamluk realm. As in Iranian art, no precursor for the style is found in pre-Mamluk art before the advent of the Mongols, but the lotus motif suddenly emerged in Mamluk territory in an already highly stylised form, especially in metalwork and glass, and prevailed in almost all possible types of pictorial and decorative art produced in Egypt and Syria in the fourteenth century. In terms of variety of media, the lotus is integrated into Mamluk decorative concepts more deeply than into those of Ilkhanid Iran. In addition to the vogue for lotus decoration in Mamluk textiles (Atıl 1981a, no. 116) and ceramics (ibid., nos 90–1), lotuses often appear in architectural decoration (see, e.g., a carved stone relief with floral ornament inserted in the decoration of the *madrasa* of Sultan Hasan, Cairo (1356–60); Rogers 1970–1, fig. 9, n. 26). The Mamluk attachment to lotus motifs can be seen in various pictorial examples, including playing cards (Mayer 1971, figs 40–1) and manuscript painting (Haldane 1978, pls 3, 5). Surviving Mamluk copies of the Qurʾan, especially those executed in the reign of Sultan Shaʿban (r. 764/1363–778/1377; Atıl 1981a, nos 4, 5; James 1988, figs 98–9, 131–2, 134–5 and 141–2), pay great attention to flavouring the naturalistic elements in their illuminations by the subtle incorporation of lotus patterns. The Iranian type of lotus decoration is likely to have been introduced through the medium of Ilkhanid

artefacts, especially textiles, as the role of textiles in the introduction of Ilkhanid decorative repertoires into Mamluk glass workshops has been suggested (Carboni and Whitehouse 2001, 265–7). Yet, in the case of Mamluk lotus decoration, direct influences from Chinese objects as well as Indian connections are also plausible. There was an established trade network from major ports located in southern China to Alexandria; Maʿbar, on the eastern coast of India, flourished as a transit point (Allsen 2001a, 41; for further information, see Tampoe 1989). One can also correlate the occurrence of Chinese-derived lotus decoration in Mamluk art with the growing settlement of Mongol Oirats in Mamluk Syria; these men, who had a strong influence on the Mamluk court circle, may have brought Chinese products to Mamluk territory (Baker 1995, 72). Whether from Ilkhanid Iran, directly from China or via India, such readily available lotus decoration from both Iran and China enabled the motif to reach its mature phase in a relatively short period and resulted in the interchange of this motif between several media of Mamluk art. Examples of lotus-bearing Mamluk metalwork are numerous (Atıl 1981a, nos 19, 25 and 30). They cannot be classified in exact chronological order due to the lack of information about their precise date of production, but the bulk of them are datable to the period between the 1320s and 1370s, perhaps owing to the increased availability of Ilkhanid products after the Peace of Aleppo in 723/1323 (see the Gdansk textile in Chapter 1). A large brass basin (OA 1851.1–4.1, BM; Ward 1993, pl. 88), which has been ascribed to the period between 1330 and 1341, epitomises the vogue for lotuses in Mamluk metalware of the period. The motif here essentially functions as an appealing decorative pattern. It remains to be seen, however, whether this motif also carries religious, perhaps even funerary, connotations in Mamluk contexts. Another popular medium showing the prevalence of the lotus in Mamluk design is glass. The lotus appears in Mamluk glassware to fit well with the smooth and shiny surfaces of glass. In mosque lamps typical of the Mamluk period (Carboni and Whitehouse 2001, cat. no. 118), the decorative impact made by the repetition of lotus motifs works in an attractive way, creating an image of a flowering landscape. The motif gives an effect of the garden of paradise if the lamp is lit. Finally, the lotus of Ilkhanid origin began to appear in Italian Renaissance art, a topic that I hope to explore in a separate study.

169. See Laing 1991; 1995; Ma 2004.
170. Pinder-Wilson 1991, 140. For Roman and Sasanian glass found in China, see An c. 1987, 2–9.
171. Most of the earlier Chinese glass artefacts are stratified glass eye beads of diminutive size, which show a strong indebtedness to Roman and Mesopotamian examples (see *Sekai*, 2, 250–1). The skill of glass blowing was finally introduced from Islamic lands to China in the fifth century under Sui rule (see Jenyns and Watson 1963–5, 2, 119). For a summary of the glass industry in China, see Dohrenwend 1980–1.
172. See Schafer 1963, 235–7.
173. Moore 1998.
174. See Laing 1991, 109–12.
175. See An 1991, 123–30.
176. See Kröger 1995, 8. For the glass trade of Nishapur, see ibid. 33–4.

177. Hirth and Rockhill 1911, 227–8. See also *Song shi* 1985, ch. 490, 14118–22.
178. Ma 1994.
179. See Hardie 1998. According to Hardie, Mamluk glass came to China through the overland or overseas trade in the fourteenth century, but it eventually found its way to Europe and North America.
180. See Carboni 2001; Carboni and Whitehouse 2001; Goldstein 2005.
181. See Carboni and Whitehouse 2001, 23–4, figs 11–12.
182. See Fyodorov-Davydov 1984, 158–70; Kramarovsky 1998.
183. e.g. Grabar and Blair 1980, nos 39, 56.
184. See, e.g., Carboni 2001, cat. nos 85, 99. Much can be said about Mamluk glass and its Chinese connections. Most key chinoiserie motifs – e.g. lotuses, dragons and phoenixes – were brought to Mamluk glass workshops perhaps through Ilkhanid mediation (see Carboni and Whitehouse 2001, 206), but Mamluk glass is also susceptible to the form of Chinese ceramics. The impact of Chinese celadon ware is clearly reflected in the use of dragon-like handles with pendant rings in a type of Mamluk vase (ibid. 265–6).
185. See, e.g., a tenth–eleventh century Iranian glass bowl in the Khalili collection (GLS.588; Goldstein 2005, no. 250), whose finely proportioned shape evokes that found in contemporary Chinese ceramics or Chinese-inspired Iranian ceramics.
186. For a survey of Iranian woodwork, see Wolff 1966, 74–101; Golmohammadi 1989.
187. In the case of Tang China, it seems that the import of foreign wood was more encouraged than the export of Chinese wood; it became fashionable among Tang nobles to have objects made from imported wood (Schafer 1963, 133–8).
188. For the use of wood in Chinese architecture in general, see Steinhardt et al. 2002, 7–8. For Chinese woodwork, see 'China: wood-carving' in *DA*, 138–42.
189. See Li and Watt (eds) 1987.
190. Curatola 1987.
191. The decoration used in the *sanduq* in the Imamzada at Qaydar (Curatola 1987, figs 1–10) is, for example, composed of several star- or polygon-shaped units, each of which is filled with stylised scroll patterns or inscriptions. The same decorative element can be seen in the simplified *minbar* depicted in the Edinburgh al-Biruni (fo. 61^{v}; see Soucek 1975, fig. 1). The doors in the Imamzada Qasim at Qaraqush (Curatola 1987, fig. 12) vary their ornamentation. The doors are more elaborately patterned, with eight-pointed stars and palmettes, echoing those seen in the doors in the mosque of the shrine of Bayazid Bistami at Bistam (707/1307–709/1309; *SPA*, pl. 1463; Curatola 1987, 99; see also a door in the Masjid-i ʿAli at Quhrud, which is datable to the early fourteenth century (Watson 1975, pls VI–VIIa)), though the decoration as a whole persists in forming a geometric composition.
192. Smith 1938.
193. See Grabar and Blair 1980, nos 6, 9–10, 14–15, 17, 40, 43, 46, 50, 52 and 55–6. See also the doors depicted in the Edinburgh al-Biruni (Soucek 1975, figs 6, 9 and 18); the Freer Balʿami (Fitzherbert 2001, pls 3, 19 and 33); and the *Jamiʿ al-Tawarikh* manuscripts (Rice 1976, E1, E29, E31, E36, E38, E54–E55 and E59; Blair 1995, K3, K20 and K27). Some doors

found in these Ilkhanid paintings are painted in various colours, ranging from blue to red, while others are painted in brown, clearly intended to depict wooden doors. Chinese elements are, however, less pronounced on the decoration of these doors.

194. Grabar and Blair 1980, nos 40, 43.
195. For costumes and textiles, see Kadoi (forthcoming a); for carpets, see Ettinghausen 1959a, 99–105; for metalwork, see Melikian-Chirvani 1987, 121–2.
196. This example is intended to be placed in the mausoleum for eternity (*Legacy*, 281), an idea that is close to the Chinese custom of burying pieces of precious wood in tombs.
197. Pourjavady (ed.) 2001, 3, 216–17. This *minbar* is now preserved in the Islamic Arts Museum, Tehran (no. 3276) and is dated 771/1369.
198. See, e.g., Berlin 2001, 60–1.
199. This stand has customarily been attributed to Central Asia (e.g. Lentz and Lowry 1989, 330). On the other hand, O'Kane has recently proposed its Iranian provenance (*Legacy*, 282).
200. See Lentz and Lowry 1989, 206–10.
201. Two examples of pre-Timurid lacquerwork are known to survive: a wooden bowl discovered at Ribat-i Sharaf in north-east Iran (see Kiani 1982); and a plate in the Victoria and Albert Museum (see Watson 1982). These are, however, devoid of Chinese elements.
202. For instance, the development of Timurid lacquer industry has often been discussed in relation to bookbinding (see Aslanapa 1979).
203. Fehérvári 1982, 225.
204. Pointed out in Fehérvári 1982, 226; Watson 1982, 238.
205. See, e.g., Diba 1989; Khalili et al. 1996–7, passim.
206. See Watson 1995, 61–8.
207. Garner 1979, 63–121.
208. For a further discussion of Chinese lacquer and Islamic design, see Crowe 1996.
209. See also lacquered thrones depicted in the Edinburgh al-Biruni (Soucek 1975, figs 17, 19) and in the Great Mongol *Shahnama* (Grabar and Blair 1980, nos 17, 39, 40 and 58). For thrones depicted in Ilkhanid painting, see Donovan 1988–9.
210. For Chinese lacquered furniture, see Medley 1982.
211. For this monument, see O'Kane 1979. According to Wilber, some ten Ilkhanid monuments that display the use of stone are known to survive. Except for the shrine in the court of the Masjid-i Jami' at Shiraz (751/1351), all are located in Azerbaijan (see Wilber 1955, 51–2, 89).
212. Scarcia 1975; Curatola 1982. I am most grateful to Dr Alireza Anisi for having provided this photograph for me.
213. See the discussion of Islamic-type dragons in Chapter 4.
214. For dragons used in Chinese tombstones, see Rawson 1984, 95–6.
215. See Chen (ed.) 1984.
216. See, e.g., ibid., figs 88–2, 148, 152 and 154.
217. *Legacy*, cat. no. 205.
218. Lentz and Lowry 1989, 208–11.
219. Chinese jade has been well studied; in particular, see Rawson 1995.
220. Melikian-Chirvani 1997b, 127–9; Bosworth 2002, 297.
221. Schafer 1963, 223–7; Rawson 1995, 75.
222. For later Chinese jade, see Rawson 1995, 321–412.

223. However, Melikian-Chrivani (1997b, 148–61) has attributed some Iranian jade objects to the first half of the fourteenth century. For pre-Timurid Iranian jade, see Jenkins and Keene 1982, no. 12; Melikian-Chirvani 1997b; Keene 2004.
224. Similar dragon-shaped protomes, made not of jade but of stone, have been discovered in the territory of the Golden Horde (see *GH*, 208–9, nos 2–3). See also a related example from Yuan China (Kessler 1993, fig. 111; *Legacy*, cat. no. 204).
225. See also Rice 1976, E16 and E18; Blair 1995, K23; İpşiroğlu 1971, Abb. 23.
226. See Skelton 1972; Lentz and Lowry 1989, 221–6.

CHAPTER FOUR

Manuscript Painting I

As mentioned in the Introduction, the Chinese contribution to the development of Iranian painting, notably to the establishment of the style of the Mongol school, has often been emphasised. While 'China' seems to be a key word for studies in Ilkhanid painting, a satisfactory and comprehensive overall view of Chinese elements in late thirteenth- and early fourteenth-century Iranian painting is still lacking.

Several intricate aspects of this issue make it difficult to assess the exact course of the introduction of Chinese pictorial arts into Iran. First, the multiple borrowings of motifs and techniques of East Asian origin seem to have been taken not from one Chinese source but from various ones. Handscroll painting was not the only medium for conveying Chinese pictorial traditions to Iran. More likely sources should be sought in other media of the pictorial arts beyond the category of fine arts – for example, in maps and medical books. In addition, since some distinctive motifs derived from Chinese decorative arts often occur in late thirteenth- and early fourteenth-century Iranian painting, one should, at some point, recall the patterns of the adoption and adaptation of Chinese themes in Iranian textiles, ceramics and metalwork, which have been discussed at length in the preceding chapters.

Secondly, comparisons between Iranian and Chinese painting have tended to be made on the basis of only scanty knowledge of Chinese painting. This was partly due to the lack of archaeological and literary evidence for the arrival of Chinese painting in Iran; the question whether Chinese painters were active at Ilkhanid ateliers has never been answered satisfactorily. Yet, because copying and imitating the works of masters was the preferred Chinese way of learning and creating paintings, it is, to some extent, possible to generalise about the forms of Chinese painting over a period of several hundred years.[1]

Thirdly, the long scholarly neglect of Chinese painting under the Mongols and other non-Han tribes was a major obstacle to a clear understanding of the artistic relationship between Iran and China. Re-evaluation of Liao, Jin and Yuan painting, which has made great strides during the second half of twelftieth century,[2] has helped to identify Chinese sources more precisely and to characterise more clearly each Chinese theme in late thirteenth- and early fourteenth-century Iranian painting.

The following three chapters address the early development of chinoiserie in Iranian painting until the 1330s – namely, before the Great Mongol *Shahnama* (c. 1335), when the painters began to take a different approach to Chinese pictorial traditions. Since the early fourteenth century was a productive period in Iranian painting, relevant available examples are so numerous that there is the risk of making the chapters merely a summary of early fourteenth-century Iranian painting. Thus in order to form a clear picture of the absorption of Chinese motifs and pictorial techniques into Iranian painting, a more restricted discussion is essential. The main thrust of the three chapters on manuscript painting is therefore focused on the Ilkhanid painting that flourished in north-west Iran, but some works of the Isfahan school are also dealt with, for one of the foremost interests in the chapters on manuscript painting lies in the provincial differences in the quality of chinoiserie between north-west and central Iran. It is hoped that the present study will encourage the exploration of hitherto unexamined Chinese connections in the development of Jalayirid and Muzaffarid painting and will lead to a reconsideration of the Chinese elements in early Timurid painting.

The Iranian encounter with East Asian pictorial traditions

Very little is known about Iranian painting before the eleventh century. The general supposition is that its early development owed much to Sasanian pictorial traditions,[3] and that Manichaean painting exerted an influence over Iranian pictorial concepts during their formative period.[4] There seem to have been continuous artistic contacts between Iran and Central Asia from the early Islamic period onwards, which were brought to West Asia by the Uighurs, the Sogdians and later by the Saljuqs. While it remains a matter of speculation how far Chinese pictorial traditions were understood and influential in Iran before the eleventh century, the Chinese were already famed for their high pictorial skills in Iran and the Middle East. The so-called older preface to the *Shahnama* of Firdausi, datable to the middle of the tenth century, yields information about the possible contribution of Chinese painters to the production of Iranian book painting during this period.[5]

The art of painting must have been at a developmental stage in Iran under the domination of the Saljuq Turks, judging by the high quality of the figural decoration in contemporary ceramics and metalwork.[6] The first substantial evidence for the arrival of artistic impact from China, or more broadly from East Asia, is found in the illustrations of the *Kitab Suwar al-Kawakib al-Thabita* ('The Book of Fixed Stars') of al-Sufi in the Bodleian Library in Oxford (probably Fars, 400/1009; MS Marsh 144).[7] The illustrations are characterised by their fine drawing technique, recalling the Chinese-style ink painting called *baimiaohua*.[8] The art of drawing (*rasm*) had already been established in the Middle East during the early Islamic period,[9] yet the subtle linear drawings of the al-Sufi manuscript are more likely to have been indebted to those used in figure painting of Chinese or Central Asian origin.[10]

Furthermore, the Iranian reaction to East Asian themes is reflected in the details of costumes, particularly draperies and ribbons. Among draperies of the constellations, those of Andromeda's robe are conspicuous by their cloud-like rich folds (Figure 4.1). Here vermicular drapery folds are more elaborately depicted than the draperies of the two well-known dancers in the ʿAbbasid wall painting discovered at Samarra.[11] Rather, ninth- and tenth-century examples from Turfan appear to be more relevant counterparts.[12] This type of drapery-fold convention seems to have been familiar throughout Central Asia and was perhaps first introduced into China by the seventh century thanks to the cultural unification that occurred under Tang rule. It reached the Middle East by the eleventh century through Sogdian mediation.[13] It is thus little wonder that there is a striking resemblance between the draperies of the constellations in Marsh 144 and those seen in seventh-century works of the famous Khotanese painter, Weichi Yiseng (Weichi the Younger), whose distinctive foreign style was highly regarded in the context of Tang exoticism (Figure 4.2).[14]

Compared with draperies, representations of ribbons are less prominent in the Oxford al-Sufi manuscript, apart from the flying ribbons attached to Sagittarius' turban (fo. 272),[15] whose fluttering movement and gentle folds are reminiscent of those used in Buddhist painting as found in Bezeklik.[16] This supports the assumption that this ribbon convention was introduced into Iran through Buddhist sources, such as hangings in Buddhist monuments or illustrations in Buddhist texts. Although none of these has yet been found in Iran, the norm of East Asian beauty was gradually incorporated into Iranian visual vocabulary along with the westward spread of Buddhism into the Iranian world,[17] and the heavenly movement of ribbons could have been part of this. As will be seen later, the Iranian attachment to ribbons became increasingly stronger; in early fourteenth-century Iranian painting, ribbons appear not only to be attached to clothes but also to be used for decorating interior settings.

Some signs of artistic inspiration from East Asia are discernible in the *Varqa va Gulshah* manuscript (Hazine 841, TSM),[18] which is regarded as the only surviving illustrated manuscript that can safely be attributed to the Saljuq school. The manuscript is datable to the middle of the thirteenth century and was probably made in Anatolia

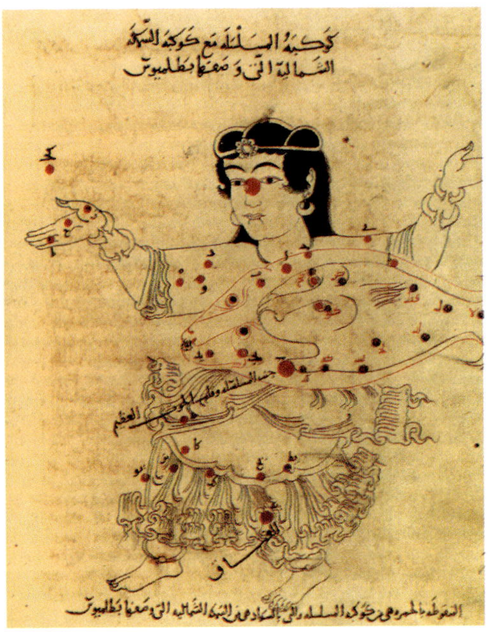

Figure 4.1 Kitab Suwar al-Kawakib al-Thabitah *of al-Sufi: Andromeda. Probably Fars, 400/1009.*

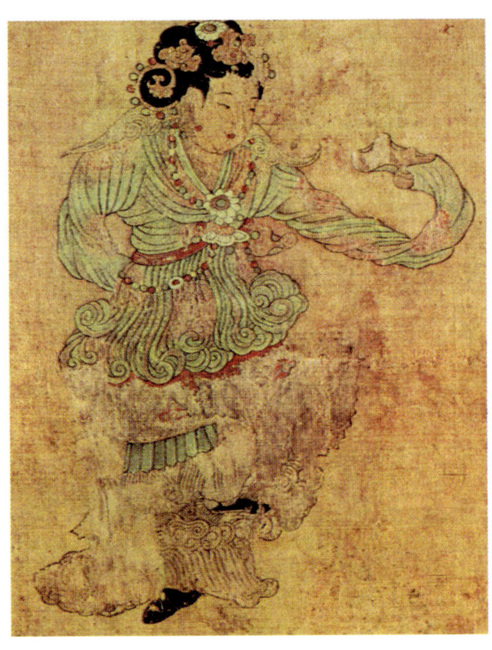

Figure 4.2 *The Berenson scroll:* A Dancer. *China, eleventh-century copy of a seventh-century painting by Weichi Yiseng.*

or north-west Iran, for similar haloed figures can be identified in contemporary metalwork and *minaʾi* wares produced in these regions.[19] Its seventy-one miniatures also contain elements derived from contemporary Mesopotamian painting, in which stylised plants are decoratively arranged, recalling those seen in the works of the thirteenth-century Mosul school.[20] However, evidence for the impact of East Asian pictorial traditions is found in the representations of faces, which consist of arched eyebrows and almond eyes set in a round face. This reflects the fashion for the East Asian type of face in Anatolia and north-west Iran of the period, where the so-called moon-face or *mahruy* was gradually associated with ideal beauty in the course of the spread of Buddhism and became highly regarded as *bot-i mahruy* ('the moon-faced Buddha').[21] As Melikian-Chirvani has pointed out, this facial type was not based on the depictions of actual individuals in a realistic way but is more likely to have been developed within a religious context, perhaps, like ribbons, through Buddhist hangings and illustrations; its archetypes were eventually idealised to suit Iranian aesthetics.[22]

The preceding discussion has revealed that the introduction of Chinese pictorial traditions into Iran during the eleventh, twelfth and thirteenth centuries was fragmentary, depending as it did on a few scraps of information about broadly 'Far Eastern' painting, which were mainly derived from Buddhist sources. The Iranian

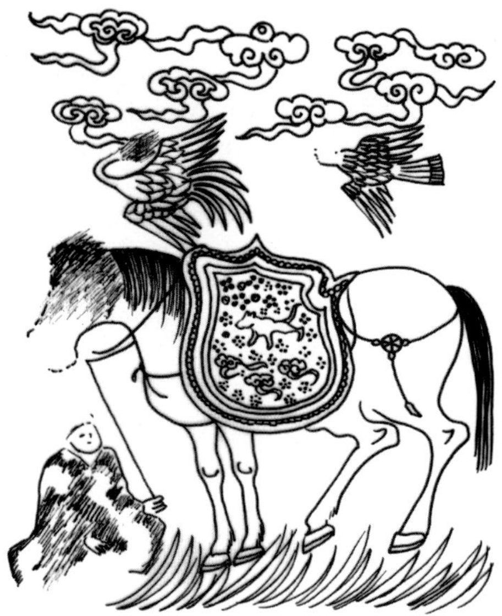

Figure 4.3 Tarikh-i Jahan-gusha *of Juvaini: frontispiece. Baghdad, 689/1290.*

reception of Chinese artistic conventions took a new turn in the late thirteenth century. Indications of chinoiserie can be recognised in the landscape depicted in book illustrations produced at the turn of the century in Baghdad – a city that still functioned as an important cultural centre in the Middle East even after its fall to the Mongols in 656/1258.[23] Importantly, however, the painters seem to have become familiar with Chinese landscape elements in the context not of Chinese pictorial arts but of the decorative arts, especially textiles. Images of flying birds amid a group of clouds seen in the right side of the double-page frontispiece of the *Tarikh-i Jahan-gusha* ('History of the World Conqueror') of ʿAla al-Din ʿAta Malik Juvaini dated 689/1290 (suppl. per. 205, BN; Figure 4.3),[24] for example, do no more than duplicate conventional bird-and-cloud patterns derived from Chinese textiles.[25] Little effort is made to create a naturalistic background by a rearrangement of clouds and birds more suitable for this scene. A notable improvement in the depiction of trees and flowers is observable in the *Marzubannama* of Saʿd al-Din al-Varavini (698/1299),[26] a contemporary manuscript produced in Baghdad. In comparison with the landscape depicted in the *Varqa va Gulshah*, several improvements can be observed in the rendering of nature. Tree trunks are well proportioned, and each flower is carefully modelled. On the whole, however, landscape representations remain out of harmony with figures; flowering trees merely function as pictorial supplements. From these examples, it is hard to ascertain exactly how Chinese pictorial traditions were introduced into late thirteenth-century Baghdad.

The growth of Iranian interest in landscape: the Morgan Bestiary

Re-examination of the illustrations of the *Manafiʿ-i Hayavan* of Ibn Bakhtishuʿ (M.500, the Pierpont Morgan Library, New York),[27] known as the Morgan Bestiary, is a real starting point for understanding Chinese themes in Iranian painting. The manuscript contains 103 miniatures and was executed probably in 697/1297 or 699/1299[28] at Maragha, the capital of the Mongol realm under Ghazan Khan. The style of the miniatures can be divided into several groups based on the understanding of Chinese conventions, especially landscape, which varies according to each group: (1) fos 3ᵛ–20ᵛ; (2) fos 22–9; (3) fos 30–49ᵛ and (4) fos 50–83.[29]

Chinese impact on the first thirteen miniatures of the manuscript is rather limited. In these miniatures, the landscape is customarily composed of tufty grass, nodding flowers and delicate leafy trees, which are arranged decoratively to fill the empty space.[30] Features of trees with birds sitting on the branch bear a great similarity to those seen in thirteenth-century Mesopotamian painting.[31] Similarly, representations of animals are based on the old traditions of depicting animals – namely, those of the *Kalila wa Dimna*, the most popular bestiary in the medieval Islamic world.[32] More attention is paid to the lifelike re-creation of animals, but their figures betray limited movements. On the whole, there is no real harmony between the landscape and the animals. In spite of stereotyped landscape elements, however, the two figures in the painting of Man and Woman (fo. 4ᵛ)[33] display some new features. While halos and round faces are reminiscent of thirteenth-century Mesopotamian painting and even of *minaʾi* ware of the period,[34] the robes are not typically Middle Eastern. In contrast with Byzantine-inspired clinging robes predominantly used in pre-Mongol painting,[35] the rich folds of clothing here are more suggestive of East Asian artistic impact – for instance, similar loose robes can be seen in Buddhist painting, especially in that depicting the lohans (*arhat* in Sanscrit), which were popular imagery of the Southern Song period.[36]

Stylistic and technical innovations became apparent first in the depictions of two foxes (fo. 22),[37] and later where the landscape was rendered in a more naturalistic manner. In particular, pictorial advancements are visibly seen in the illustration of *A Mare Followed by a Stallion* (fo. 28; Figure 4.4). The landscape is compositionally simple, but the illustration clearly shows a good knowledge of Chinese landscape conventions. The technique of cutting the treetop by the margins, and the sense of continuity from right to left by using only the head of the black stallion, provide important visual evidence to confirm the echoes of Chinese painting in the handscroll format – for example, Zhao Meng-fu's (1254–322) horse painting (Figure 4.5).[38] This horse painting raises yet another question about

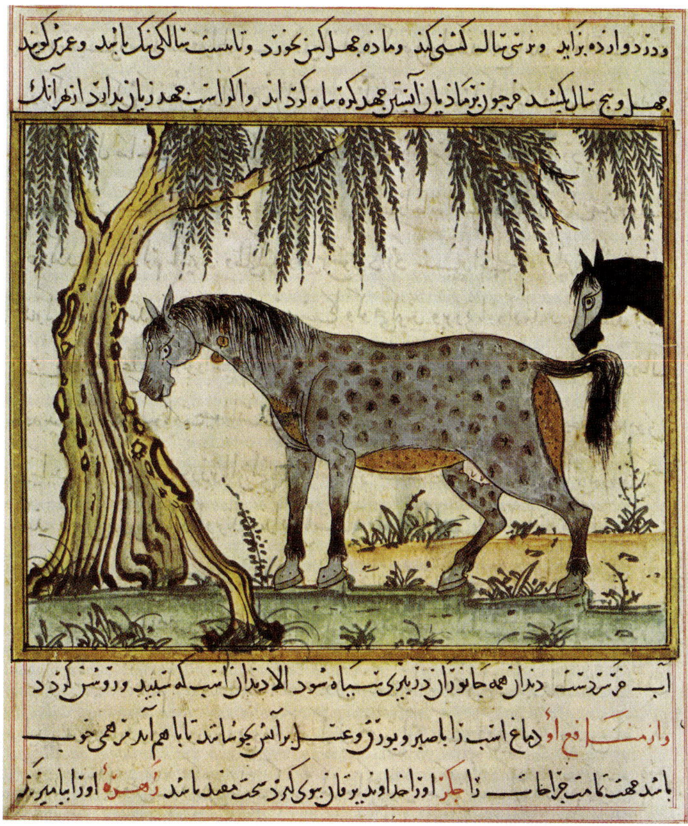

Figure 4.4 Manafiʿ-i Hayavan *of Ibn Bakhtishuʿ*: A Mare Followed by a Stallion. *Maragha, c. 1300.*

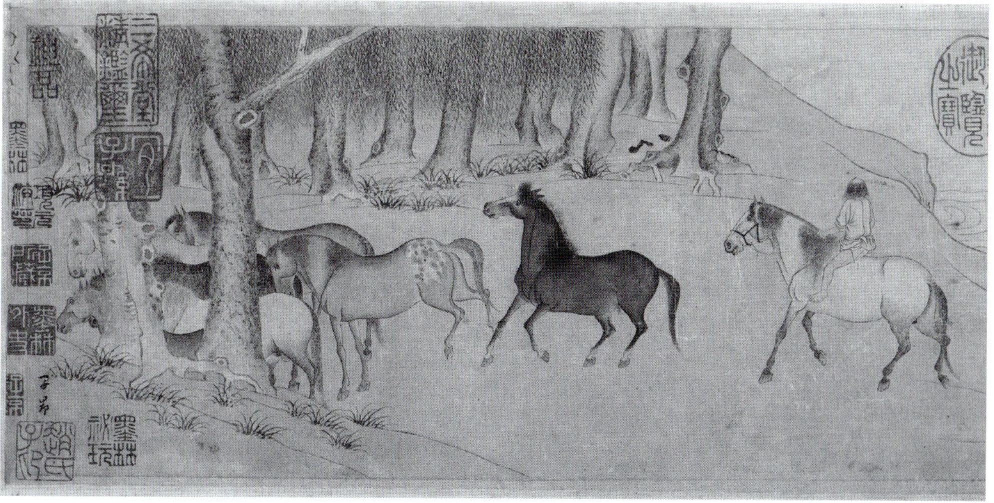

Figure 4.5 *Zhao Meng-fu:* Horses and Grooms Crossing a River. *Handscroll, ink on paper. China, Yuan dynasty.*

the likelihood of the Chinese impact on the rendering of horses of this manuscript.[39]

Each blade of grass in this illustration is expressively depicted with quick strokes; the arrangement of tufty grass in receding lines is a clear difference from the single line of grass as depicted in the miniatures of the first group. This type of grass is called 'Mongol grass'[40] – a key element to understanding the stylistic development in early fourteenth-century Iranian painting. Chinese contributions to the establishment of this grass convention are undeniable, for similar tapering brush strokes and the way of showing distance can be traced back to several media of Chinese pictorial arts, ranging from hand-scroll painting (Figure 4.5) to wall painting to woodblock prints.[41] One of the interesting points about the representations of grass in this illustration is the appearance of double outlines on the grassy ground. This convention seems to have come about in the course of refining representations of the ground surface under the inspiration of monochrome ink tones used in Chinese painting; as will be seen later, the use of double outlines recurred in the miniatures of other groups and indeed persisted in later Ilkhanid painting.

Increased information about Chinese landscape conventions in Ilkhanid Iran is also reflected in the representations of willow trees. The handling of the brush strokes is smooth and elegant. Fissures in the tree bark are also rendered in many different ways: in the illustration of the mare, for example, they are delicately drawn by using vertical black lines and are further accentuated by graded colour and ink washes. Such a subtle treatment of trees is distinctly different from the old conventions of depicting trees – in the *Maqamat* of al-Hariri, for instance, tree trunks were often divided into segments (Figure 4.6). Another possible Chinese impact can be seen in the distinctive root-like forms of the lower parts of the trees. Their arrangement is somewhat adjusted to compositional purposes, as if they were bridges between different ground levels, but the use of such pictorial devices is effective enough to suggest several distances. Trees were never depicted like this in pre-Mongol painting; such ideas would not have occurred without the knowledge of Chinese tree conventions.

The painter in charge of illustrations from folios 30 to 49^{v} was more enthusiastic in creating a new style by using Chinese conventions than any of the other painters of the manuscript, where other major landscape elements, such as clouds, rocks and water, were eventually introduced. Yet the major problem was how to accommodate these landscape elements derived from several different sources, ranging from painting to decorative objects, and to integrate their Chinese conventions into new stylistic concepts. The adoption of Chinese landscape conventions was thus still experimental and was not always successful.

In the illustration of two asses (fo. 31; Figure 4.7), the tree and grass are apparently rendered by the same conventions as those used

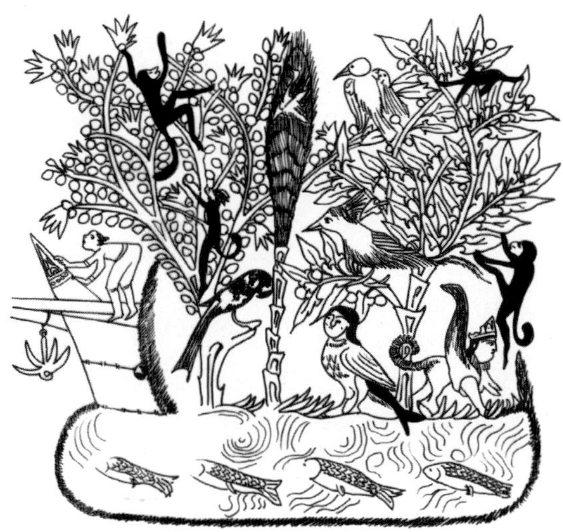

Figure 4.6 Maqamat *of al-Hariri:* The Eastern Isle. *Baghdad, 634/1237.*

in the scene of the mare. The texture of the gnarled tree trunks is recognised, but there is no proper balance in size between the tree branches and the peony-like flowers, recalling those seen in the left side of the double-page frontispiece of the *Tarikh-i Jahan-gusha.*[42] The rendering of grass is in some ways distorted: in comparison with the careful approach to Chinese grass conventions of the earlier group, in which Chinese-inspired tufty grass – the 'Mongol grass' – is punctuated with vigorous strokes, representations of grass here are more simple and repetitive; the same type of grass is found at regular intervals. Chinese elements are ultimately diluted in such clichéd grass representations. Presumably this is because the painter was dependent on the grass conventions that already prevailed at Ilkhanid ateliers rather than on his own observation of actual Chinese examples. Moreover, because the ground is divided into different areas of grass, which run parallel to each other, the space is strongly compartmentalised. Spatial recession is thus not recognised enough for verisimilitude. This results in the unnatural positioning of the animals. Similar spatial devices can be seen in a mural of the Jin period (Figure 4.8),[43] though a sense of horizontality in the Jin example is reduced, thanks to the sketchy treatment of ground lines. In the illustration of two asses, double outlines are, again, intentionally used for the division of the grassy ground. They are further accentuated by a number of small circles, whose origin is something of a puzzle – perhaps they are intended to represent stones in case they combine with the grass; or the use of circular patterns could be an alternative way of shading the ground surface.

A group of clouds situated in the left corner of folio 31 is not unique to this illustration. In fact, there is a growing fascination

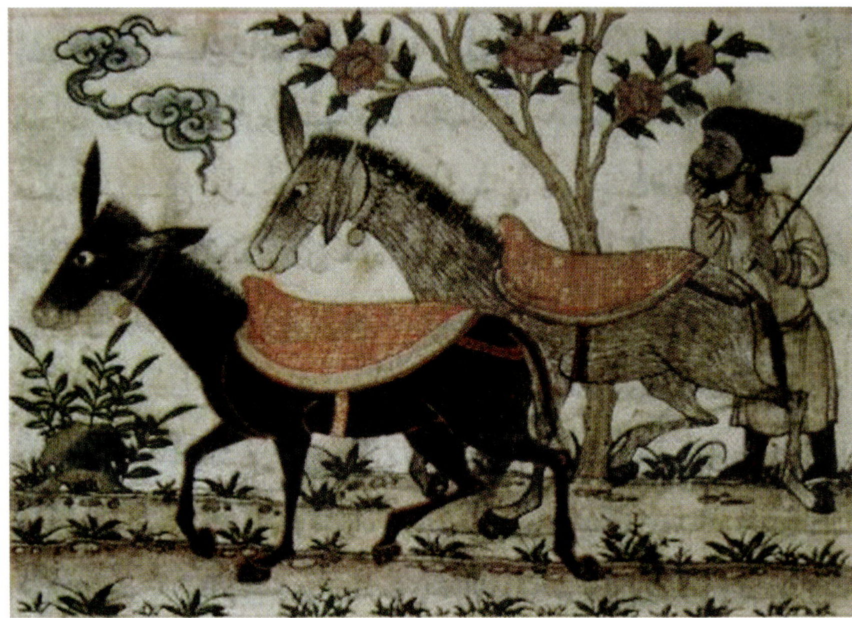

Figure 4.7 Manafiʿ-i Hayavan *of Ibn Bakhtishuʿ*: Two Asses. *Maragha, c. 1300.*

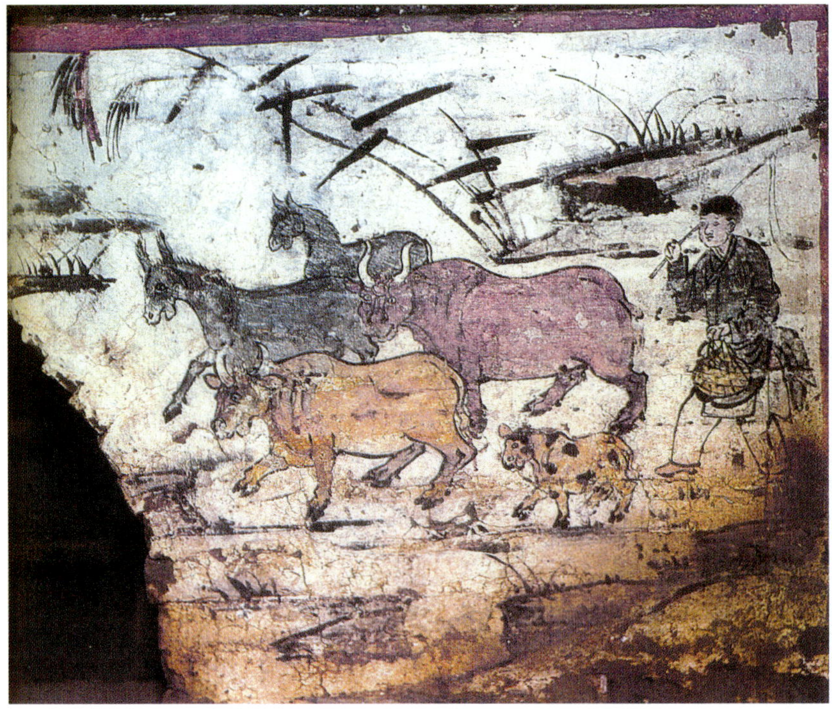

Figure 4.8 *Pasturage. Mural on the south wall of the Shizhuang tomb, Hebei province. China, Jin dynasty.*

with the rendering of clouds for the following illustrations, where the painters explore a variety of cloud forms. For Ilkhanid painters the use of clouds for pictorial arts must have been a great discovery – this enabled them not only to create outside scenes but also to fix compositional layouts in an easy yet more precise way. The clouds here are intrinsically of Chinese ancestry, but some of them are considerably transformed through Ilkhanid interpretations. The clouds can be classified into three types: the first type is of the clouds illustrated in folio 31 and used predominantly in the rest of the miniatures of this group,[44] which are evidently the *lingzhi* clouds. Distinctive features of mushroom-like heads linked with long wisps recall those used in contemporary Chinese textiles, such as the Hermitage example (Figure 1.9). Clouds have been equally important in Chinese painting for both secular and religious themes. In addition to enriching mountain scenery in landscape painting, they are significant as vehicles of immortality and as images of Heaven in Buddhist and Daoist pictorial traditions (Figure 5.28). Curiously enough, unlike clouds used in Chinese decorative arts, this type of cloud is often coiled around trees, transforming itself into a serpent-like creature. This may stem from the painter's misinterpretations about Chinese cloud conventions used in both decorative and pictorial contexts. The second type is of the cumulus-like convoluted clouds, as seen in the illustration of a mule (fo. 30).[45] They often appear almost hidden in the top corner of the illustration, but both their size and their position are suitable for creating a naturalistic background. The diagonal arrangement of clouds and a mass of rock, which is situated in the bottom corner of the illustration, are compositionally effective in setting the image at a wide angle. It is, however, difficult to compare this type of cloud with the clouds represented in Chinese painting; they are perhaps derived from Chinese decorative arts, though there is a great degree of modification. The third type is of the fanciful clouds depicted in the upper-right corner of folio 35v[46] – whose Chinese sources can hardly be detected either in painting or in the decorative arts. Here the central part of clouds is decorated with radial patterns as well as some dots placed beside the contours, betraying the poor capacity of the painter for shading. These clouds appear to be unimportant elements of the landscape; nor do they carry any symbolic meanings. Thus, perhaps because of the lack of careful supervision by the masters at the workshop, the choice of cloud types is inconsistent in the miniatures of this group; moreover, different types of cloud exist side by side (fo. 47).[47]

The illustration of two asses provides information about the Iranian reaction to another feature of Chinese art – namely, rock conventions.[48] The features that differentiate the Manafiʿ rocks from those used in thirteenth-century Mesopotamian painting[49] are that rocks are outlined in bold; they have Taihu-like holes and concavities.[50] On the whole, rock modelling is visibly improved. Bunches

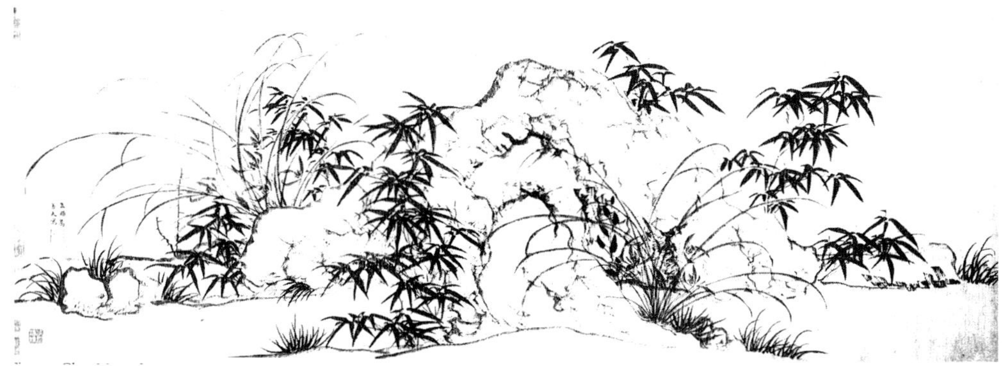

Figure 4.9 *Zhao Meng-fu:* Bamboo, Rocks and Orchid. *Handscroll, ink on paper. China, late thirteenth–early fourteenth centuries.*

of flowers or plants are often shown behind the rocks, evoking Zhao Meng-fu's rock painting (Figure 4.9). However, the painter clings to the use of double outlines to model rocks. Lichens on rock surfaces are depicted as patterns, and some additional lozenge-shaped decoration merely suggests lustrous surfaces. The rocks here are employed in enlivening the landscape setting, together with a flowering tree and clouds. Yet their compositional role is less prominent; their position, which is close to the clouds, is insufficient to convey spatiality. Among the rocks in this manuscript, representations of rocky crags in the illustration of two gazelles (fo. 36^v; Figure 4.10) must have posed a challenge for the painter. Of particular significance is that, even though there is no division of the ground, the rocky crags appear to stretch backwards, creating a sense of depth. Indications of vegetation around the contours are sufficient to suggest rocky crags in the distance. More importantly, the painting succeeds in showing an advanced compositional idea similar to the so-called high distance – one of the Chinese ways of representing perspective developed in the Northern Song period.[51] The highest background peak is in striking contrast to those rendered in the Northern Song manner – for example, that of Fan Kuan (c. 960–c. 1030) (Figure 4.11).

The painters of the last group (fos 50–83) are equally familiar with Chinese art traditions, but their approach to Chinese conventions is clearly different from that of the earlier painters. In a number of small miniatures from folio 50 onwards, the painters characteristically pay more attention to the details of animals and creatures. This reflects not only the tradition of Arabic scientific treatises, which was taken over by Iranian scientists,[52] but also the growth of cosmographical and encyclopaedic interest in Iran under the patronage of Ghazan for scientific activities around his capital Maragha.[53] In terms of chinoiserie, there is an interesting parallel between these detailed drawings with scientific accuracy and the illustrations in Chinese pharmacological treatises, some of which were certainly brought to

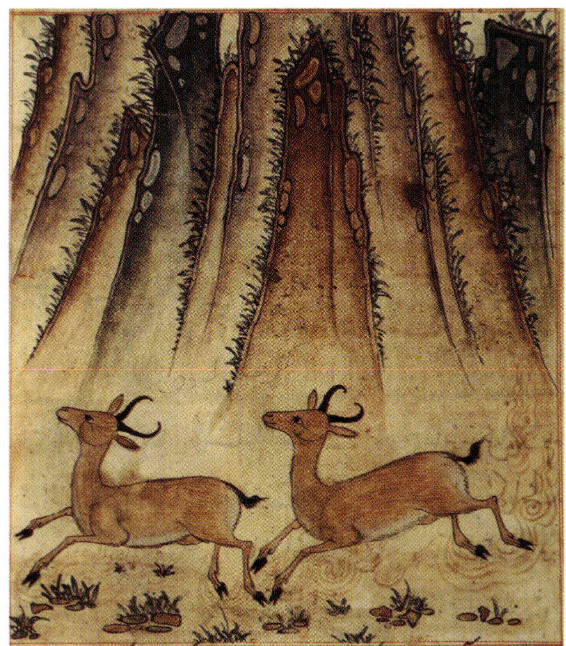

Figure 4.10 Manafi'-i Hayavan *of Ibn Bakhtishu'*: Two Gazelles. *Maragha, c. 1300.*

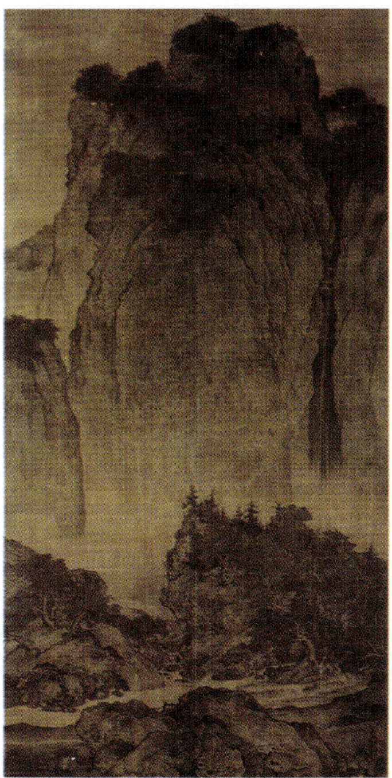

Figure 4.11 *Fan Kuan:* Travellers by Streams and Mountains. *Hanging scroll, ink on silk. China, c. 1000.*

Iran and were translated into Persian during the Mongol period.[54] The development of Chinese medical texts can be traced back to the Northern Song period, when an increasing interest in the natural world led to the compilation of major medical texts classifying plants and creatures.[55] Tang Shenwei's (1012–67) *Chongxiu Zhenghe jingshi zhenglei beiji bencao* ('The Revised Pharmacopoeia of the Zhenghe Era') published in 1116 was among the most popular texts of this kind (Figure 4.18) and had been extensively reprinted by the Yuan period.[56]

The landscape in this group is rendered in the same way as that of the second group. However, advanced compositional ideas can be seen in the miniatures of this group, where, instead of grass, trees play an intrinsic part in suggesting distances. In addition, there is a great similarity between an atmospheric picture of the *kalagh* (a type of Asian crow) (fo. 59^{v}; Figure 4.12) and a painting of the Southern Song period (Figure 4.13), revealing that the painter's knowledge of Chinese tree conventions seems to have ranged from landscape painting to bird-and-flower painting, all of which were already established genres in the Song period.[57] Of representations of grass, although there is retention of double outlines and adherence to the division of the ground, they become more diversified and so accurate that it is possible to identify the grass species: for example, a bank of reeds is vividly depicted in some small paintings.[58] On the other hand, clouds and rocks play a negligible role in landscape settings in the miniatures of this group. Both are rendered in ready-made formulas: the *lingzhi* clouds are always used in outdoor scenes that contain birds, mostly a group of flying birds (fo. 62^{v});[59] the use of Chinese-inspired rocks is confined to lone-bird scenes (Figure 4.14).[60]

Water conventions vary from painting to painting. While some illustrations retain Mesopotamian water conventions,[61] in which water movement is expressed by strong scroll and zigzag lines, more decorative representations of water are found in folio 69^{v} (Figure 4.14) and other miniatures of this group.[62] The origin of such ornamental patterns remains uncertain. The patterns, which can be called 'imbricated' or 'segmental' wave patterns, seem to have been rooted in pre-Islamic Iran, as similar patterns are used to suggest water in Sasanian silverware.[63] Yet information about their later development in Iranian art is relatively limited. The patterns are more reminiscent of the so-called *shuicang* (literally 'blue water') patterns in Chinese ornament.[64] The use of ornamental water patterns is uncommon in textiles of the Song and Yuan periods, whereas the patterns often appear in Yuan blue-and-white porcelain (Figure 2.17).[65] In Chinese pictorial arts, although not fine art proper, the use of similar patterning is recognised in the maps of the Song and early Yuan periods, where rivers and lakes are often filled by geometric wave patterns (Figure 5.9).[66]

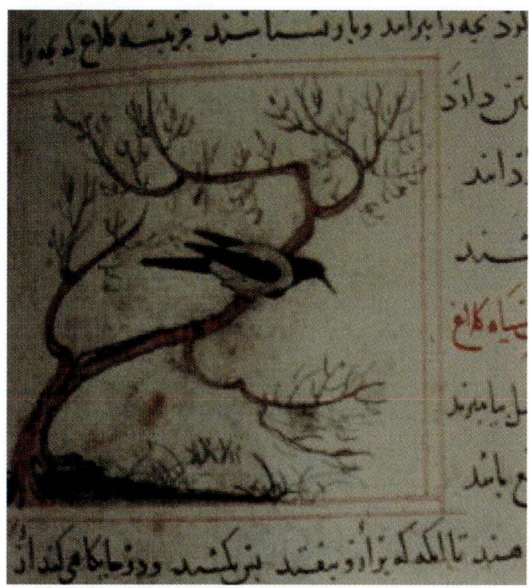

Figure 4.12 Manafiʿ-i Hayavan *of Ibn Bakhtishuʿ*: Kalagh. *Maragha, c. 1300.*

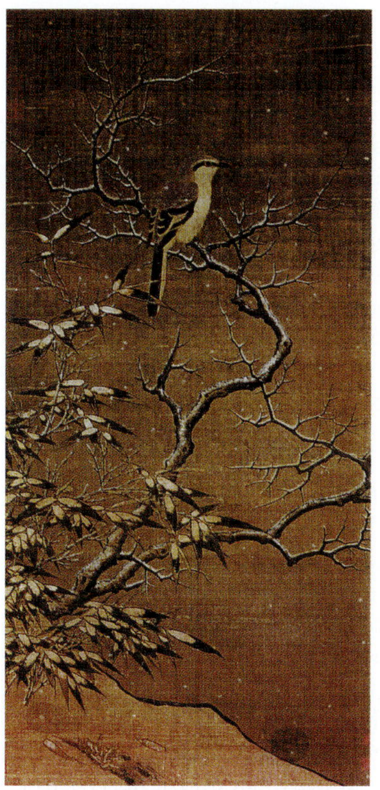

Figure 4.13 *Li Di:* Shrike on a Winter Tree. *Hanging scroll, ink and colour on silk. China, 1187.*

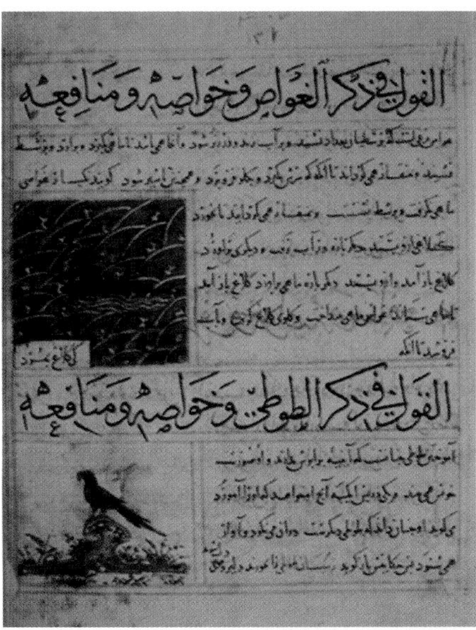

Figure 4.14 Manafiʿ-i Hayavan *of Ibn Bakhtishuʿ:* Diver Bird *(top);* Parrot *(below). Maragha, c. 1300.*

Ostensibly, chinoiserie adheres to an unforgettable image of the *simurgh* (*ʿanqa*) (fo. 55; Figure 4.15), but this illustration reflects a mélange of old and new conventions. As regards the bird, it seems that its image derives not so much from actual descriptions of the animal in the text as from other iconographic sources[67] – for instance, the Chinese *fenghuang* or phoenix is one of the possible sources of inspiration for this *simurgh*. By the end of the thirteenth century, the Chinese phoenix had certainly been known in Iran through the Mongols, as has been observed in the previous chapters on the decorative arts, and it played a vital role in the establishment of the visual concept of the *simurgh* in Iranian art.[68] It is, however, noticeable that the bird here is not entirely indebted to prototypical Chinese phoenixes – for example, those used in contemporary Chinese textiles (Figure 1.12). Rather, some distinctive features, such as falcated tails, are evocative of those found in an image of the rooster in the *Varqa va Gulshah* manuscript.[69] Judging by the fact that the same conventions are used in the illustration of a rooster (fo. 63),[70] there seems to have been no particular attempts to distinguish the *ʿanqa* from other birds. A more interesting aspect of this painting can be seen in the way of visualising inaccessible islands where the fabulous bird lives according to the text.[71] The painter subtly avoids the difficulty of illustrating a water-surrounded island seen from above by using framing devices; here water is framed by vibrant curves decorated with rich grass and plants. Water is depicted by the old Mesopotamian conventions previously used in the miniatures

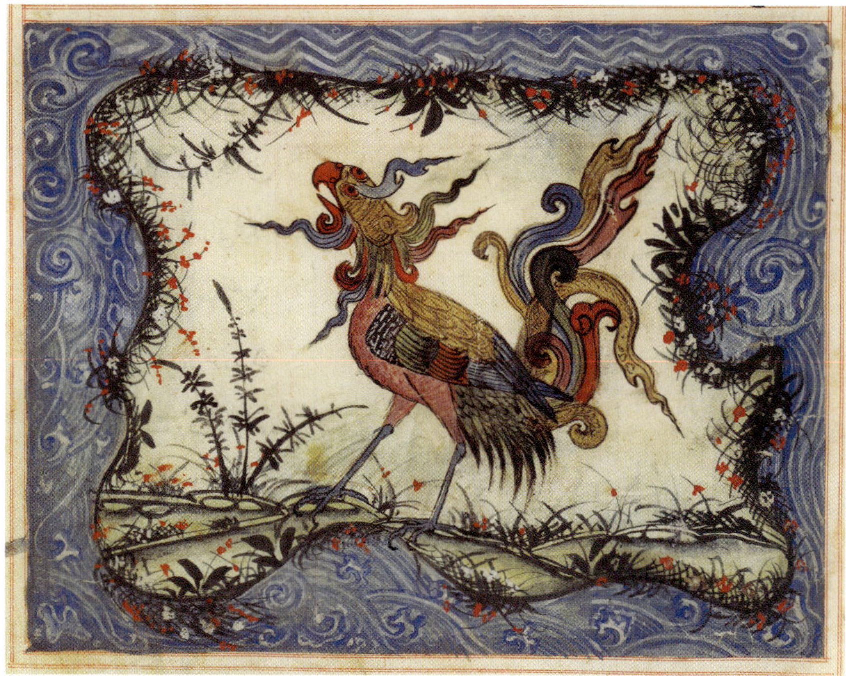

Figure 4.15 Manafiʿ-i Hayavan *of Ibn Bakhtishuʿ*: Simurgh. *Maragha, c. 1300.*

of this group, but new water conventions are blended into the lower parts. The continuous and dynamic forms of this type of water create a sense of fluid movement. It seems that these artistic improvements, including delicate depictions of water sprays, are indebted to Chinese water conventions, presumably not so much to its decorative arts as to its pictorial arts, for similar representations of water are found in landscape paintings of the twelfth and thirteenth centuries (Figure 4.16).

The understanding of the conventions of the Morgan Bestiary is indispensable for recognising not only the process of the early adoption of Chinese conventions, but also the role of China in the formation of the style of the Mongol school. The rendering of landscape elements was markedly developed, and this was, to a large extent, indebted to the Chinese conventions used in both painting and decorative objects. In particular, Iranian familiarity with Chinese printed sources is self-evident.[72] Yet the adoption of Chinese conventions was, in most cases, still at an experimental stage; Chinese elements did not entirely displace old Mesopotamian conventions – perhaps the painters were unaware of the full repertoire of Chinese landscape conventions or did not yet fully understand the significance of landscape.

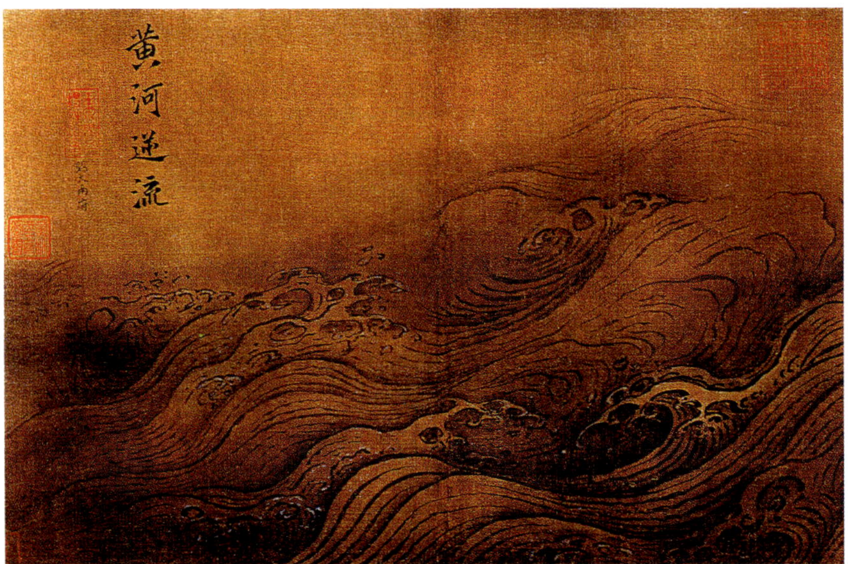

Figure 4.16 *Ma Yuan:* Twelve Phases of Water *(detail). Handscroll, ink and colour on silk. China, Southern Song dynasty, thirteenth century.*

The age of experimentation 1: the London Qazwini

An Arabic copy of the *ʿAjaʾib al-Makhluqat* ('Wonders of Creation') of al-Qazwini (Or. 14140, BL)[73] provides another rich source of information about the development of Ilkhanid painting at the turn of the fourteenth century. The so-called London Qazwini was probably executed in the years between 694/1295 and 701/1302 – just after the production of a complete copy of the *ʿAjaʾib al-Makhluqat* (Wasit, 678/1280) now in Munich (Cod. Ar. 464, Staatsbibliothek)[74] – and perhaps in Mosul under the patronage of the governor Fakhr al-Din ʿIsa (d. 701/1302).[75] A total of 368 miniatures in this manuscript display various influences derived from different artistic traditions; in particular, those of the northern Jazira and south-east Anatolia are prominent.[76] The additional significance of the miniatures lies in their close relationship with the Morgan Bestiary,[77] in which very similar landscape elements are found in the miniatures; to a certain extent, the Qazwin manuscript shares interests in Chinese landscape conventions with the Morgan codex. Furthermore, there is a new important piece of visual evidence in this manuscript that links it to China – namely, the dragon.

Since most landscape representations in the London Qazwini bear a striking resemblance to those seen in the Morgan Bestiary, whose Chinese connections have already been discussed in enough detail, only the more important points will be mentioned. Although representations of trees in this manuscript are visibly influenced by the

Morgan codex – for instance, striking features of Chinese-inspired root forms that extend into different grassy ground levels (fo. 39)[78] resemble those often seen in the miniatures of the second and fourth groups in the Morgan manuscript[79] – the London Qazwini takes a more quasi-scientific approach to the depictions of trees, thus echoing Arabic scientific treatises. This is because most trees in this manuscript are illustrated not for artistic but for more practical purposes (Figure 4.17). Though the rendering of trees is not accurate enough to be truly useful – for example, to identify each tree species – the relationship between texts and illustrations is closer than that of thirteenth-century Arabic medical texts;[80] each illustration is arranged to adjoin the texts, as seen in Song medical texts (Figure 4.18).

In the rendering of grass, the difference in quality and style indicates that, as in the Morgan manuscript, more than two painters with different artistic backgrounds were probably involved in the execution of the miniatures. The grass in this manuscript can be classified into three major types.[81] The most common one is Type 1 (Figure 4.19, below)[82] which consists simply of a range of short grass, sometimes with the addition of bunches of dark green plants. The grass of this type is placed frontally, but each tuft of grass is depicted more realistically than the kind that appears in thirteenth-century Mesopotamian painting (Figure 4.6).[83] This grass is rather reminiscent of that predominantly used in the first thirteen miniatures of the Morgan manuscript.[84] Type 2 often appears in the illustrations of the Vegetable Kingdom (fos 77^{v}–98^{v}), where the grass functions as decoration rather than as a landscape element: the ground is filled with either distinctive spiralling grass (Figure 4.17, top and middle)[85] or *shuicang*-like patterned grass (Figure 4.17, below).[86] The grass with *shuicang* patterns is unique to the London Qazwini, which differs from the Morgan Bestiary in the respect that the patterns are not used for depicting grass. The first two types of grass thus remain the components of the vegetal foreground, where chinoiserie is less apparent. Type 3 is, on the other hand, largely inspired by Chinese grass conventions, recalling those often seen in the Morgan Bestiary from folio 22 onwards (Figure 4.4). For example, the grass in folio 39[87] serves to create a three-dimensional setting by using receding lines to suggest distance; the use of double outlines recurs, and some pebbles are also depicted. The source of inspiration for this grass convention can be traced back to Song and Yuan painting, but it is more likely that the painter here repeats a formula already known to Ilkhanid ateliers rather than observing actual Chinese examples. It is clear that representations of grass in the London Qazwini are closely associated with those used in the Morgan codex, demonstrating that these conventions for depicting grass had already spread throughout north-west Iran, the northern Jazira and south-east Anatolia by the end of the thirteenth century.

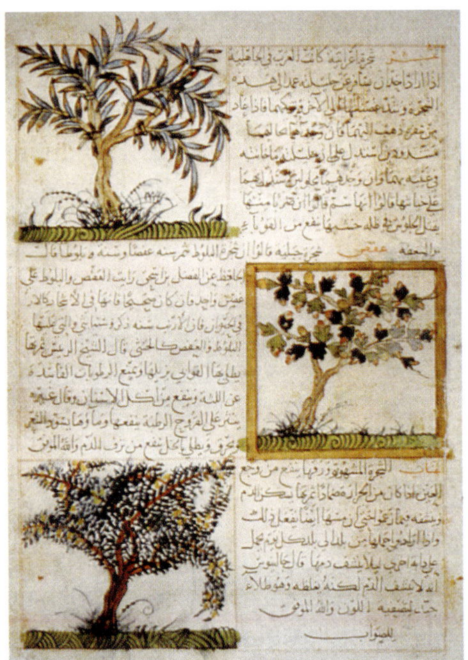

Figure 4.17 ʿAjaʾib al-Makhluqat *of al-Qazwini:* Milkweed *(top);* Gall Tree *(middle);* Jujube Tree *(below). Probably Mosul, c. 1300.*

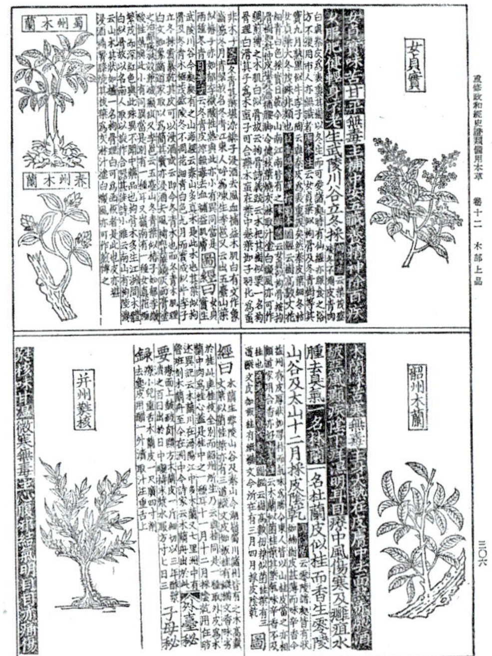

Figure 4.18 *Tang Shen-wei:* Chongxiu Zhenghe jingshi zhenglei beiji bencao. *China, 1116.*

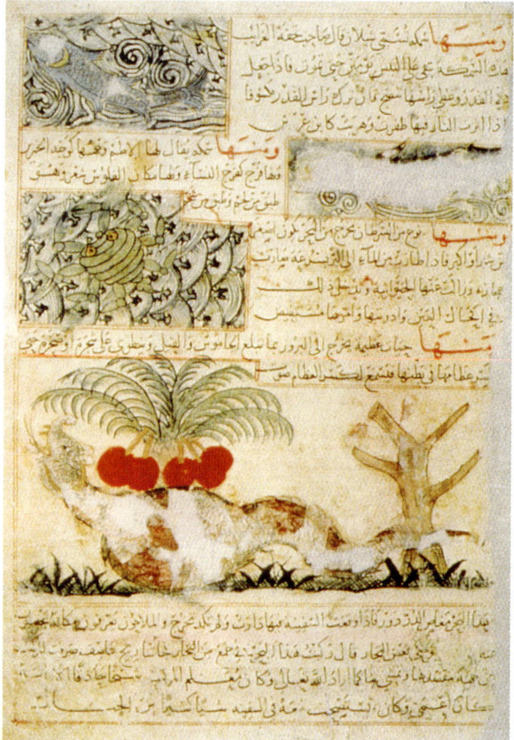

Figure 4.19 ʿAjaʾib al-Makhluqat *of al-Qazwini:* A Fish that a Man is Able to Catch Only after Fishing Two Days *(top)*; Sea Cow *(damaged)*; Crab *(middle)*; Serpent *(below)*. *Probably Mosul, c. 1300.*

The possible impact of the Morgan codex is also evident in representations of water. Depictions of the undulating swells in the scene of the River Nile (fo. 62ᵛ)[88] are comparable to those seen in folios 42 and 48ᵛ in the Morgan manuscript.[89] Similarly, there is a close stylistic affinity between decorative water patterns used in folio 33 (Figure 4.19) and those that occur in several illustrations of the last group in the Morgan manuscript (Figure 4.14). The choice between these two types of water remains vague. Seemingly, the former is used for the scenes that include human figures; the latter is used for those that combine water creatures. The source of inspiration for the water with sprays that appears in folio 99ᵛ[90] is presumably the same as that of the water partially used in the image of the *ʿanqa* (Figure 4.15) – namely, Chinese water conventions (Figure 4.16).

Clouds seem to have caught the fancy of the painters of the London Qazwini, but only to a very limited extent. Clouds situated above the body of a sea-dragon (Figure 4.20) are, so far as one can recognise, the only relevant example of the adoption of Chinese clouds in this manuscript. They have a clear function – namely, to accentuate the form of the dragon according to Chinese conventions. Their sources of inspiration are conceivably the same as those of the Morgan codex – namely, the dragon-and-cloud motif often used in Chinese and Central Asian textiles (e.g. Figure 1.1) – although, as will be examined, this sea-dragon itself is not entirely a Chinese prototype. While clouds play a wide variety of roles in the Morgan Bestiary, no attempt is made to integrate clouds with landscape in the London Qazwini. The lack of attention to clouds is presumably attributable not to the ignorance of Chinese cloud conventions but to the nature of the text itself, which discourages redundant elements.

Among the animal representations in the London Qazwini, three images of dragons or snakes stand out.[91] In the text Qazwini distinguishes the dragon, the sea-dragon and the snake, and describes their physical characteristics.[92] Yet these vivid images of dragons are more likely to have been derived from other iconographic sources, not only Islamic but also Chinese ones.

As already noted, an image of the dragon-and-cloud on folio 48 (Figure 4.20) is initially of Chinese derivation. Interestingly, however, while the dragon's head follows the Chinese convention, showing a protruding tongue and curling proboscis, its body is replaced by one of Islamic type. This type of dragon in a looped form without clawed legs and dorsal or pectoral fins seems to have been ubiquitous in the northern Jazira and south-east Anatolia during the thirteenth century, as often seen in the stone reliefs of thirteenth-century Anatolia[93] and in illustrated manuscripts produced in the Mosul area – for example, the double frontispiece of the Paris *Kitab al-Diryaq*[94] and an image of the looped dragon accompanied by Chinese *lingzhi* clouds in the *Tarjama-yi Tarikh-i Tabari* ('History of the Prophets and the Kings') of Balʿami (probably Iraq or the Jazira, c. 1300; F1957.16, 1947.19 and 1930.21, FGA; fo. 116, F.1957.16).[95] Similar observations can be made about the conspicuously knotted dragon on folio 128.[96] In spite of the use of the Chinese-type head, a serpentine knotted body dominates the image. The iconographic source of the knotted dragon can, again, as has been discussed at length by Carboni, be traced back to stone reliefs in Anatolia and the northern Jazira of the twelfth and thirteenth centuries.[97]

What significance, then, do these complex images of dragons have? Intrinsically, they follow traditional Islamic dragon designs. The looped or knotted dragons here, according to their symbolic meanings in Islamic iconography, carry a certain astronomical significance, representing ecliptic dragons.[98] In particular, the image of the knotted dragon must be associated with *al-Jawzahr*,[99] an Islamic astronomical term indicating two lunar nodes. According to this, the pseudo-planet dragon is separated into two parts; 'head', implying the moon's orbit, and 'tail', suggesting the ecliptic. In order to convey such an astronomical significance, the knot is used as a connection between the head and the body. The two dragons in the London Qazwini are, therefore, more likely to be indigenous products, but reconfigured with the newly acquired Chinese dragon head. It is difficult to determine with certainty the motive behind the use of the Chinese-type head, but its effect is clear. It serves to isolate the head from the body, emphasising this intrinsic astronomical idea.

The dragon in folio 127 (Figure 4.21) deserves special attention in the present discussion – this is one of the first Chinese-type dragons to be fully adopted into Iranian painting.[100] The dragon is characterised by its scaly twisted body, two legs with two- or three-clawed feet, impressive fins and a horned head, which is apparently not derived from an Anatolian prototype but is much more reminiscent of conventional Chinese dragons (*long*) – although this type of dragon usually has four legs. Since this is among the most popular type of Chinese dragon depicted throughout the ages, its sources can be detected in several media of Chinese art: while Chinese ceramics and metalwork[101] are the ostensible sources of inspiration for this dragon, the distinctive feature of a band of the flame around the dragon's body evokes thirteenth-century Chinese or Central Asian textiles (e.g. Figure 1.1).[102] In addition, such meticulously detailed depictions of the flaming dragon with threatening gestures indicate a possible association with dragon paintings in China (Figure 4.22).[103] This is evident if a comparison is made with earlier Iranian adoptions of the Chinese dragon derived predominantly from Chinese or Central Asian textiles, such as the dragon tile found at Takht-i Sulayman (Figure 2.6). The Qazwini dragon may thus have relied on the more convincing and abundant information about Chinese dragon conventions that began to be available in the northern Jazira and south-eastern Anatolia by the end of the thirteenth century. The debt to China is also shown in the dragons depicted in other contemporary Jaziran manuscripts – namely, a five-clawed dragon in the Freer Balʿami (Figure 4.23).[104]

The preceding discussion of the London Qazwini has revealed that the end of the thirteenth century was a transitional period in the establishment of dragon conventions in Ilkhanid painting, a time when conventional Islamic dragons and newly acquired features from Chinese dragons intermingled. The unmistakable Anatolian and Jaziran elements permeate Qazwini dragons enough to justify the current attribution of this manuscript to Mosul. Yet of more note here is that some painters, fascinated by the head parts of Chinese dragons, attempt to integrate the head into traditional Islamic dragon design; others must have had a far-reaching knowledge of Chinese dragon conventions.

In sum, the miniatures in the London Qazwini show the fusion of different artistic influences, ranging from contemporary Ilkhanid painting – namely, the Morgan Bestiary – to thirteenth-century Mesopotamian and Mosul school styles, as well as Chinese decorative and pictorial arts. Chinoiserie is unmistakable in the representations of landscape. However, the more scientific intention of this

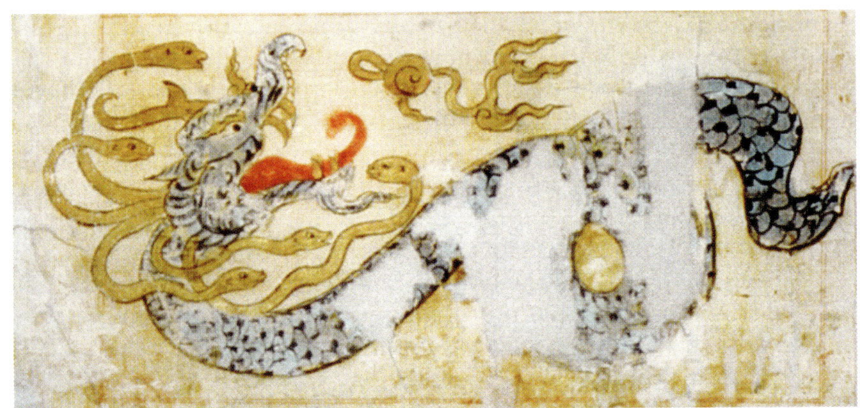

Figure 4.20 ʿAja'b al-Makhluqat *of al-Qazwini:* Sea-Dragon. *Probably Mosul, c. 1300.*

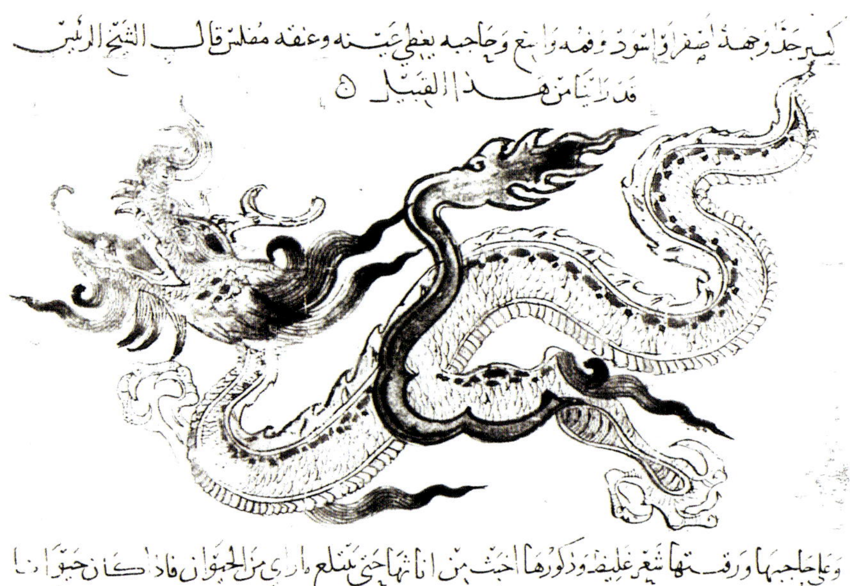

Figure 4.21 ʿAja'b al-Makhluqat *of al-Qazwini:* Giant Snake. *Probably Mosul, c. 1300.*

manuscript is reflected in the treatment of nature, and the knowledge of Chinese landscape conventions seems to have been obtained through the models already established at Ilkhanid ateliers rather than through the first-hand observation of Chinese specimens. The key sinicising elements in this manuscript are in fact the dragon, demonstrating the gradual penetration of Chinese art and culture into Ilkhanid Iran through the Mongols.

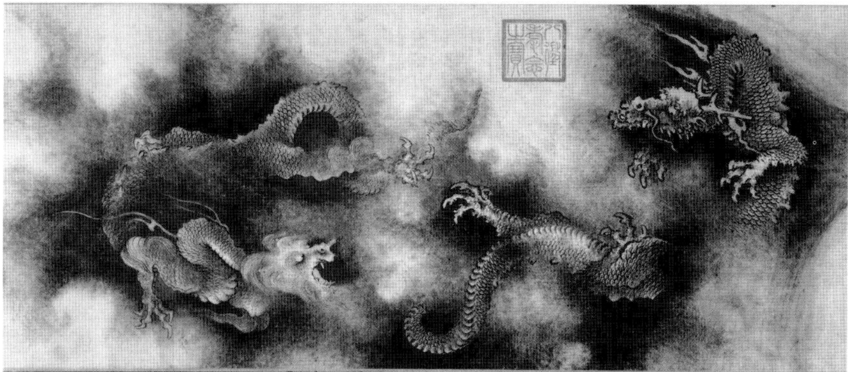

Figure 4.22 *Chen Rong:* Nine Dragons Appearing through Clouds and Waves *(detail). Handscroll, ink and colour on paper. China, 1244.*

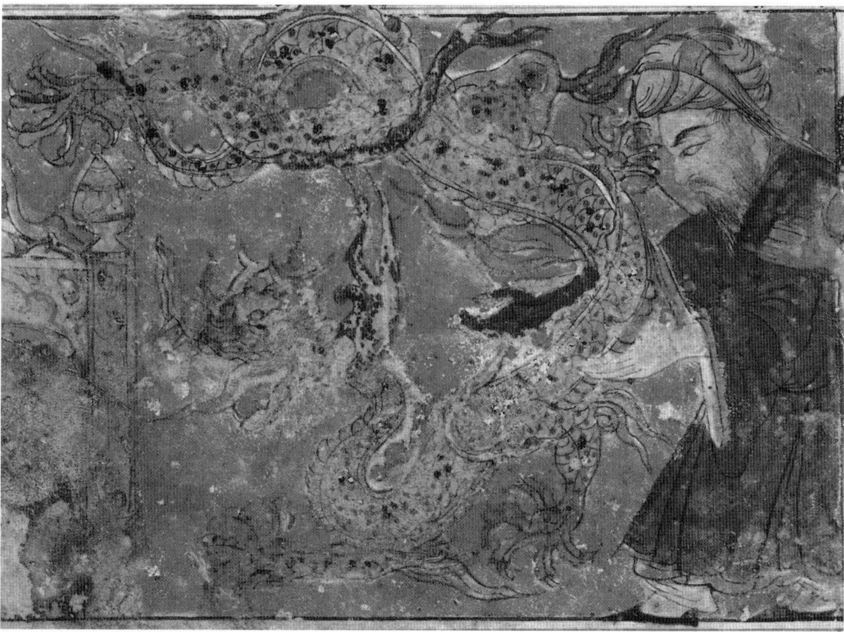

Figure 4.23 Tarjama-yi Tarikh-i Tabari *of Balʿami:* Musa Frightens Firʿawn by Turning his Staff into a Serpent *(detail). Probably the Jazira, c. 1300.*

The age of experimentation 2: the Edinburgh al-Biruni

The last key manuscript in the formative period of Ilkhanid painting is the *al-Athar al-Baqiya* ('Chronology of Ancient Nations') of al-Biruni dated 707/1307 (MS Arab 161, Edinburgh University Library),[105] whose relatively few yet distinguished miniatures have aroused continued interest among specialists in Ilkhanid painting.

The survival of old conventions derived from thirteenth-century Mesopotamian painting, such as haloed figures, the arrangement of the groups of people and two-dimensional architectural settings, have frequently been pointed out, but little effort has hitherto been made to explore Chinese themes in the miniatures more comprehensively.

As far as landscape is concerned, the miniatures show clear artistic continuity from the previous two Ilkhanid manuscripts, namely the Morgan Bestiary and the London Qazwini. The al-Biruni codex inherits their Chinese-inspired landscape conventions, but some are duplicated somewhat inaccurately; others are completely reinterpreted. Rocky backgrounds in the scene of *Ahriman Tempts Mish and Mishyana* (Figure 4.24) are meant to show a hilly terrain, and are apparently under the inspiration of Chinese landscape painting (Figure 4.25). The painter of the al-Biruni illustration, however, modifies the rocky composition used in the *Manafiʿ-i Hayavan* – for example, in the scene of two gazelles (Figure 4.10) – to suit the size and context of this painting. As a result, its grandeur is largely reduced, and the sense of space is expressed inadequately. The other difference from the Morgan example is that the rocks are modelled not by careful brush strokes but by intense deep colours. Each glossy rock has double outlines akin to those used in the Morgan manuscript, but its contours are crowded with trees and plants situated in unnatural positions. The single Taihu-like rock on the right side again functions as a *repoussoir*; yet, because of the use of deep blue colour and stiff outlines, its Chinese taste is ultimately diluted. The Mongol type of grass, which is characterised by the careful depiction of each blade of grass, recurs in the al-Biruni manuscript.[106] In folio 129^{v},[107] for instance, the grassy ground lines are arranged vertically, evoking the third type of grass used in the London Qazwini,[108] and each line is used merely to arrange groups of people. Finally, the water in the scene of the *Baptism* (fo. 140^{v})[109] is, despite Chinese-inspired water sprays on the left side, still rendered predominantly in the old Mesopotamian conventions.[110] Thus, the aforementioned landscape elements in the al-Biruni manuscript show little stylistic innovation, and new direct influences from Chinese decorative and pictorial arts remain hypothetical.

Most miniatures of outside scenes customarily depict convoluted blue clouds with white outlines often adorned with tail-like appendices,[111] which seem to have been developed from the type 2 cloud used in the Morgan manuscript. The clouds in this manuscript are rather conventional, but the menacing thunder cloud set against a dark blue sky in the scene of the *Day of Cursing* (fo. 161)[112] is a notable exception and conveys a certain symbolic meaning. The artists manipulate cloud forms to intensify the dramatic moment of the encounter of two groups of people based on the Shiʿite version of this episode.[113] It should be noticed that the clouds tinged with red and gold over the heads of the Prophet and his family clearly

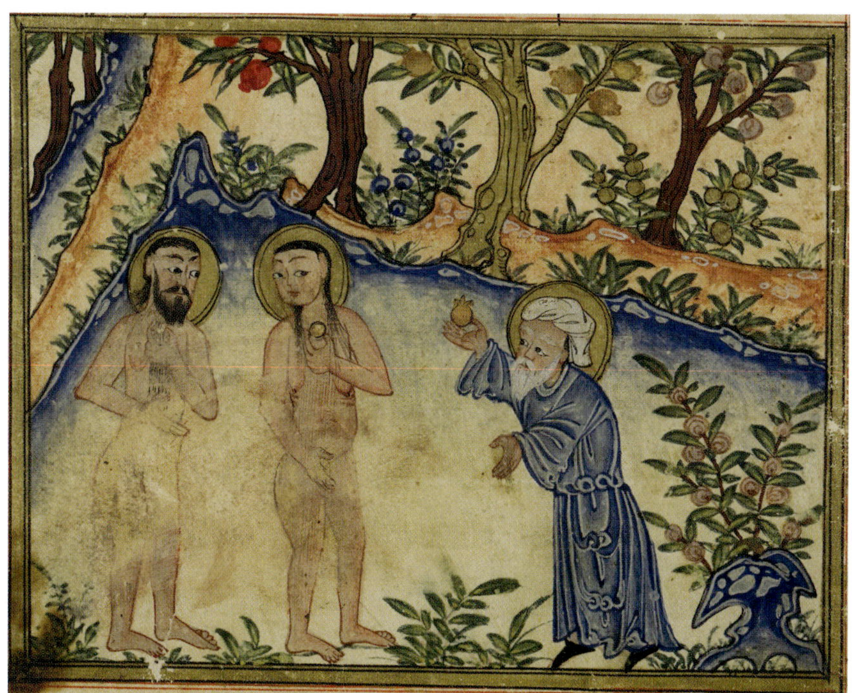

Figure 4.24 Al-Athar al-Baqiya *of al-Biruni:* Ahriman Tempts Mish and Mishyana. *North-west Iran or Mosul, 707/1307.*

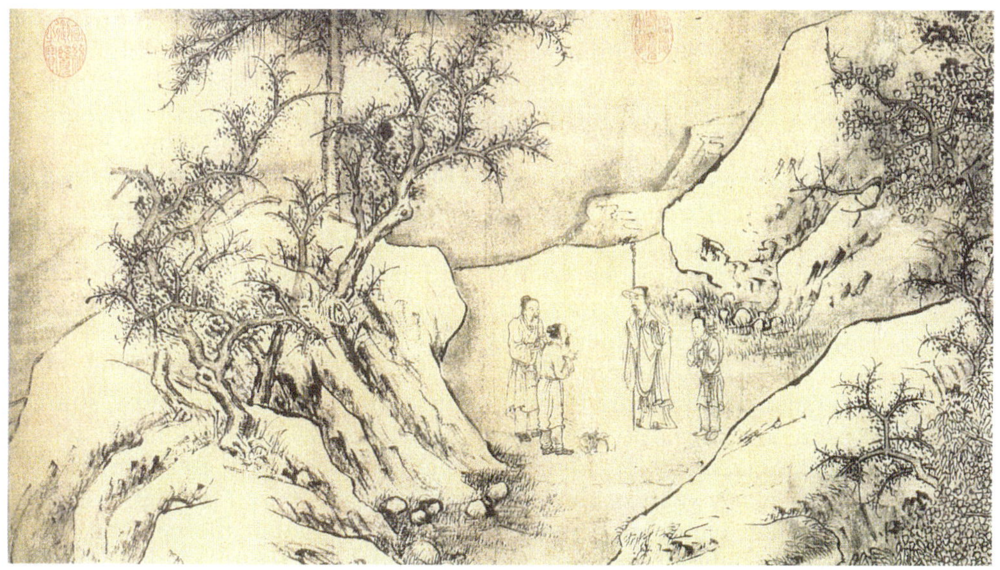

Figure 4.25 *He Cheng:* Returning Home. *Handscroll, ink on paper. China, Yuan dynasty.*

serve to distinguish them from the three Christians on the left side of the painting and to dramatise a theological debate between them.

In spite of clichéd elements, the landscape in the illustration of the *Investiture of ʿAli* (fo. 162; Figure 4.26) is remarkable from a compositional point of view – for the upper and lower land masses are separated by expanses of blank space. The two landscapes are unrealistically separated by the empty space, but this unique strong vertical and horizontal format is effective in enhancing the emotional moment in this Shiʿite story.[114] While the foreground is given over to the five characters, the background is used for visualising the high tension of this ceremony more metaphorically by contrasting an inanimate clump of trees with a large menacing mushroom cloud. This kind of landscape style is less common in contemporary Chinese landscape painting and seems more likely to have arisen at Ilkhanid ateliers. However, such a unique space compartmentalisation can be paralleled with those seen in landscape paintings by later Yuan painters. Among the Four Great Masters of the Yuan dynasty, Ni Zan (1301–74) is famous for landscapes in this style (Figure 4.27).[115] It is interesting to compare these two landscape styles, although the Chinese examples link two land masses through the expanse of water, and thereby make the stretching interval between foreground and distance more atmospheric.

Amongst other features, the appearance of Buddhist elements in the Edinburgh al-Biruni manuscript is worthy of reconsideration in the context of the present discussion. As has been discussed earlier in this chapter, the Iranian reaction to Buddhist pictorial traditions became obvious in depictions of draperies and ribbons in pre-Mongol Iranian painting. Yet the next spreading of the faith, brought by the Mongols during the Ilkhanid period, had a more fundamental influence in Iran, and this is clearly reflected in the fashion for lotus decoration in Ilkhanid art. Buddhist temples themselves are not depicted in the al-Biruni manuscript,[116] but the scenes of *Abraham Destroys the Idols* (fo. 88^{v})[117] and *Bukhtnassar Orders the Destruction of the Temple* (fo. 134^{v})[118] reflect an actual event that happened in Ilkhanid Iran – namely, the destruction of Buddhist temples and idols accompanied by the conversion of Ghazan to Islam in 694/1295.[119]

The *Annunciation* (Figure 4.28) is, in this respect, the most intriguing miniature in this manuscript. The iconographical sources here are initially derived from Byzantine conventions,[120] which became accessible through close contacts with the Byzantine world in the early years of the fourteenth century;[121] yet, more profoundly, Buddhist elements penetrate into this Christian theme. The Angel Gabriel, who holds streamers connected to a flaming halo in his left hand instead of the sceptre tipped with the fleur-de-lis as conventionally used in its Byzantine models,[122] is portrayed with Chinese,

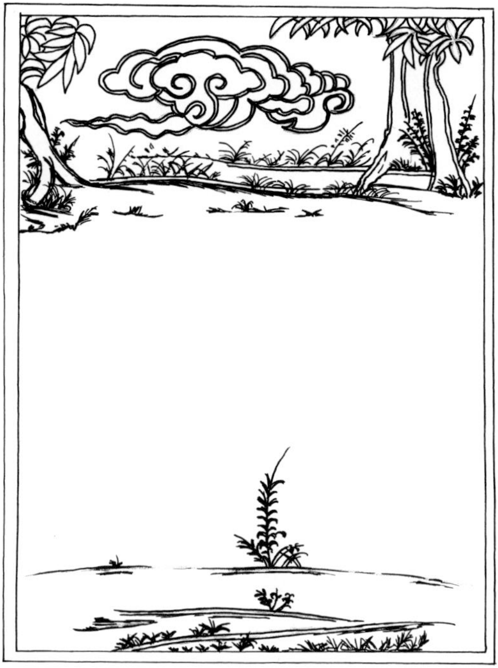

Figure 4.26 Al-Athar al-Baqiya *of al-Biruni:* The Investiture of ʿAli (*landscape detail*). *North-west Iran or Mosul, 707/1307.*

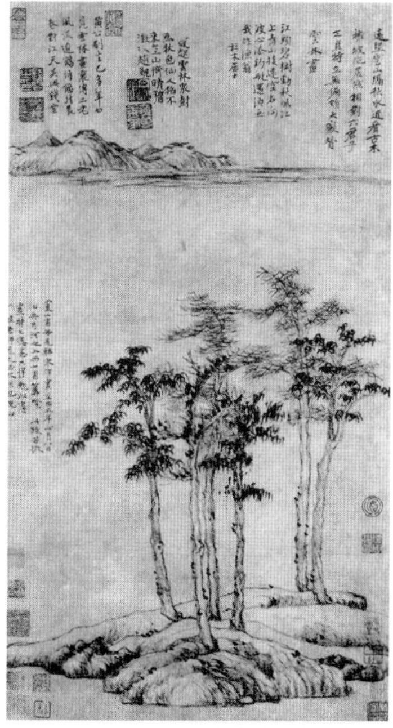

Figure 4.27 *Ni Zan:* The Six Gentlemen. *Handscroll, ink on silk. China, 1345.*

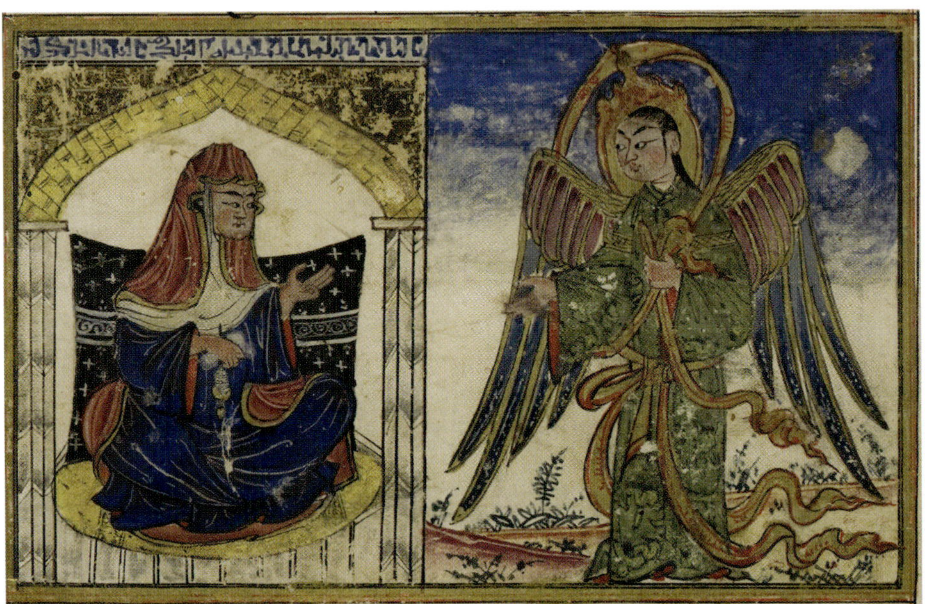

Figure 4.28 Al-Athar al-Baqiya *of al-Biruni:* The Annunciation. *North-west Iran or Mosul, 707/1307. This treatise discusses calendrical systems, as well as the customs and religions of different peoples known to the author. Reflecting the tenacity of pre-Mongol conventions and the experimental stage of chinoiserie in Iranian painting, the pictorial style of the Edinburgh manuscript is essentially eclectic. The scene of the annunciation displays an iconographic interest in both Christian and Buddhist traditions.*

or more broadly East Asian, features. The Buddhist flavour in this image of the Angel is increased by the deliberate depictions of the floating ribbons, whose visual impact on Iranian painting has been discussed with reference to the Oxford al-Sufi's manuscript, as well as the flaming halo, which often appears as an attribute of the Buddha and the Bodhisattvas,[123] even though his robe has Mesopotamian-type wrinkly draperies and armbands of Islamic origin, known as *tiraz* bands.[124] On the other hand, in spite of her Islamic surroundings – a cushioned throne[125]and the architectural frame with a pointed arch and Arabic inscriptions[126] – the Virgin Mary herself also bears a certain East Asian cast. It is difficult exactly to determine the reliable sources of the image from long-established Buddhist art in East Asia, but her slant-eyed face and headgear show a great degree of resemblance to those seen in a ninth-century painting depicting the goddess Hariti found near Turfan (Figure 4.29). The illustration of the Annunciation in the Biruni manuscript is evidence enough to make the following deductions: that Buddhist beliefs took root in Iran and survived for a while because of the syncretic nature of Ghazan's Islam;[127] and that non-Iranian artists, notably Uighur artists, whose style was still under old Central Asian Buddhist and Manichaean

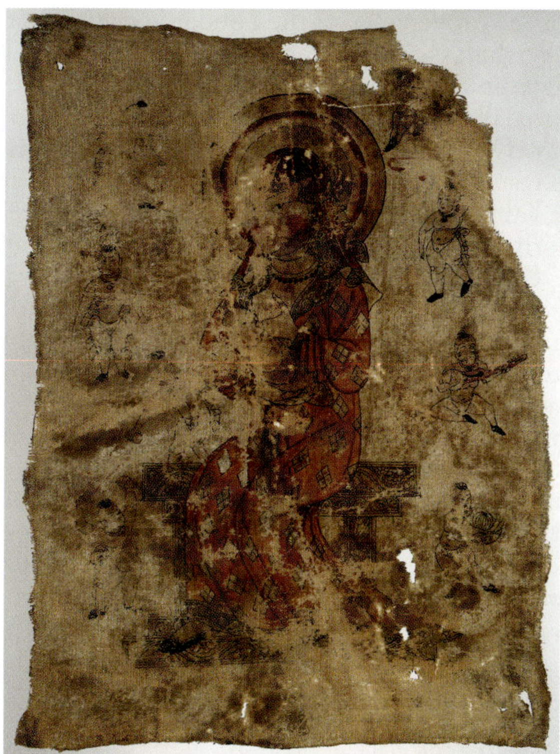

Figure 4.29 *Goddess Hariti (detail). Painting on ramie. Yarkhoto, ninth century.*

traditions, were involved in the production of the miniatures of this manuscript.[128]

The Edinburgh al-Biruni is considered to have been produced either in Maragha – a scientific centre of Ilkhanid Iran – or in Tabriz, not only a capital city but also a hub of commercial and cultural activities in early fourteenth-century Eurasia.[129] In spite of the lack of resemblance to the works of the Rashidiyya near Tabriz in the 1310s, the latter city is the most likely provenance of this manuscript, thanks to the fact that the miniatures include multiple elements derived from non-Islamic sources, such as Jewish, Byzantine and Buddhist, which reflects the growth of interest in other beliefs around the capital of Ilkhanid Iran. Another possible place of origin of this manuscript is Mosul.[130] It is probable that, judging by Christian imagery confidently depicted in some miniatures, the al-Biruni manuscript was produced at an atelier where Christian iconographic sources were easily accessible to the painters. The fact is that Christianity was rooted in the area of Mosul more deeply than in Tabriz and Maragha.[131] In terms of figural representations, the painters of the al-Biruni manuscript seem to have had the same artistic background as that of some painters in the London Qazwini – a point that Carboni has stressed in his attribution of the provenance of the London Qazwini to the northern Jazira.[132] Nevertheless, the statements with reference to the provenance of the Edinburgh codex remain hypothetical and will need to be substantiated by future studies.

The twenty-five miniatures of the Edinburgh al-Biruni manuscript are not mere visual supplements to a treatise on calendrical systems. But they are valuable mirrors of Iranian culture under the Mongols and particularly reflect religious movements in Ilkhanid Iran. These aspects differentiate this manuscript from the Morgan and Qazwini manuscripts. Iconographic approaches here are remarkable in the way that multiple elements derived from not only Islamic but also Christian and Buddhist sources come together harmoniously. On the other hand, although there are a few exceptions – the painters succeed in integrating Chinese clouds into the last two Shiʿite images – most of the landscape representations in this manuscript remain stale borrowings from those already used in previous Ilkhanid manuscripts. This suggests that the experimental stage of the adoption of Chinese landscape conventions of Ilkhanid painting in its first great phase came to an end in the first decade of the fourteenth century.

Notes

1. Fong and Watt 1996, 31.
2. For Liao mural painting, see Johnson 1983; Rorex 1984. For Jin painting, see Bush 1965; Laing 1988–9. The standard work on Yuan painting is Cahill 1976. See also Weidner 1989.
3. Arnold 1924, 9–14.
4. Ibid. 14–23; Azarpay 1981, 170–80.
5. According to the older preface, one of the Samanid rulers, Nasr ibn Ahmad (301/914–331/943), ordered the poet Rudaqi to make a metrical version of the *Kalila wa Dimna*, and this poem with illustrations by Chinese artists delighted the ruler (Minorsky 1956, 168).
6. For the relationship between Saljuq ceramics and contemporary book painting, see Hillenbrand 1994b. For the figural decoration in pre-Mongol Iranian meitalwork, see Melikian-Chirvani 1982, 55–230, passim.
7. Marsh 144: Wellesz 1959; 1965; *AP*, 51–3. Soudavar (1999, 262–4) has proposed the twelfth and thirteenth centuries as the date of the manuscript. However, his arguments deserve detailed consideration in the context of a close examination of the manuscript itself. See also the so-called 519/1125 Sufi manuscript (Baghdad; Sotheby's 1998, lot 34). Similar East Asian-inspired linear drawings are found in a late thirteenth-century copy of the al-Sufi manuscript now in London (probably Maragha; Or. 5323, BL; Carey 2001). Except for this drawing technique, however, the London al-Sufi retains Arab pictorial traditions. See also the Istanbul al-Sufi (probably Iran, 647/1249; Ayasofya 2595, Suleimaniyye Library; *Turks*, no. 56).
8. The artistic value of ink painting had already been acknowledged in China since ancient times, but it was during the Tang dynasty that ink painting became an established genre in Chinese painting. Li Gonglin

(c. 1041–1106), one of the greatest painters of the Song dynasty, contributed to the reappraisal of Tang-style ink painting (see Barnhart 1993).

9. See, e.g., frescoes found in Qusayr ʻAmra (Almagro et al. 1975, 152–9, 190–3, pls IV–X, XLII–XLV) and Qasr al-Hayr al-Gharbi (*AP*, 35, 37). For further information about drawing in the Islamic world, see Brend 1995.
10. See, e.g., painter's sketches at Dunhuang (Fraser 1999; 2004). The technique of pouncing, which seems to have originated in China, was transmitted across Central Asia and eventually reached Iran about 1400, although surviving examples of pricked drawings belong to post-Ilkhanid periods (Bloom 2001, 190).
11. *AP*, 191, fig. 6.
12. e.g. Yaldiz et al. 2000, 257, pl. 378.
13. The significance of Sogdian painting in the westward influence of drapery conventions has been discussed at length by Azarpay (1981, 171–5).
14. I could not find any detailed studies of the development of clothing folds in Chinese painting at the time of writing this book, except for Wang's brief discussion (1995, 43–8) about the methods of painting clothing folds in China.
15. Wellesz 1959, fig. 14.
16. See Le Coq 1913, pl. 37. For similar ribbons in Sogdian painting, see Azarpay 1981, 169, pl. 28. See also ribbons depicted in Dunhuang painting (Whitfield 1982–5, vol. 1, colour pls 1–4, 7, 9–10, 39 and 42–6).
17. See the discussion of the incense-burner in Chapter 3.
18. Hazine 841: Melikian-Chirvani 1970b; Daneshvari 1986.
19. Pointed out in Titley 1983, 15, fig. 15. It has been suggested that the calligrapher who copied the *Varqa va Gulshah*, ʻAbd al-Mu'min b. Muhammad of Khoy, is mentioned in a *waqf* dated 649/1251 of the Karatay madrasa at Konya (O'Kane 2003, 46, n. 19).
20. e.g. the Paris *Kitab al-Diryaq* ('Book of Antidotes') (probably northern Iraq, 595/1199; Arabe 2964, BN; *AP*, 84–5).
21. Melikian-Chirvani 1972, 60–3. According to Melikian-Chirvani, the term *bot* often occurs in early Persian romances, such as the *Varqa va Gulshah* and Gurgani's eleventh-century romance *Vis u Ramin*. For the term *bot*, see Bailey 1931. For further information about the penetration of East Asian type of beauty into Iranian aesthetics, see Esin 1979.
22. See Melikian-Chirvani 1970b, 43–5; 1972, 63.
23. See Simpson 1982a.
24. Suppl. pers. 205: Simpson 1982a, 111–14; Fitzherbert 1996; Richard 1997a, no. 7.
25. See, e.g., *WSWG*, nos 9, 60.
26. M216: Simpson 1982a, 94–115. The manuscript has three miniatures. Chinese-inspired landscape elements can be seen in fos 2 and 7 (Simpson 1979, figs 109–10).
27. M.500: Hillenbrand 1990; Schmitz 1997, 9–24, figs 1–38.
28. For the discussion of the date of production, see Schmitz 1997, 11.
29. This classification is based on Schmitz (ibid. 12–15). Grube, on the other hand, has divided the miniatures into ten groups and several subgroups (Grube 1978b, 164–8). A number of miniatures that have been repainted in the nineteenth century (e.g. 3^v, 6^v, 23^v, 25^v, 36, 47^v, 58^v, 72^v, 78 left, 78^v, 84 and 84^v) can be left out of this analysis.

30. See, e.g., *PP*, 20–3.
31. See the Paris (*AP*, 84–5) and Vienna *Kitab al-Diryaq* (Northern Iraq, c. 1215–50, A.F.10, Nationalbibliothek, Vienna; Brandenburg 1982, 74, pl. 23).
32. See the Paris *Kalila wa Dimna* (probably Syria, c. 1220; Arabe 3465, BN; *AP*, 62–3). However, Ettinghausen has pinpointed Chinese associations with the depictions of the *kargadan* (rhinoceros; fo. 14^{v}; Ettinghausen 1950, 106–7).
33. Hillenbrand 1990, 155–6, fig. 31.
34. See, e.g., *AP*, 91. For related *minaʾi* ware, see *SPA*, pl. 653.
35. See, e.g., *AP*, 98–9.
36. See Fong 1992, 267–9, pl. 75. The same convention is used in robes on the miniature of Cain and Abel (fo. 6^{v}; however, this is a modern miniature; Schmitz 1997, fig. 4) and the loose folds of skin on the painting of two elephants (fo. 13; ibid., fig. 5).
37. For this illustration, see ibid. 18, fig. 11.
38. See also his *Horses Drinking in the Autumn Woods* (1312, Palace Museum, Beijing; Yang (ed.) 1994, 1, 194–7, pl. 78). For his horse painting, see Li 1968.
39. Horses were traditional subjects of Chinese painting, associated with the imperial heavens. Horse painting had been continuously produced since the Tang period, and it was an established genre during the Yuan period. It is assumed that the Mongols especially enjoyed horse paintings, associating with their nomadic heritage. For horse-painting traditions in China, see Sung 2002. The fact that Zhao Meng-fu was famous for his horse painting may be related to his close association with the Mongols (Cahill 1976, 38). On the other hand, the influence of thirteenth-century Arab horse depictions on this horse has been pointed out (Canby 1993a, 29). See also exhibition catalogues of the images of horses in Islamic art (Alexander (ed.) 1996; Paris 2002).
40. Schmitz 1997, 18.
41. For wall painting, see *Sekai*, 5, pl. 63; for woodblock prints, see Chen and Ma 2000, 4, 73.
42. Richard 1997a, 41.
43. This mural also recalls one of the illustrations in the *Divan* of Sultan Ahmad (probably Baghdad, c. 1400; F1932.29–37, FGA; Klimburg-Salter 1976–7, fig. 1).
44. See fos 32^{v} (unpublished), 35 (*SPA*, pl. 819a), 37 (Hillenbrand 1990, fig. 32), 39^{v} (Ettinghausen 1950, pl. 11), 42 (Schmitz 1997, fig. 20), 42^{v} (ibid., fig. 21), 44^{v} (Hillenbrand 1990, fig. 38), 47 (Natural History 1958, 561), 48^{v} (Schmitz 1997, fig. 22) and 49^{v} (ibid., fig. 23).
45. Schmitz 1997, 19, fig. 15. See also fos 44^{v} (Hillenbrand 1990, fig. 38) and 49^{v} (Schmitz 1997, fig. 23).
46. Hillenbrand 1990, 156, fig. 33. See also fo. 32^{v} (unpublished). Clouds in folio 33^{v} (Hillenbrand 1990, fig. 42) may also belong to this group.
47. Schmitz 1997, 20. However, scudding clouds here are more likely later additions.
48. See also fos 30 (ibid., fig. 15), 32^{v} (unpublished), 35^{v} (Hillenbrand 1990, fig. 33), 38 (unpublished), 39^{v} (unpublished), 42 (Schmitz 1997, fig. 20) and 44^{v} (Hillenbrand 1990, fig. 38). For Chinese rock conventions, see Cahill 1969.
49. See, e.g., *AP*, 89.

50. In China, Taihu rocks, taken from the Great Lake (Taihu), were especially admired for their fantastic shapes from the time of the Northern Song dynasty onwards (Munakata 1991, 61).
51. See Fong et al. 1984, 21. Guo Xi (after 1000–c. 1090) played an important part in the development of the idea: in landscape painting, mountains and rocks are carefully arranged in order to convey the impression of perspective in height, level and depth. For his treatise, the *Linquan gaozhi* ('The Lofty Ambition in Forests and Streams') (c. 1080), see Bush and Shih 1985, 141–2,150–4.
52. For example, a cosmography entitled *'Aja'ib al-Makhluqat* was written by al-Qazwini after his retirement at the fall of Baghdad in 656/1258. The manuscript will be referred to hereafter in this chapter.
53. *CHI*, 5, 396–7, 673. For the famous observatory at Maragha set up by Nasir al-Din Tusi under the patronage of Hulagu, see Wilber 1955, 107, fig. 5; Vardjavand 1979. In Yuan China, astronomical and scientific activities were greatly encouraged during the reign of Khubilai. He patronised Iranian astronomers and finally established the Institute of Muslim Astronomy (*Huihui sitianjian*) in 1271 (Rossabi 1988, 125–6).
54. Soucek 1980, 89–91. For example, the *Tanksuqnama* (713/1313; no. 3596, Aya Sofya, Istanbul) is the Persian translation of Chinese medical texts, including the famous Jin dynasty (265–317) physician Wang Shuhe's *Maijing* ('Classic of Pulse') (see Gölpinarli 1939; Needham 1954-, 1, 218–19). For further discussion of the impact of Chinese physicians in Iran, see Allsen 2001a, 141–60.
55. Fong 1992, 186.
56. Soucek 1980, 91.
57. For the development of bird-and-flower painting, see *CP*, 67–77. As a motif, bird-and-flower decoration was widely adapted to various media in the decorative arts of China throughout the ages (see, e.g., Figures 1.11, 1.13 and 2.16). For further discussion, see Chen 2000. As for Iranian imitations of Chinese bird-and-flower decoration, see the discussion of Sultanabad wares in Chapter 2.
58. See fos 53 (Schmitz 1997, fig. 25), 72 (unpublished), 76 (unpublished) and 76^{v} (unpublished).
59. Schmitz 1997, 22; Carboni 1992, pl. 42. See also fos 64^{v} (unpublished), 67^{v} (unpublished) and 68^{v} (unpublished).
60. See also fos 55^{v} (unpublished), 56 (Martin 1912, pl. 26c) and 59 (Schmitz 1997, fig. 29).
61. e.g. fo. 65^{v} (Schmitz 1997, 22, fig. 31). For Mesopotamian counterparts, see Folsach 2001, no. 22. See also representations of water in the second group (fo. 42; Schmitz 1997, 20, fig. 20), which are not entirely bereft of Mesopotamian water conventions; water movement is expressed by obscure wavy lines, as in *Maqamat* water conventions (Figure 4.6).
62. See fos 75 (unpublished), 76^{v} (unpublished) and 78^{v} (Schmitz 1997, fig. 36).
63. See *SPA*, pls 217, 225A and 232A–B.
64. The patterns are often referred to in books and dictionaries on Chinese art. However, as far as I know, no articles have ever been devoted to the study of their development.
65. Similar water patterns are seen in Song ceramic design (Wirgin 1979, pls 54 j–k).

66. For Chinese maps of these periods, see Cao et al. 1990. Similar water patterns can be found in Song and Yuan painting, but only to a limited extent (see, e.g., Barnhart et al. 1997, fig. 142). In relation to the impact of Chinese maps on the Iranian world, comparison can be made between Chinese maps and gritted architectural plans in the eastern Islamic world (see Bloom 2008).
67. Stewart 1967, 131. For further information about the *simurgh* and the *ʿanqa*, see Büchner 1934; Pellat 1960; Schmidt 1980; Blois 1997.
68. Baer 1965, 41.
69. See Daneshvari 1986, 56–67, fig. 36. A similar rooster-like *ʿanqa* occurs in the London Qazwini (fo. 122v; Schmitz 1997, fig. 27).
70. Schmitz 1997, 22, fig. 30.
71. Stewart 1967, 131.
72. For further discussion on the westward spread of Chinese paper making and printing technology, see Allsen 2001a, 176–85.
73. Or. 14140: Carboni 1988–9; 1992.
74. For the Munich Qazwini, see *AP*, 138–9. There are three more related manuscripts: a fourteenth-century copy in Gotha (probably Shiraz, c. 1330–40; MS A1506, Forschungsbibliothek); a fragmentary copy sold at Sotheby's in 1990 (probably Syria, c. 1350), and the so-called Sarre Qazwini (Diyarbakir, c. 1400; F1954.33–114 and 57.13, FGA; Spencer coll. MS 45, New York Public Library). For each detailed reference, see Carboni 1992, ch. 2, nn. 4–6 and 8 respectively. See also the 722/1322 Qazwini in the Suleimaniyye Library (probably Shiraz; Yeni Cami 813; Berlekamp 2007).
75. The provenance and commissioner of this manuscript have been discussed in detail by Carboni 1992, 523–38. Fitzherbert (2001, 347–61) has discussed the association between Fakhr al-Din ʿIsa and the Freer Balʿami.
76. For further discussion, see Carboni 1992, 447–90.
77. This has already been pointed out: ibid. 434–41; Schmitz 1997, 12–15.
78. Carboni 1988–9, fig. 3.
79. See Figure 4.4; fos 60v (Hillenbrand 1990, fig. 41), 61 (Natural History 1958, 562) and 63 (Schmitz 1997, fig. 30).
80. See *AP*, 72–3.
81. This classification is based on that of Carboni (1992, 390–2). He has subdivided Type 1 into two other types according to the degree of simplicity. The distribution of these three types of grass is uneven, which is not the case in the Morgan codex.
82. See also fos 100 (Carboni 1988–9, pl. VIC), 100v (ibid., pl. VID), 101v (ibid., fig. 1), 104 (ibid., fig. 5), 109 (Schmitz 1997, fig. 14), 112 (Carboni 1988–9, fig. 2) and 122 (ibid., pl. VIIIB).
83. See also *AP*, 117, 119.
84. See *PP*, 20.
85. See also fo. 86v (Carboni 1992, 176, cat. no. 169). It seems likely that the spiralling grass convention was developed from the stylised grass band used in thirteenth-century Syriac manuscripts (e.g. Add. 7170, BL; Siriaco 559, Biblioteca Apostolica, Vatican City; Leroy 1964, figs 77–1, 77–4, 79–1) or Mosul school painting (e.g. the Vienna *Kitab al-Diryaq*; Nassar 1985, 92–3, fig. 4). Similar spiralling grass can be seen in the Morgan manuscript, but only in one of the miniatures (fo. 65v; Schmitz 1997, fig. 31).
86. See also fo. 88v left (Carboni 1988–9, pl. VIIC).

87. Carboni 1988–9, fig. 3. See also fos 83, 88 (Carboni 1992, pls 30b–c).
88. Carboni 1988–9, 17, pl. VIIA.
89. Carboni 1992, 438. For these miniatures, see Schmitz 1997, figs 20, 22.
90. Carboni 1992, pl. 14.
91. There are five representations of dragons in the London Qazwini, but dragons in fos 33 (Figure 4.19) and 47 (Carboni 1992, pl. 29a) are depicted so obviously as snakes that they can be left out of this analysis. For discussion about the dragons in the London Qazwini, see ibid. 495–7.
92. Ibid. 131, 269, 271, and ch. 1, n. 143.
93. Öney 1969, figs 11–12, 17–18; Gierlichs 1996, 92–9.
94. Farès 1953, 29–33, pls III–IV; Azarpay 1978. See also the looped dragon in the Oxford al-Sufi (Wellesz 1959, fig. 20) and in the London al-Sufi (Huxley 1979, 83).
95. F1957.16, 1947.19 and 1930.21: Fitzherbert 2001. For this dragon image, see ibid., pl. 16.
96. Carboni 1992, 271, pl. 9.
97. Ibid. 475–9. Otto-Dorn (1978–9, 128–30) has pinpointed its Chinese origin, but, as far as I know, Chinese examples of the knotted dragon – for example, those found in a T-shaped silk painting from Tomb no. 1 at the Mawangdui (mid-second century BC; Watson 1995, fig. 147), are insufficient to demonstrate a Chinese contribution to the development of the knotted dragon in Islamic art.
98. Carboni 1992, 477. For further discussion about the dragon in Islamic iconography, see Hartner 1938, 135–44; Curatola 1989, 45–81; Gierlichs 1993, 10–17. In the study of the Paris *Kitab al-Diryaq*, Farès (1953, 32) has pointed out talismanic, magical and therapeutic significances of the knotted dragon in Islamic iconography, as seen in a number of monumental Saljuq buildings – for example, the city gate at Sinjar (c. 1300) and the Talisman gate at Baghdad (c. 1220).
99. Hartner 1938, 131–4; 1965.
100. It should be noted that Chinese dragon themes are found in Armenian manuscripts produced in the 1280s – e.g. the Gospel manuscript of 1286 (no. 979, Matenadaran, Erevan; Kouymjian 1986, figs 2–3). This topic has been examined in a series of articles by Kouymjian (1986; 2006). Chinese-type dragons were known in Armenia perhaps through textile designs in the course of friendly relations between the Armenian kingdom of Cilicia (1198–1375) and the Mongol Empire (Kouymjian 1986, 417, 449–51). For Armeno-Mongol relations, see Wolff and Hazard (eds) 1969, 651–9.
101. See, e.g., Wirgin 1979, figs 11c–d; Zhu 1998, 24–9, figs 4–6.
102. The flame is also a key chinoiserie element. As has already been mentioned in the chapter on textiles, the dragon carrying flames has a symbolic meaning in China. However, as the flame was known in Iran through conventional Chinese dragon motifs, its original significance was gradually lost; Iranian painters began to incorporate it into some other animals – for example, the *karg* (e.g. the Freer Balʿami, F.1957.16, fo. 107; Fitzherbert 2001, pl. 14). I shall return to this point in the final chapter.
103. The convention of dragon painting was developed especially among Chan painters during the Southern Song period (see Sirén 1956–8, 2, 148–51).

104. This dragon is undoubtedly of Chinese derivation. Yet, compared with the Morgan manuscript and the London Qazwini, Chinese artistic influence in the miniatures of the Freer Balʿami is, on the whole, less apparent.
105. Arab 161: Soucek 1975; Hillenbrand 2000a. It is interesting to compare the Edinburgh al-Biruni with a sixteenth-century copy of the al-Biruni treatise now in Paris (Arabe 1489, BN; Blochet 1926, 58–60, pls XIV–XV; *SPA*, 1833, pls 824–5). The Paris al-Biruni faithfully copies the miniatures from the Edinburgh codex. Barrucand has compared some, but not all, images of the Edinburgh copy with those of the Paris copy (Barrucand 1999, 22–3, pls III.1–IV.4). I am most grateful to Professor Barrucand for having sent me a copy of this article.
106. See, e.g., fos 92^{v} (Soucek 1975, fig. 8), 95 (ibid., fig. 11), 140^{v} (ibid., fig. 21), 141^{v} (Figure 4.28), 161 (Soucek 1975, fig. 24) and 162 (Figure 4.26).
107. Soucek 1975, fig. 18.
108. See Carboni 1992, pl. 7.
109. Soucek 1975, fig. 21.
110. For similar Mesopotamian-style water in the Morgan Bestiary, see Schmitz 1997, fig. 31.
111. See fos 10^{v} (Soucek 1975, fig. 2), 16 (ibid., fig. 3), 92 (ibid., fig. 7), 92^{v} (ibid., fig. 8), 93^{v} (ibid., fig. 9), 94a (ibid., fig. 10), 95a (ibid., fig. 11) and 104^{v} (ibid., fig. 17). A cloud in fo. 91 (ibid., fig. 6) is exceptionally yellowish.
112. Ibid. 151–4, fig. 24.
113. For this story, see ibid. 154.
114. For this story, see Hillenbrand 2000a, 134–5.
115. For his works, see Cahill 1976, 114–20, pls 48–50.
116. For example, the place of worship is not depicted as a Buddhist temple in the scene of *Indians Celebrate the Autumnal Equinox* (fo. 129^{v}; Soucek 1975, 141, fig. 18).
117. Ibid. 114–18, fig. 5. Similar cross-legged idols are also to be found in the Freer Balʿami (F1957.16, fo. 126; Fitzherbert 2001, 144–5, pl. 19).
118. Soucek 1975, 143–5, fig. 20.
119. According to the *Jamiʿ al-Tawarikh*, 'When the Load of Islam, Ghazan, became a Muslim, he commanded that all the idols should be broken and all the pagodas destroyed, together with all the other temples the presence of which in Muslim countries is forbidden by the shariʿa . . .' (quoted in *CHI*, 5, 542).
120. Soucek 1975, 148. See, e.g., Rice 1959, pl. XXXVIII.
121. For example, an ambassador from the Byzantine Emperor Andronicus II came to Iran in 1302 (Spuler 1955, 101). Christianity, particularly Nestorian Christianity, flourished in Iran (Morgan 1986, 159–60), and was widespread among the women of the Ilkhans' family (Browne 1933, 148–78; Holmberg 1993; Ryan 1998, 413–18).
122. Buckton (ed.) 1994, 203.
123. See, e.g., *CP*, 51. For images of the Bodhisattvas in Central Asian Painting, see Bussagli 1963, 91.
124. Pre-Islamic Central Asian associations with this practice have been suggested by Rice 1969. Yet more convincing evidence for this suggestion needs to be found.
125. This type of throne can be traced back to the Saljuq period, as seen in the *Varqa va Gulshah* manuscript (Daneshvari 1986, figs 13, 41)

and *mina'i* ware (Atıl 1973, pls 52–3). The cushioned throne suits the cross-legged pose in nomadic culture. For further discussion, see Otto-Dorn 1982. Similar cushioned thrones are also to be found in the *Maqamat* (Schefer Hariri) and the Vienna *Kitab al-Diryaq* (*AP*, 121; Brandenburg 1982, pl. 22). The Freer Bal'ami has several throne scenes: central figures usually sit on cushioned thrones with crossed legs (Fitzherbert 2001, pls 1, 15, 17), but the thrones are much more rigid with solid frames and poles on both sides.

126. This architectural structure recalls, for example, the *mihrab* of the *Masjid-i Jami'* at Bistam (Wilber 1955, 127–8, pl. 36). For further discussion on the representations of architecture in the Edinburgh al-Biruni, see Barrucand 1986a, 128–31.

127. Amitai-Preiss 1996, 9. Ghazan maintained Mongol custom and traditions, which contradicted the precepts of his new religion. Melville (1990, 171) has argued that Ghazan converted to Islam mainly because of political reasons to secure his position and to win Muslim support in his struggle against Baidu. The sincerity of his conversion, therefore, remains a matter for speculation.

128. For further discussion about Uighur artists at Ilkhanid ateliers, see Esin 1963, 141, n. 2.

129. Soucek 1975, 156; Carboni 1992, 422. Tabriz has been suggested as the place of production by Gray (*PP*, 26–7).

130. Barrett 1952, 6; *Legacy*, 145.

131. For the survival of Christianity at Mosul and in the area of the northern Jazira during the thirteenth and fourteenth centuries, see Fiey 1975.

132. Carboni 1992, especially 421–8.

CHAPTER FIVE

Manuscript Painting 2

The evolution of Ilkhanid painting: the London and Edinburgh *Jamiʿ al-Tawarikh*

AN EPOCH-MAKING development in Iranian painting took place during the second decade of the fourteenth century at the Rabʿ-i Rashidi ('Quarter of Rashid'), a cultural complex near Tabriz that was established by the eminent Ilkhanid vizier Amir Rashid al-Din Fadl-Allah (d. 718/1318).[1] Under his supervision, a considerable production of illustrated and unillustrated books was undertaken at the workshops of the Rabʿ-i Rashidi until the destruction of the quarter in 718/1318. One of the most outstanding productions of this period is the compilation of the history of the world entitled the *Jamiʿ al-Tawarikh* ('A Compendium of Chronicles') under the commission of Ghazan and Uljaitu. The miniatures of the two earliest surviving but fragmentary manuscripts – one is held in the Edinburgh University Library (Arabic MS 20)[2] and the other is now in the possession of the Nasser D. Khalili Collection (MS 727)[3] – provide the most vivid impression of the inaugural moment of the Rashidiyya style.

The 103 miniatures of these two Arabic fragments can be distinguished from earlier Ilkhanid manuscript paintings by their high degree of artistic and technical excellence. While manuscript paintings produced in the first decade of the fourteenth century are relatively conservative in their repetition of established conventions, the style used in the two *Jamiʿ al-Tawarikh* manuscripts, both of which are now thought to have originally been part of the same manuscript and to have been produced in 714/1314,[4] became further enriched by means of elements derived from several artistic traditions. This certainly reflects the prosperity of Tabriz – the principal Ilkhanid capital as well as an important entrepôt for commercial activities between East and West, where goods of various origins were exchanged on a large scale.[5] The city was also a melting pot of several religious traditions. Thanks to the Mongol policy of religious tolerance, several written and pictorial sources of Christianity, Judaism and Buddhism became more widely available and accessible to Ilkhanid artists.[6] In such an international atmosphere, the style of the Rashidiyya school was born, and very soon it had its first flowering.

The two Arabic *Jamiʿ al-Tawarikh* manuscripts are also of great documentary value, for they project the political concern of the Ilkhanids and, moreover, mirror Mongol universalism.[7] Fully illustrated copies of this work were distributed throughout the major cities of the Ilkhanid realm each year, one written in Arabic and the other in Persian, in order to legitimise Mongol rule in Iran. The contents of the four volumes of the *Jamiʿ al-Tawarikh* were carefully composed so as to proclaim the glory of the Mongol Empire.[8] Of course, not all the distinctive elements of the manuscripts can be satisfactorily interpreted in the context of legitimacy. Yet it is also true that, as a result of courtly involvement in the production of the pictorial programme, the relationship between art and patronage in the Ilkhanid court became stronger than ever before.

The Edinburgh and London manuscripts have attracted much scholarly attention for a high degree of assimilation of Chinese elements into their illustrations.[9] The tutelage of Chinese art is prominent in the extensive use of line and shading, which are of paramount importance in discerning the turning point of chinoiserie in Iranian painting. Such revolutionary elements are, as some scholars have mentioned, indicative of the involvement of artists who were of Chinese origin or, at least, were trained in Chinese art traditions.[10] An even more decisive factor for these stylistic and technical innovations may lie in the use of a variety of Chinese sources, both in quality and quantity – to take one example, the impact of Chinese woodblock prints (Figure 5.1)[11] is pronounced in the format of illustrations with long narrow frames.[12] In addition to the increased availability of and hence familiarity with a wide range of Chinese pictorial and decorative arts, the unusual large size of the sheets of paper used must also have encouraged the painters to adopt Chinese elements more confidently and unreservedly.[13]

What is remarkable is that the painters of the *Jamiʿ al-Tawarikh* manuscripts attempted to assimilate Chinese landscape settings to their conception of composition both in scale and perspective. This is evident when one observes the interest of the painters in chinoiserie elements. The floating *lingzhi* clouds and grassy ground lines that are ubiquitous in earlier Ilkhanid paintings disappeared from the painters' repertoires, being replaced by a more sophisticated representation of landscape and a more developed sense of spatial recession.[14] The key landscape elements are thus rocks, trees, mountains and water, and all of these permit interesting comparisons with Chinese examples of various media.

Rocks particularly illustrate a pattern of adoption and adaptation of Chinese landscape conventions in the *Jamiʿ al-Tawarikh* manuscripts. The painters responsible for the first few miniatures of the Edinburgh codex were enthusiastic in adopting Chinese rock

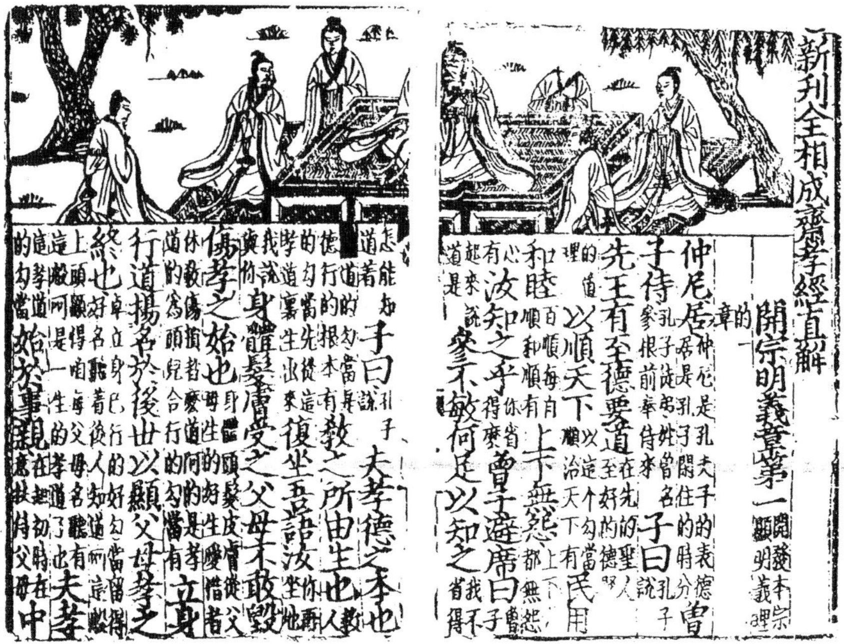
新刊全相成齋孝經直解

開宗明義章第一

仲尼居曾子侍子曰先王有至德要道以順天下民用和睦上下無怨汝知之乎曾子避席曰參不敏何足以知之

子曰夫孝德之本也教之所由生也復坐吾語汝身體髮膚受之父母不敢毀傷孝之始也立身行道揚名於後世以顯父母孝之終也夫孝始於事親中

Figure 5.1 *Page from the* Xiaojing. *Yongzhong imprint of 1308.*

conventions. In the illustration of *The Finding of Musa* (E9; Figure 5.2),[15] for instance, the contours of rocks are represented not by vague double outlines but by well-defined calligraphic ones. The improvement of rock modelling also serves to enhance the elegance and sharpness of rocks, giving them a similar appearance to the rocks delicately rendered by Chinese masters (Figure 4.9). A more noteworthy point is that, compared with the mass of rocks unnaturally placed in the foreground in earlier Ilkhanid paintings (e.g. Figures 4.7, 4.24), an intensive attempt is made to incorporate various shapes and sizes of rocks into the background. In the subsequent miniatures, however, the painters often failed to capture the essence of Chinese rocks. In spite of the use of highlights and shading, the rocks depicted in the scene of *Muhammad Receives his First Revelation* (E32)[16] are visibly deformed. The upper parts of the rocks are oddly enlarged and transformed into cauliflower-shaped objects. Finally, as often happened in the later stages of the adaptation of foreign imagery in Iranian art, the rocks lost their original significance as landscape elements and were modified to suit the demands of the painters. The representation of rocky beds in the scene of the *Death of Musa* (K33),[17] though effective in visualising a dramatic moment, betray only a veneer of knowledge of Chinese rock conventions. The rocks here lack volume and have unusual angular shapes. An excessive use of brush strokes for rock surfaces merely results in providing an impression of folds within the rocks.

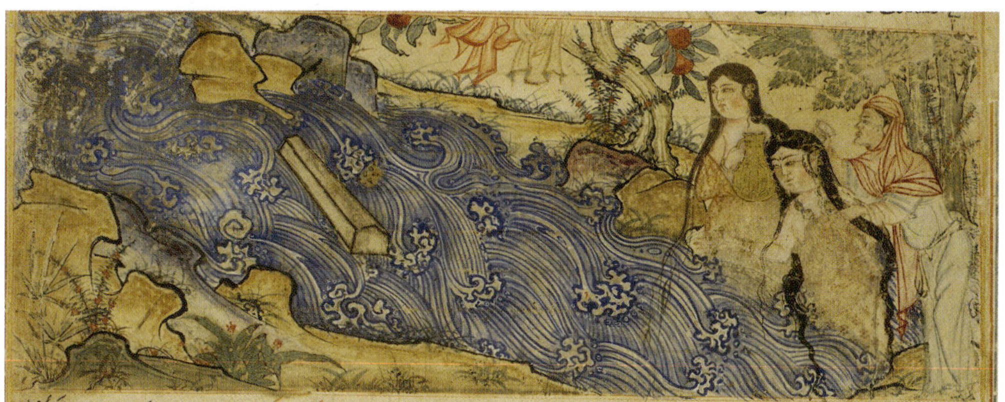

Figure 5.2 Jamiʿ al-Tawarikh *of Rashid al-Din:* The Finding of Musa. *Tabriz, 714/1314.*

These brief observations on rocks reveal a variable degree of adoption and adaptation of Chinese landscape conventions in the Edinburgh and London *Jamiʿ al-Tawarikh.* Earlier illustrations towards the beginning of the Edinburgh manuscript echo Chinese conventions for depicting rocks, while in the subsequent illustrations it is increasingly hard to trace the impact of Chinese landscape styles.[18] Such inconsistencies in the understanding of Chinese landscape conventions are indicative of the uneven quality of the painters and of the careless supervision exercised by the masters at the workshop.

Despite the emphasising of tree trunks by vigorous strokes,[19] the understanding of Chinese tree conventions in the *Jamiʿ al-Tawarikh* manuscripts appears to be defective. In the illustrations towards the beginning of the Edinburgh codex, even though each tree is rendered in a careful manner (e.g. Figure 5.17), little attempt is made to harmonise trees of various kinds with each other and with other landscape elements. The illustrations towards the middle of the London manuscript show how the painters gradually lost their interest in duplicating Chinese tree conventions; some of the illustrations betray degenerate tendencies in using trees as decorative space-fillers.[20]

Exceptions are the trees depicted in the two illustrations located in the history of India (K25, K26),[21] where the painters show a fine command of Chinese tree conventions. The trees depicted in both illustrations are distinct from those seen in other illustrations in terms of form and arrangement. They are, as in a certain Chinese woodblock print (e.g. Figure 5.1), effective in suggesting several distances within the landscape, whereas speculations as to the definitive sources of inspiration for the trees of these illustrations have remained inconclusive. In the case of the illustration of *Shakyamuni Offers Fruits to the Devil* (K25; Figure 5.3), it has been pointed out that the composition may have been derived from illustrated sources brought by Indian monks,[22] such as the Indian Buddhist monk called

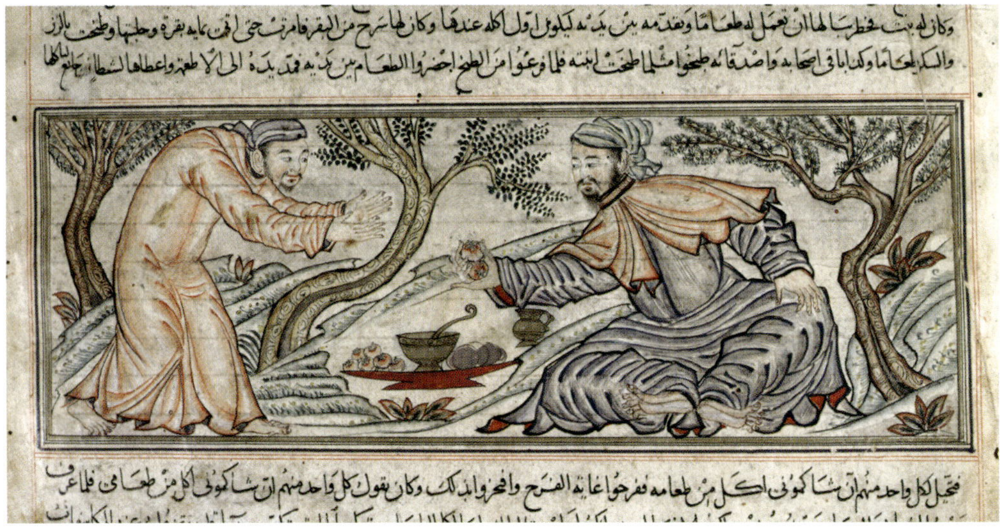

Figure 5.3 Jamiʿ al-Tawarikh *of Rashid al-Din:* Shakyamuni Offers Fruit to the Devil. *Tabriz, 714/1314.*

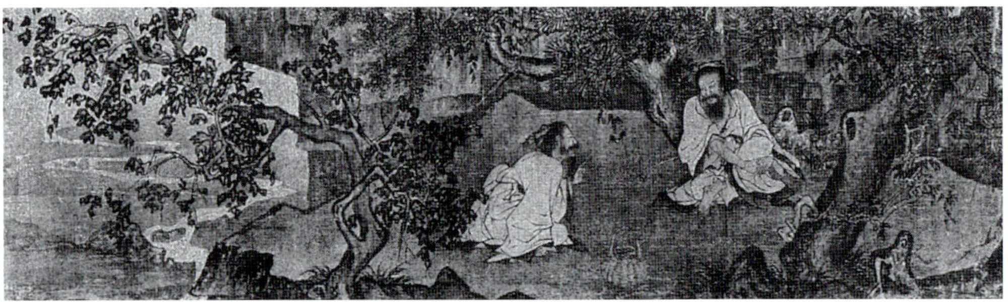

Figure 5.4 *Li Tang:* Two Men Picking Roses. *Handscroll, ink on silk. China, Southern Song dynasty.*

Kamalashri who served in the Mongol court and brought Sanskrit sources for the life and teaching of the Buddha to Rashid al-Din.[23] Another scholar has noted that there is a possible association between this illustration and Chinese medical texts in terms of the careful treatment of individual trees.[24] Judging by the way that the trees are cut off at a lower point by the upper margins, the painting retains an artistic link not only with woodblock prints (e.g. Figure 5.1) but also with Chinese painting in the horizontal scroll format – for instance, a scroll painting of two persons under trees by Li Tang (fl. c. 1120–40) (Figure 5.4).

Another intriguing illustration located in the history of India is *The Grove of Jetavana* (K26; Figure 5.5). Each tree is carefully arranged, showing the concern of the painters for spatial depth. The

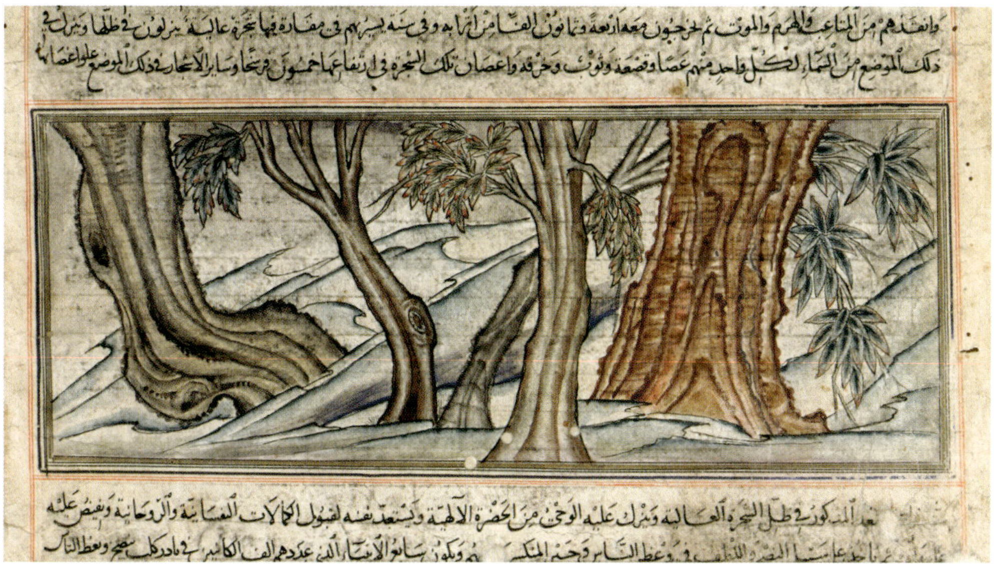

Figure 5.5 Jamiʿ al-Tawarikh *of Rashid al-Din:* The Grove of Jetavana. *Tabriz, 714/1314. The depiction of landscape in this illustration should be viewed as a pinnacle of chinoiserie in Ilkhanid painting.*

unbalanced shapes of the large leaves are suggestive of the continuation of earlier Ilkhanid tree conventions (e.g. Figure 4.7), yet representations of tree trunks are much improved under the inspiration of Chinese tree conventions – where the texture of tree trunks is expressed by lighter and much more delicate colouring. The difficulty is, however, to determine their definitive Chinese sources: while Canby has stressed the stylistic similarities between the trees depicted in this illustration and those seen in Song painting, adducing the work of Fan Long (fl. 1227–62),[25] Blair has alleged their iconographic association with Buddhist pictorial sources.[26] Whether the sources are secular or religious, it is significant that the painters took their artistic inspiration from various sources, owing to an increase in the Iranian stock of knowledge of Chinese and broadly East Asian art traditions, and exerted themselves to adjust newly acquired elements to their own pictorial settings.

More conclusive evidence confirming the impact of Chinese landscape conventions is found in the representations of mountains. Again, the painters in charge of the history of India were susceptible to new styles of depicting mountains brought from China. *The Mountains of India* (K19) and *The Mountains between India and Tibet* (K20) deserve careful examination for a proper understanding of the association with Chinese pictorial sources, both in the handscroll format and in other types of media. The former illustration (Figure 5.6) is often regarded as the first known pure landscape painting produced in the Islamic world, not just because of the absence

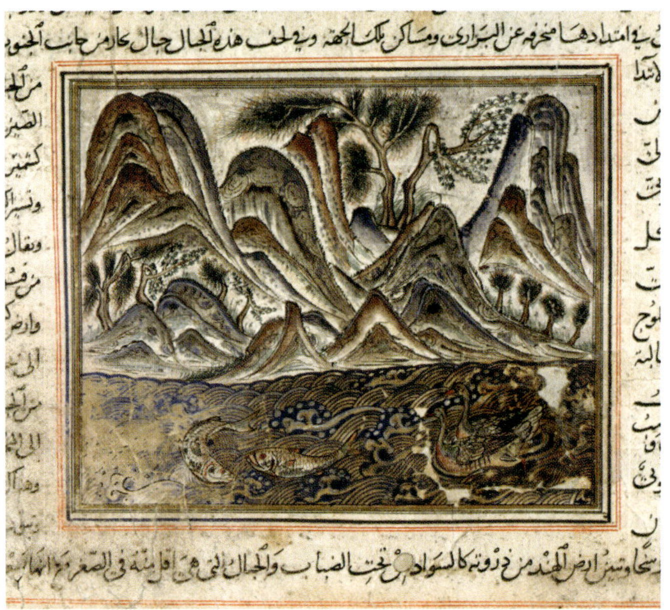

Figure 5.6 Jami' al-Tawarikh *of Rashid al-Din:* The Mountains of India. *Tabriz, 714/1314.*

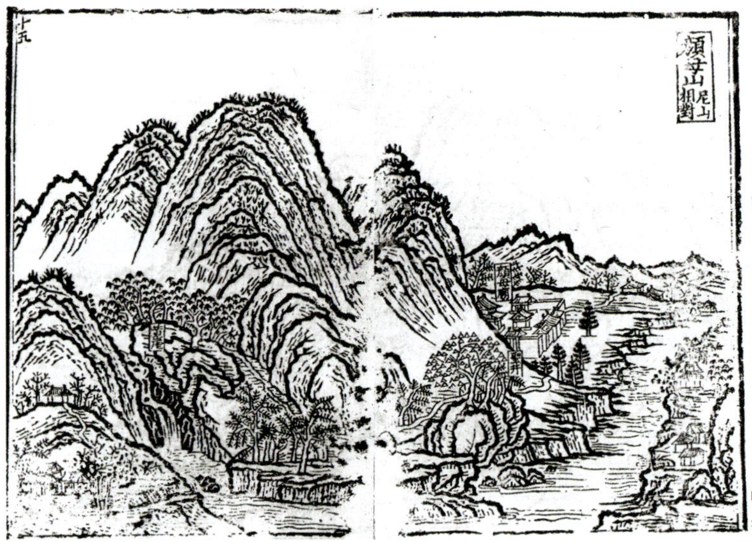

Figure 5.7 Kongshi zuting guangji *of Y. Kong:* The Yanmu Mountain. *Qufu imprint of 1242.*

of figures but because of the adequate attention paid to the relationship between mountains and distances. The image is also striking in the way that the main scene is set back, creating a panoramic view. This feature differentiates the mountains of this illustration from those depicted in thirteenth-century Mesopotamian painting – for example, in the Wasit Qazwini (678/1280; MS 464, Bayerische Staatsbibliothek, Munich),[27] the mountain ranges are rendered in a rapid and sketchy manner but are devoid of the sense of depth. The detail of mountains in *The Mountains of India* also has a distinctive feature: to add verisimilitude, fingerprint-like patterns are put around the mountainsides. The appearance of blue-and-green colours around the mountain tops may have been inspired by the colour schemes often used in early Yuan landscape painting.[28] However, touches of Chinese woodblock prints lie behind the overall treatment of mountains (Figure 5.7),[29] particularly the way of showing the overlaps of mountain ranges and of arranging trees.

In *The Mountains between India and Tibet* (Figure 5.8), still more striking similarities can be noted between the mountains depicted here and those seen in Chinese printed examples. The narrow streams are, as typically found in contemporary Chinese maps (Figure 5.9), represented by segmental patterns. Thus, clearly, the painters of the illustrations in the history of India had a good understanding of Chinese mountain conventions, especially those used in woodblock prints.

Despite a certain indebtedness to Chinese pictorial sources, however, they were unable to overcome difficulties in understanding the balance of size between mountains and other pictorial elements – namely, fish, two women and temples. Not only is this the case in the two illustrations discussed above, but it also seems to have been a common problem among the painters of the *Jamiʿ al-Tawarikh* manuscripts. The mountains depicted in the illustration of *Muhammad, Abu Bakr and the Goats* (E37),[30] for example, reveal how the painters tackled the problem of painting the grandeur of mountains and hills. It seems that they intended to depict a scene where two persons and animals are surrounded by mountain peaks. Yet, because of the lack of sense of space, the mountain ranges here function merely as framing devices. The whole composition of this illustration fails to bring creatures and nature into a close relationship.

There is a variety of water representations in the *Jamiʿ al-Tawarikh* manuscripts. Some painters are conversant with Chinese water conventions, while others follow earlier Ilkhanid or Mesopotamian ways of depicting water. In the *Finding of Musa* (Figure 5.2), the flow of water from the upper left to the lower right is expressively rendered, displaying an unmistakable dependence on Chinese models for the depiction of water (Figure 4.16). The painters succeed in evoking a certain dynamism by using water sprays, an attempt that had remained experimental in earlier Ilkhanid painting – the water movement represented in most illustrations of the Morgan Bestiary, the London Qazwini and the Edinburgh al-Biruni is represented by obscure wavy outlines or ornamental water patterns with indications of water sprays (e.g. Figure 4.19). The waves

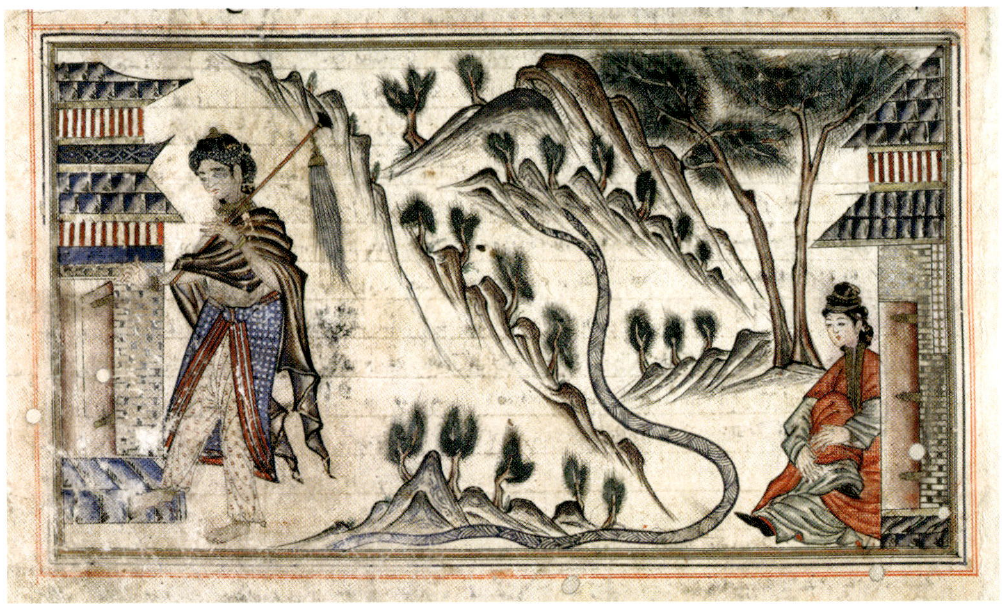

Figure 5.8 Jamiʿ al-Tawarikh *of Rashid al-Din:* The Mountains between India and Tibet. Tabriz, *714/1314.*

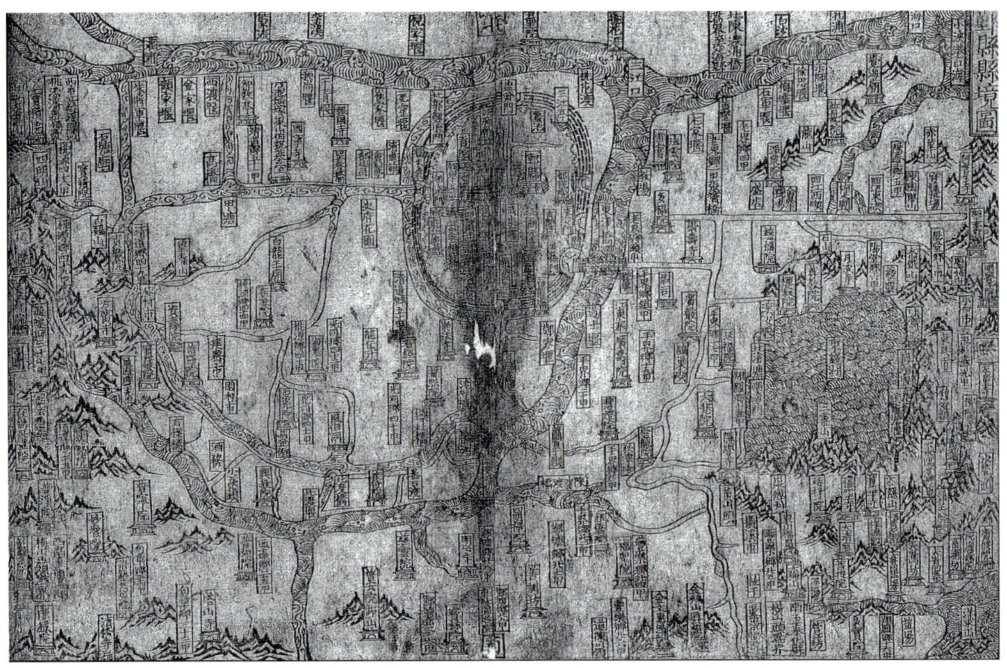

Figure 5.9 *A Map of Yinxian Border (Ningbo) from the* Baoqing Simingzhi. *China, 1272.*

depicted in the illustration of Musa and Aaron (E11)[31] are also rendered in a descriptive way, but their continuous and rhythmic forms are more evocative of the breaking wave patterns used in contemporary Chinese porcelain.[32] Apart from these new conventions for depicting water, ornamental water patterns re-emerge from the illustrations towards the middle of the Edinburgh codex (Figure 5.8)[33] As seen in some illustrations of the Morgan Bestiary (e.g. Figure 4.14), waves are depicted as alternatively arranged imbricated patterns. The last water convention to be discussed here occurs in the two illustrations concerning the biblical story in the Khalili portion (K28, K35).[34] The water movement here is rather sluggish, failing to give adequate attention to the fluidity of water. The water is neither of Chinese origin nor of earlier Ilkhanid derivation, but is more likely to have been developed from pre-Mongol conventions of depicting water – for example, that used in the *Maqamat* of al-Hariri (Figure 4.6). The unnatural arrangement of fish also points to the persistency of Mesopotamian water conventions.

There are marked differences in landscape style between the miniatures depicting specific events and those depicting battle scenes. In the latter, the painters seem to have been more interested in inventing unique devices than in imitating Chinese landscape conventions. This was, perhaps, intended to avoid monotony or to satisfy a variety of compositional requirements. The first device is apparently derived from the form of mountains (K21; Figure 5.10). For the sake of giving the painting a good sense of action, the background is filled with the summary indications of mountains. It appears, at first glance, that triangular patterns are haphazardly arranged in the background purely for decorative purposes, but their

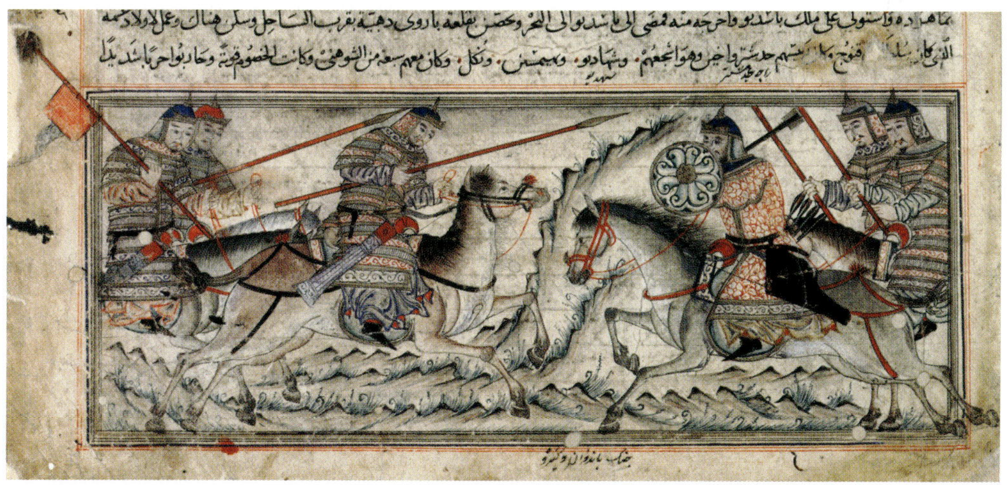

Figure 5.10 Jamiʿ al-Tawarikh *of Rashid al-Din:* Battle of the Pandavas and Kauravas. *Tabriz, 714/1314.*

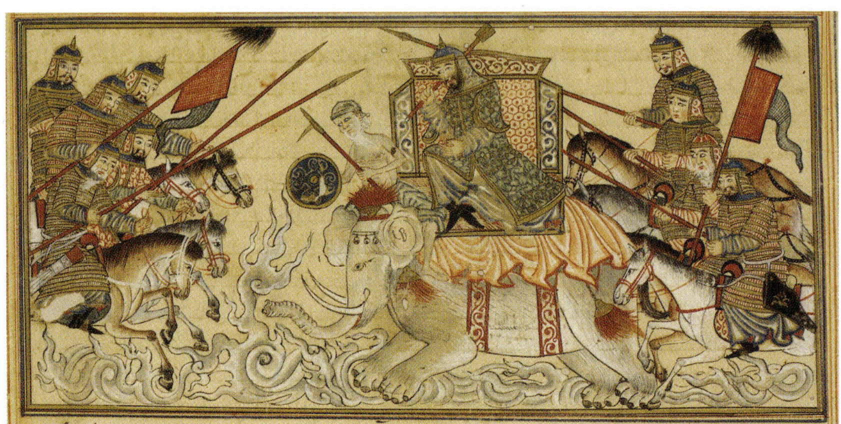

Figure 5.11 Jamiʿ al-Tawarikh *of Rashid al-Din:* Fighting between Mahmud and Ismaʿil. *Tabriz, 714/1314.*

positions keep rhythm with the movement of the horsemen. The second invention is the arrangement of a mass of rocks between two armies.[35] Although devoid of the stylistic traits of Chinese rocks, the rocks here serve to highlight the wildness of the battlefield.[36] Compositionally, however, this is not a successful adaptation of landscape elements. The rocks provide a clear division within the picture and thus interfere with the pictorial movement. The third device is a dusty cloud (E48; Figure 5.11). Despite the decline in landscape function, the use of dusty clouds for the battle scenes is among the most successful reinterpretations of landscape elements in the manuscripts, for the painters manipulated the serpentine form of clouds to add drama and force to the scene. This device is certainly an Ilkhanid invention, but the clouds themselves seem more likely to have relied on Chinese models – apart from cloud patterns used in Chinese decorative arts, Buddhist texts are in this case also plausible sources for providing the images of smoky clouds permeating ground level (Figure 5.28).

The second matter to be addressed is costumes.[37] Types of robe and headgear are varied, reflecting the mingled cultures of Ilkhanid Iran. A certain degree of consistency can, however, be recognised in the choice of clothing. The painters adopt classical modes of attire for characters of the biblical story,[38] while Arab-type kaftan dress, sometimes with the addition of *tiraz* bands on the sleeves, is predominantly used in the illustrations of the story of Muhammad.[39] Mongol styles permeate the miniatures dealing with historical events and battle scenes.[40]

Of particular note is the strong sartorial bias noticeable in enthronement scenes, in which, regardless of dynastic origin, Mongol elements are fully integrated into the clothing of rulers and attendants. Both a standing ruler and Mongol attendants in the scene of Mahmud ibn Sebuktegin (E50; Figure 5.12), for example, wear a dress with a right–left diagonal crossed fastening, recalling those depicted in Yuan murals[41] and actual Mongol robes discovered in Inner Mongolia (Figure 5.13).[42] The design of the robes of the attendants is rather standardised: except for some use of chequered or flowered patterns, most of the robes are plain, apart from some additional folds. The chest or shoulder parts of the robes are sometimes ornate with flame-like decoration, perhaps intending to depict embroideries woven in gold, as seen in a Yuan painting depicting Khubilai Khan's hunting in Taipei.[43] In contrast with the lightly clad attendants, the importance of the ruler is reinforced by a richly woven overcoat, which can be identified as a robe of honour (*khil'a*).[44] The depiction of the overcoat is accurate enough to enable one to find a similar multicoloured striped design in contemporary Iranian textiles.[45] This indicates that, in addition to *nasij*-type gold robes, this type of polychrome robe was acknowledged as royal apparel in West Asia. This enthronement scene appears, to some extent, to have reflected actual Mongol wardrobes on ceremonial occasions. The attendants' costumes are uniform in style, though they differ according to the ethnic origin of the attendants.[46] The choice of headgear in the enthronement scenes is also distinctive: rulers wear the so-called Saljuq crown, a feature that differentiates them clearly from their uncrowned attendants. While Arab attendants wear turbans in association with kaftan dress,[47] the identification of Mongol attendants can easily be made by virtue of their elaborate headdress, such as double-brimmed hats.[48] Such a variety of headgear is illustrative of the significant role of headdress in the distinction of social classes and ethnic groups in Mongol society.

However, the extent to which the painters were familiar with Chinese costumes proper remains dubious. A series of illustrations depicting the successive emperors of China (K4–K18) shows little concern for accuracy and coherence in representing Chinese imperial costumes. In the illustration of Song emperors (K17; Figure 5.14), for example, Mongol robes are inaccurately combined with Chinese scholar-type caps. The emperors of the Song dynasty should have been depicted as being dressed in traditional Chinese robes with fastenings in front, as seen in a portrait of the first Song emperor produced in China (Figure 5.15). Similar iconographic confusion is often found in other illustrations of Chinese emperors in the manuscripts, thereby betraying the painters' scant knowledge of Chinese costumes. The scarcity of information about the Chinese tradition of depicting the genealogical trees of emperors also makes it difficult to demonstrate an actual Chinese association with the images of Chinese emperors in the *Jami' al-Tawarikh* manuscripts or even to deduce possible Chinese sources of inspiration for them. The images of emperors arranged in several compartments are rarely seen in

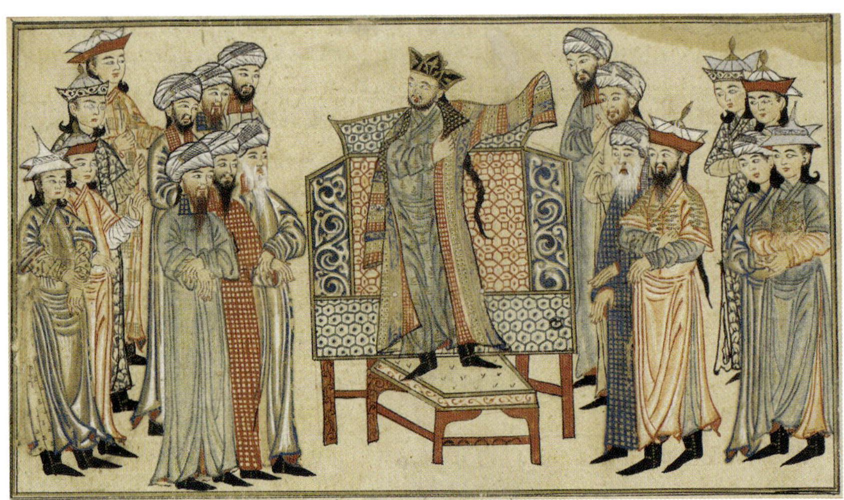

Figure 5.12 Jamiᶜ al-Tawarikh *of Rashid al-Din:* Mahmud ibn Sebuktegin Receives a Robe of Honour from the Caliph al-Qadir Biʾllah in 1000. *Tabriz, 714/1314. As in Islamic society, the robe of honour constitutes a major part of the Mongol practice of investiture. Detailed depictions of each dress in this manuscript suggest the cultural and political importance of clothing in the social structure of Ilkhanid Iran.*

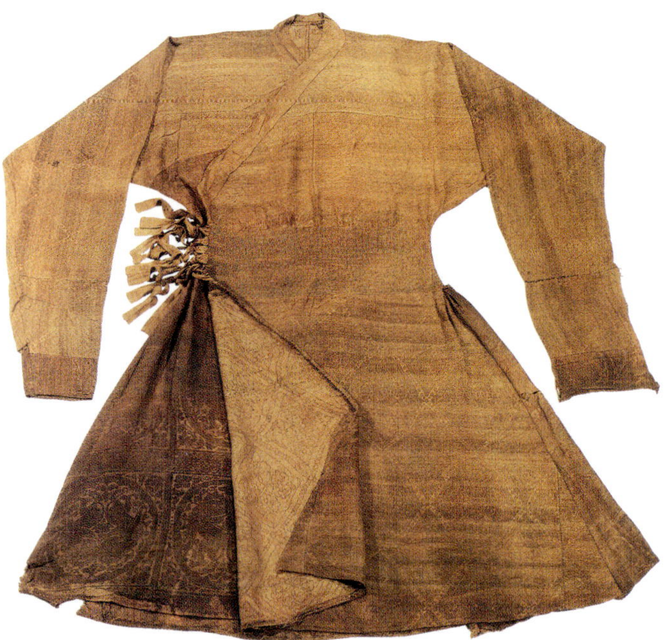

Figure 5.13 *Yellow-lined silk robe. Mongolia, c. 1300. This magnificent Mongol robe from Onggut tombs at Dasujixiang Mingshui in Daerhanmao Mingan United Banner is a testament to the luxury of nomadic material culture. This type of robe, whose front opening overlaps to the right as opposed to the left, is traditionally worn with trousers suitable for riding.*

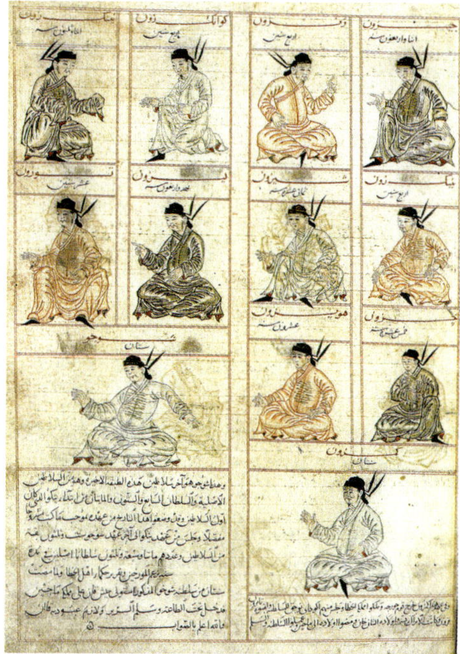

Figure 5.14 Jamiʿ al-Tawarikh *of Rashid al-Din:* Twelve Emperors of the Song Dynasty. *Tabriz, 714/1314.*

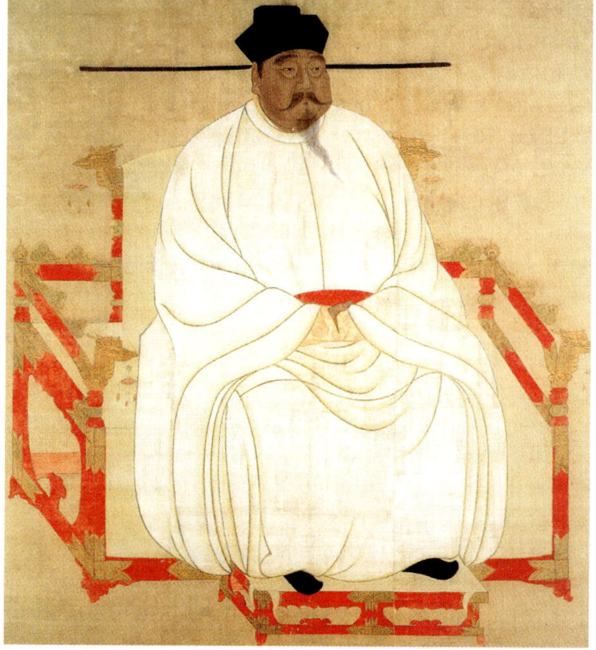

Figure 5.15 *Portrait of Song Taizu. Hanging scroll, ink and colour on silk. China, Song dynasty.*

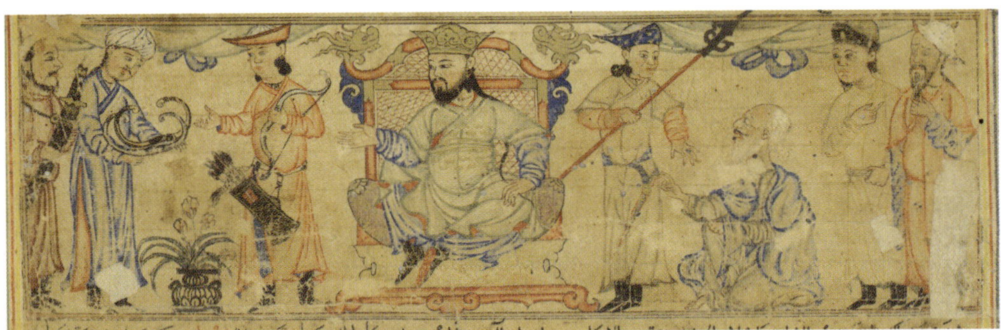

Figure 5.16 Jamiʿ al-Tawarikh *of Rashid al-Din:* Jamshid. *Tabriz, 714/1314.*

Chinese imperial portraits, and such ideas may rather have relied on indigenous Middle Eastern pictorial sources.[49] In terms of legitimacy, however, it is possible to explain the insertion of distinctive Mongol elements into the images of Chinese emperors as an intention to propagate the genealogical association between the Mongol and Chinese royal families.

The enthronement scenes are enlivened not only by costumes but also by interior settings, such as thrones and curtains. There are several distinctive types of throne in the *Jamiʿ al-Tawarikh* manuscripts, some of which display a close association with thrones and chairs used in China.[50] One of the popular types is the pedestal throne (Figure 5.16).[51] This type of throne is predominantly used for the scene of an enthroned ruler in frontal posture, as found in pre-Ilkhanid iconography.[52] The detail of the throne is, however, reminiscent of that of Chinese imperial thrones proper – for example, that depicted in a Song imperial portrait (Figure 5.15).[53] Both thrones are tinged with a red lacquer finish and are backed by a screen; the edges of the backrest are accentuated by dragon-headed carvings, evoking, as mentioned in the discussion of stone carving, those made of jade (Figure 3.20). The obvious difference is the use of a cushion in the Ilkhanid example – which is a remnant of Middle Eastern-type thrones.[54]

Another major type of throne is characterised by its tripartite backrest, high legs and footstool (Figure 5.12).[55] Although evidence for the use of triple panels in Chinese imperial thrones is scarce before the Ming period,[56] screen devices in general, such as free-standing painted screens, had prevailed in China since the Tang period.[57] The choice of patterns for the triple panel in the enthronement scenes is uneven, ranging from spiral to geometric.[58] In some thrones of this type, the boundless Iranian interest in East Asian themes is prominent in the adaptation of lotus or peony patterns for the decoration of the backrest.[59] It is possible to find similar flowery patterns in several media of Chinese decorative arts, but the patterns adapted for the backrest are particularly evocative of those

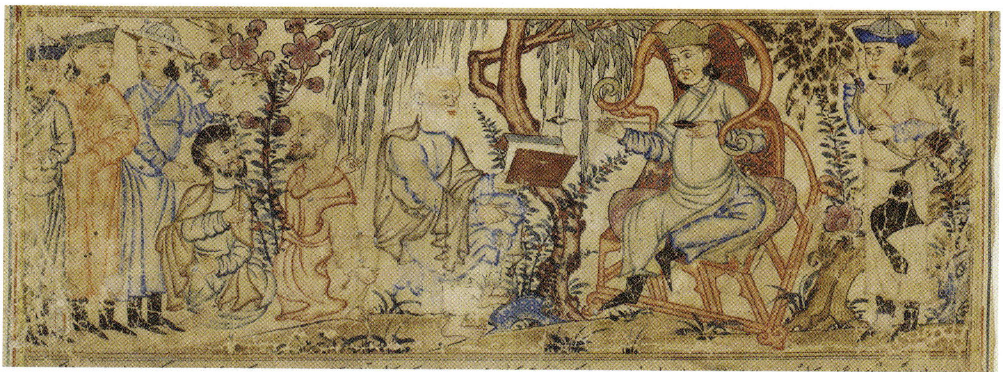

Figure 5.17 Jamiʿ al-Tawarikh *of Rashid al-Din:* Hushang, the King of the World. *Tabriz, 714/1314.*

used in lacquer wares of the thirteenth and fourteenth centuries (Figure 2.12).

Among folding chairs found in the enthronement scenes,[60] an imaginative throne depicted in the scene of Hushang (E3; Figure 5.17) is worth observation. While the horseshoe arm support of the upper part may have been derived from folding chairs used in contemporary China – for example, those identified in Yuan murals[61] – the open panelled dais composed of the bottom part seems to have been inspired by Chinese models of rather old-fashioned style.[62] The painters place pictorial emphasis on the detail of the throne, but their depiction is inaccurate in that the throne is rendered in a two-dimensional manner, showing a serious confusion of perspective. Thus, though archaeological and literary evidence for the actual use of the thrones discussed above in the Ilkhanid court is still limited, it is highly probable that Chinese-type thrones or chairs were known in Ilkhanid Iran.

Another distinctive feature of the enthronement scenes is the incorporation of curtains into the interior settings.[63] Curtains in the enthronement scene of Jamshid (Figure 5.16) are hung horizontally and are decorated with ribbons in places. This unique device appears to have been newly developed by Iranian painters, perhaps with the intention of giving the scene a more theatrical appearance, or to indicate awnings under the inspiration of Mongol tents. In pursuing the question of the Chinese associations of the curtain device in the *Jamiʿ al-Tawarikh*, one is tempted to compare it with the curtains often depicted in Chinese wall paintings of the thirteenth and fourteenth centuries. Very similar compositional ideas are in fact found in a Yuan mural discovered in Liaoning province,[64] where the curtains hung above a coffin, and the female attendants are well incorporated into the background, obeying compositional harmony. The curtains depicted in this Yuan mural are also comparable to those seen in the illustration of the bier of Mahmud ibn Sebuktegin

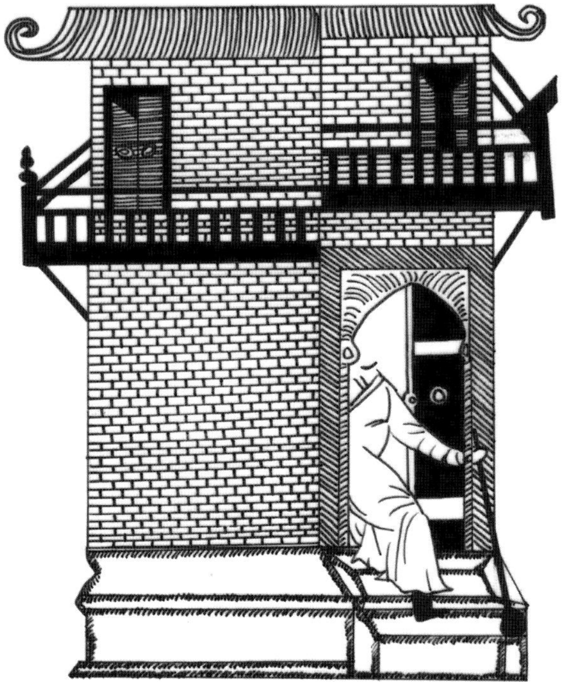

Figure 5.18 Jami' al-Tawarikh *of Rashid al-Din: City of Iram (detail). Tabriz, 714/1314.*

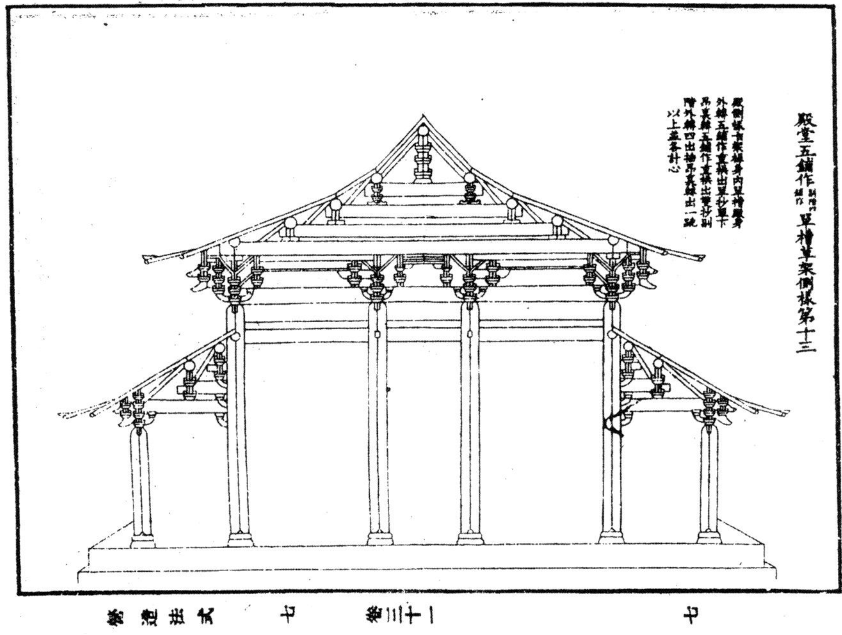

Figure 5.19 *Page from the* Yingzao fashi. *China, 1103.*

(E64)[65] in that curtains serve to solemnise a funeral ceremony. It is thus important to note that a variety of curtain devices were developed in both Iranian and Chinese pictorial arts under the Mongols.

The final point to be noted is the appearance of outlandish buildings, particularly those with horn-like projections at the four corners of the roof (Figure 5.18).[66] Rice identified this feature simply as a Chinese element without giving any concrete evidence.[67] But this type of roof ending is atypical of Song and Yuan buildings. As demonstrated in the Song manual of architecture entitled the *Yingzao fashi* (Figure 5.19), the standard Chinese roof of the period favours either straight or slightly curved lines but lacks strongly marked projections. In the case of important buildings, such as the main hall of a temple, a pagoda or a palace, the roof is dignified by its inward curve and upturned corners.[68] The corners are often decorated with animal figurines, but horn-shaped decoration for corners is unknown. Conceivably, when the traditions of Chinese architecture proper began to be known in Ilkhanid Iran, perhaps through Chinese architects, Chinese artists who served at the Ilkhanid court, or pictorial sources – for example, illustrations of Buddhist texts, maps and illustrated books[69] – the roof form of Chinese buildings was misunderstood. The curved line of the roof or the decoration of animal figurines was exaggerated by degrees, perhaps thereby implanting the image of buildings with horn-shaped roof endings in the minds of Ilkhanid artists. The painters of the *Jamiʿ al-Tawarikh* seem to have associated the roof with horned projections not so much with buildings in China as with those located in distant countries or imaginary places, for it occurs in scenes of the earthly paradise (Figure 5.18) and the temple of the Philistines (E15).[70] What is fascinating is that this Iranian reaction to Chinese artistic ideas has much in common with that of eighteenth-century European designers and architects – whose strong obsession with roof corners of unusual shape is evident in their chinoiserie designs, though these owe much to a superficial knowledge of Chinese architecture based on the reports of travellers and limited pictorial sources.[71]

To conclude this section, it should be emphasised that the painters of the *Jamiʿ al-Tawarikh* manuscripts broke the bond of an uneasy marriage of the old and new styles and succeeded in taking the art of painting to new heights, owing to their use of a much larger and more varied repertoire of landscape and other pictorial elements. The extensive use of Chinese landscape conventions in the Edinburgh and London codices invites serious discussion of their sources, especially woodblock prints. No printed examples of this form of Chinese art datable to the thirteenth and fourteenth centuries have been discovered in Iran, yet this is in the main due to the nature of paper – less durable than objects – and does not mean the unavailability of Chinese printed materials in Ilkhanid Iran. In fact, Rashid al-Din could not have completed the *Jamiʿ al-Tawarikh* without these;[72] his achievements, as a historian and a physician, undoubtedly owed something to direct access to Chinese medical texts and maps, through which he must have been aware of the potential role of paper and printing.[73] On the other hand, the illustrations of the manuscripts show tangible evidence of the introduction of costumes, furniture and architecture of East Asian origin into West Asia. Taken together, it is highly conceivable that the increased availability of printed sources as well as information about the art and culture of China could have familiarised Iranian painters with Chinese art traditions. The Iranian love for chinoiserie thus took a new turn, which held sway throughout the next generation.

The establishment of Rashidiyya conventions and the role of China

The next step is to observe the immediate effects of the aforementioned two Arabic copies of the *Jamiʿ al-Tawarikh* on other illustrated manuscripts attributable to the works of the Rashidiyya school and the diversification of Rashidiyya conventions. The works in question are two Persian copies of the *Jamiʿ al-Tawarikh* that are now held in the Topkapı Saray Museum, as well as detached manuscript paintings that are preserved in albums in Berlin and Istanbul. Both Istanbul and Berlin examples are of great value for reconstructing the stylistic changes that followed, and it is therefore necessary to place them securely in the history of Ilkhanid painting and to pinpoint their characteristics, taking account of their Chinese connections.

The Istanbul Jamiʿ al-Tawarikh

The two Persian copies of the *Jamiʿ al-Tawarikh* in Istanbul, known as Hazine 1653 (714/1314)[74] and Hazine 1654 (717/1317),[75] contain seventy-one miniatures (sixty-eight and three respectively) stylistically related to the Rashidiyya school. In general, the Ilkhanid illustrations of the Istanbul manuscripts reveal a certain stylistic indebtedness to the two Arabic copies of the *Jamiʿ al-Tawarikh* manuscripts in Edinburgh and London, such as horizontal formats, subdued colouring and emphases on outlines and shading; furthermore, these manuscripts share the same interest in iconography.

Pictorial themes in the Istanbul manuscripts are rich in variety, ranging from enthronement scenes, battle scenes to outdoor and indoor scenes. As in the enthronement scenes of the two Arabic manuscripts, the interior settings are enlivened by richly decorated thrones and satin-like curtains in the Istanbul manuscripts.[76] Two enthronement scenes found in folio 5, Hazine 1654, for instance, depict an enthroned ruler in the centre and courtiers grouped on either side, a pictorial layout that is typically used in the enthronement scenes of the Edinburgh and London manuscripts.[77] Comparison can also be made between folio 5^{v}, Hazine 1654, together with a

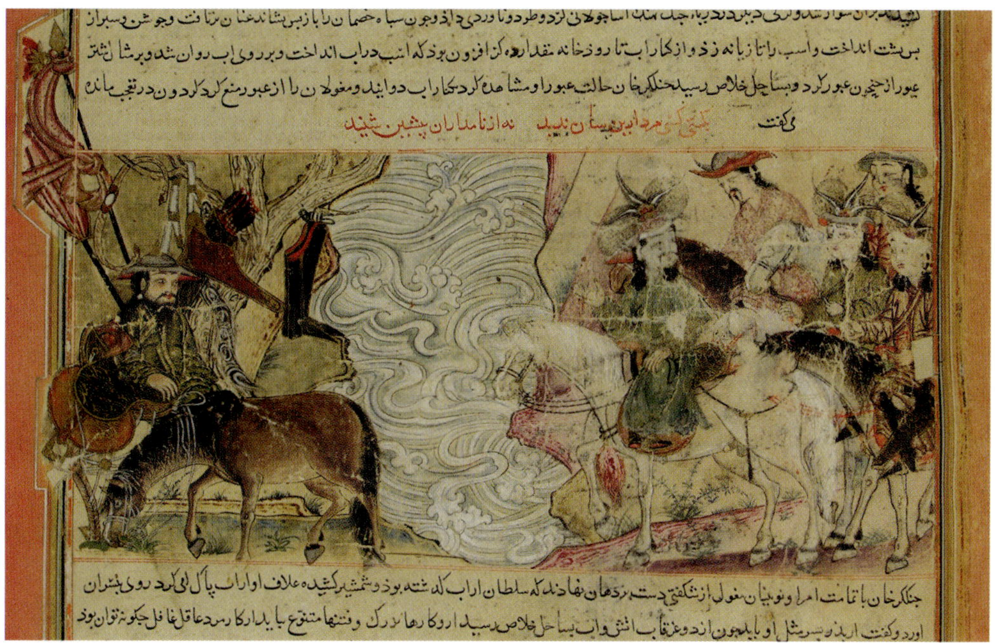

Figure 5.20 Jamiʿ al-Tawarikh *of Rashid al-Din:* Jalal al-Din and the Army of Genghis. *Tabriz, 714/1314. This fourteenth-century Persian copy of the* Jamiʿ al-Tawarikh, *which found its way to the library of Shahrukh (r. 807/1405–850/1447) as an incomplete volume, is now preserved in a manuscript together with a replacement text written by the Timurid historian Hafiz-i Abru (d. 833/1430).*

post-Ilkhanid illustration in folio 31^{v}, Hazine 1653, and the scene of Ibrahim captured into a fire in the Edinburgh portion (E7) in terms of iconographic treatment.[78] Yet figural types and costumes are visibly standardised and simplified in the Istanbul illustrations. The image is rather crowded with excessive pictorial elements, which makes it somewhat unbalanced.

Miniatures depicting exterior scenes show a certain degree of artistic response to Chinese landscape conventions. In folio 335, Hazine 1653 (Figure 5.20), an attempt is made to diversify the image of Mongol-clad riders and horses by means of a variety of landscape elements, including a rapidly flowing river in the centre. However, landscape here is not rendered in a wholly Rashidiyya manner. It is more likely that it owed much to earlier Ilkhanid manuscripts – for instance, the gnarled trees and the Mongol grass evoke those seen in the Morgan Bestiary (e.g. Figure 4.4). Above all, this picture lacks a sense of depth.

Similarly, battle scenes in the Istanbul manuscripts are evocative of those found in the Arabic manuscripts, such as the arrangement of lances and arrows on the ground in order to suggest a pictorial movement,[79] but they are not entirely reliant on the Rashidiyya convention. One of the predominant features is that not only clouds

– which are reminiscent of those found in the Edinburgh battle scene (Figure 5.11) – but also water sprays are deeply incorporated into the Istanbul battle scenes.[80] On the other hand, it remains unclear how far the painters of the Istanbul manuscripts were aware of the potential of other landscape elements, such as rocks and mountains, which play a pivotal role in the formation of landscape in the Arabic manuscripts.

A series of illustrations depicting Chinese emperors in the Istanbul manuscripts[81] are, from the iconographic point of view, rendered in the same way as in the London codex. Mongol-type robes and Chinese scholar caps are, yet again, inaccurately combined. However, some important decorative elements of the robes found in the London manuscript – for example, shading and indications of chest decoration – are absent in the images of Chinese emperors in the Istanbul manuscripts.

Thus, despite a certain association with the Edinburgh and London copies of the *Jamiʿ al-Tawarikh* manuscripts, the impact of Chinese pictorial and decorative arts was no longer vital in the Istanbul manuscripts. A certain degree of mannerism is observable in their pictorial style. Such paintings of rather pedestrian quality are, as Blair has pointed out,[82] indicative of the intention to speed up production and to reduce cost. Besides, a qualitative distinction between the Arabic and Persian copies of the *Jamiʿ al-Tawarikh* manuscripts may suggest that the Istanbul Persian copies were designed to be distributed throughout the Ilkhanid realm, while the Edinburgh and London Arabic copies were intended to be preserved in the Rabʿ-i Rashidi.[83]

The Diez Albums, group 1

Some forty leaves of the Diez Albums are relevant to the subject of this section.[84] Folio 71 contains eleven diminutive miniatures, each depicting a couple. All are similar in shape and size, and none bears texts.[85] These miniatures can be divided into two subgroups: an enthroned couple painted in vivid colour (Figure 5.21 – right and left images only) and a similar couple drawn in pale colour.[86] These two subgroups of miniatures are likely to have come from different manuscripts, but both share common features in terms of costumes and settings. All the couples are beautifully attired, indicating their high position in Mongol society. Men wear typical Mongol robes and feathered hats similar to those often depicted in the Edinburgh and London *Jamiʿ al-Tawarikh*. Women's costumes are also evidently of Mongol style. Their elaborate headdress, known as the *gugu*, is characterised by its chimney-like shape.[87] Yuan imperial portraits – for example, a portrait of Chabi executed by a Nepali artist[88] – point to the accuracy of the depiction of the *gugu* in the Diez miniatures. Such a distinctive headdress, presumably of Uighur origin,[89] seems to have been incorporated into Mongol costumes by the 1220s and

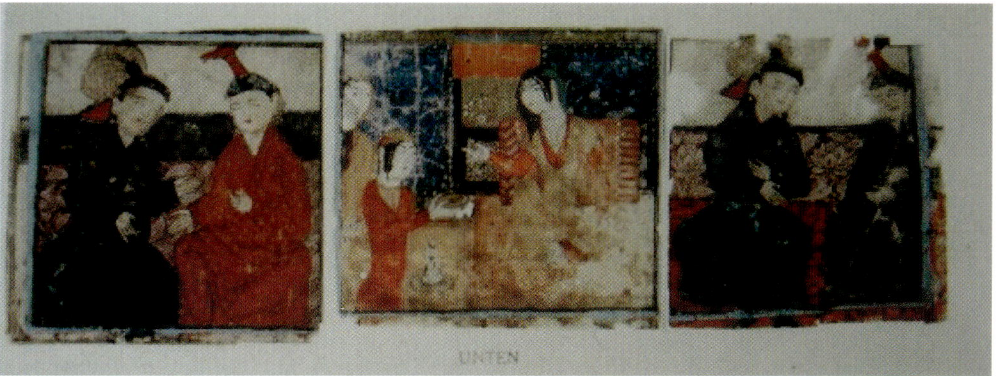

Figure 5.21 Mongol Ruler and Consort *(two scenes). Illustration from the Diez Albums. Probably Iran, early fourteenth century.*

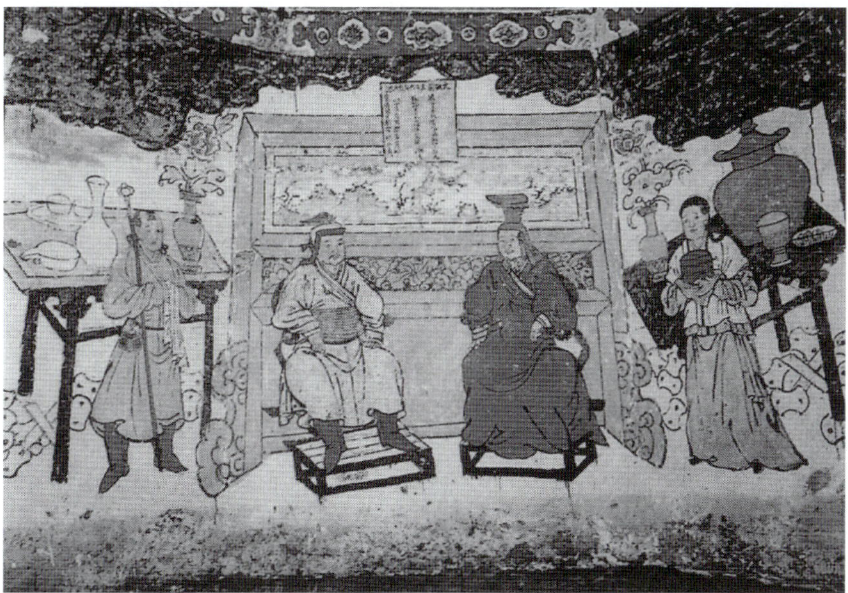

Figure 5.22 Mongol Couple. *Mural on the north wall of a tomb in Dongercun, Pucheng County, Shaanxi Province. China, c. 1270.*

became a component of formal dress in the Yuan court in order to single out the social rank of wearers.[90] The Diez miniatures are thus suggestive of the prevalence of this type of headdress in West Asia. In both subgroups of miniatures, couples take a relaxed pose devoid of formality.[91] They seem to be having a conversation with each other. Women are predominantly placed to the left side of men from the viewer's direction, following the traditional position used by the Mongols on ceremonial occasions.[92] Another point of interest is the representations of thrones. While the couples of the second subgroup of miniatures are seated on cushion-type thrones, the thrones depicted in the first subgroup have solid backrests with flower-based decoration. It remains uncertain, however, whether the choice of throne type reflects the painter's knowledge or a certain social hierarchy in Mongol society.

One of the most widespread explanations for the function of these small miniatures is that they were intended for use in the genealogy charts of the first volume of the *Jamiʿ al-Tawarikh* – namely, the *Tarikh-i Mubarak-i Ghazani*.[93] This is a most plausible interpretation, and, as in a Tashkent copy of the *Jamiʿ al-Tawarikh* manuscript (No. 1620, Abu Rayhon Biruni Institute of Orientology of the Uzbek Academy of Sciences),[94] the Diez miniatures may originally have been inserted in the beginning of the narrative of each Khan.[95] It is, however, also conceivable that these miniatures were, like some of the illustrations of Chinese emperors in the London *Jamiʿ al-Tawarikh* (Figure 5.14), put together to form a genealogical tree. The Diez miniatures thus appear to depict Genghis Khan's successors and their wives. Each face is rendered in a slightly different way, but its depiction is not sufficiently distinct to characterise each couple. This seems to have stemmed not so much from the lack of drawing skills as from the lack of intention to distinguish each couple by facial appearance, as revealed in Figure 5.21.[96]

It could plausibly be argued that the prototype of enthroned couples was indigenously developed in Iran. A seated couple is in fact a common theme in thirteenth-century Iranian ceramics,[97] and the tradition of depicting a couple was well incorporated into later Iranian painting.[98] Yet it is worth attempting in the context of this book to find other possible iconographic sources from contemporary Chinese examples. For example, there is an interesting parallel between the Diez miniatures and a number of Yuan murals found inside tombs that depict tomb occupants as a couple, in particular that discovered in Shaanxi (Figure 5.22). This Yuan mural is very comparable to the Diez miniatures in that the couple is seated and clad in traditional Mongol garb. The key difference is, however, that the Yuan mural produces a ritual atmosphere. This is because in China portraiture was closely associated with ancestor worship on the basis of Buddhist doctrine.[99] In addition to imperial portraiture, whose production was developed from the Song dynasty onwards,[100] portraiture became a popular subject to be painted on the walls of tombs among Mongol elites.[101] In spite of the discrepancies between the Diez miniatures and the Yuan murals in terms of function, the stylistic similarities between them raise the hypothesis that the Diez miniatures relied for their prototypes on Yuan sources, such as cartoons of portraits brought from China. In the light of the stylistic impact of Chinese murals on Ilkhanid painting, which has been emphasised in the previous discussion, the involvement of painters with a wall-painting background in the execution of the Diez miniatures is not entirely without foundation. Textiles are another possible medium that could have conveyed the style of Yuan portraiture to West Asia. The fact is that in Yuan China portraiture was not only painted but also woven into the silk textiles and tapestries used in religious rites.[102] The best-known example of Yuan religious textiles is a *mandala*, dated about 1330, now in the Metropolitan Museum of Art (1992.54),[103] in which the donors are depicted as a couple. The practice of producing *kesi* tapestries with portraiture can safely be traced back to the reign of Chengzong (1293–307), when, according to a historical record, numerous orders were given to produce painted cartoons depicting emperors and empresses, which were eventually to be woven in silk.[104] Of course, the Diez miniatures are merely suggestive of an association with Yuan portraiture, and thus the actual introduction of Yuan burial customs into Ilkhanid Iran remains speculative.[105]

The Diez miniatures depicting a couple, though small in size, provide much information about the Sino-Iranian artistic relationship under the Mongols. What has become certain from the above considerations is the role of murals and textiles in the artistic interaction across Mongol Eurasia. These two media must not be overlooked in any discussion of chinoiserie in Iranian art.

The second major group of miniatures consists of those evidently concerned with specific events described in the first volume of the *Jamiʿ al-Tawarikh*. Identification of some individual images has tentatively been made by some scholars,[106] yet, because of the lack of texts, it is difficult to reconstruct any of the sequences of their pictorial cycles with assurance. A more precise classification of these miniatures, according to their style, is also open to question. In this study, however, only those marked features of this group of miniatures that are relevant to the discussion of the development of the Rashidiyya style are considered.

On the whole, the reliance of this group of miniatures on drawing techniques used in the Edinburgh and London manuscripts is undeniable. Yet, in terms of landscape, architectural and facial representations, the painters of this group are not entirely subject to current pictorial fashion. This group of the Diez miniatures also differs from the Edinburgh and London illustrations in the way of depicting enthronement scenes.

There are two subgroups of miniatures containing landscape representations. In one subgroup, early Ilkhanid and Rashidiyya styles are well blended (Figure 5.23).[107] The picture shown here subtly displays a visual progression from right to left by using horses' steps and facial direction, suggesting a continuation to adjoining illustrations – for example, a picture that has recently been identified as a royal procession of Hulague's envoy (Fol. 71.S.50).[108] The landscape

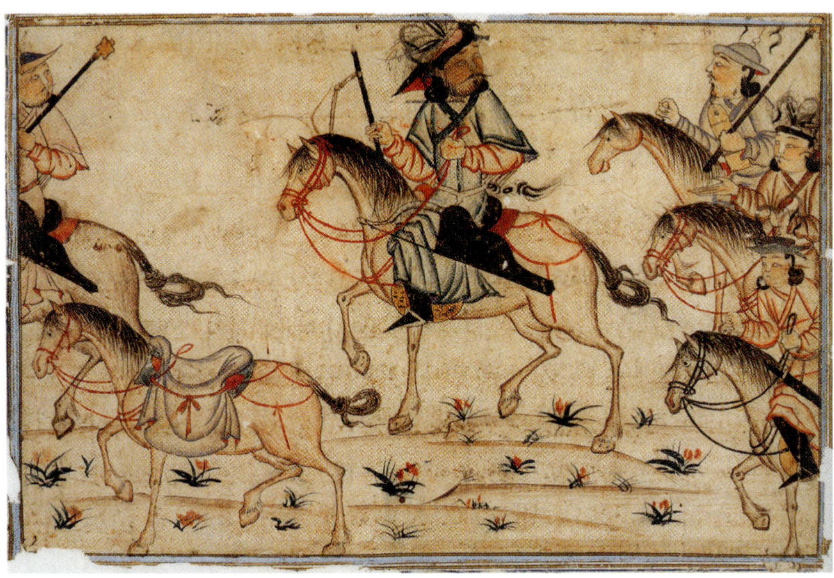

Figure 5.23 Mongol Travelling. *Illustration from the Diez Albums. Probably Iran, early fourteenth century.*

in this picture is simply composed of tufty grass and ground lines, and these two elements are arranged at appropriate intervals. The combination of horses and grassy lines bears a striking resemblance to that seen in earlier Ilkhanid painting – for example, the illustration of a mare in the *Manafiʿ-i Hayavan* (Figure 4.4). Besides showing the Rashidiyya preference for light and delicate drawing, the painters of this subgroup add the finishing touches of red to faces and flowers, making a good contrast with inky outlines. The mingling of early Ilkhanid and Rashidiyya conventions is also retained in another subgroup of miniatures (Figure 5.24).[109] These miniatures can be distinguished from the subgroup of miniatures mentioned above by their washes and the softer tones used in modelling figures and landscape elements. The landscape here, again, betrays an inclination to adopt earlier llkhanid conventions – for example, those used in the Morgan Bestiary – rather than Rashidiyya ones, for instance showing the revived interest in depicting clouds coiled around trees.[110] The rocks also remain mere duplications of early Ilkhanid models – for example, evoking those often depicted in the Morgan Bestiary and the Edinburgh al-Biruni (see, e.g., Figures 4.7, 4.14 and 4.24). Chinese themes are thus decidedly secondary.

In addition, battle scenes are of importance for discerning the developing style of landscape.[111] Despite the absence of distinctive landscape elements – for example, the jagged mountain edges conventionally used in the Edinburgh and London manuscripts – the careful arrangement of galloping horses and archers is sufficient

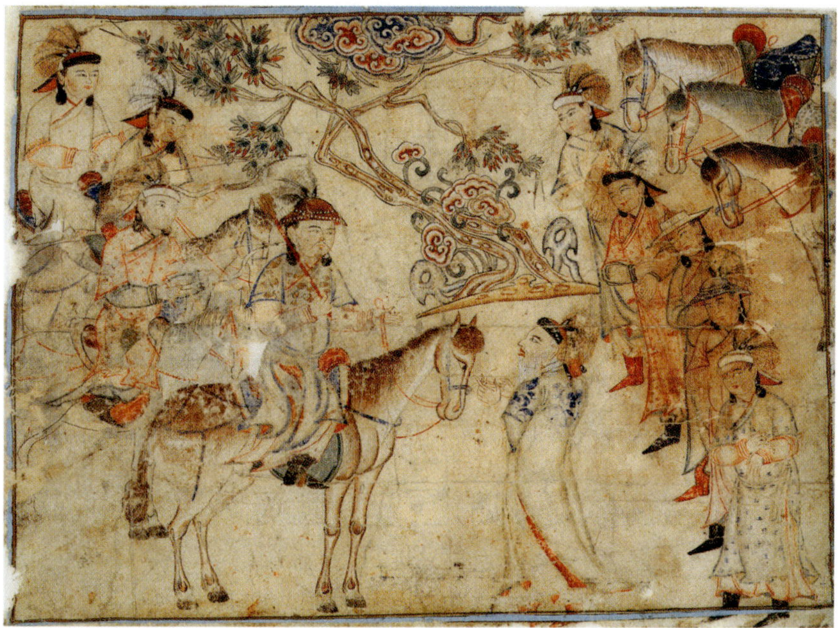

Figure 5.24 Negotiations. *Illustration from the Diez Albums. Probably Iran, early fourteenth century.*

to make the scene come alive. Some of the battle scenes are even more impressive for their theatrical display of fighting between two confronted armies.[112] Attention here is paid to a dramatic encounter of armies on each side of the river. The pulse of each troop of warriors is not expressed by their gestures, but the surging waves of the river are effective in implying the gradual increase in tension between the two sides. The same theatrical setting on the river side can be seen in the Istanbul *Jamiʿ al-Tawarikh* (Figure 5.20), suggesting a certain stylistic relation between the Istanbul and Berlin examples.

Another subgroup of miniatures can be defined according to the degree that they incorporate architectural settings. Three of this subgroup of miniatures, including two pictures associated with the episode of the *Capture of Baghdad* (Fol. 70.S.4 and S.7),[113] show a growing concern for the full-scale use of an architectural complex. The main interest lies in the depiction of a citadel on a proper scale, keeping the balance with other pictorial elements. This is noteworthy as evidence for the emerging post-Rashidiyya style, which is based not on landscape but on architecture, though the use of architectural settings in the Diez miniatures is still at an embryonic stage in comparison with the highly developed spatial conventions of Jalayirid and Timurid painting.[114] Examples of the partial use of an architectural complex are rare in the Diez Albums,

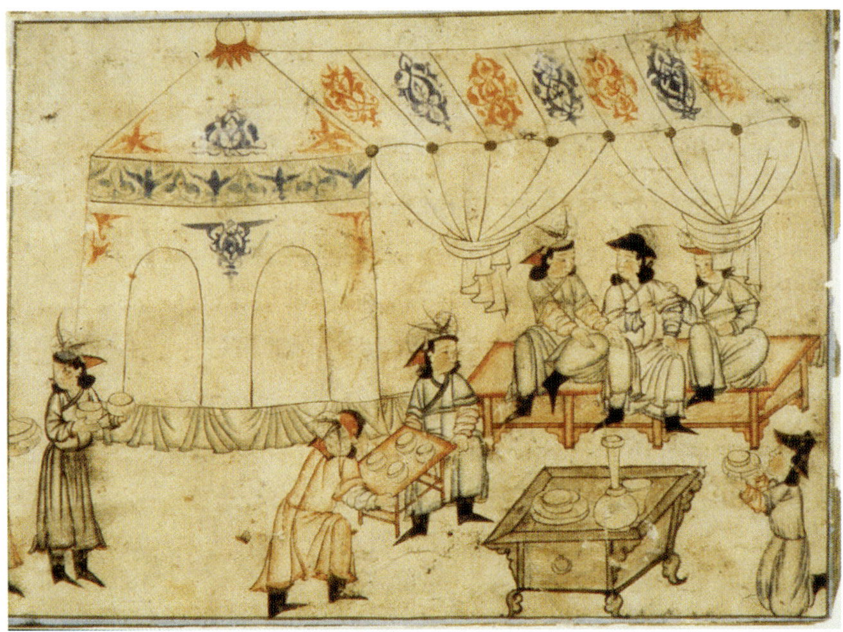

Figure 5.25 Preparations for a Banquet. *Illustration from the Diez Albums. Probably Iran, early fourteenth century.*

yet a fragmentary miniature associated with the *Jamiʿ al-Tawarikh*, which is now preserved in Paris (probably Iran, c. 1300–50; suppl. pers. 191, fos. 10 and 27, BN),[115] may have been a remnant of this convention coming into vogue at Rashidiyya workshops at that time. In the Paris example, a citadel standing on rocky crags is rendered in more subdued colour, owing to the delicate tones of red colour. In other Diez miniatures of this subgroup, tents too play their compositional role (Figure 5.25).[116] The painters make good use of a tent to dramatise some events described in the Mongol history of the *Jamiʿ al-Tawarikh*. The tent depicted here is indeed reminiscent of that portrayed by Muslim and Western travellers of the Mongol period[117] and of that still used among nomads in Mongolia, known as the *ger*.[118] The exterior of the tent is relatively simple; it has a white ground overlaid with blue or red patterns. The literary descriptions of the exterior decoration used in Mongol tents are not articulate enough to generalise, but the patterns depicted in this picture appear to be of Islamic rather than of Central Asian or Chinese origin.[119] Although not depicted here, the typical interiors of Mongol tents of the thirteenth and fourteenth centuries were, judging by the accounts of Muslim travellers,[120] ornate with hangings woven in gold. An extant set of oblong Mongol textiles richly decorated with medallions (Figure 1.14) is undoubtedly a masterpiece of its kind.

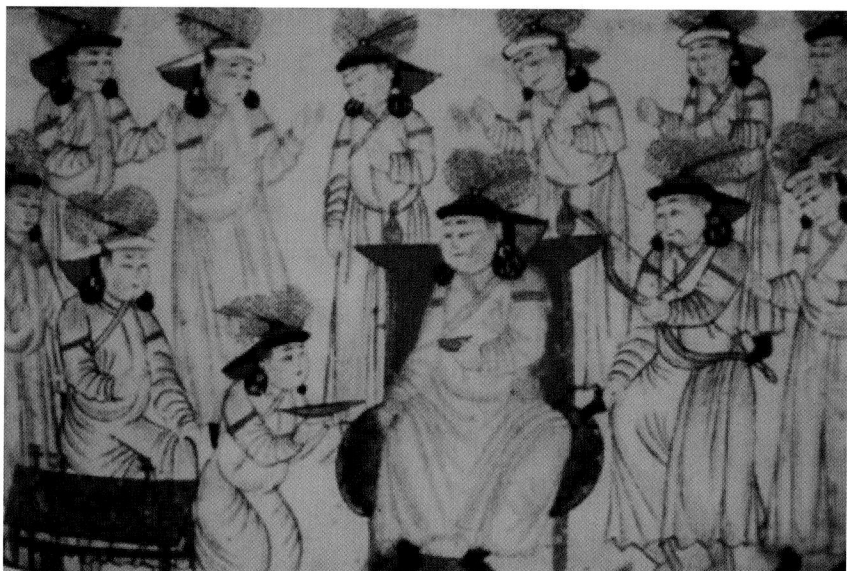

Figure 5.26 Enthroned Ruler Surrounded by Attendants. *Illustration from the Diez Albums. Probably Iran, early fourteenth century. This anonymous illustration is now found in the Diez Albums, together with other paintings and drawings from disparate sources. The ruler and attendants, who are neatly attired in Mongol garb, are placed in an enthronement setting, following Ilkhanid pictorial conventions.*

The third subgroup of miniatures is characterised by the subtle articulation of figural and facial features (Figure 5.26).[121] The painters deliberately show the stocky appearance and bold countenance of the men, all of whom wear feathered hats. Their faces are further highlighted by the lifelike depiction of almond-shaped eyes. A comparison between the Diez miniatures and the illustrations of the Anthology of *Diwans* (M132, BL),[122] dated between 713/1314 and 714/1315, serves to elucidate how this convention operated at Ilkhanid ateliers of the second decade of the fourteenth century. In the London Anthology, the approach to facial representation is much neater, thanks to the softness of outlines. Extra lines are added to the outer corner of the eyes of men, whether crowned or turbaned, with intent to depict them as Mongols. Some of them pucker up their mouths, while others have smiling faces. Such a variety of facial representations in the Berlin and London examples is symptomatic of the growth of physiognomic interest in the Mongols on the part of painters in Ilkhanid Iran. While in earlier Ilkhanid painting costumes help to identify a Mongol ethnic origin, the Diez examples show a more straightforward reaction to the facial peculiarities of the Mongols: their slant eyes, small mouths and round jaws seem to have left a great impression on Iranian painters of the period.

Interestingly, despite the coincidental increase of Chinese interest in the Mongols as an object to be depicted, representations of the Mongols in Yuan China differ significantly from those in Ilkhanid Iran: the physical properties of the Mongols in Chinese pictorial examples are, to a certain extent, modified to make them more acceptable to Chinese taste.[123] Eyes of the Mongols here are rounder than those depicted in the Diez miniatures; the use of delicate outlines and warm hues results in giving them gentle countenances. In Yuan imperial portraiture, Mongol rulers are clearly depicted as being of Chinese descent – namely, as the legitimate successors of Song emperors.[124]

The last point to be noted is that some painters of this group display a highly innovative compositional idea, which is particularly marked in enthronement scenes. Six large oblong miniatures depicting enthronements stand alone from the compositional point of view (Figure 5.27).[125] Three of the miniatures depict overcrowded scenes, whereas the remainder show an enthroned couple surrounded by courtiers and relatives. These miniatures are now separately mounted. Yet, judging by similar double-page structures found in post-Ilkhanid manuscripts of the *Jamiʿ al-Tawarikh*,[126] it may be assumed that the two different types of miniatures were bound together as double-page spreads in the second section of each narrative;[127] perhaps, as shown in Figure 5.27, an illustration of the couple may have been placed on the right page. It remains unclear whether these six leaves of the Diez Albums were originally in pairs or were derived from different manuscripts. Compared with the enthronement scenes illustrated in the Edinburgh and London manuscripts, more emphasis is laid on verticality than horizontality in the Diez miniatures. What they lack, however, is a sense of spaciousness. The predominant emphasis is on the groups of people, each of which is arranged in parallel lines without the aid of sparse grass or receding ground lines. This is insufficient to create a feeling of depth, with the result that each group of people is oddly present against a plain surface. The origin of this type of composition is rather puzzling. Approximately contemporary compositions can be found in the Istanbul Saray Albums (H.2153, fo. 23 and fo. 148v),[128] suggesting that this was not a style unique to the Berlin examples but an established style used at Rashidiyya workshops. An attempt to find Chinese sources for this composition might suggest a possible debt to how figures in illustrations of Buddhist texts are depicted (Figure 5.28), though in the Buddhist tradition the imagery of floating figures is essential for implying divinity and immortality. Stylistically, however, the Diez enthronement pictures have little aesthetic appeal. Figural types are rather standardised and undiversified. Clothing is emphatically delineated, displaying an awareness of Rashidiyya-style ink drawing, but its depiction seems to have lost some of the fineness of Rashidiyya drawing techniques.

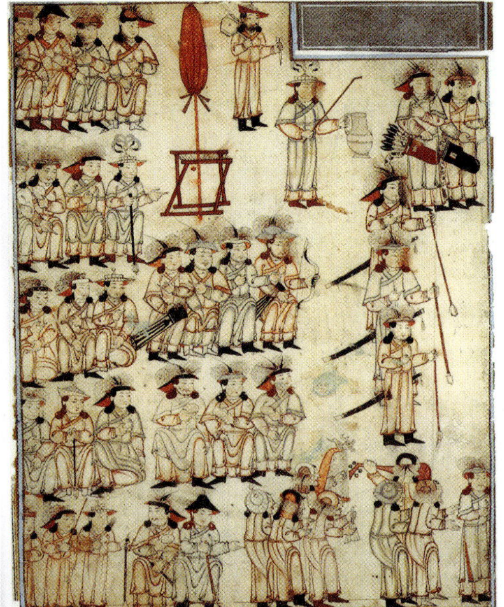

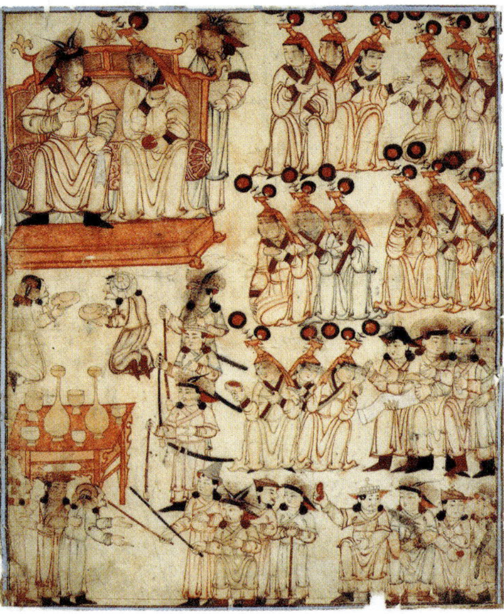

Figure 5.27 *Enthronement scenes. Illustrations from the Diez Albums. Probably Iran, early fourteenth century.*

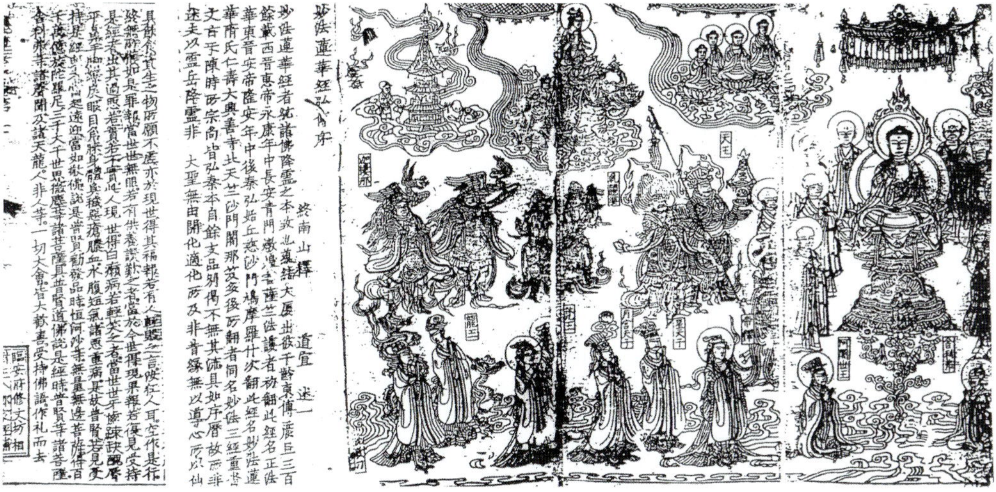

Figure 5.28 *Page from the Lotus Sutra. China, Southern Song dynasty.*

In conclusion, a group of early fourteenth-century miniatures in the Diez Albums offers glimpses into many different aspects of Iranian painting as a consequence of the upsurge in artistic activities in the Rashidiyya cultural complex. The discussion of the Diez miniatures has also certified the continuation of the far-flung artistic and cultural impact of China on Iran during the period between 1314 and 1335. Indeed, the Berlin leaves have a high documentary value concerning the history of early fourteenth-century Iranian painting; their significance should be reassessed as an equivalent to the two monumental manuscripts of the *Jami' al-Tawarikh* in Edinburgh and London.

Notes

1. For the Rab'-i Rashidi, see Wilber 1938; 1955, 129–31; Blair 1984. For the life of Rashid al-Din, see D. Morgan 1995.
2. MS 20: Rice 1976.
3. MS 727: Gray 1978; Blair 1995.
4. Blair 1995, 16–23.
5. The greatness of Tabriz was described by Polo and Ibn Battuta (Polo 1993, 1, 74–6; Ibn Battuta 1958–2000, 2, 344–5).
6. For a multi-religious phase of Ilkhanid Iran, see *CHI*, 5, 538–49. It is more likely to be the case that the Mongols were simply indifferent, not tolerant, to the religious beliefs of the peoples whom they conquered (Baldick 2000, 123).
7. Allsen 2001a, 197.
8. The first volume is the history of the Mongols, known as the *Tarikh-i Mubarak-i Ghazani*; the second one deals with the history of the rest of the world, parts of which correspond to the Edinburgh and London manuscripts; the third one, *Shu'ab-i Panjgana* ('the Five Genealogies'), is a sort of anthropological study of the Arabs, Jews, Mongols, Franks and Chinese; and the last volume, though still missing, is thought to have dealt with geography. For further discussion, see Jahn 1964.
9. See, e.g., Kadoi 2000.
10. For the painters of the *Jami' al-Tawarikh* manuscripts, see Rice 1970; 1976, 5–9; Ivanov 2000.
11. The Classic of Filial Piety (*Xiaojing*) was the most frequently illustrated of all the Confucian classics (Barnhart 1993, 74).
12. Except for 13 square and 1 stepped formats, most of the illustrations have rectangular formats (Blair 1995, 44).
13. The pages of the Edinburgh portion now measure 42 x 32 cm, while those of the Khalili portion measure 43.5 x 30 cm. Since the margins have been trimmed, the original pages of both manuscripts would have measured about 50 x 36 cm (Blair 1995, 38). The increased availability of paper may also have spurred an explosion in the production of large-sized illustrated manuscripts in Iran at that time. For further discussion of the role of paper in the development of Iranian painting, see Bloom 2000; 2001, 161–201.
14. Examples of clouds are relatively few in the Edinburgh and London manuscripts (e.g. E10, E36 and K2: Rice 1976, 58–9, 110–11; Gray 1978, 25). As will be discussed later, the role of clouds in the battle scenes appears to be different from their role in the historical scenes. The occurrence of grassy ground lines is also scarce in the manuscripts (e.g. E1, E3 and E19: Figures 5.17–18; Rice 1976, 76–7). The grass arranged in the background of the scene of the *Mi'raj* (E36: ibid.

110–11), is, for example, depicted as vegetation around the hill tops.
15. See also E2 (ibid. 42–3).
16. Ibid. 102–3.
17. Gray 1978, 37–8. It has been suggested that the composition of this painting was derived from deathbed scenes in Byzantine manuscripts (Allen 1985, 124).
18. As Rice (1976, 70–1) has noted, the painters' interest in imitating Chinese conventions languished from the illustration of Sultan Luhrasp (E16) onwards, perhaps because of a change of the master.
19. See, e.g., E9 (Figure 5.2), E17 (Rice 1976, 72–3), E19 (ibid. 76–7) and E21 (ibid. 80–1).
20. See, e.g., K27 (Gray 1978, 34–5), K29 (ibid. 36), K32 (ibid. 37) and K34 (ibid. 38).
21. For Rashid al-Din's Indian History, see Jahn 1965.
22. Gray 1978, 33.
23. Allsen 2001a, 84. For the life of Kamalashri, see Jahn 1956a. For the political relationship between Kashmir and the Mongol court, see Jahn 1956b.
24. Soucek 1980, 91.
25. Canby 1993b, 303. For this painter, see Cahill 1980, 84–5.
26. Blair 1995, 78.
27. *AP*, 138–40.
28. For this convention, see *CP*, 101–4, and in particular Qian Xuan's style (ibid. 102).
29. The book entitled the *Kongshi zuting guangji* was originally published in 1227 and was reprinted in 1242. The illustrations of this book have been mentioned by Bush (1965, 171–2) in her article on Jin painting.
30. Rice 1976, 113–14.
31. Ibid. 60–1.
32. Waves had been popular in ceramic design since the twelfth century (see, e.g., Wirgin 1979, pl. 8; Rawson 1984, fig. 101). Similar braking wave patterns are also found in Song bronze objects (Kerr 1990, pl. 31).
33. See also E25, E52 and E62 (Rice 1976, 88–9, 142–3, 162–3).
34. Gray 1978, 35–6, 38.
35. See E51 (Rice 1976, 140–1), E56 (ibid. 150–1).
36. The role of rocks in the battle scenes of the manuscripts has been discussed by Brend (1980, 115–17).
37. Costumes in the Edinburgh manuscript have been discussed by Rice (1976, 16–23).
38. See E9–E15 (Rice 1976, 56–69) and K28–K35 (Gray 1978, 35–8).
39. See E29–E32 (Rice 1976, 96–103) and K1–K3 (Gray 1978, 24–5). For further discussion of the images of Muhammad in the Edinburgh manuscript, see Hillenbrand 2000a.
40. The Mongol arms and armour depicted in early fourteenth-century Iranian painting have been discussed by Gorelik 1979, 38–41. See also Nicolle 1990.
41. See, e.g., Tonko bunbutsu kenkyusho (ed.) 1982, 5, cat. no. 162. For Mongol costumes depicted in Yuan murals, see Shen 2001.
42. Similar Mongol robes are now preserved in several museums outside China and Mongolia (e.g. Thompson 2004, cat. no. 18; Paris 2007, cat. no. 13).

43. For this painting, see Fong and Watt 1996, 269–72.
44. N. A. Stillman 1986. It is said that Abaqa received a robe of honour from Khubilai at the time of his investiture to symbolise his authority (Allsen 2001a, 25).
45. See, e.g., *Legacy*, cat. no. 75.
46. Investiture ceremonies were of profound importance in Mongol society, not just because they demonstrated royal majesty but because they created a sense of solidarity (Allsen 2001b, 309). According to Allsen, participants were required to wear a robe of one colour in the Mongols' *jisün* feasts, which served to create a sense of separation from outsiders and moreover to reduce the social distance between the participants (ibid.).
47. Although this does not occur so often, turbans are sometimes used in conjunction with Mongol robes (see E65, K23 and K30–K31: Rice 1976, 168–9; Gray 1978, 32, 36–7).
48. The classification of headgear in the manuscripts has been made by Schroeder and Rice (Schroeder 1939, fig. 1; Rice 1976, 20–3).
49. See, e.g., a page of the Vienna Galen (A.F.10, fo. 1^{v}, Nationalbibliothek; Brandenburg 1982, pl. 22). See also a leaf depicting the genealogical trees of the Timurids (Hazine 2152, fo. 33^{v}, TSM; Lentz and Lowry 1989, fig. 37).
50. For further discussion, see Donovan 1988–9.
51. See also E4, E6, E8 and E65–E68 (Rice 1976, 46–7, 50–1, 54–5, 168–75).
52. See Otto-Dorn 1982; Donovan 1988–9, 3–16.
53. Very few thrones or chairs are known to have survived from before the Ming period. Judging by literary and visual evidence, the use of chairs in China can safely be traced back to the Tang dynasty. For further discussion of the development of chairs in China, see Fitzgerald 1965.
54. Donovan 1988–9, 24. See, e.g., *AP*, 114.
55. See also E16, E18, E20, E26–E27, E34, E47, E50, E69, E70, K22–K23 and K30–K31 (Rice 1976, 70–1, 74–5, 78–9, 90–3, 106–7, 132–3, 138–9, 176–9; Gray 1978, 32, 36–7). Similar thrones can be found in the Edinburgh al-Biruni (fo. 133^{v}; Soucek 1975, fig. 19).
56. See, e.g., Stuart and Rawski 2001, fig. 3.11.
57. Wu (1996) has discussed the development of screens in China. For Chinese triple screen panels depicted in thirteenth-century painting, see ibid., figs 124–5, 134 and 136.
58. For further discussion, see Donovan 1988–9, 41–64.
59. In particular, see E16 and E18 (Rice 1976, 70–1, 74–5).
60. See E4, E8, E65 and E69 (Rice 1976, 46–7, 54–5, 168–9, 176–7). A folding chair is also depicted in the scene of *Ibrahim Catapulted into a Fire* (E7; ibid. 52–3). For folding chairs in the Middle East, see Kurz 1972.
61. Rawson 1984, 150; Donovan 1988–9, 20. For relevant Yuan murals, see *ZMQ*: Painting, 12, 68, pl. 184.
62. Donovan 1988–9, 20–2.
63. See E4, E6, E8, E14, E45 and E65–E68 (Rice 1976, 46–7, 50–1, 54–5, 66–7, 128–9, 168–75).
64. See *ZMQ*: Painting, 12, pls 169, 184, 186.
65. Rice 1976, 166–7.
66. See also E15 (Rice 1976, 68–9). For representations of architecture

in the Edinburgh and London manuscripts, see Barrucand 1986a, 131–6.

67. Rice 1976, 41, 69.
68. For Southern Song temples and pagodas, see *Sekai*, 6, pls 234–6, 244.
69. See, e.g., Chen, Wu and Yue (eds) 1999, 12–13, 16, 124–6; Chen and Ma 2002, 24–5, 47–50.
70. Rice 1976, 68–9.
71. See, e.g., Impey 1977, 143–59.
72. Rashid al-Din began to be acquainted with Mongolian and Chinese history through various printed materials brought from China, including the *Altan Debter* and the *Secret History*. See Franke 1951; Allsen 2001a, 88–90.
73. For his medical and cartographic works, see Allsen 2001a, 103–4, 107, 144–6. For his interest in Chinese printing, see ibid. 179–80.
74. Hazine 1653: Aga-Oglu 1934; Ettinghausen 1955; İnal 1965; 1975, 115–43.
75. Hazine 1654: İnal 1963. Ilkhanid illustrations found in Hazine 1653 and Hazine 1654 have long been neglected since İnal's study on these manuscripts. Hazine 1653 was exhibited at the Turks exhibition in 2005 (*Turks*, cat. no. 34).
76. For other enthronement scenes in Hazine 1653, see (unpublished otherwise cited) fos 277^{v}, 280^{v}, 301 (İnal 1975, fig. 1), 303^{v} (İnal 1965, pl. XIB), 304, 306, 308^{v} (ibid., pl. XIII), 310, 311^{v}, 313 (ibid., pl. XIVA), 316 (ibid., pl. XIVB), 317, 320, 322 (ibid., pl. XVIA), 323, 325^{v} (ibid., pl. XVIB), 362 (ibid., pl. XXVB), 373 and 375^{v} (ibid., pl. XXVA). One enthronement scene is set outside (fo. 268^{v}).
77. Cf. fo. 5, Hazine 1654 (İnal 1992, fig. 2; one illustration only) and E5–E6 (Rice 1976, 49–52). See Blair 1995, 91.
78. See Rice 1976, 53–4.
79. See fos 269^{v}, 283 (İnal 1963, pl. VIB) and 376 in Hazine 1653.
80. For other battle scenes with clouds in Hazine 1653, see fos 165^{v} (İpşiroğlu 1980, no. 9), 169 (İnal 1965, pl. IIB) and 291^{v} (ibid., pl. VIIB). For those with water sprays in the same manuscript, see fo. 347^{v} (Grube 1975, pl. 3B).
81. Published in Jahn 1971.
82. Blair 1995, 90–2.
83. Ibid. 92.
84. After İpşiroğlu's publication of an incomplete catalogue of the Diez Albums in 1964, the Albums were remounted and renumbered in a conservation project undertaken in 1971–2 (Appel and George 1971). However, the catalogue of the Albums has not yet been revised. Rührdanz's article is perhaps the first comprehensive study of the Diez Albums, which attempts to reconstruct fourteenth-century miniatures dealing with the *Jamiʿ al-Tawarikh* (Rührdanz 1997). Some leaves of the Diez Albums were displayed in recent exhibitions (see *Legacy*, cat. nos 17–32; Bonn/Munich, cat. nos 279–309).
85. S.41.Nr.4 (unpublished), S.42.Nr.4 (Figure 5.21 right), S.42.Nr.6 (Figure 5.21 left), S.45.Nr.5 (unpublished; woman image only), S.46.Nr.6 (unpublished), S.63.Nr.1 (*Legacy*, fig. 133), S.63.Nr.2 (ibid.), S.63.Nr.3 (ibid.), S.63.Nr.5 (ibid.), S.63.Nr.6 (ibid.) and S.63.Nr.7 (ibid.).
86. See, e.g., Fol. 71. S.63. Nr.2–Nr.3, Nr.5–Nr.7 (ibid.).
87. For this headgear, see Boyer 1952, 17–18; Basilov (ed.) 1989, 112–13.

88. See Jing 1994. See also the *gugu* found in Yuan wall painting (Tonko bunbutsu kenkyusho (ed.) 1982, 5, cat. no. 161).
89. See Franke 1978, pl. 2; Yaldiz et al. 2000, pl. 326; *Turks*, cat. no. 14. Allsen (1997, 16) has briefly discussed its origin.
90. Jing 1994, 72.
91. For further information about sedentary postures in Turco-Mongol iconography, see Esin 1970–1.
92. Both Carpini and Rubruck refer to this position (cited in Steinhardt 1990–1, n. 29). There are, however, exceptions (S.41.Nr.4 and S.63. Nr.1), indicating that some painters did not understand the significance of this position. See also Figure 5.27.
93. Roxburgh 1995, 116; Rührdanz 1997, 297–8. It is also possible to assume that they belonged to the third volume of the *Jamiʿ al-Tawarikh*, namely the *Shuʿab-i Panjgana*, perhaps in the section of Turco-Mongol dynasties (Esin 1979, 290).
94. No. 1620: Ismailova et al. 1980, 20–3, pls 1–2; Poliakova and Rakhimova 1987, 264–5, pls 6–8. Since the Tashkent manuscript was not available for consultation at the time of writing this book, I was obliged to rely on Ismailova's short caption for this manuscript.
95. Ismailova et al. 1980, 22; Rührdanz 1997, 298.
96. For instance, very similar miniatures are placed in the beginning of the story of Ogodai and of Hulagu in the Tashkent copy (Ismailova et al.1980, 22; Poliakova and Rakhimova 1987, 264, pls 6–7).
97. See, e.g., Atıl 1973, nos.41–2.
98. See, e.g., Grabar and Blair 1980, pl. 56. A rare example of the image of a Mongol royal couple is found in a Jacobite–Syrian Lectionary of Gospels (Mosul, 1260; fo. 223^{v}, Siriaco 559, Biblioteca Apostolica, Vatican City), which is identifiable as Hulagu and his wife, Doquz Khatun (Leroy 1964, fig. 99-2; Fiey 1975, 23).
99. Stuart and Rawski 2001, 40–1.
100. For Song imperial portraits, see Fong and Watt 1996, 141–3.
101. For further discussion of Yuan murals, see Steinhardt 1990–1.
102. Stuart and Rawski 2001, 41.
103. *WSWG*, no. 25.
104. Ibid. 60–1; Stuart and Rawski 2001, 41.
105. As yet little is known about Ilkhanid murals. To take one example of the surviving Ilkhanid mausoleums, the interior of the mausoleum of Uljaitu (Figure 6.14), Sultaniyya, is decorated with curved and painted plaster. The design is, however, based on geometric patterns, resembling those used in contemporary book illumination (see Sims 1982; 1988). For fourteenth-century fresco decoration in central Iran, see Kadoi 2005b.
106. See, e.g., Barthold and Rogers 1970; Brentjes 1978; Blair 2005.
107. See also Fol. 70.S.18.N.2 (Rührdanz 1997, fig. 6) and Fol. 70.S.22 (*Legacy*, fig. 84, cat. no. 19).
108. Blair 2005. The oval object attached to the body of a bearded man who precedes the entourage has been identified as a *paiza* (ibid. 50).
109. For other miniatures of this group, see Fol. 71.S.57 (unpublished) and Fol. 72. S.16.Nr.1 (Rührdanz 1997, Abb. 10).
110. See Schmitz 1997, figs 20–1.
111. See Fol. 70.S.9.Nr.1 (unpublished), Fol. 70.S.19.Nr.1 (İpşiroğlu 1964, Tafel VI), Fol. 71.S.58 (Kühnel 1959a, Tafel 5), Fol. 71.S.59 (Bonn/ Munich, cat. no. 282; mirror image), Fol. 71.S.60 (Bonn/Munich,

cat. no. 284), Fol. 71.S.61 (unpublished) and Fol. 72.S.17 (unpublished).

112. See, e.g., Fol. 70.S.9.Nr.2 (unpublished).
113. For these miniatures, see Brentjes 1978. An architectural complex with a domed building found in Fol. 70. S.13 has been identified as the Gunbad-i ʿAli, the tomb of Ghazan (Rührdanz 1997, 300–1, Abb. 5).
114. For a study of space in Timurid painting, see Hillenbrand 1992.
115. Suppl. pers. 191: Richard 1997a, no. 15.
116. See also Fol. 70.S.8.Nr.1 (İpşiroğlu 1964, Tafel VIII) and Fol. 70.S.18.Nr.1 (*Legacy*, 251–2, fig. 86, cat. no. 30). See also tents depicted in an illustration of the Edinburgh codex (E55; Rice 1976, 148–9).
117. Allsen 1997, 13–16.
118. For Mongol tents, see Berger and Bartholomew 1995, 20–2. See also Andrews 1999, 271–665.
119. See tents depicted in the *Varqa va Gulshah* (Hazine 841, TSM; fos 26^{v}, 27^{v}, 34^{v}, 40, 41, 42, 43^{v} and 46; Melikian-Chirvani 1970b, figs 26–7, 34, 39, 40–1, 43 and 46) and those found in the Istanbul 731/1330 *Shahnama* (Hazine 1479, TSM; Rogers, Çağman and Tanındı 1986, figs 33, 40).
120. Allsen 1997, 13–16.
121. See also Fol. 71.S.47 (Bonn/Munich, cat. no. 287), Fol. 71.S.48 (unpublished), Fol. 71.S.49 (Rührdanz 1997, Abb. 8), Fol. 71.S.52 (ibid., Abb. 2), Fol. 71.S.55 (*Legacy*, fig. 122), Fol. 71.S.56 (ibid., fig. 161), Fol. 71.S.63.Nr.4 (ibid., fig. 133) and Fol. 72.S.16.Nr.2 (Rührdanz 1997, Abb. 10).
122. M132: Robinson 1976, 4–10.
123. See, e.g., Taipei 2001, pl. I-13, 291; Fong 1992, pls 25, 62, fig. 83.
124. Jing 1994, 73-4.
125. See also Fol. 70.S.5 (Bonn/Munich, cat. no. 286), Fol. 70.S.10 (ibid.), Fol. 70.S.11 (Rührdanz 1997, Abb. 3) and Fol. 70.S.21 (ibid.).
126. For example, see a late fourteenth-century copy of the *Tarikh-i Mubarak-i Ghazani* (fos 154^{v}–155; MS 1820, Reza Library, Rampur; Blair 1995, figs 60–1). Rührdanz has compared the Diez double-page miniatures with those seen in the Paris *Jamiʿ al-Tawarikh* (Herat, c. 1430; suppl. pers. 1113, fos 227^{v}–228, BN; Rührdanz 1997, 299).
127. Rührdanz 1997, 298; Blair 1995, 95.
128. Rogers, Çağman and Tanındı 1986, 69, pls 43–4. Hazine 2153 contains miscellaneous manuscript paintings, whose dates range from the early fourteenth century to the middle of the fifteenth century (see, e.g., Ettinghausen 1959b, 52–6, figs 6–7 and recently Istanbul 2004; *Turks*, cat. nos 100–41, 143). There is no space to discuss the detail of these miniatures, except to note that they were certainly executed by the painters with the same artistic background as those involved in the production of the Diez miniatures. For further discussion, see Karamağarali 1966–8.

CHAPTER SIX

Manuscript Painting 3

The divergence of chinoiserie traditions in Iranian painting

HAVING ASSESSED THE development of the Iranian understanding of Chinese artistic traditions and the reception of Chinese themes in the capitals of the Ilkhanid dynasty up to the second decade of the fourteenth century, we can now turn to the subject of what happened in the pictorial arts produced in other areas of Ilkhanid territory, especially in the semi-autonomous regions in central Iran during the Mongol period, and of how the Iranian reaction to Chinese pictorial and decorative arts was reflected in the manuscript painting of local provincial schools. To consider this issue may seem to be inconsistent with the chronological discussion of Iranian painting adopted in the previous chapter. Yet this approach will help, not only in better comprehending the degree of adoption and adaptation of Chinese artistic themes in early fourteenth-century Iranian painting as a whole, but also in offering a further insight into the artistic relationship between China and Iran during the Mongol period. Another aim of this chapter is to give a clear view of the revolutionary development of both style and technique of Iranian painting during the four decades of the fourteenth century, which was achieved in a remarkable manner by the painters of the Great Mongol *Shahnama*.

The Small Shahnama manuscripts

The manuscripts to be discussed first are the earliest surviving copies of illustrated *Shahnama* manuscripts; they are generically, though not entirely accurately, known as the Small *Shahnamas*.[1] The term is generally used to refer to a *Shahnama* with small-size miniatures, most of which are now housed in the Freer Gallery of Art, Washington, DC, and the so-called First and Second Small *Shahnamas*, whose miniatures are scattered throughout the world. The importance of the Small *Shahnama* manuscripts has been much emphasised in the study of fourteenth-century Iranian painting, especially in the context of the iconographical development of *Shahnama* illustrations.[2] However, the Small *Shahnama* manuscripts have not generally been taken as evidence for how Iranian painting developed stylistically under the inspiration of Chinese art. This is partly due to the former attribution of the Small *Shahnama* manuscripts to Isfahan or Shiraz,[3] whereby preconceptions about manuscript painting executed in early fourteenth-century central and southern Iran – *horror vacui*, patterned designs and a two-dimensional setting – seem to have discouraged scholars from looking closely at any impact that might conceivably have been exerted by Chinese pictorial and decorative arts. Even after Simpson's detailed study of the Small *Shahnama* manuscripts, in which she proposed Baghdad and about 1300 as the provenance and date of these manuscripts,[4] most remarks on Chinese elements in the Small *Shahnama*s feature brief and somewhat shallow comments on the Mongol features of stocky personages and Chinese-inspired landscape elements. Yet chinoiserie does certainly occur in the Small *Shahnama* manuscripts. Besides showing the inheritance of sinicising motifs from late thirteenth- and early fourteenth-century painting produced in the western parts of Ilkhanid territory, some distinctive landscape elements and costumes place the Small *Shahnama* manuscripts in a unique position in the history of the chinoiserie traditions in Iranian painting.

These points direct attention towards reconsidering the provenance of the Small *Shahnama*s. Of course, in terms of chinoiserie, the miniatures of the Small *Shahnama* manuscripts differ in many details from those executed around the Ilkhanid capitals, and it seems inappropriate to discuss the impact of Chinese artistic traditions on all manuscript paintings of Ilkhanid date as if they came out of a single workshop. Rather, one would expect different versions of chinoiserie at different workshops in Ilkhanid territory.

Although the manuscripts share the same basic composition of landscape, the degree of the retention of pre-Mongol Central Asian and thirteenth-century Mesopotamian conventions and of the adaptation of newly acquired Chinese conventions varies from manuscript to manuscript. Mesopotamian or Central Asian conventions are predominantly used in the depictions of landscape in the Freer Small *Shahnama* manuscript. Some basic landscape elements are often present against the gold background, but each element is rendered in a two-dimensional manner, which merely increases the impression of pattern-like designs. The painters characteristically depict a green gently sloping hillock with a bunch of flowers at the feet of hunting or standing persons.[5] The hillock is presumably meant to be grassy ground, but no attention is paid to the detail of the grass; the decorative arrangement of flowers or plants recalls those often seen in thirteenth-century Mesopotamian painting. Moreover, since no receding lines of grass are used to suggest distance, little spatial development is observable in the miniatures of the Freer Small *Shahnama*. Compared with the mountains of the

*Jami*ᶜ *al-Tawarikh* – for example, those atmospherically depicted in the illustration of *The Mountains of India* (Figure 5.6) – the rocky mountains of the Freer Small *Shahnama*, in which there is no indication of shading and perspective, are far from a literal description of such features. The height of the mountains is highlighted by means of multiple shadowy wavy lines, perhaps intended to depict overlapping mountain ranges.[6] This mountain convention is more closely associated with that used in Central Asian painting of the pre-Mongol period (Figure 6.5).[7] Clouds are often represented in outside scenes, and they are mostly of a *lingzhi* style. Most of the floating clouds, which are now heavily oxidised, seem to have owed much to their Chinese prototypes, namely cloud patterns derived from Chinese textiles – whose significance has been referred to repeatedly in the preceding chapters. Such a landscape setting, consisting of green hills, spongy mountains and wispy clouds, became a set image, especially in the background of the hunting scenes of Bahram Gur.[8] Since, however, the painters do not successfully manipulate grass, mountain and clouds as free pictorial elements, artistic unity is somehow missing in the landscape of the Freer Small *Shahnama*. This seems to have resulted in a separation of people and landscape.

Much more can be said about the rendering of landscape and its Chinese connections in the First Small *Shahnama* manuscript. As seen in the illustration of *Bahram Gur Kills the Dragon* (Figure 6.1), each landscape element is rendered with a more naturalistic bent. Both people and animals are well incorporated into the landscape. The foreground is filled with distinctive spiralling grass, recalling the type often seen in the London Qazwini (Figure 4.17, top and middle). Anonymous flowering plants are arranged at appropriate intervals on the grassy border. Some of the tall plants apparently play a compositional role, whereas others function as mere space-fillers. Other landscape elements, such as clouds and mountains, are also found in the First Small *Shahnama* (Figure 6.2). Floating *lingzhi*-style clouds bear a great resemblance to those that occur in the Freer manuscript.[9] Each cloud is attached to its neighbours, and consequently the clouds appear to be flying ribbons. In the scene of Faridun and Zahhak (Figure 6.2), however, one more advanced idea can be seen in the representation of Mt Damavand. The painters superbly visualise Zahhak silhouetted against the mountain, which is certainly effective in conveying his agony.

What is unique in the landscape of the First Small *Shahnama* is that, as seen in the illustration of Zahhak, the painters vividly depict the sun with brilliant rays.[10] This may have stemmed from the text, which describes the landscape setting articulately enough to evoke the image of the sun.[11] Another possibility is that its prototype came from contemporary Ilkhanid pictorial and decorative arts. The sun of the First Small *Shahnama* is more realistically depicted than

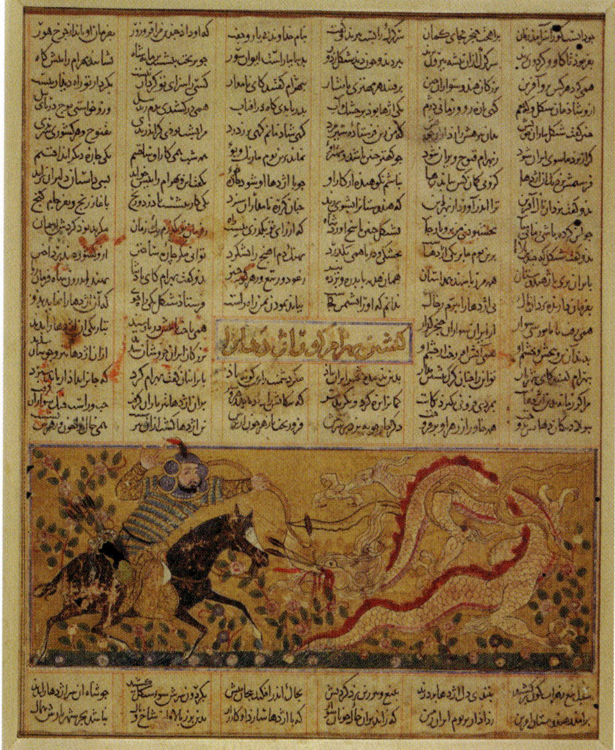

Figure 6.1 Bahram Gur Kills the Dragon. *Page from the First Small* Shahnama. *North-west Iran or Baghdad, c. 1300.*

those seen in Mesopotamian painting – for example, the Paris *Kitab al-Diryaq*.[12] Perhaps the sun in the two illustrations of the Arabic copies of the *Jamiʿ al-Tawarikh* is the best counterpart.[13] The sun has astrological significance in the Middle East, and is often represented in the decorative arts as a human face surrounded by rays.[14] In the interior decoration of thirteenth- and fourteenth-century metalwork, the sun is often encircled by fish and whorl patterns. Baer has interpreted the so-called fish-pond ornament as an allegory of the source of life.[15] On the other hand, any Chinese association with the sun of the Small *Shahnama*s remains dubious: the use of the sun here is unlikely to be the result of the impact of Chinese landscape painting, for landscape painters of the Song and Yuan periods seem to have preferred to depict cloudy and misty scenery and to have been less fascinated with depicting a clear sky with the radiant sun.[16] Despite its great significance in Chinese thought – for example, *yang*, one of the principal forces in the universe, stands for the sun and light[17] – the sun was rarely adapted for use among the decorative patterns of Chinese ceramics, metalwork and textiles throughout the ages.

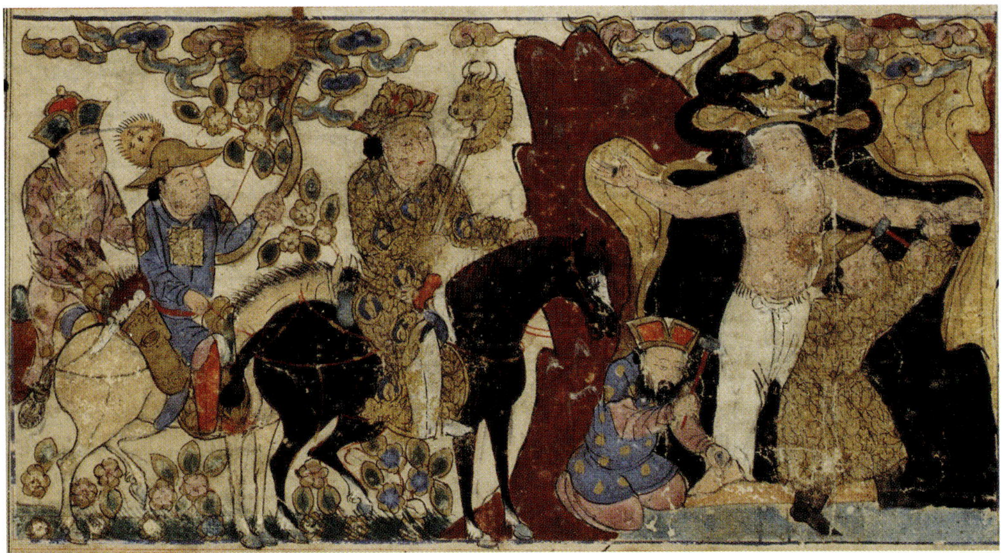

Figure 6.2 Faridun Binds Zahhak to Mt Damavand. *Page from the First Small* Shahnama. *North-west Iran or Baghdad, c. 1300.*

In spite of an awareness of Ilkhanid landscape conventions, the painters of the Second Small *Shahnama* were unable to follow and adopt them satisfactorily. In fact, the landscape of the Second Small *Shahnama* remains simple and shows little evidence for the direct impact of Chinese pictorial arts. The Second Small *Shahnama* can clearly be distinguished from the Freer and the First Small *Shahnama* manuscripts in that, instead of spiralling-grass borders, wavy ground lines are predominantly used on the bottoms of the illustrations, which make the foreground hilly and uneven.[18] Trees seem to have been acknowledged as landscape elements in the Second Small *Shahnama* manuscript.[19] However, gnarled surfaces and roots are emphatically depicted, revealing the painter's disregard for both Chinese and Ilkhanid tree conventions.

Further evidence for the Ilkhanid provenance of the Small *Shahnama* manuscripts lies in the distinctive East Asian features in costumes. A majority of people wear long-sleeved robes coloured in red, blue and green. The robes of rulers and heroes, especially those depicted in the First and the Second Small *Shahnama*s, sometimes appear to be woven in gold with elaborate patterns, suggesting that *nasij*-type textiles were prevalent throughout Ilkhanid territory in the Middle East. Because of the small size of the miniatures, most patterns used in the robes can be recognised only generically as flowers.[20] The costly robes of some characters are decorated with rhomboidal or polygonal patterns, evoking Yuan-dated Mongol robes discovered in Inner Mongolia (Figure 5.13).

There are a few words to be said about square-shaped accessories

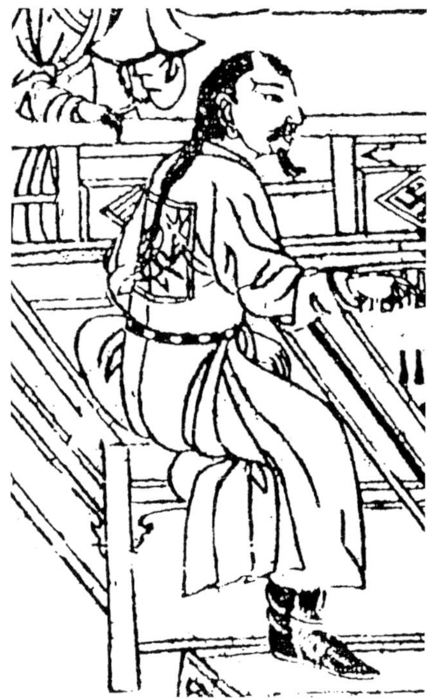

Figure 6.3 *Page from Y. Chen's* Shilin guangji *(detail). Chunzhuang Academy imprint of 1328–32.*

that can be identified on the robes depicted in the Small *Shahnamas* (Figure 6.2). They are the so-called Mandarin square[21] – insignia badges called *buzi* ('garment patch') in China. Both early literary and archaeological evidence of this peculiar costume is surprisingly limited: the Mandarin square is unlikely to be of ancient Chinese origin but is most probably of Uighur derivation.[22] The square had been introduced into China through the Mongols by the early fourteenth century, judging by the earliest depictions of Mongol nobles wearing decorative squares placed on the chest and back of their robes in Yuan woodblock prints – for example, the *Shilin guangji* ('Vast Record of Varied Matters') (1328–32) (Figure 6.3) and recently discovered examples of Mongol square badges datable to the thirteenth century,[23] – and it was eventually developed into an emblematic distinction of dress.[24] The squares of the robes in the Small *Shahnamas*, together with those found in the London Qazmini (fo. 63^{v})[25] and in the Edinburgh al-Biruni (fo. 104^{v}),[26] are thus of importance as the earliest visual evidence of the Mandarin square found outside China.[27] Compared with the early Ilkhanid manuscripts, the ubiquity of the Mandarin square is much more obvious in the Small *Shahnama* manuscripts.[28] This is indicative either of the painters' awareness of the Ilkhanid convention of depicting square badges or of the current fashion for the Mandarin square in the general area where the Small *Shahnamas* were made. Judging by published illustrations, the Mandarin square also appears in the scene of the hero or ruler surrounded by attendants or in the tripartite audience scene that is centred on an enthroned ruler, though there seems to be no particular distinction between the badges of rulers and those of attendants. The square seems more likely to have been at this stage a mere cliché used for the decoration of robes. The bulk of square badges in the Small *Shahnamas* are depicted as being woven with flower motifs, but the depiction of the Mandarin square here is inaccurate in that it is placed over the fold of robes. This suggests the disregard of Small *Shahnama* painters for depicting costume elements with fidelity.

The varied type of headgear also betrays a close awareness of the multicultural nature of Ilkhanid society, and is reminiscent of the Rashidiyya fashion. Hats of Mongol origin are easily recognisable throughout the illustrations; conversely, no Chinese scholar-type caps are depicted in the Small *Shahnamas*.

The dragon occurs in all three Small *Shahnama* manuscripts – for example, in the illustrations of the Bahram Gur cycle.[29] While chinoiserie is less apparent in representations of the dragon in the Freer manuscript,[30] in which it is transformed into a griffin-like creature, most of the dragons depicted in the First and the Second *Shahnamas* conform to a Chinese-type dragon (Figure 6.1) – a creature with a long wriggling body, a horned head, dorsal fins and four legs with clawed feet. Each dragon has an elegantly proportioned form. This type of dragon must have been based on the same East Asian models, as the dragon used in some paintings of the London Qazwini and the Freer Balʿami (Figures 4.21, 4.23). The use of a red colour for dorsal fins is comparable to those seen in Central Asian-type dragons in Bezeklik (Figure 6.5). Yet a band of flame emanating from the dragon's body is particularly evocative of that often seen in dragons woven in Chinese and Central Asian textiles of the eleventh to the fourteenth century.[31]

The flame is indeed a key chinoiserie element in Iranian art – perhaps it shows the most typical process of how Iranians adopted foreign imagery. In China, the flame in itself is symbolic in the Buddhist context, in which it is primarily associated with the immortal soul.[32] But the flame bears a more powerful visual message when it appears with mythical creatures. The Chinese dragon was originally bereft of flames,[33] but the combination of flame and dragon emerged as a standard prototype in both the pictorial and the decorative arts during the Tang dynasty, following the expansion of Buddhist thought into China.[34] The adoption of the flame for the dragon thus resulted in enhancing the artistic value of this animal as a symbol of eternal authority, and eventually the dragon became a symbol of the Chinese emperor himself. During the Mongol period, the flame was known in Iran through conventional Chinese animal patterns, presumably those used in Chinese or Central Asian textiles with dragon motifs (e.g. Figure 1.1). What is interesting is that, because Iranian artists were unaware of the original significance of the flame in Chinese conventional animal patterns, they began to incorporate the flame into other creatures, mainly those associated with myths or those rarely observed in Iran.[35] In the Small *Shahnamas*, along with the dragon, the flame is customarily combined with the *karg*.[36] As Ettinghausen has discussed,[37] the possibility of Chinese sources for this unicorn-like single-horned creature is undeniable. The *karg* could be regarded as equivalent to the *qilin* or the *xiniu* (rhinoceros) in Chinese art.[38] Yet, despite their popularity, examples of the *qilin* and the *xiniu* depicted with flames are rather limited in Chinese pictorial and decorative arts before the Ming period.[39] This indicates that the flame associated with the *karg* most probably came from the dragon motifs, once again, used in Chinese or Central Asian textiles. It is presumed that for the painters of the Small *Shahnamas* the flame was a convenient device to enhance an image of the mythical *karg*. Or, as a similar *karg* design is used in the decoration of Ilkhanid metalwork (Figure 3.6), an image of the flame-bearing *karg* had already taken root among Ilkhanid artists.

It is thus clear that the appearance of Chinese themes in the Small *Shahnama* manuscripts is something more than a provincial reflection of the impact of Chinese artistic traditions and cultures. The discussion so far has shown that some basic chinoiserie elements are present in landscape representations. Most of these elements seem to have been derived from earlier Ilkhanid painting, especially of the type epitomised by the Morgan Bestiary and the London Qazwini.[40] Chinese-inspired landscape elements must have provided an incentive to add something new, but the admiration of the painters of the Small *Shahnamas* for Chinese landscape conventions was insufficient to promote a drastic stylistic change in the formation of landscape. Perhaps, then, the principal significance of the Small *Shahnamas* in the context of chinoiserie lies in the minute rendering of costumes of Chinese and Mongol origins.

The Gutman Shahnama and paintings of the Isfahan school under the Mongols

In the light of the question of how Chinese conventions entered early fourteenth-century central Iran, the Gutman *Shahnama* (1974.290, MMA)[41] requires some specific comments. The provenance of this manuscript, like that of some of the fourteenth-century *Shahnamas*, had generally been thought to be Inju-ruled Shiraz, but Swietochowski has suggested Isfahan as the likeliest location.[42] The date of production of this manuscript is now considered to be the years around 736/1335, when Isfahan was still under Ilkhanid rule.[43] The forty-two

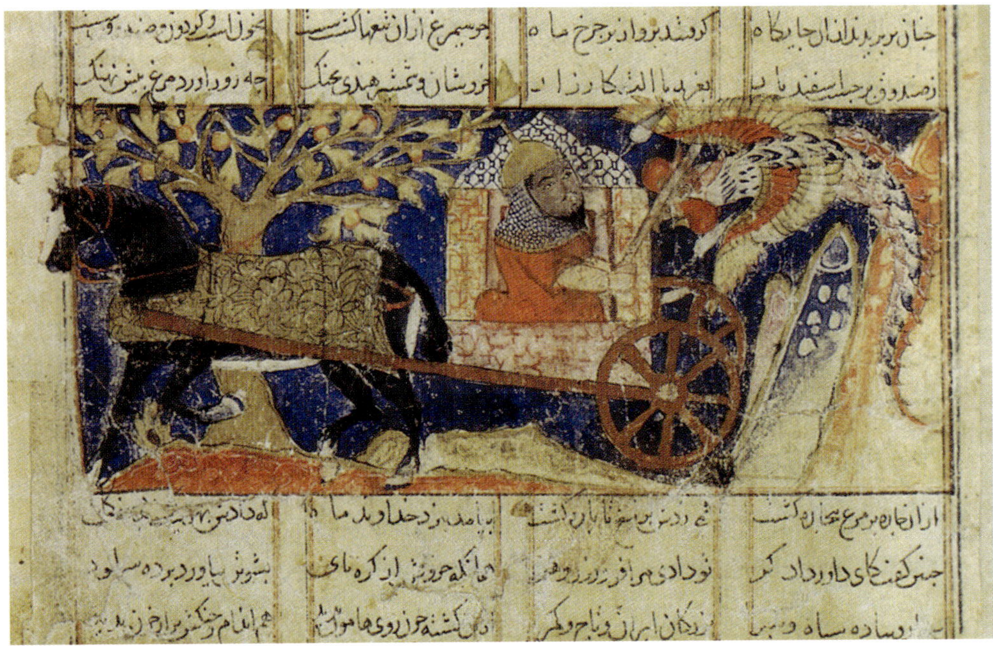

Figure 6.4 Isfandiyar Slays the Simurgh. *Page from the Gutman* Shahnama. *Probably Isfahan, c. 1335.*

miniatures of the manuscript have rarely been discussed in relation to the evolution of early fourteenth-century Iranian painting.

Yet the fact is that some distinctive landscape elements of the Gutman *Shahnama* correspond closely to those seen in Ilkhanid painting, and also follow Ilkhanid reactions to Chinese landscape conventions more clearly than the Small *Shahnama*s or any other paintings produced in southern Iran under the Mongols. Although sketchy, the mountains of the Gutman *Shahnama* are different from those depicted in the Small *Shahnama*s, for they lack rippling outlines and multiple contours (Figure 6.4). The mountains here, which have triangular forms, at first glance recall those often seen in Inju painting, whose prototypes can be traced back to Central Asian wall painting (Figure 6.5).[44] Yet the detail of the mountains – for example, the use of multiple contours and spots – is more suggestive of a close association with earlier Ilkhanid painting.[45] Similar soaring rocky crags are found in the Morgan Bestiary and the Edinburgh al-Biruni (Figures 4.10, 4.24). The painters of the Gutman *Shahnama* draw trees in a realistic way.[46] Although root forms are not strongly emphasised, tree trunks and fruit-bearing branches are carefully represented.

Similarly, the multiple ground levels in the Gutman *Shahnama* evoke those seen in earlier Ilkhanid painting, though the foreground here is not clearly divided by straight lines.[47] As for representations of grass, however, the Gutman *Shahnama* seems unlikely to

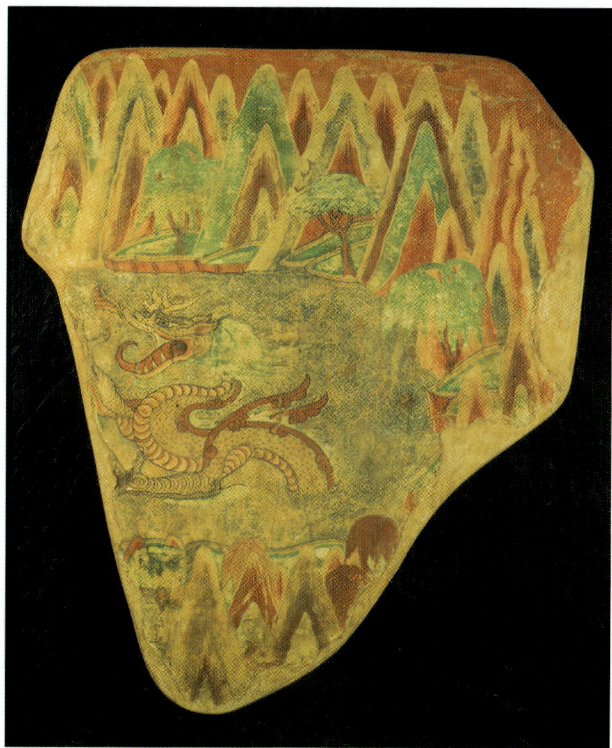

Figure 6.5 Dragon in a Lake. *Wall painting. Bezeklik, Temple 19, ninth century.*

have inherited its grass conventions from earlier Ilkhanid painting: neither 'Mongol' grass, which first occurs in the Morgan Bestiary, nor spiral grass decoration of the type found in the London Qazwini is recognisable in the landscape of the Gutman *Shahnama*. Some of the miniatures contain representations of sparsely scattered grass,[48] a characteristic that later became conventional in manuscript painting produced under the Jalayirids and Muzaffarids.[49] The arrangement of flowering plants is random, but some plants are employed to separate groups of people.[50]

There are two types of cloud in the illustrations of the Gutman *Shahnama*. Scalloped clouds coloured in either gold or light purple are often situated in the upper centre of the miniature.[51] These are Ilkhanid-type clouds, which especially evoke those frequently used in the Edinburgh al-Biruni.[52] The other type is the dust cloud,[53] which was perhaps originally invented by the painters of the *Jamiʿ al-Tawarikh* manuscripts in order to dramatise furious battle scenes (Figure 5.11). The stylistic association with earlier Ilkhanid painting is also obvious in the depiction of rocks.[54] Mushroom-like rocks with holes bear a close resemblance to those in the Morgan Bestiary and the Edinburgh al-Biruni (Figures 4.7, 4.24). Finally, the painters of the

Gutman *Shahnama* adopt one of the Ilkhanid water conventions, especially that used in the Morgan Bestiary, which was derived from thirteenth-century Mesopotamian painting.[55] Thus, the Gutman *Shahnama* betrays the unmistakable impact of earlier Ilkhanid painting, especially the Morgan Bestiary. However, neither direct influence from Chinese landscape painting nor a new interpretation of Chinese landscape conventions can be proposed for this manuscript.

Among the animals pictured in the Gutman *Shahnama*, some remarks should be made about two particular animals in relation to their connection with China – namely, the dragon and the *simurgh*. The Gutman dragon is likely to be a composite of Central Asian, Chinese and indigenous dragons.[56] The painters show an interest in depicting dragons' faces, such as the proboscis and round eyes, yet the main difference from the conventional Chinese dragon in that the Gutman dragon's face is devoid of menace. An even more visible difference is the absence of the flame around the dragon's body.[57] The large-size scaly body is somehow disproportionate to the head. Of equal interest is the depiction of the *simurgh*. In the Gutman *Shahnama*, there are two examples of this mythical bird in agitated flight (Figure 6.4),[58] both of which deviate from Chinese prototypes of phoenixes. Compared with the *simurgh* used in the Morgan Bestiary (Figure 4.15), the head of the Gutman *simurgh* appears to be that of a rooster. Its body is also atypical of Chinese phoenixes. Its plumage is less fluttering, having been transformed into a reptilian tail.

The Gutman *Shahnama* provides a rich source of information about the costumes coming into vogue in central Iran during the early fourteenth century. The painters add a variety of decoration to the robes of rulers and attendants.[59] The elaborate flower motifs used in some of the robes[60] and even saddles (Figure 6.4) are seemingly of the same kind as those seen in the Small *Shahnama*s.[61] The design seems to have been inspired by lotus decoration, whose Chinese prototypes can be found in various media of Chinese decorative arts (Figures 1.12, 3.12). Headgear is also minutely depicted in nearly all illustrations. In particular, warriors' helmets bearing two-ring designs are characteristic of this manuscript,[62] though these are unlikely to be of Chinese origin.

It is possible to make the same observation for some leaves of the Diez Albums, which are now miscellaneously bound together with other paintings, as occurs on Folio 71.[63] Swietochowski has reached a conclusion from a detailed comparison between these leaves and the Gutman *Shahnama* illustrations that the Diez leaves might also have been produced in the Isfahan school under the Mongols.[64] Besides the fact that they share colour schemes, the stylistic affinity between them can be confirmed from representations of landscape and animals.[65] The clouds depicted on the Diez leaves take the shape of convoluted banks in the upper margins;[66] instead of straight horizontal lines of grass, mountain ranges play a major compositional role. No dragons are depicted in the Diez leaves. However, as seen in the Gutman *Shahnama*, the *simurgh* pictured in one leaf is obviously just a rooster.[67] Perhaps the major difference between the two manuscripts lies in the rendering of trees. The tree leaves in the Diez Albums are somehow overweight and out of proportion to the spindly tree trunks. The source of this balloon-like foliage remains uncertain: it does not correspond closely to tree leaves found in contemporary Ilkhanid painting – for example, the Great Mongol *Shahnama*;[68] nor is it comparable to those naturalistically depicted in Chinese landscape painting. The tree conventions of the Diez leaves are thus likely to have been indigenously developed.

Another manuscript attributable to the Isfahan school of the Mongol period is the incomplete manuscript entitled *Mu'nis al-ahrar fi daqa'iq al-ash'ar* ('The Free Men's Companion to the Subtleties of Poems') (Isfahan, 741/1341).[69] Thirty-nine folios of the manuscript are extant, and, except for its double frontispiece, all eleven illustrations are to be found in the six folios that once formed Chapter 29 of the *Mu'nis al-ahrar*. The illustrations of the *Mu'nis al-ahrar*, like those of some fourteenth-century *Shahnama*s, had long been attributed to the school of Shiraz.[70]

As far as chinoiserie is concerned, the illustrations of the *Mu'nis al-ahrar* reveal little further information about the artistic relationship between China and central Iran and do not reveal any notable new interpretations of Chinese artistic conventions. On the whole, the landscape here remains primitive. Grass and plants are decoratively arranged against the red background. The appearance of distinctive rocks with holes is the only evidence that the painters were perhaps aware of the landscape conventions used in Ilkhanid painting.[71] The animals of the *Mu'nis al-ahrar* are equally devoid of Chinese characteristics. Only the dragon's head found in one page follows a Chinese convention.[72] Thus, the absence of naturalistic treatment and the decisive sinicising elements in the rendering of landscape and animals indicate that the style of the painters of the *Mu'nis al-ahrar* was remote from that practised in the capital area of the Ilkhanid dynasty.

However, the double-page frontispiece (Figure 6.6) of the *Mu'nis al-ahrar* ensures that the manuscript holds an important position in the history of fourteenth-century Iranian painting. As has already been noted by Carboni, there is a close stylistic resemblance between the landscape of the right page showing a hunting scene and that of both the Gutman *Shahnama* and some Diez Album leaves.[73] Similar cone-shaped mountains with double contours, which evoke, yet again, Central Asian mountain conventions (Figure 6.5), can be recognised throughout these manuscripts.[74] The left page is evidently based on the standard fourteenth-century tradition of depicting an enthronement scene.[75] What is important in the context of chinoiserie is that Chinese or Mongol elements are apparent in the depiction

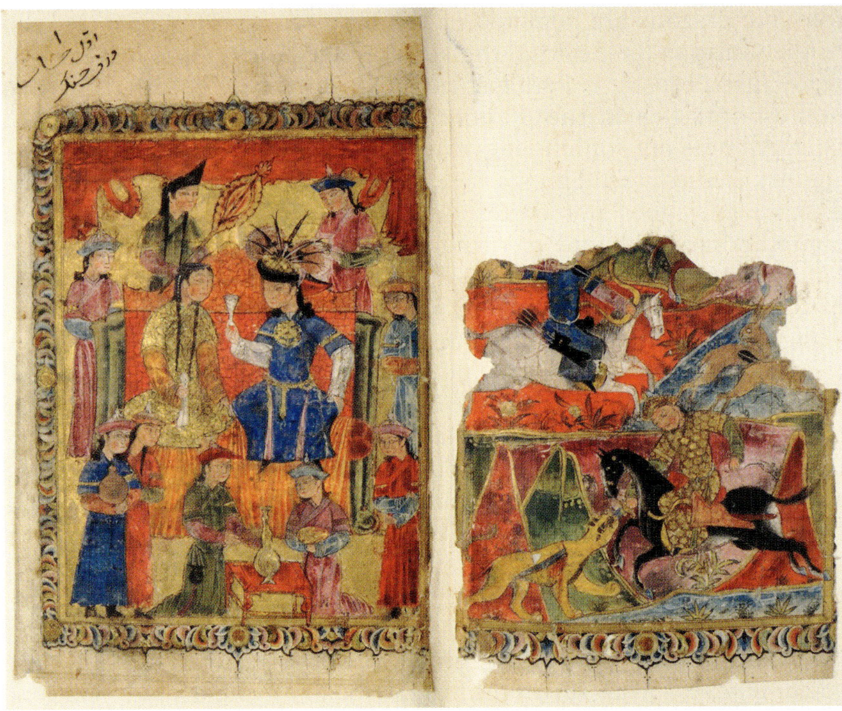

Figure 6.6 *Double-page frontispiece from the* Mu'nis al-ahrar. *Isfahan, 741/1341.*

of costumes. In particular, the ruler's clothing is quite distinctive: in addition to his elaborate feathery hat, a round badge on his blue robe serves to enhance his royal image. While the ruler's hat is of Mongol origin, the appearance of the gold round badge in his robe should be observed as the earliest visual evidence for the penetration of Chinese costumes into central Iran. China has a long tradition of the wearing of a round badge as a type of insignia: the round badge had already gained popularity among Chinese nobles during the Tang dynasty,[76] and the tradition of employing it was taken over by the people inhabiting the northern part of China, especially the Khitans.[77] Robes with round badges seem to have existed until the Ming dynasty, but it was during the Qing period that imperial garments with dragon medallions began to be known as dragon robes.[78]

Despite the fact that the occurrence of Chinese themes in the Gutman *Shahnama*, the Diez leaves and the *Mu'nis al-ahrar* does not deviate significantly from Iranian chinoiserie traditions, chinoiserie remains a suggestive but not conclusive element in manuscript painting of the Isfahan school produced during the third and fourth decades of the fourteenth century. Compared with the situation in earlier Ilkhanid and Rashidiyya painting, an artistic confrontation of the painters with Chinese decorative and pictorial arts is less observable in these manuscripts. The direct impact of Chinese pictorial and decorative arts on early fourteenth-century Isfahani painting thus remains uncertain.

The Ilkhanid Kalila wa Dimna manuscripts and other related works

The discussion of chinoiserie in late thirteenth- and early fourteenth-century Iranian painting would be incomplete if one neglected the illustrations of the *Kalila wa Dimna* manuscripts that have been attributed to the early Ilkhanid period. Originating in the Indian animal tales known as the *Pančatantra*, the story of the *Kalila wa Dimna* has been one of the most popular animal tales in the Arab world since it was first translated from Pahlavi into Arabic in the eight century.[79] Its pictorial traditions seem to have been developed first in Syria and Egypt under Ayyubid rule[80] and subsequently in the eastern Islamic world under the Saljuqs.[81] Yet there was a long interim period taken up by the emerging Mongol style until the artistic explosion of the *Kalila wa Dimna* illustrations achieved by Jalayirid painters.[82] Thus the works discussed below, though in the main undated and of uncertain provenance, serve to provide a more clear-cut idea about the process of the reorientation of Arab pictorial traditions as a result of contact with Persian visual culture, and the development of Iranian manuscript painting during the late thirteenth and early fourteenth centuries. Analysis of Chinese elements in these manuscripts also reveals their relationship with securely localised and dated Ilkhanid illustrated manuscripts.

There are three *Kalila wa Dimna* manuscripts attributable to the early Ilkhanid period, though their dating and provenance remain controversial. The best-known manuscript of this group is the British Library *Kalila wa Dimna* (707/1307).[83] Despite its Ilkhanid date, which is equivalent to the time of production of the Edinburgh al-Biruni manuscript, the manuscript has long been neglected in the study of Mongol school painting and its miniatures have hitherto not been published in their entirety. The reason for this perhaps lies in their stylistic crudity; they reveal a penchant for Mesopotamian conventions and a foretaste of the Inju school style. Yet the British Library *Kalila wa Dimna* deserves special attention as providing an insight into the formation of a provincial style in early fourteenth-century Iranian painting.

Some distinctive Mesopotamian characteristics can easily be identified in the rendering of landscape,[84] which is depicted in a cursory manner without any naturalistic bent. In the miniature depicting a leopard and a lion (fo. 74),[85] the background is overcrowded with tooth-shaped rocks built up in layers and balloon-like trees with haloed birds. Both the rocks and the trees depicted here are not drawn from Chinese sources but seem to have relied on models that were developed in pre-Mongol painting of the Mosul school – for example, those used in Syriac Jacobite Gospels.[86] Compositionally, too, no attempt is made to recreate a Chinese feeling of space. Unlike most of the miniatures in the Morgan Bestiary with their elaboration of spatial devices, the bases of the miniatures in the London *Kalila wa Dimna* are, again as in pre-Mongol painting of the Mosul school,[87] simply bordered with thick grass with indications of flowers at intervals. The absence of *lingzhi* clouds is also illustrative of the non-Chinese nature of this manuscript. Atmosphere is generated by a suffusion of red, which is typical of Inju painting, with the result that the background merely stresses two-dimensionality. There is thus little sign of ideas borrowed from China; nor can any striking elements derived from Ilkhanid painting be detected in the landscape of the London *Kalila wa Dimna*.[88]

Similarly, in its human figures and costume, the London manuscript is stylistically remote from painting of the Mongol school. None of the human figures is unmistakably depicted as Mongols by headgear and robes. The figures are either crowned or turbaned, and they wear robes decorated with flower-like patterns. Rather, the debt to Saljuq-style painting is undeniable, for similar figures are customarily represented in thirteenth-century *mina'i* ware[89] and are also found in the illustrations of the *Varqa va Gulshah* manuscript.[90]

An as yet comparatively little-known earlier Persian copy of the *Kalila wa Dimna* is preserved in Paris (supp. pers. 1965, BN).[91] This diminutive manuscript contains twenty small but compelling illustrations. Owing to a complex range of stylistic influences exerted by old and new conventions, the attribution of this manuscript has been among the most perplexing problems in the study of early *Kalila wa Dimna* manuscripts. Suggested datings range from the mid-thirteenth to the mid-fourteenth century, and its place of origin has been ascribed to various centres, from Inju to Mamluk territory.[92]

The landscape in the Paris manuscript is prosaic and less varied than that of the London manuscript. Plants predominate in the formation of backgrounds, and rocks and grass are rarely incorporated into landscape settings. Tall swaying flowering plants, recalling those seen in Mosul school painting – for example, in the Vienna and Paris *Kitab al-Diryaq* manuscripts[93] – are set beside figures or thrones. The plants depicted in this manuscript are difficult to identify, but an exception is found in folio 16^{v}, where a blooming flower identifiable as a lotus appears between the lion and the jackal.[94] This indication of chinoiserie brings the date of this manuscript into the Mongol period. But its appearance remains isolated, as in the *Marzubanmana*,[95] and differs from the lotus motif that is an integral feature of Ilkhanid pictorial and decorative concepts. Another point to be noted is the depiction of water in folio 8^{v}.[96] The fluid movement of water is suggested not only by the use of circular patterns but by the depiction of sprays, showing a resemblance to one of the types of water representation used in the Morgan Bestiary, which was, in turn, dependent on Chinese models.[97]

Chinese or Mongol traits are less obvious in the depiction of costumes in the Paris manuscript. The dress and headgear of the figures contain elements derived from disparate sources, mainly those conventionalised in thirteenth-century Mesopotamian painting. A close parallel for the double-outlined haloes is, as O'Kane has suggested, a double frontispiece in the *Rasa'il Ikhwan al-Safa' wa khullan al-wafa'* ('Epistles of the Brethren of Purity and the Loyal Friends') (Baghdad, 686/1287; Esad Efendi 3638, Suleimaniyye Library, Istanbul),[98] while the elaborately pleated robes of the haloed figures are more evocative of those seen in thirteenth-century Mosul school painting.[99] Another feature that differentiates this manuscript from the manuscript painting of the Mongol school is the emphasis on ribbons. Wind-blown ribbons are exaggeratedly depicted, giving a strong impression of fast movement. This convention was, as has been noted earlier, associated in earlier Iranian art with the sphere of Buddhist culture – representations of lifelike ribbons had already excited the imagination of Iranian painters before the Mongol invasion.

In contrast to such conspicuous costume elements, the interior setting is relatively austere, being composed simply of thrones or curtains. Several types of throne appear in the audience scenes, such as those with cushions with concave tips and those with backrests and poles on the corners,[100] yet none of these shows stylistic affinities with those thrones embodying strong Chinese associations that are frequently depicted in Rashidiyya painting. The thrones in the Paris manuscript are more reminiscent of those that occur in *mina'i* ware.[101] Likewise, no impact of Chinese themes can be discerned in the decoration on the curtains, most of which are decorated with arabesque-derived patterns.[102]

It is assumed that the medley of different pictorial styles in the Paris *Kalila wa Dimna* – for instance, the retention of the Mesopotamian style and the emergence of Chinese elements – reflects the political and social upheaval in Iran in the aftermath of the Mongol invasion. This suggests that the manuscript was executed during the late thirteenth and early fourteenth centuries, but the very mixed styles make it hard to pin down the provenance of the manuscript. On the grounds of the experimental use of Chinese elements, Baghdad is one of the likeliest places of origin,[103] taking account of the artistic milieu of this city in the late thirteenth century,[104] though the red background is suggestive of a link of this manuscript with Inju-ruled southern Iran.[105]

The most telling example of this group is an Arabic copy of the *Kalila wa Dimna* in Rabat (MS 3655, Bibliothèque royale).[106] This manuscript had been virtually unknown until the publication by Barrucand and has been placed outside the mainstream of Iranian

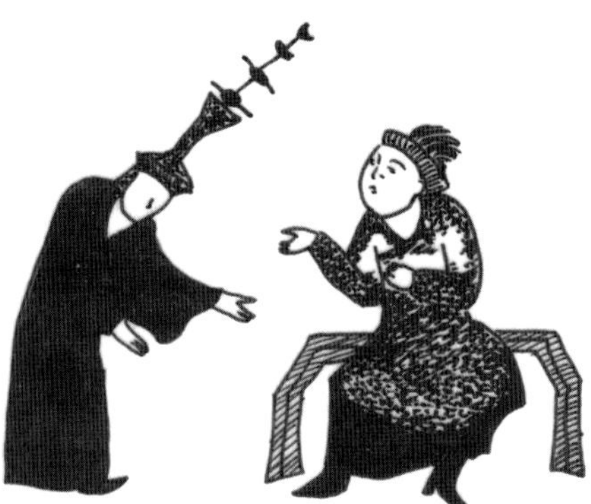

Figure 6.7 The King and his Wife. *Page from the* Kalila wa Dimna. *Probably Baghdad, c. 1300.*

painting. The manuscript is lavishly illustrated, but only about a third of the 122 miniatures have been published.[107] As far as the published illustrations are concerned, the Mesopotamian tradition is pronounced in the entire treatment of landscape, such as isolated plants, undulating horizons and multi-contoured rocks,[108] recalling Mesopotamian landscape conventions.[109] These meagre elements are sufficient to indicate the landscape, but there is no attempt to think afresh about the naturalistic rendering of backgrounds.

Of unique importance in the Rabat *Kalila wa Dimna* is that the miniatures display two very different types of costumes. Although some characters are shown as typical Arabs, judging by their turbans and kaftan-type clothing, the others are dressed in clearly Mongol garb (Figure 6.7)[110] – namely, cylinder-shaped headgear for women and feathered hats for men in the manner of Mongol aristocrats. Published illustrations of the Rabat manuscript do not, however, reveal satisfactorily how far the painters distinguished between Arab and Mongol types of costume. On the other hand, an interesting parallel can be made between these images and Mongol royal portraits in the Diez Albums that are considered to have been inserted in the *Jamiʿ al-Tawarikh* manuscripts (Figure 5.21).[111] Both examples closely resemble each other in terms of costumes, but the Rabat example does not follow the traditional position of men and women for ceremonial occasions in Mongol society.

Once again, such mixed conventions, absorbing old and new pictorial styles, make the date and provenance of this manuscript uncertain; in particular, the occurrence of distinctive Mongol apparel presents something of a puzzle. Barrucand has suggested a date of production between 1265 to 1280, citing in comparison paintings from or assigned to late thirteenth-century Baghdad.[112] Unmistakable Mongol elements in the costumes, however, which are absent from the London and Paris manuscripts, enable one to expand with confidence the time frame of this manuscript up to the beginning of the fourteenth century, when Mongol-clad figures became ubiquitous in Iranian painting. As for the provenance of the Rabat manuscript, the absence of Inju characteristics, such as red backgrounds and patterned robes, indicates its stylistic distance from the Mongol protectorate in southern Iran. The cosmopolitanism of the Rabat manuscript suggests its links to north-west Iran or perhaps some other major cultural sphere of Mongol territory in the late thirteenth and early fourteenth centuries, such as Baghdad or Mosul.

The above remarks on the *Kalila wa Dimna* manuscripts underline their importance in the history of Iranian painting as a forerunner of regional styles, which were late developed into the establishment of the distinctive Inju style, as well as the development of the iconographic traditions of animal painting in the Iranian world under Mongol rule. Although the roots of chinoiserie in the illustrations of the early *Kalila wa Dimna* manuscripts remain shallow and the use of Chinese elements is somewhat cursory, without further translation into Iranian idioms, these manuscripts are illustrative of how Chinese themes gradually became acclimatised to the pictorial traditions of Iran and how they were bit by bit integrated into the new pictorial concepts of early fourteenth-century Iranian painting.

Of equal relevance to this section is a dispersed Persian *Manafiʿ-i Hayavan*.[113] Despite its unique position in the history of Iranian painting, especially its visual correspondence to animal painting of the Mongol school, such as the Morgan Bestiary and the London Qazwini, it has never been satisfactorily discussed within the framework of Ilkhanid painting. It has rather been dealt with in the context of Mamluk painting, owing in part to several similarities with the *Manafiʿ-i Hayavan* of Ibn al-Duraihim al-Mausili, known as the Escorial Bestiary (probably Syria, 755/1354; MS Ar. 898, Biblioteca Real).[114] Given the present dispersed state of the miniatures, which are in collections over much of the world, the reconstruction of their original pictorial cycle is a difficult task. It is nevertheless possible to some extent to trace the echoes of Mongol style in these images and, in turn, the impact of Chinese conventions.

Compared with the Ilkhanid *Kalila wa Dimna* manuscripts, the landscape in the dispersed *Manafiʿ-i Hayavan* is free from the impact of the styles of the thirteenth-century Baghdad and Mosul schools. Landscape elements are not treated as isolated pictorial clichés but are physically related to each other. The illustration of two mares (Figure 6.8) remains two-dimensional, but space is suggested by the imaginative arrangement of the vegetation. Thick tufty grass is defined by the emphasis of linear details, following an inherited grass convention of the Mongol school, as in one of the types used in the London Qazwini (Figure 4.19). Representations of flowering plants are rather sketchy, but their composition and types are varied in each illustration. The lotus blossoms, which occur with frequency in the surviving illustrations of the manuscript,[115] are confidently depicted,

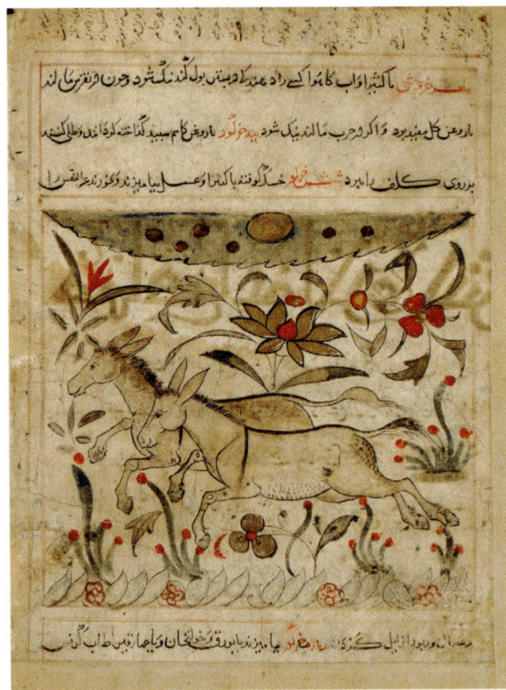

Figure 6.8 Two Mares. *Page from a dispersed* Manafiʿ-i Hayavan *of Ibn Bakhtishuʿ. Iran, c. 1300. Two galloping mares are presented against a two-dimensional landscape background. Apart from the presence of a lotus blossom, this illustration contains few chinoiserie elements.*

indicating a reliance on specific models – for example, those seen in the decoration of Ilkhanid artefacts (e.g. Figure 3.13). Trees are also employed in the formation of landscape, yet interestingly, though this is perhaps merely coincidental, two of the surviving miniatures that contain representations of trees have a Chinese association – willows (No. 12) and bamboos (No. 11).

Another determinant of the Ilkhanid origin of this manuscript is the occurrence of Chinese-inspired clouds. The painters of the dispersed *Manafiʿ-i Hayavan* seem to have explored new means of expressing landscape, experimenting with various forms of cloud, ranging from prototypical *lingzhi* clouds,[116] used in the same way as in the Morgan Bestiary, to serpentine clouds diffused all over the ground[117] – a foretaste of the Rashidiyya style (Figure 5.11).

With regard to animals and human figures, the surviving miniatures of the dispersed *Manafiʿ-i Hayavan* manuscript are insufficient to give a clear idea of the overall treatment of Chinese-related animals and costumes. Judging by the illustration of phoenixes, a painting that shows marked dependence upon Chinese models (No. 10), some painters who were involved in the production of the manuscript seem to have been familiar to some extent with Chinese animal iconography. A few examples contain human figures (No. 11). The woman in the scene of a goat appears to be a Saljuq-type haloed beauty with a moon face and long black hair, evoking the women depicted in *mina'i* ware of the late twelfth and early thirteenth centuries, rather than a Mongol female aristocrat distinguished by her headgear and robe with elaborate decoration.

Another remaining problem is the occurrence of framing devices (No. 15), an element that is uncommon in the illustration of the Morgan Bestiary[118] and is different from the architectural devices often incorporated into the illustrations of the Edinburgh al-Biruni.[119] In addition to decorative vertical panels on both sides, the arch is embellished in its spandrels with large lotus blossoms. A more noteworthy point is the elaborate decorative frieze of lobed arches arranged between the text and the animal image, which is reminiscent of that found in Uljaitu's *mihrab* in Isfahan (Figure 3.14). Although it is difficult to generalise from this isolated instance, this is a possible indication of the growing awareness of the role of marginal decoration in the image structure in animal painting and perhaps Iranian painting in general.

A certain degree of stylistic relationship between the dispersed *Manafi'-i Hayavan* and animal painting of the Mongol school provides a key for an approximate dating and provenance for this manuscript, namely north-west Iran in the period between 1300 and 1320. Additionally, the occurrence of decorative frames in association with contemporary Iranian monuments reinforces the Ilkhanid dating of this manuscript.

The last phase of chinoiserie in Iranian painting: the case of the Diez Albums, group 2

The key material that fills the gap in styles between the 1320s and 1330s – a politically turbulent yet artistically productive time associated with the inauguration of the Jalayirid style[120] – are, again, some of the fragmentary miniatures in the Saray Albums. The albums, now divided between Istanbul and Berlin, have long been known to scholars of Iranian painting, yet scholarly discourse about the miniatures, especially those possibly produced between the period immediately before and after the Great Mongol *Shahnama*, remains unsatisfactory. As in the previous section dealing with a group of early fourteenth-century paintings in the same albums, both the Istanbul and Berlin examples encourage a detailed scholarly investigation of their links to the pictorial traditions that evolved in Iran during the late Ilkhanid period.

Because of the absence of texts attached to these images, the distinctions between the paintings that I have identified as belonging to Group 1 and 2 rest on their styles, and in particular on the degree of assimilation of Chinese elements. Group 1 is characterised by inherited conventions of the Rashidiyya school, while Group 2 has resonances of the Demotte style and attempts to remodel or to persianise Chinese themes. Some of the Istanbul and Berlin leaves belonging to Group 2[121] also provide a clue for a better understanding of paintings probably produced between the 1340s and 1350s under the Jalayirids, whose stylistic chronology is still incomplete.[122] Yet this section centres on the examples that can be regarded as safely belonging within the context of later Ilkhanid painting.

Since this group of miniatures is more discrete than those in Group 1, it is difficult to reconstruct the original context in which the miniatures would have been painted and viewed. But the bulk of the miniatures in this group are *Shahnama* images that were initially incorporated into books or were possibly individual paintings.[123] To take an example, six small miniatures, perhaps originating from one manuscript but now pasted together in disorder on one page, illustrate several phases of furious battles (Diez A. Fol. 71.S.43). On the whole, the impact of Rashidiyya conventions lingers in these miniatures. The visual emphasis is placed on horizontality; the pictorial movement is predominantly set from right to left by means of the movement of horses. Yet a point that distinguishes the battle scenes of the Diez miniatures from those of the Rashidiyya school lies in the treatment of nature, in which the proportions of landscape elements are adjusted not to decorative purposes but to compositional requirements. One miniature (Fol. 71. S.43. Nr.6; Figure 6.9), for example, shows a striking originality in the composition of landscape. Here the human figures in the foreground are swallowed up by the massive rock formation in the background. The layers of rocks drawn by speedy brush strokes, which slant dynamically towards the left, serve to distract the viewer's attention from the formal arrangement of riders. This unusual way of suggesting the physical relationship between human figures and landscape elements is an antecedent of later Ilkhanid conventions – namely, those evolved in the Great Mongol *Shahnama*.[124] The landscape in this miniature is constructed under the spell of Chinese inspiration, especially that exerted by Chinese woodblock prints (Figure 6.10).[125]

Some scholars have suggested that the Istanbul Saray Albums contain certain illustrations that were split from the Great Mongol *Shahnama* manuscript, or at least some that were executed at subsidiary workshops, evoking the now-lost illustrations of the Demotte *Shahnama* manuscript.[126] Among the putative Demotte leaves in Istanbul, the image of Zal shooting a water bird (Hazine 2153, fo. 65^{v}, TSM)[127] stands out for its variety of modes of expressing landscape. The entire space is boldly divided at a diagonal angle by an expanse of the rapidly flowing river. Perhaps generated by a current interest in the manipulation of water in the landscape structure in Iranian painting,[128] the billowing streams in this scene of Zal are rendered in the vein of Rashidiyya painters, as in the illustration of the River

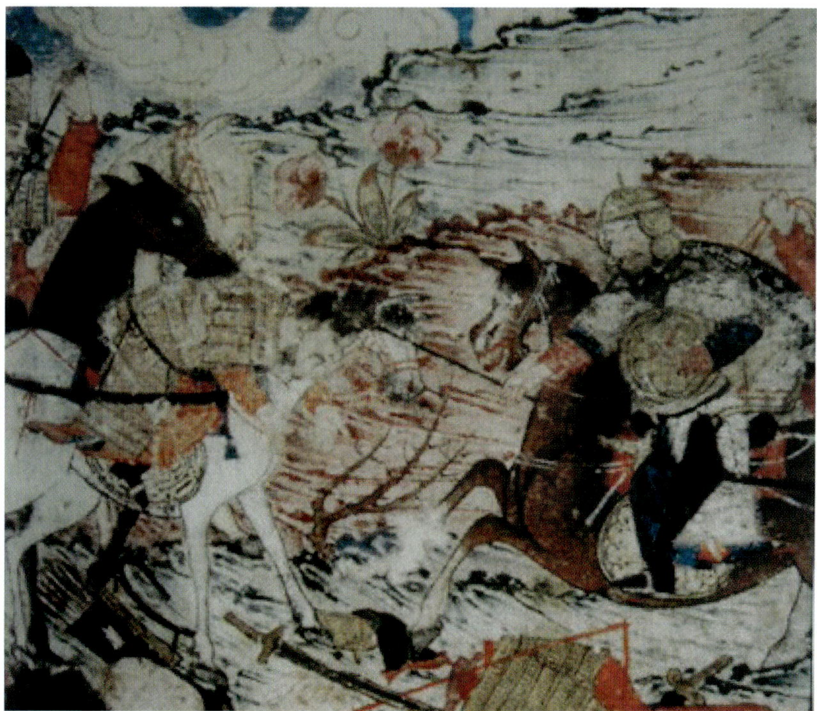

Figure 6.9 *Battle scene. Page from the* Shahnama. *Iran, c. 1300–50.*

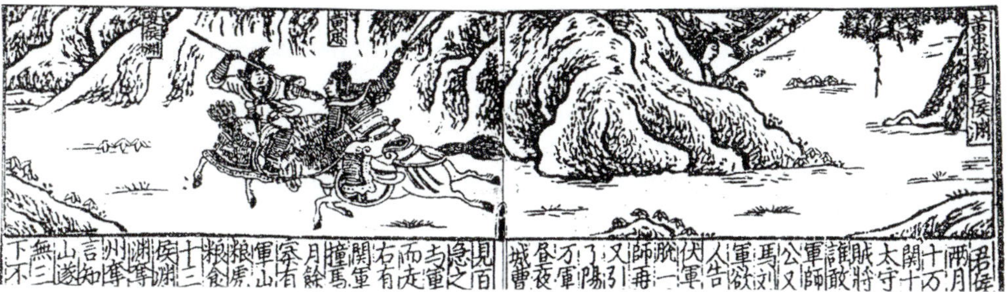

Figure 6.10 Huang Zhong Slaying Xiahou Yuan. *Page from the* Sanguozhi. *Xinanyu imprint of 1321–3.*

Nile in the Edinburgh *Jamiʿ al-Tawarikh* manuscript (Figure 5.2), with the additional use of white colour for both sprays and currents. What is unique to this painting is that the river serves to enhance the dynamic spatial relationship between the images, which are divided into two land masses, and thus to highlight Zal's mastery of shooting in a more effective way. While the near space is crowded with vigorously rendered low bushes and neatly arranged short grass, the landscape on the opposite side of the fast-flowing stream conveys an elegance of rose-like flowering plants and lichened rocks.

The following three miniatures deserve special attention as landmarks of the reinterpretation of Chinese landscape conventions in later Ilkhanid painting. A leaf known as *Winter Landscape* (Fol. 70. S.10; Figure 6.11)[129] is painted with a remarkable feeling of harsh weather in winter. The delicacy of depiction is conveyed by deciduous trees in both the foreground and the background. The painter's artistry is manifest in a careful modelling of sinuous tree trunks and a detailed depiction of bent twigs that taper to sharp points, a mode depending largely on Chinese prototypes. The spiky trees depicted in this miniature are particularly evocative of old trees depicted by Chinese painters, which is one of the popular genres in Yuan painting.[130] The trees depicted with such sensitivity serve to create a melancholic atmosphere. A feeling of gloom is further enhanced by the spare arrangement of elongated rocks. The rocks here focus on recreating double contours and superficial holes under the inspiration of Mongol school conventions (e.g. Figure 4.24). But they also have an illusionistic bent, owing much to the use of intense colour schemes. Another highlight in the landscape of this painting is the depiction of water. The tracts of water serve to divide the whole landscape composition into three parts. The painter adopts one of the water conventions appearing in earlier Ilkhanid painting (e.g. Figure 5.2), which was ultimately of Chinese origin. Yet, in contrast with the lyrical treatment of nature in the background, the movement of water, which is soberly controlled by the simple repetition of curled waves and sprays and by the use of subdued colours, stresses simplicity and bleakness. As a result of the subtle juxtaposition of two different types of landscape, however, the miniature succeeds in making an unforgettable visual impression on the viewer.

Chinoiserie is in the ascendant in an Istanbul leaf known as *Autumn Landscape* (Hazine, 2153, fo. 68; Figure 6.12). Such a large-scale landscape may not have been alien to Iranian painters by the 1350s, when the miniatures of Group 2 were possibly compiled. In comparison with the landscape paintings found in the *Jamiʿ al-Tawarikh* (Figures 5.5–6), the Istanbul leaf provides a superb bird's-eye view of the grandeur of nature, with the intention of integrating Chinese compositional ideas. Like prototypical Chinese landscape painting in a hanging format, this miniature displays an entire composition at one time. The image is stretched backwards by the use of overlapping mountain peaks. Compared with *The Mountains of India* (Figure 5.6), it is clear that the painter of the Istanbul leaf places special value on distance rather than on height. Sparsely arranged grass and misty clouds that emerge in the distance are also effective in displaying a panoramic view. The impact of Chinese landscape conventions remains intact in the rocky formation to the right. Though less dynamic than these rocks, the overhanging cliffs reproduce the idyllic ambience of the mountainside. The appearance of small waterfalls suffices to suggest a picturesque atmosphere, an

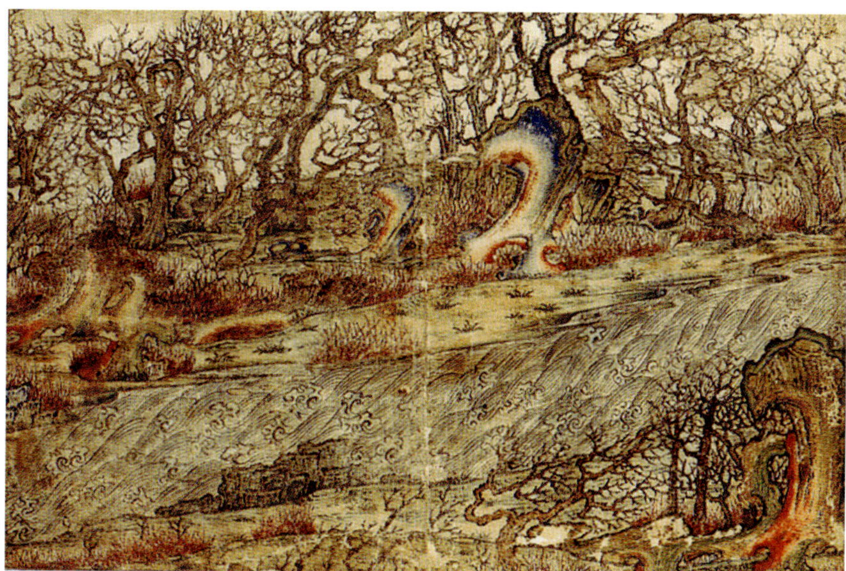

Figure 6.11 Winter Landscape. *Illustration from the Diez Albums. Iran, c. 1300–50. By the middle of the fourteenth century, landscape had been fully incorporated into the pictorial genre of the Iranian world. The horizontal arrangement of leafless trees, curling waves and elongated rocks serves to create a dramatic landscape setting.*

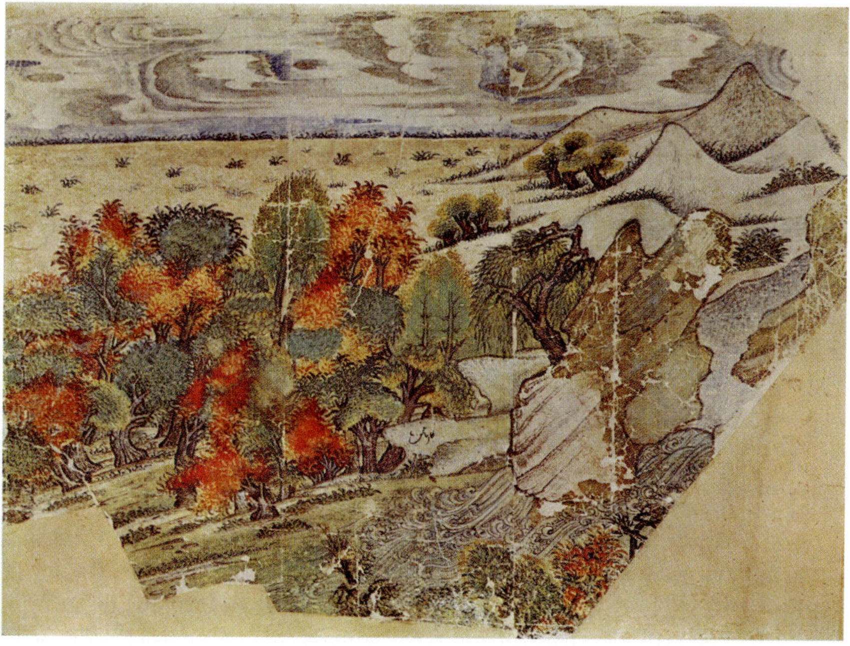

Figure 6.12 Autumn Landscape. *Illustration from the Istanbul Saray Albums. Iran, c. 1300–50. An autumnal atmosphere is generated by the polychromic treatment of trees in this panoramic view of a valley.*

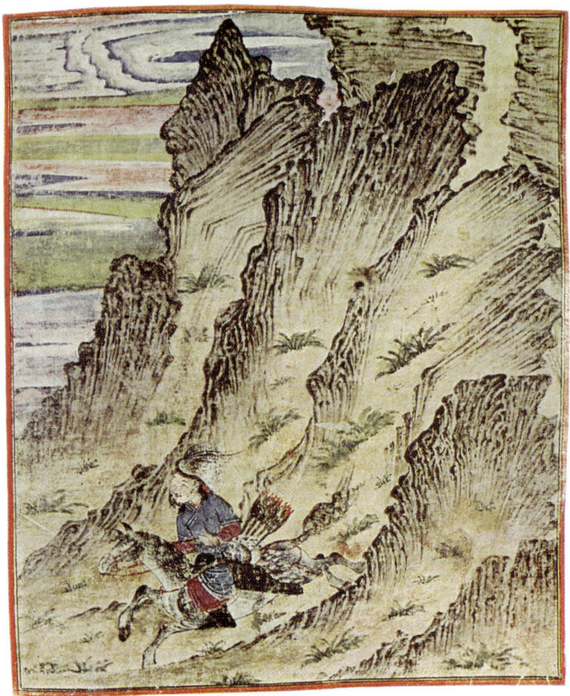

Figure 6.13 Hunter against Cliffs. *Illustration from the Diez Albums. Iran, c. 1300–50.*

idea that may have stemmed from Chinese models – for example, those seen in Song landscape painting (Figure 4.11). The underlying pictorial concept in this landscape, however, lies not only in the lifelike depiction of each landscape element or the pursuit of naturalism in its structure, but also in its tonality. A subtle sense of colour is shown in the stand of trees aflame with red and orange leaves placed in the middle of the scene. Such colour schemes make the whole image pleasing and restful to the eye.

An illustration of a Mongol-clad hunter is distinguished by its spatial and compositional elegance (Fol. 71.S.28. Nr.1; Figure 6.13). He is dramatically set against a rocky landscape rendered in monumental proportions. The elevated cliffs here have a quality of composition and force of structure that suggest Chinese models – for example, they give rise to visual tension in almost the same way as that found in the Northern Song landscape (Figure 4.11). The painter uses ink monochrome techniques for the contours and surfaces of cliffs, complementing the density of texture, while the sky, which is imaginatively pigmented in rainbow colours, creates an interesting contrast to the cliffs, with an emphasis on lifelike details. Similar emotional effects generated by directional thrusts can be observed in other related examples in the Istanbul Albums, such as the images of two hunters (Hazine 2153, fo. 28, TSM)[131] and of the *simurgh* and Zal (Hazine 2153, fo. 23, TSM),[132] indicating that this type of rocky landscape came to be treated as a standard compositional structure in Iranian painting during the middle of the fourteenth century.

The Diez Albums contain another subgroup of miniatures with a comparable emphasis on colour. In one miniature (Diez A. Fol. 71.S2),[133] the painter's concern is not to depict landscape in a naturalistic way but rather to parade his skills in the play of colour. While there is a remnant of chinoiserie elements – for example, in the exaggerated way of modelling rock – tonality is further stressed in the rendering of rocks. Instead of showing graded shading techniques with thickening and thinning lines, rocks are intensely pigmented in separate colour schemes. A similar colour concept can be seen in painting of the Tang period and also in early Yuan painting, which shows an archaic tendency.[134] Yet a bold combination of various colours used in the Diez miniature, ranging through orange, brown, purple, green and blue, highlights brightness and creates exquisite colour harmony. This mode, which came to dominate later Iranian painting, is important in that it documents the emergence of nascent Jalayirid conventions.

In sum, a group of miniatures in the Berlin and Istanbul albums reveal aspects of the high level of manuscript painting in the Iranian world in the 1320s and 1330s. The stylistic vocabulary used in these miniatures varies from subgroup to subgroup, perhaps as a reflection of the political and social disturbances following the decline of Mongol supremacy, but they exploit new pictorial techniques and repertoires among Iranian painters of the third and fourth decades of the fourteenth century. Some miniatures in Group 2 are supplementary documents for the development of *Shahnama* iconography, in which landscape is ingeniously incorporated into the whole image structure. In several examples of pure landscape painting, the painters of the Diez and Istanbul leaves have been adept in following Chinese landscape conventions, but have further developed their interest in compositional structure and colour – a phenomenon that heralds the Jalayirid style.

Illumination

One of the major emphases of this book is to identify coherence in the use of Chinese elements in several media of Iranian arts. The detailed analysis of illumination is therefore appropriate in looking into what happened in the art of the book in Mongol-ruled Iran and how this correlated with the development of Iranian pictorial and decorative concepts during the late thirteenth and early fourteenth centuries.

The art-historical significance of illumination has been widely recognised in association with the study of Qur'anic manuscripts.[135]

The techniques of illumination had already reached maturity in the Islamic world before the advent of the Mongols thanks to the continuous demand for a high standard of production of Qurʾanic manuscripts. As in some of the decorative arts of Iran, however, the use of Chinese themes is almost unprecedented in Iranian illumination before the Mongol period. Pre-Mongol Qurʾanic manuscripts are essentially adorned with non-representational decoration of vegetal, geometric and epigraphic type.[136] Equally, in the illumination inserted into the treatises of the pre-Mongol date – for example, in the *Kitab al-Diryaq*[137] – the design is in the main composed of arabesque scrolls interwoven with geometric ornamentation.

Surviving examples of Ilkhanid illuminated manuscripts, either in the form of the Qurʾan or in the *shamsa* and border decoration of illuminated books,[138] are relatively scarce; thus it is relatively difficult to pinpoint the nature of Ilkhanid illumination and especially its relationship with China. None of the Iranian illumination that predates the fourteenth century reveals decisive Chinese elements, except limited attempts to assert naturalism with some accents of blossom-like motifs.[139] Yet keys to the understanding of the decorative achievements of Ilkhanid illumination, including its reaction to Chinese themes, are found in the exquisite Qurʾanic manuscripts commissioned by Uljaitu. The first of these Qurʾans was made in 704/1304–707/1307 by a calligrapher from Baghdad; the second is the so-called Mosul Qurʾan of Uljaitu, which was completed about 712/1312; and the final and most renowned one is the Qurʾan made in Hamadan in 713/1313, which was later sent to Cairo.[140] This range of towns suggests that the art of illumination evolved particularly in the western parts of Ilkhanid territory in the early fourteenth century.[141]

Apart from their dedication to Uljaitu's mausoleum (Figure 6.14), the three manuscripts are not wholly identical in the style of illumination: the degree of assimilation of Chinese elements also varies. The decoration of the copy made in Baghdad depends largely on its geometric composition. Here the intricacy of palmettes and scrolls is enhanced by meticulous details and by a wide range of colour schemes. Lotus blossoms occur in the border of one decorative page now in Leipzig,[142] but their artistic value remains inconspicuous, for they yield to overwhelming vegetal scrolls.

Chinese elements are more recognisable in the other two manuscripts, though they are reflected in a different way. In the Mosul manuscript, a cloud collar is boldly integrated into the upper part of the frame (Figure 6.15).[143] This flamboyantly arched frame, together with a palmette frieze above, serves to enhance the sumptuousness of the calligraphy, which is written in gold script outlined in black. The cloud collar was initially recognised as a costume element in Mongol-ruled Iran, but the combination of inscriptions and multi-lobed arches creates an architectural atmosphere, evoking that found

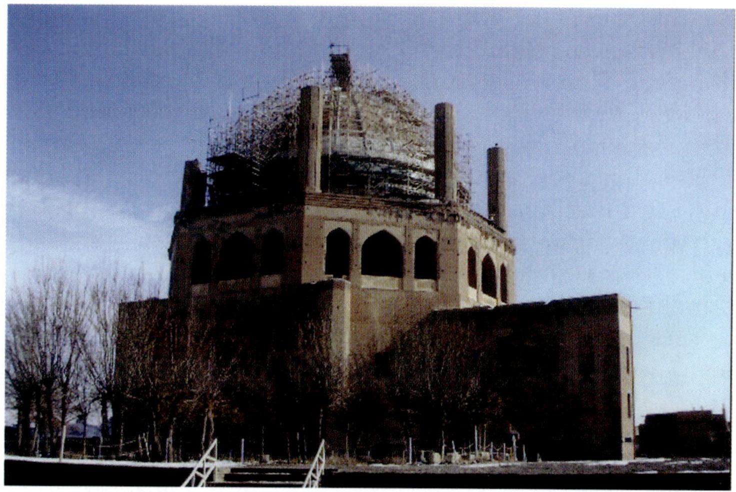

Figure 6.14 *The Mausoleum of Sultan Uljaitu. Sultaniyya, 1315–25. Built as a summer capital under Arghun, the city of Sultaniyya ('the imperial') became the Ilkhanid capital under his son Uljaitu. Once the centre of a pious foundation, only this gigantic tomb, at more than 50m height, survives until the present. The interior also remains impressive for its richly painted decoration.*

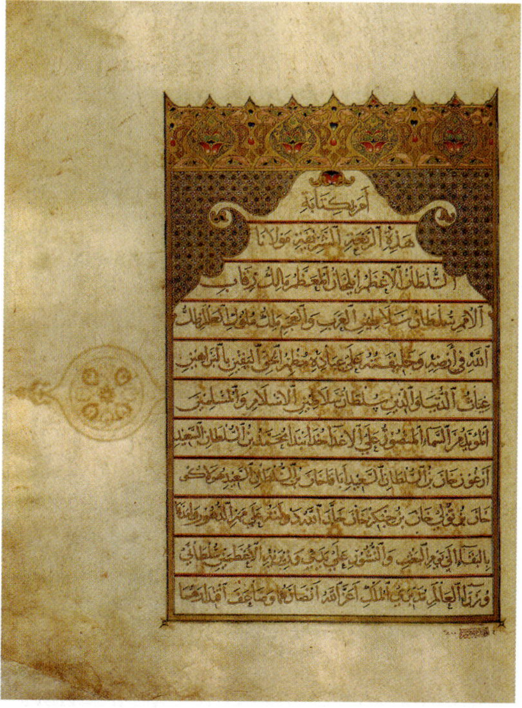

Figure 6.15 *Uljaitu's Qur'an.* Juz' *21. Mosul, 710/1310.*

in lustre *mihrab*s of the Ilkhanid period.[144] In fact, similar cloud-collar framing devices are found in the decoration of Uljaitu's mausoleum in Sultaniyya (Figure 6.14) and his *mihrab* in Isfahan (Figure 3.14),[145] suggesting a close stylistic relation between architectural decoration and manuscript illumination at that time. Evidence for the fashion for cloud-collar decoration can be found in successive examples of Ilkhanid illumination,[146] but this seems to have become outmoded as a design for illumination in the Timurid period.

Despite its adherence to geometry, which echoes one of the decorative principles of Uljaitu's mausoleum (Figure 6.14),[147] some illuminated pages of the Hamadan Qur'an betray touches of Chinese floral themes. This is particularly evident in the scrolling flowers projecting into the border decoration.[148] Compared with the flowery scrolls built into the design of earlier Ilkhanid illumination,[149] the floral motifs used in the Hamadan manuscript are rendered in a more articulate and fluid manner. Such features as multi-petalled flowers elegantly interlacing with foliate arabesques, perhaps intended to depict peonies, are evocative of those seen in Yuan blue-and-white porcelain (Figure 2.17). Such peony-like flower motifs are thus well assimilated into the scrolling decoration in the border, but lotus-bearing scroll decoration is rarely seen in either the Hamadan Qur'an or the other two Qur'anic manuscripts under discussion. Some fragmentary illumination of the Mongol period, however, suggests an awareness of the combination of lotus motifs and arabesque-based scrolling patterns among Ilkhanid illuminators[150] as well as the northward transmission of such decoration into Caucasus and eastern Anatolia.[151]

While in the illumination of the Uljaitu Qur'an the use of Chinese themes is confined to headings and border decoration, some Ilkhanid illuminators seem to have discovered the potential of Chinese elements as a principal background decoration of Qur'anic inscriptions. The curious mixture of disparate Islamic and Chinese elements, such as treating Arabic scripts as if they were swimming in patterned water, is found in a double-page frontispiece from a Qur'an that was produced at Maragha after the death of Abu Sa'id in 736/1335 (Figure 6.16).[152] This type of water convention is first seen in an Islamic context in representations of rivers or seas in manuscript painting at the turn of the fourteenth century – for example, in the Morgan Bestiary (Figure 4.14). It soon became one of the landscape conventions most typical of Mongol school painting. Unlike Ilkhanid painters, who used such decorative water patterns predominantly for suggesting a stream (e.g. Figure 5.8) or sometimes for embellishing costumes,[153] the illuminators of this Qur'anic manuscript exploited the possibility of this pattern as a type of ornamentation reconcilable with Arabic scripts. The gentle repetition of the imbricated patterns matches the smoothness and elegance of execution of the holy words. Another point of interest is the cloud-like contour panel that is used to outline the text; this device is known as *abri*.[154] The

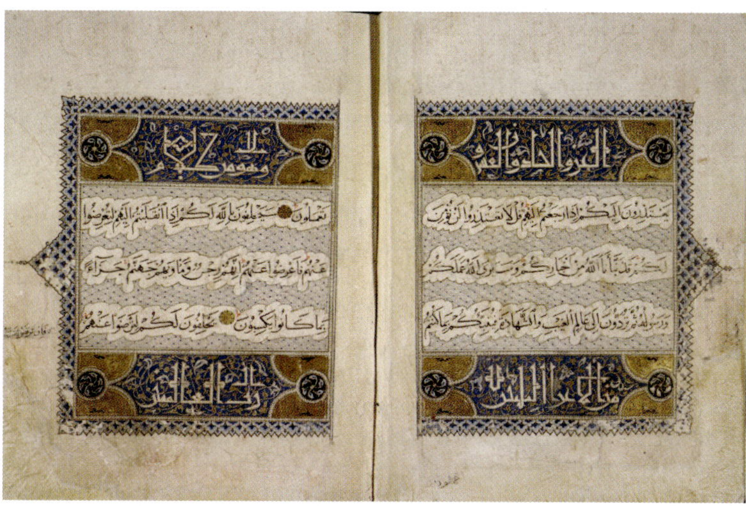

Figure 6.16 *Opening pages from the Qur'an.* Juz' *11. Maragha, 738/1338–739/1339.*

technique, though it seems unlikely to have had the same Chinese source of inspiration as the cloud motifs that evolved in Iranian pictorial and decorative art from the late thirteenth century onwards,[155] functions as a device to separate the script itself from the background of imbricated water patterns.

Though little remains, surviving illumination of the Inju school,[156] in particular that executed between 1330 and 1370, is a good point of reference for the evolution of the art of illumination in southern Iran. As in the illumination executed in the Ilkhanid centres in the west of the empire, there seems to have been an inclination to add an air of China to the decoration of Inju illumination, especially in floral decoration. One of the earliest dated examples of Inju illumination is the title-page of the Istanbul 733/1331 *Shahnama* frontispiece (Figure 3.16),[157] where lotus blossoms are emblematically present in the central and four small medallions at the corners. This was perhaps allied with the frequent occurrence of lotus blossoms in the illustrations of this manuscript.[158]

More sophisticated decorative ideas occur in the illumination of an Inju Qur'an manuscript in the Khalili Collection (fos 2^{v}–3, QUR 182),[159] which was produced perhaps subsequently to the 733/1331 *Shahnama*. Floral sprays here are gracefully arranged over the whole page. They are vividly rendered in brush strokes, recalling ink painting, a device that is in marked contrast to the arabesque scroll grounds used in some Ilkhanid Qur'an manuscripts.[160] A sense of geometry is absent, which distinguishes this Qur'an from the Hamadan Qur'an. Inju illuminators were clearly more absorbed in suggesting a naturalistic background on a grand scale than in the partial adoption of Chinese-inspired floral motifs. The overall impression of the texts is thus softened, thanks to the presence of foliage patterns delicately depicted in watercolour-like technique.

In spite of a tendency to abstraction and geometry, Iranian illuminators of the Mongol period gradually developed a more positive attitude towards unconventional decoration. By the early fourteenth century, they had become conversant with Chinese themes, including cloud-collar decoration and lotus or peony patterns. Owing much to inspiration from East Asia, they succeeded in introducing fresh decorative ideas into their repertoires of illumination. This accords with the time when Iranian decorative schemes were revolutionised under Uljaitu's patronage. The occurrence of the same decorative ideas in illumination, architectural decoration and manuscript painting demonstrates the collaboration of manuscript illuminators, architectural decorators and painters at Ilkhanid workshops, in which they seem to have worked together from common sources. Pre-eminent among these were probably drawings on paper.[161] Another important finding in this section is the decorative achievement of Inju illuminators. This is indicative of the versatility of the art of illumination in the early fourteenth-century Iranian world.

Detailed comparisons between Chinese elements in paintings of some key manuscripts produced in Iran under the Mongols and the Chinese conventions that they use made it possible to trace the pattern of the adoption and adaptation of Chinese themes in late thirteenth- and early fourteenth-century Iranian painting, as well as to identify possible Chinese sources. The examples discussed in the above three chapters are particularly useful in highlighting the significance of pictorial techniques, landscape elements, animal themes and decorative schemes of Chinese origin. Ilkhanid and Inju illumination has given additional evidence for chinoiserie in the art of the book in Iran at that time. It is thus no great leap to conclude that China had a profound impact on the stylistic and iconographic development of Iranian pictorial arts during the late thirteenth and early fourteenth centuries.

Notes

1. For the Small *Shahnama*s, see Simpson 1979. Some of the illustrations are now available online (http://shahnama.caret.cam.ac.uk; accessed 10 July 2008).
2. As has already been discussed at length, the illustrations of the Small *Shahnama*s are closely associated with those found in ceramics and tiles of the twelfth and thirteenth centuries. For a discussion of the prototype of Small *Shahnama* illustrations, see Simpson 1979, 208–48. The so-called Freer beaker (F1928.2, FGA) has often been cited as evidence for the iconographic development of the *Shahnama*

in Iran prior to the fourteenth century (see Guest 1943; Schmitz 1994).

3. For former attributions of the Small *Shahnamas*, see Simpson 1979, 16–32.
4. Ibid. 272–307.
5. See, e.g., ibid., figs 50, 53, 76 and 80–1 (NB: no archival information about each Small *Shahnama* leaf is mentioned, owing to the shortage of space).
6. The best example of this mountain convention can be seen in the illustration of *Kayumars Enthroned in the Mountains with Siyamak* (*PP*, 59).
7. Central Asian elements in the Small *Shahnama* illustrations have often been pointed out, especially in the course of discussing the association with Inju school painting (Simpson 1979, 31–2).
8. See, e.g., ibid., figs 4, 37, 39 and 53.
9. For other examples, see ibid., figs 4, 37, 39, 81 and 71.
10. For other examples, see ibid., figs 75, 78. No sun is depicted in the extant illustrations of the Freer Small *Shahnama*, while the sun in the Second Small *Shahnama* has a face (ibid., fig. 106).
11. See Firdausi 1905–25, I, 166–70.
12. See Farès 1953, 40–1, pl. XIII.
13. See Rice 1976, E13; Blair 1995, K3. See also the sun depicted in the Morgan Bestiary – namely, fos 37 (Hillenbrand 1990, fig. 32) and 73^{v} (Schmitz 1997, fig. 35).
14. See Fahd et al. 1997; Carboni 1997, 1–9. For the sun used in ceramics of the twelfth and thirteenth centuries, see Watson 1985, pl. B; Carboni 1997, pl. 7. Milstein (1986, 548–9) has pointed out the possible association between the sun and the true faith of Islam.
15. Baer 1998, 105.
16. This idea is closely associated with idealism and naturalism in Chinese painting. For further information, see Rowley 1959, 29–32.
17. For *yin–yang* dualism, see Rawson 1984, 91–2.
18. See, e.g., Grube 1962, fig. 17; Simpson 1979, figs 2, 15 and 98.
19. See, e.g., Grube 1962, pl. 16; Simpson 1979, figs 21, 86, 90 and 102. Examples of tree representations in the Freer Small *Shahnama* are relatively limited (e.g. ibid., fig. 65). For trees depicted in the First Small *Shahnama*, see Ettinghausen 1950, pl. 24; Arberry et al. 1959, pls 4a, 7c, 9b and 13; Simpson 1979, figs 5, 27, 29, 38, 69, 73–5, 89 and 101.
20. According to my close observations on some thirty leaves of the Freer Small *Shahnama*, the decoration of robes contains deer-like animal patterns painted in red, perhaps intended to depict kneeling *djeirans* (e.g. F. 1929.37 (unpublished)).
21. For the Mandarin square, see Cammann 1944; Garrett 1990.
22. For example, similar square-shaped chest decoration is found in tenth-century Manichean painting found in Gaochang (Turfan) (Yaldiz et al. 2000, pl. 358).
23. Zhao 1999, 290–1, pl. 09.09. The *Yuan shi* does not mention this special badge.
24. Chinese official records indicate that the Ming court adopted the *buzi* in 1391 in order to denote ranks of civil and military officials (*Ming shi* 1974, ch. 67, 1638; see also the list of the *buzi* in the Ming court, Huang and Chen 2001, figs 9.36–7). The establishment of this tradition

is confirmed by portraits of Ming officials (e.g. a portrait of Jiang Shunfu (1453–1504); Garrett 1994, fig. 1.17; Xie Huan's *A Literary Gathering in the Apricot Garden* (1437); Vinograd 1992, 26, pl. 3) and by actual surviving examples of Ming court robes (Yang (ed.) 1994, 4, pl. 1347).

25. Carboni 1992, 148–9, pl. 10.
26. Soucek 1975, fig. 17.
27. Indeed these are peculiar examples of the Mandarin square in Ilkhanid painting: in the Freer Bal'ami, Bahram Gur wears a coat with roundels on his chest (Fitzherbert 2001, pl. 16), but not squares (see also fo. 90ᵛ, F.1957.16; ibid., pl. 13); nor is the Mandarin square found in the Edinburgh and London *Jami' al-Tawarikh*, even though most parts of the costume in this manuscript are heavily under Mongol influence. It is, however, found in the Demotte *Shahnama* (Tabriz, c. 1335; Grabar and Blair 1980, pl. 47). Well-known enthronement scenes in both the Istanbul Saray and Berlin Diez Albums (Hazine 2152, fos 60ᵛ–61; Diez A. Fol. 71.S.46.Nr.4; İpşiroğlu 1971, pls 22–4; İpşiroğlu 1964, pl. 4) – which have been generally attributed to the works of the Mongol school at the turn of the fourteenth century (though their exact date of production is still a matter of controversy) – also provide further information about the existence of the Mandarin square in early fourteenth-century Iran. For further discussion, see Kadoi 2005a.
28. See also Simpson 1979, figs 7, 13, 18, 22, 31–2, 34, 48–9, 51, 63–4, 66, 73, 89–90, 93–4 and 113.
29. For this episode, see Firdausi 1905–25, 2, 48–50. The dragon occurs in the illustrations of the Bahram Gur, Hushang, Faridun, Gushtasp and Isfandiyar cycles in the Small *Shahnama*s: Arberry et al. 1959, pl. 4d (First); Simpson 1979, figs 42 (First), 58 (Freer), 91 (First) and 92 (Second); Fitzherbert 2001, fig. 81 (First).
30. See Simpson 1979, fig. 39. See also a dragon depicted in the illustrations of the Faridun cycle of the Freer Small *Shahnama* (ibid., fig. 58).
31. See *WSWG*, figs 16, 22, 26, cat. nos 13–14, 17 and 22.
32. See 'kaen-mon', in Nakamura and Hisano (eds) 2002, 163.
33. For the early stylistic development of the dragon in Chinese art, see Hayashi 1993.
34. Xu 2001, 48.
35. In the Morgan Bestiary, the flame appears in the body of a porpoise (fo. 27ᵛ; Grube 1978b, fig. 2) and of a hippopotamus (fo. 29ᵛ; Ettinghausen 1950, pl. 48, bottom). The flame is not used for the *simurgh* in either Mongol school painting or the Small *Shahnama*s (see Figure 4.15; Simpson 1979, figs 1 (Freer), 2 (Second), 3 (First) and 15 (Second)).
36. See Arberry et al. 1959, pl. 9b (First); Ettinghausen 1950, pls 24 (First) and 25 (Freer); Simpson 1979, 177–9, figs 37 (Freer), 38 (First), 59 (First), 60 (Second) and 61 (Freer). However, the rhinoceros in the Morgan Bestiary (fo. 14ᵛ; Brandenburg 1982, 48) and the London Qazwini (fo. 112; Carboni 1988–9, fig. 2) does not emanate flames.
37. Ettinghausen 1950, 101–6.
38. Ibid. 68–70. For the *qilin* in Chinese art, see Wirgin 1979, 200. For the *qilin* in Islamic art, see Paris 2001, 105–7. For the rhinoceros in Chinese art, see Jenyns 1954–5; Wirgin 1979, 196–8.

39. See, e.g., Rawson 1984, 107–10, fig. 92.
40. This suggests that the manuscripts may have been produced at workshops located in areas inside Mongol political control, most probably in north-west Iran or the northern Jazira, where both Ilkhanid conventions and cultural information of China and Mongol were easily accessible to the painters.
41. 1974.290: Swietochowski 1994.
42. Ibid. 79–81.
43. After the death of Abu Saʿid, Isfahan was indirectly dominated by the Chubanids, but finally the Injus took the city under their control in 741/1341. For further discussion, see Boyle 1977b.
44. Pointed out in Swietochowski 1994, 75. For representations of mountains in Inju painting, see İpşiroğlu 1967, pls 4–5.
45. See also fos 2^{v} (Swietochowski 1994, pl. 8), 7^{v} (ibid., pl. 13), 23^{v} (ibid., pl. 30), 26 (ibid., pl. 32), 32^{v} (ibid., pl. 38) and 33^{v} (ibid., pl. 39).
46. See also fos 2^{v} (ibid., pl. 8), 6 (ibid., pl. 12), 18^{v} (ibid., pl. 24), 25 (ibid., pl. 31), 27 (ibid., pl. 33), 30 (ibid., pl. 36), 31 (ibid., pl. 37), 33^{v} (ibid., pl. 39), 36 (ibid., pl. 41) and 35^{v} (ibid., pl. 42).
47. See also fos 6 (ibid., pl. 12), 20 (ibid., pl. 16) and 35^{v} (ibid., pl. 42).
48. See, e.g., fo. 16 (ibid., pl. 26).
49. See, e.g., Canby 1993a, figs 21–4.
50. See fos 9^{v} (Swietochowski 1994, pl. 15) and 10 (ibid., pl. 17).
51. See fos 4^{v} (ibid., pl. 10), 8 (ibid., pl. 14), 20 (ibid., pl. 16), 11 (ibid., pl. 18), 13 (ibid., pl. 20), 14 (ibid., pl. 21), 21v (ibid., pl. 27) and 34^{v} (ibid., pl. 40).
52. See Soucek 1975, figs 2–3, 6–11 and 17.
53. See fos 5^{v} (Swietochowski 1994, pl. 11), 12 (ibid., pl. 19), 26 (ibid., pl. 32) and 42 (ibid., pl. 48).
54. See fo. 31 (ibid., pl. 37).
55. See fo. 17 (ibid., pl. 23). See also fo. 65^{v} in the Morgan Bestiary (Schmitz 1997, fig. 31) and the water depicted in the Paris *Maqamat* (Figure 4.6).
56. There are three examples of the dragon in the Gutman *Shahnama*: see fos 24 (Swietochowski 1994, pl. 30), 26 (ibid., pl. 32) and 36 (ibid., pl. 41).
57. The adaptation of the flame for other creatures is rarely seen in the Gutman *Shahnama*. For example, the rhino-wolf (*karg*; fo. 23^{v}; ibid., pl. 29) bears no flames.
58. For other examples, see ibid., pl. 8. See also the rooster depicted in the Morgan Bestiary and the rooster-like *simurgh* depicted in the London Qazwini (Schmitz 1997, figs 27, 30).
59. See, in particular, fo. 3 (Swietochowski 1994, pl. 9).
60. See fos 9 (ibid., pl. 15), 21^{v} (ibid., pl. 27), 22 (ibid., pl. 28), 32^{v} (ibid., pl. 38), 38 (ibid., pl. 44) and 39 (ibid., pl. 45).
61. See *Legacy*, figs 176–7.
62. Swietochowski (1994, 72) has discussed this type of helmet.
63. Seven of the leaves related to the Gutman *Shahnama* were first published by İpşiroğlu 1964, 1–7, pls 1–6. According to my findings, the other six leaves in Fol. 71 (Diez A, Fol. 71.S.6.Nr.5, S.7.Nr.1, S.11.Nr.1, S.40.Nr.1, S.41.Nr.1 and S.42.Nr.1) can be categorised as belonging to the same group as the Gutman *Shahnama*.
64. See Swietochowski 1994, especially 68–75.
65. See ibid. 69, fig. 14.

66. See Diez A. Fol. 71.S.6.Nr.5 (unpublished), S.7.Nr.11 (unpublished), S.11.Nr.1 (unpublished), S.30.Nr.2 (Swietochowski 1994, fig. 19) and S.42.Nr.2–Nr.3 (ibid., figs 13–14).
67. See Diez A. Fol. 71.S.7.Nr.2 (ibid., fig. 17).
68. See the illustration of *Nushirvan at the House of Mahbud* (Grabar and Blair 1980, 168–9).
69. See Carboni 1994.
70. For former attribution of this manuscript, see ibid. 11–12.
71. See ibid., pls 4-b, 5-a and 7-c.
72. See ibid., pl. 6-d.
73. Ibid. 14.
74. See, e.g., Figure 6.4; Diez A. Fol. 71.S.42 (Swietochowski 1994, figs 13–14).
75. See, e.g., the double frontispiece of the 733/1333 *Shahnama* in St Petersburg (Adamova and Giuzal'ian 1985, 40–4; Carboni 1994, fig. 6).
76. See Huang and Chen 2001, 148–9.
77. See *WSWG*, pl. 51, 176–9; Zhao 1999, pl. 09.01, 270–1.
78. See Cammann 1952.
79. For further information, see Grube 1990–1, n. 2; O'Kane 2003, 22–31.
80. Arabe 3465, BN (O'Kane 2003, app. 1) is considered to have been made in Syria in the early thirteenth century. For a useful survey of the early illustrations of the *Kalila wa Dimna*, see Raby 1987–8, 381–98.
81. For example, No. 527, Fondation Martin Bodmer, Geneva (probably Konya, 661/1262; but its paintings were added in the late sixteenth century at an Ottoman workshop; O'Kane 2003, app. 10).
82. The rich pictorial tradition of the *Kalila wa Dimna* in the fourteenth century has been elucidated by O'Kane 2003.
83. Or. 13506: Waley and Titley 1975. Closely related to the London manuscript is a Persian version of the *Kalila wa Dimna* in Istanbul (Hazine 363, TSM; İpşiroğlu 1971, pls 7–14; Rogers, Çağman and Tanındı 1986, 50–1, pls 25–31). The Istanbul manuscript has customarily been attributed to thirteenth-century Anatolia (Konya) or Iraq (Mosul). However, O'Kane has reattributed it to the Ilkhanid period, suggesting that it was made in Baghdad between 1260 and 1285 (O'Kane 2003, 228). Published illustrations of the Istanbul manuscript show no trace of Chinese influence.
84. See, e.g., ibid., figs 5, 13, 23 and 32.
85. *Legacy*, fig. 266.
86. See Leroy 1964, figs 76–2, 78–2, 78–4 and 86–2.
87. See, e.g., *AP*, 91. Waley and Titley (1975, 50) have pointed out a similar use of haloed birds in the frontispiece of the Vienna *Kitab al-Diryaq*.
88. Further to the problems of chinoiserie in the London *Kalila wa Dimna*, it is worth recalling the discussion of the distinctive border design used in a double-page frontispiece and in successive title pages that was named as the 'lotus-petal' design by Waley and Titley (ibid. 44, figs 3–4). Their theory that this design is evidential of the stylistic association between the London *Kalila wa Dimna* and Inju painting is convincing (ibid. 44–6 and 56–7). This serves to substantiate a southern Iranian origin for this manuscript. Yet what is inappropriate is the use of the term 'lotus-petal' for this design – in which crescent-like patterns spread out left and right from the centre – because this

term merely causes gross confusion as to whether or not it was intrinsically associated with the lotus-petal design that is of Chinese origin.

89. See, e.g., Atıl 1973, nos 28–31, 33, 35, 39, 42, 46, 48, 52–3 and 69.
90. See Melikian-Chirvani 1970b, passim.
91. Suppl. pers. 1965: Richard 1997a, no. 11.
92. For a summary of the attributions suggested for the Paris *Kalila wa Dimna*, see Grube 1990–1, 378–9.
93. See Farès 1953, figs 8–9, pls XVI–XIII. This type of plant recurs in mid-fourteenth-century Mamluk bestiaries: e.g. the Oxford *Kalila wa Dimna* (probably Syria, 755/1354; Pococke 400, Bodleian Library; Atıl 1981b); the Milan *Kitab al-Hayawan* of al-Jahiz (probably Syria, c. 1350; MS 140, Inf. S.P.67, Biblioteca Ambrosiana; Hillenbrand 1990).
94. *SPA*, pl. 817A. The occurrence of lotuses has been pointed out by O'Kane 2003, 44, 229. One of the blossoms represented in fo. 21ᵛ can also be identified as a lotus (ibid., fig. 23), though it appears to be a redundant pictorial device.
95. See Simpson 1979, fig. 110.
96. See Corbin et al. 1938, pl. XIV-2. A good reproduction of this picture is not yet available.
97. See Figure 4.15. See also fo. 32ᵛ in the Istanbul *Kalila wa Dimna*, in which water is rendered in a Mesopotamian manner (İpşiroğlu 1971, pl. 8).
98. O'Kane 2003, 229. For this frontispiece, see *AP*, 98–9; Hillenbrand 2006.
99. See Leroy 1964, pls 75.3–4 and 76.
100. See fos 1ᵛ (unpublished), 2ᵛ (Blochet 1926, pl. XVIII-A), 7ᵛ (ibid., pl. XVIII-C), 9ᵛ (unpublished), 18ᵛ (Blochet 1926, pl. XVIII-E), 19ᵛ (ibid., pl. XVIII-F), 20ᵛ (unpublished), 21ᵛ (O'Kane 2003, fig. 23) and 24 (Richard 1997a, 43).
101. See Atıl 1973, pls 44 and 51–3.
102. See fos 4ᵛ (Blochet 1926, pl. XVIII-B), 15ᵛ (*SPA*, pl. 817B) and 20ᵛ (unpublished).
103. O'Kane 2003, 229.
104. For further discussion, see Simpson 1982a.
105. Richard 1997a, 43.
106. MS 3655: Barrucand 1986b.
107. Ibid., figs 1–32; O'Kane 2003, figs 2, 8 and 35.
108. See, e.g., Barrucand 1986b, figs 2, 3, 7, 12, 15–16, 18, 20–3 and 25.
109. See *AP*, 108, 112, 116 and 122.
110. See also Barrucand 1986b, figs 2, 6, 17, 19, 25–6 and 28–32.
111. See also one of the miniatures found in the Tashkent manuscript (fo. 50; Ismailova et al. 1980, pl. 1).
112. Barrucand 1986b, 29–32.
113. According to Contadini (1992, 162–5), 32 leaves and 28 miniatures of this manuscript have been identified. The present location and publication details of the illustrated leaves that I could trace at the time of writing this book are as followed: (1) 'the asses' (unknown; Binyon, Wilkinson and Gray 1933, 42, pl. IX.B); (2) 'the crows' (Garett Collection; Moghadam and Armajani 1939, 87, no. 197); (3) 'the unicorn' (FGA; Ettinghausen 1950, pl. 46); (4) 'the eagle' (Fogg Art Museum; Schroeder 1961, fig. 4); (5) 'the wild ass' (Fogg Art Museum;

Grube 1962, pl. 5); (6) 'the oxen' (MMA; Grube 1962, pl. 4); (7) 'the stags' (Minneapolis Institute of Art; Grube 1962, pl. 6); (8) 'the lizards' (unknown; Sotheby's 1967, lot 6); (9) 'the crab' (Hans P. Kraus Collection; Grube 1972, no. 26); (10) 'the phoenixes' (Keir Collection; Robinson 1967, 133, pl. 13, III.1); (11) 'the goat' (unknown; Sotheby's 1977, lot 32; Sotheby's 1981, lot 13); (12) 'the herons' (FGA; *SPA*, pl. 821); (13) 'the mares' (al-Sabah Collection, Dar al-Athar al-Islamiyya, Kuwait; Jenkins (ed.) 1983, 97); (14) 'the eagles' (MMA; Metropolitan Museum of Art 1987, 70); (15) 'the ram' (Art Institute of Chicago; Schmitz 1997, 16, fig. 3); (16) 'the water-birds' (Aga Khan Collection; Paris 2007, no. 11); (17) 'the doves' (FGA; unpublished); (18) 'the ibexes' (McGill University Library, Montreal; Binyon, Wilkinson and Gray 1933, 42, no. 18 (C)); (19) 'the scorpions' (Contadini 1992, pl. 64a); (20) 'the owls' (FGA; unpublished); (21) 'the viper' (Art Institute of Chicago, unpublished).

114. Schmitz 1997, 16. For the Escorial Bestiary, see Lorey 1935b; Contadini 1988–9. This manuscript has also been published in colour facsimile by a Spanish bank (C. R. Bravo-Villasante, *El libro de las utilidades de los animales de Ibn al-Durayhim al-Mawsili* (Madrid, 1981); personally unconsulted).
115. See Nos 1, 4–6, 7, 9–10 and 14.
116. See Nos 3, 6–7 and 10.
117. See No. 12.
118. However, the Kufic heading in this illustration is reminiscent of those seen in the Morgan Bestiary.
119. See Soucek 1975, figs 5, 12 and 14.
120. Literary evidence for the importance of this period in the history of Iranian painting is found in Dust Muhammad's preface to the Bahram Mirza Album (951/1544, Hazine 2154, TSM). See Thackston 1989, 345.
121. Of particular note are the earliest ascension miniatures in Istanbul – namely, the *Miʿraj-nama* (Hazine 2154, TSM), which can be dated to the middle of the fourteenth century (Ettinghausen 1957b; İpşiroğlu 1967, 60–7). Splendid as the paintings are, chinoiserie elements relevant to the subject of this book are scarce in them. For further discussion on the fourteenth-century *Miʿraj-nama*, see Gruber 2005, 108–79.
122. There are three dated manuscripts that were produced in the early Jalayirid period: the *al-Maʾ al-Waraqi waʾl-ard al-Najmiyyah* (740/1339; but its paintings were added later; Ahmet III, 2075, TSM; Farès 1959); the *Kalila wa Dimna* (744/1343; but its paintings are later additions; MS Fars 61, National Library, Cairo; Kühnel 1937); and the *Garshasp-nama* (755/1354; Hazine 674, TSM; Ettinghausen 1959b, 60–5, figs 13–17). For a brief discussion of these manuscripts, see Grube 1978b, 18–19.
123. The following Diez leaves are equally relevant to the discussion of *Shahnama* iconography in late Ilkhanid and possibly early Jalayirid painting: Fol. 71.S.6.Nr.6 (unpublished), Fol. 71.S.26.Nr.2 (unpublished), Fol. 71.S.40.Nr.1 (unpublished), Fol. 71.S.44.Nr.1–Nr.5 (unpublished), Fol. 71.S.45.Nr.2–Nr.3 (unpublished), Fol. 71.S.46.Nr.2–Nr.3 and Nr.5 (unpublished).
124. See, e.g., Grabar and Blair 1980, nos 30, 33–4, 36, 38, 41–2, 47, 49, 51 and 53 in particular.

125. I am indebted to Dr Teresa Fitzherbert for valuable information about this Chinese material.
126. e.g. Hazine 2153, fo. 156ᵛ (suggested by Grube 1976, n. 64; Atasoy 1970, fig. 7), fo. 55 (suggested by Sims 2002, no. 102), 112 and 118 (suggested by Grabar 2000, 46; Atasoy 1970, figs 16, 2). Fo. 55ᵛ (Sims 2002, no. 221) is also closely related to the style of the Great Mongol *Shahnama*.
127. *PP*, 42.
128. See, e.g., representations of water in the Istanbul *Miʿraj-nama* (Ettinghausen 1957b, figs 2, 4) and some leaves of the Diez Albums datable to the late Ilkhanid period (İpşiroğlu 1964, Tafel, XV, XI).
129. İpşiroğlu (1967, 33–4) has regarded this painting as part of the Rashid al-Din manuscript.
130. See Fong 1992, pls 92–4.
131. See Rogers, Çağman and Tanındı 1986, pl. 49.
132. See ibid., pl. 50.
133. İpşiroğlu 1964, 39, Tafel XIV. See also Fol. 71.S.36 (ibid., Tafel XV), Fol. 71.S.39 (ibid., Tafel XVI) and Fol. 72.S.29 (*Legacy*, cat. no. 26).
134. *CP*, 102. For colour in Chinese painting in general, see Yu 1988.
135. See Lings 1976; James 1992.
136. See, e.g., ibid. 22–3, nos 1–9.
137. See Farès 1953. For other examples, see the *ex libris* of the *Kitab Khalq al-Nabi wa Khulqih* (1050–3, Ghazna; MS 437, Leiden University Library; Stern 1969, fig. 1).
138. For a list of dated illuminated manuscripts of the Mongol period, see *SPA*, 1954, n. 1.
139. Gray 1985, 137. See a frontispiece of the Qurʾanic manuscript dated 688/1289 (Arabe 6716, BN; Blochet 1926, pl. XVI).
140. For these manuscripts, see James 1988, 98–126. The stylistic relationship between the Hamadan Qurʾan and Mamluk Qurʾans has been pointed out (ibid. 103–10).
141. Gray 1985, 135. The production of calligraphy was predominant in Baghdad, where the famous master Yaqut al-Mustaʿsimi was active until his death in 697/1298 (James 1992, 58–9). Hamadan was one of the places where the tradition of calligraphy and illumination was established under Rashid al-Din (James 1988, 127–31). For the importance of Mosul in manuscript illumination in the Ilkhanid period, see James 1992, 99–101.
142. See *SPA*, pl. 937B.
143. See also *Juzʾ* 15 of the Mosul manuscript (James 1988, fig. 65).
144. See Watson 1985, figs 111, 126.
145. See also a cloud-collar device found in the interior decoration of his mausoleum (Sims 1988, figs 5–7 and 35).
146. See *SPA*, pl. 939B.
147. See Sims 1988, figs 4, 14, 17, 19–20, 27–8 and 30–2.
148. See, e.g., James 1988, figs 76-d, 79 and 82; Sotheby's 1988, lot 20.
149. See, e.g., James 1992, no. 21.
150. See, e.g., ibid., nos 10, 22.
151. See ibid., no. 49; Baykan (ed.) 2002, 198–200.
152. Another section of this Qurʾan is now in the Museum of Fine Arts, Boston (29.58; *SPA*, pl. 938B). Similar patterns occur in another fourteenth-century Qurʾan in Dublin (Is 1471, Chester Beatty Library; Lings 1976, no. 41) and in a Mamluk Qurʾan in Istanbul (Y365, TSM; James 1988, fig. 102).

153. See K33 in the London *Jamiʿ al-Tawarikh* (Gray 1978, 37–8).
154. For this device, see Ettinghausen 1977.
155. Ettinghausen (ibid. 349–50) has discussed the early development of *abri* painting in Qur'an illumination, which can be traced back to the early eleventh century.
156. For Inju illumination, see James 1992, 122–49.
157. Flower motifs, conceivably peonies, are found in the illumination of the 741/1341 *Shahnama* (Simpson 2000, pls 1–2, 12–13). The lotus motifs that occur in an illuminated page of the Stephens *Shahnama* (752/1352; Sotheby's 1998, lot 41) are more articulate than those seen in the 733/1331 *Shahnama*.
158. See Rogers, Çağman and Tanındı 1986, pls 32, 38, 40 and 42.
159. James 1992, no. 29. For other related examples, see Lings 1976, no. 60; James 1992, nos 30–1 and 33. For Muzaffarid examples of this decorative device, see Soudavar 1992, no. 18.
160. See, e.g., James 1988, figs 53, 63.
161. Bloom 2001, 191.

Conclusion

THROUGH THE CONSIDERATION of the all-pervasive impact of China on Iranian art under Mongol rule, this study has revealed the immense richness of material culture in late thirteenth- and early fourteenth-century Iran. Having experienced the gamut of decorative motifs and pictorial styles introduced from East Asia through the advent of the Mongols, Iranian artists gradually became acclimatised to such elements and consequently acquired a certain command of Chinese conventions. Their insatiable curiosity for alien aesthetics led to an extraordinary internationalisation of styles, forms and patterns in almost all media of Iranian decorative and pictorial arts. This certainly served to increase the depth and range of Iranian art.

In general, the results of this study have not contradicted the major earlier remarks on this subject. Yet the three chapters on decorative arts have provided a more nuanced view of the complex yet intriguing process of the wholesale borrowing of artistic forms of China by Iranian artists that manifested itself from the late thirteenth century onwards. As soon as Chinese themes had swept into the Iranian world, a Chinese veneer became a standard ingredient of imagery in the major decorative objects produced in Iran under the Mongols – dragons, phoenixes, lotuses and clouds. In addition to textiles, which provide a substantial body of evidence for the artistic exchanges between East and West, the westward transmission of Chinese themes was encouraged by the thriving ceramic trade between China and the Middle East. Metalwork and other miscellaneous objects are also a reservoir of information about the Sino-Iranian artistic relationship.

Similarly, the conventional theory of chinoiserie in Iranian painting has been enriched by the three chapters on manuscript painting, which shed much light on characteristics and patterns of chinoiserie in Iranian painting. Having been inspired by the intense observation of nature demonstrated by Chinese painters, Ilkhanid painters discovered the significance of landscape, which became a cardinal importance in the history of Iranian painting. Ilkhanid painters quickly absorbed Chinese conventions of depicting landscape, including the mastery of Chinese brush strokes and advanced spatial devices, into their pictorial repertoires and subtly transformed them into new pictorial concepts suitable for their own cultural sphere. What makes Iranian painting of the period especially interesting is the occurrence of elements derived from Chinese printed materials, which were no doubt diffused westwards more easily than hand-scroll paintings. Finally, the marvels of the stylistic and technical achievement of the painters of the Mongol and other provincial schools in the late thirteenth and early fourteenth centuries became the basis for new pictorial traditions in Iran, leading to the rise of the so-called classical style in the fifteenth century.

This study has aimed to illuminate hitherto obscure aspects of late thirteenth- and early fourteenth-century Iranian art. Yet the questions raised by the occurrence of Chinese elements in Iranian art under the Mongols have by no means been answered entirely satisfactorily. Many vexing problems remain to be solved. Given all the findings in this study, it should nevertheless have been made clear that Chinese art left an indelible artistic and cultural mark upon the entire art and material culture of the Iranian world. Essentially, then, chinoiserie is one of the fundamental parameters of the development of Iranian art.

References

Primary and secondary sources

Adamova, A. T. and L. T. Giuzal'ian (1985). *Miniatiury rukopisi poemy 'Shakhname' 1333 goda*. St Petersburg.

Adle, C. (ed.) (1982a). *Art et société dans le monde iranien*. Paris.

—— (1982b). 'Un Diptyque de fondation en céramique lustrée, Kâšân 711/1312 (recherche sur le module et le tracé correcteur/régulateur dans la miniature orientale, II', in Adle (ed.) (1982a), 199–218.

Aga-Oglu, M. (1934). 'Preliminary notes on some Persian illustrated MSS in the Topkapu Müzesi – part 1', *AI*, 1: 183–99.

Aigle, D. (ed.) (1997). *L'Iran face à la domination mongole, actes du colloque de Pont-à-Mousson, 26–28 octobre 1992*. Tehran.

Album, S. (1984). 'Studies in Ilkhanid history and numismatics i: a late Ilkhanid hoard (743/1342)', *SI*, 13: 49–116.

—— (1985). 'Studies in Ilkhanid history and numismatics ii: a late Ilkhanid hoard (741/1340) as evidence for the history of Diyār Bakr', *SI*, 14: 43–76.

Alexander, D. (1992). *The Arts of War: Arms and Armour of the 7th to 19th Centuries*. Oxford.

—— (ed.) (1996). *Furusiyya*, 2 vols. Riyadh.

Al-Gailani, ʿA. (1973). 'The origins of Islamic art and the role of China', unpublished Ph.D. dissertation. University of Edinburgh.

Allan, J. W. (1971). *Medieval Middle Eastern Pottery*. Oxford.

—— (1973). 'Abū'l-Qāsim's treatise on ceramics', *Iran*, 11: 111–20.

—— (1976–7). 'Silver: the key to bronze in early Islamic Iran', *KdO*, 11: 5–21.

—— (1977). 'Originality in bronze – a thirteenth century Persian school of metalworkers', *Iran*, 15: 156–64.

—— (1978). 'From Tabrīz to Siirt – relocation of a 13th century metalworking school', *Iran*, 16: 182–3.

—— (1979). *Persian Metal Technology 700–1300 AD*. London.

—— (1982). *Nishapur: Metalwork of the Early Islamic Period*. New York.

—— (1989). 'Metalwork', in Ferrier (ed.) (1989), 171–86.

—— (1991). *Islamic Ceramics*. Oxford.

—— (ed.) (1995). *Islamic Art in the Ashmolean, Oxford Studies in Islamic Art X*, 2 vols. Oxford.

—— (2000). *Persian Steel: The Tanavoli Collection*. Tehran.

Allan, J. W. and C. Roberts (eds) (1987). *Syria and Iran: Three Studies in Medieval Ceramics, Oxford Studies in Islamic Art IV*. Oxford.

Allan, J. W. and D. Sourdel (1978). 'Khātam', in *EI*², 4: 1102–5.

Allen, T. (1985). 'Byzantine sources for the Jāmiʿ al-Tawārīkh of Rashīd al-Dīn', *AO*, 15: 121–36.

Allsen, T. (1987). *Mongol Imperialism: The Policies of the Great Qan Möngke in China, Russia, and the Islamic Lands, 1251–1259*. Berkeley.

—— (1997). *Commodity and Exchange in the Mongol Empire: A Cultural History of Islamic Textiles*. Cambridge.

—— (2001a) *Culture and Conquest in Mongol Eurasia*. Cambridge.

—— (2001b). 'Robing in the Mongolian empire', in S. Gordon (ed.), *Robes and Honor: The Medieval World of Investiture*. New York, 303–13.

Almagro, M., L. Caballero, J. Zozaya and A. Almagro (1975). *Qusayr ʿAmra: Residencia y Baños Omeyas en el Desierto de Jordania*. Madrid.

Amitai-Preiss, R. (1995). *Mongols and Mamluks: The Mamluk-Ilkhanid War 1260–1281*. Cambridge.

—— (1996). 'Ghazan, Islam and Mongol tradition: a view from the Mamlūk Sultanate', *BSOAS*, 59, no. 1: 1–10.

Amitai-Preiss, R. and D. Morgan (eds) (1999). *The Mongol Empire and its Legacy*. Leiden.

An, J. (c. 1987). *Early Chinese Glassware, The Oriental Ceramic Society Translations Number Twelve*, trans. M. Henderson. *s.l.*

—— (1991). 'Dated Islamic glass in China', *BAI*, 5: 123–37.

An, L. (2004). 'Beifang youmu minzu anma shiju de chansheng he fazhan [The manufacture and development of harness in the Eurasian steppes]', *Gugong wenwu*, 21, no. 11: 106–17.

Andrews, F. H. (1920). *Ancient Chinese Figured Silks Excavated by Sir Aurel Stein at Ruined Sites of Central Asia*. London.

Andrews, P. A. (1985). 'The Turco-Mongol context of some objects shown in the Istanbul album pictures', in Grube and Sims (eds) (1985), 110–20.

—— (1999). *Felt Tents and Pavilions: The Nomadic Tradition and its Interaction with Princely Tentage*, 2 vols. London.

Anet, C. (1913). 'The "Manafi-i Heiwan"', *Burlington Magazine*, 23: 224–31, 261.

Anon. (1956). *Quanxiangben Sanguozhi pinghua* [History of the Three Kingdoms], Xinanyu imprint of 1321–3, the Cabinet Library. Tokyo. *s.l.*

Appel, K. and D. George (1971). 'Die Saray-Alben der Staatsbibliothek und ihre Restaurierung', *Jahrbuch Preußischer Kulturbesitz*, 9: 227–32.

Arberry, A. J., M. Minovi and E. Blochet (1959). *The Chester Beatty Library: A Catalogue of the Persian Manuscripts and Miniatures*, ed. J. V. S. Wilkinson, vol. 1. Dublin.

Arnold, L. (1999). *Princely Gifts and Papal Treasures: The Franciscan Mission to China and its Influence on the Art of the West, 1250–1350*. San Francisco.

Arnold, T. W. (1922). 'The Caesarian section in an Arabic manuscript dated 707 A.H.', in T. W. Arnold and R. A. Nicholson (eds), *A Volume of Oriental Studies Presented to Edward G. Browne on his 60th Birthday*. Cambridge, 6–7.

—— (1924). *Survivals of Sasanian and Manichaean Art in Persian Painting*. Oxford.

—— (1928). *Painting in Islam: A Study of the Place of Pictorial Art in Muslim Culture*. Oxford; repr. New York, 1965.

—— (1932). *The Old and New Testaments in Muslim Religious Art*. London.

—— (1981). 'Book painting: a. the origins', in *SPA*, 1809–19.

Arnold, T. W. and A. Grohmann (1929). *The Islamic Book: A Contribution to its Art and History from the VI–XVIII Century*. Paris and New York.
Ashton, A. (1934–5). 'Early blue and white in Persian MSS.', *TOCS*, 12: 21–5.
Ashtor, E. (1956). 'The Kārimī merchants', *Journal of the Royal Asiatic Society*, 45–58.
Asimov, M. S. and C. E. Bosworth (eds) (1998). *History of Civilizations of Central Asia, Volume IV, The Age of Achievement: AD 750 to the End of the Fifteenth Century, Part One, The Historical, Social and Economic Setting*. Paris.
Aslanapa, O. (1979). 'The art of bookbinding', in Gray (ed.) (1979), 59–91.
Aslanapa, O. and R. Nawmann (eds) (1969). *Forschungen zur Kunst Asiens: In Memoriam Kurt Erdmann*. Istanbul.
Atasoy, N. (1970). 'Four Istanbul albums and some fragments from fourteenth-century Shahnamehs', *AO*, 8: 19–48.
Ateş, A. (1961). 'Un Vieux Poème romanesque persan: récit de Warqah et Gulshāh', *AO*, 4: 143–52.
Atıl, E. (1972). 'Two Īl-Ḫānid candlesticks at the University of Michigan', *KdO*, 8: 1–33.
—— (1973). *Ceramics from the World of Islam*. Washington, DC.
—— (1981a). *Renaissance of Islam: Art of the Mamluks*. Washington, DC.
—— (1981b). *Kalila wa Dimna: Fables from a Fourteenth-Century Arabic Manuscript*. Washington, DC.
—— (ed.) (1990). *Islamic Art and Patronage: Treasures from Kuwait*. New York.
—— (1999). 'The Freer Bowl and the legacy of the Shāhnāme', *Damaszener Mitteilungen*, 11: 7–12.
Atıl, E., W. T. Chase and P. Jett (1985). *Islamic Metalwork in the Freer Gallery of Art*. Washington, DC.
Avery, M. (1941). 'Miniatures of the Fables of Badpai and of the life of Aesop in the Pierpont Morgan Library', *AB*, 23, no. 6: 103–16.
Ayers, J. (1978). 'The discovery of a Yüan ship at Sinan, South-West Korea: a first report', *OA*, NS 24, no. 1: 79–85.
—— (1982–3). 'Chinese porcelain of the Sultans in Istanbul', *TOCS*, 47: 77–104.
Azarpay, G. (1975). 'Some Iranian iconographic formulae in Sogdian painting', *Iranica Antiqua*, 11: 168–77.
—— (1978). 'The eclipse dragon on an Arabic frontispiece-miniature', *Journal of the American Oriental Society*, 98: 363–74.
—— (1981). *Sogdian Painting: The Pictorial Epic in Oriental Art*. Berkeley.
Badiee, J. (1984). 'The Sarre Qazwīnī: an early Aq Qoyunlu manuscript?' *AO*, 14: 98–113.
Baer, E. (1965). *Sphinxes and Harpies in Medieval Islamic Art: An Iconographical Study*. Jerusalem.
—— (1968). '"Fish pond" ornaments on Persian and Mamluk metal vessels', *BSOAS*, 31, no. 1: 14–27.
—— (1973–4). 'The Nisan Tası: a study in Persian–Mongol metalware', *KdO*, 9: 1–46.
—— (1983). *Metalwork in Medieval Islamic Art*. Albany.
—— (1998). *Islamic Ornament*. Edinburgh.
—— (2002). 'Zakhrafa', in EI^2, 11: 423–5.
—— (2004). *The Human Figure in Islamic Art: Inheritances and Islamic Transformations*. Costa Mesa.

Bahrami, M. (1949–50). 'Chinese porcelains from Ardabil in the Teheran Museum', *TOCS*, 25: 13–19.

Bailey, G. A. (1992). 'The dynamics of *chinoiserie* in Timurid and early Safavid ceramics', in Golombek and Subtelny (eds) (1992), 179–90.

Bailey, H. W. (1931). 'The word "but" in Iranian', *BSOAS*, 6, no. 2: 279–3.

Baker, P. L. (1986). 'A history of Islamic court dress in the Middle East', unpublished Ph.D. dissertation. University of London.

—— (1995). *Islamic Textiles*. London.

Baldick, J. (2000). *Animal and Shaman: Ancient Religions of Central Asia*. London.

Ball, W. (1976). 'Two aspects of Iranian Buddhism', *Bulletin of the Asian Institute of Pahlavi University*, 1–4: 103–63.

—— (1979). 'The Imamzadeh Maʿsum at Vardjovi: a rock-cut Il-khanid complex near Maragheh', *Archaeologische Mitteilungen aus Iran*, 12: 329–40.

Bar Hebraeus (1932). *The Chronography of Gregory Abū'l Faraj: the Son of Aaron, the Hebrew Physician, Commonly Known as Bar Hebraeus, Being the First Part of his Political History of the World Translated from the Syriac*, trans. E. A. Wallis Budge, 2 vols. Oxford.

Barnes, R. (1997). *Indian Block-Printed Textiles in Egypt: The Newberry Collection in the Ashmolean Museum*, Oxford, 2 vols. Oxford.

Barnhart, R. M. (1993). *Li Kung-lin's Classic of Filial Piety*. New York.

Barnhart, R. M., X. Yang, C. Nie, S. Lang, J. Cahill and H. Wu (1997). *Three Thousand Years of Chinese Painting*. New Haven.

Barrett, D. (1952). *Persian Painting of the 14th Century*. London.

Barrucand, M. (1986a). 'Les Représentations d'architectures dans la miniature islamique en orient du début du XIIIe au début du XIVe siècle', *Cahiers archéologiques*, 34: 119–41.

—— (1986b). 'Le *Kalīla wa Dimna* de la Bibliothèque royale de Rabat: un manuscrit illustré īl-khānide', *Revue des études islamiques*, 54: 17–48.

—— (1999). 'Kopie – Nachempfindung oder Umgestaltung am Beispiel arabischer mittelalterlicher Bilderhandschriften und ihrer osmanischen Kopien', in B. Finster, C. Fragner and H. Hafenrichter (eds), *Bamberger Symposium: Rezeption in der islamischen Kunst vom 26.6.–28.6.1992, Beiruter Texte und Studien, Band 61*. Beirut. 19–41.

Barthold, V. V. (1968). *Turkestan down to the Mongol Invasion*. London.

Barthold, V. V. and J. M. Rogers (trans.) (1970). 'The burial rites of the Turks and the Mongols', *CAJ*, 14: 195–227.

Basilov, V. N. (ed.) (1989). *Nomads of Eurasia*. Los Angeles.

Baykan, D. (ed.) (2002). *Museum of Turkish and Islamic Art*. Istanbul.

Beamish, J. (1995). 'The significance of Yuan blue and white exported to South East Asia', in Scott and Guy (eds) (1995), 225–51.

Behrendt, K. A. (2004). *The Buddhist Architecture of Gandhāra*. Leiden.

Berger, P. and T. T. Bartholomew (1995). *Mongolia: The Legacy of Chinggis Khan*. San Francisco.

Berlekamp, P. (2007). 'From Iraq to Fars: tracking cultural transformations in the 1322 Qazwīnī *'Ajā'ib* manuscript', in A. Contadini (ed.), *Arab Painting: Text and Image in Illustrated Arabic Manuscripts*. Leiden, 73–91.

Bernus, M., H. Marchal and G. Vial (1971). 'Le Suaire de Saint Josse', *Bulletin de liaison du centre international d'étude des textiles anciens*, 33: 22–57.

Bernus-Taylor, M. (2001). *Les Arts de l'Islam*. Paris.

Binyon. L., J. V. S. Wilkinson and B. Gray (1933). *Persian Miniature Painting*. London; repr. New York, 1971.

Bivar, A. D. H. (1970). 'Trade between China and the Near East in the Sasanian and early Muslim periods', in Watson (ed.) (1970), 1–11.
—— (2000). *Excavation at Ghubayra, Iran*. London.
Blair, S. S. (1982). 'The coins of the later Ilkhānids: mint organization, regionalization, and urbanism', *American Numismatic Society Museum Notes*, 27: 211–30.
—— (1983). 'The coins of the later Ilkhanids: a typological analysis', *Journal of the Economic and Social History of the Orient*, 26: 295–317.
—— (1984). 'Ilkhanid architecture and society: an analysis of the endowment deed of the Rab'-i Rashidi', *Iran*, 22: 67–90.
—— (1985). 'Artist and patronage in late fourteenth-century Iran in the light of two catalogues of Islamic metalwork', *BSOAS*, 48, no. 1: 53–9.
—— (1986a). *The Ilkhanid Shrine Complex at Natanz, Iran*. Cambridge, MA.
—— (1986b). 'The Mongol capital of Sultāniyya, "the imperial"', *Iran*, 24: 139–51.
—— (1987). 'The epigraphic programme of the tomb of Uljaytu at Sultaniyya: meaning in Mongol architecture', *IA*, 2: 43–96.
—— (1992). *The Monumental Inscriptions from Early Islamic Iran and Transoxiana*. Leiden.
—— (1993a). 'The development of the illustrated book in Iran', *Muqarnas*, 10: 266–74.
—— (1993b). 'The Ilkhanid palace', *AO*, 23: 239–48.
—— (1995). *A Compendium of Chronicles: Rashid al-Din's Illustrated History of the World*. Oxford.
—— (1996). 'Patterns of patronage and production in Ilkhanid Iran: the case of Rashid al-Din', in Raby and Fitzherbert (eds) (1996), 39–62.
—— (1998). *Islamic Inscriptions*. Edinburgh.
—— (2005). 'A Mongol envoy', in O'Kane (ed.) (2005), 45–60.
—— (2006). *Islamic Calligraphy*. Edinburgh.
Blair, S. S. and J. M. Bloom (1994). *The Art and Architecture of Islam 1250–1800*. New Haven.
—— (1997a). 'By the pen: the art of writing in Islamic art', in Tilden (ed.) (1997), 108–25.
—— (1997b). *Islamic Art*. London.
—— (2003). 'The mirage of Islamic art: reflections on the study of an unwieldy field', *AB*, 85, no. 1, 152–84.
—— (2006). *Cosmophilia: Islamic Art from the David Collection, Copenhagen*. Chicago.
Blair, S. S., J. M. Bloom and A. E. Wardwell (1992). 'Reevaluating the date of the "Buyid" silks by epigraphic and radiocarbon analysis', *AO*, 22: 1–41.
Blochet, E. (1926). *Les Enluminures des manuscrits orientaux, turcs, arabes, persans de la Bibliothèque nationale*. Paris.
—— (1929). *Musulman Painting XIIth–XVIIth Century*, trans. C. Binyon. London.
Blois, F. C. de (1997). 'Sīmurgh', *EI*², 9: 615.
Bloom, J. M. (2000). 'The introduction of paper to the Islamic lands and the development of the illustrated manuscript', *Muqarnas*, 17: 18–23.
—— (2001). *Paper before Print: The History and Impact of Paper in the Islamic World*. New Haven.
—— (2008). 'Lost in translation: gritted plans and maps along the Silk Road', in P. Forêt and A. Kaplony (eds), *The Journey of Maps and Images on the Silk Road*. Leiden, 83–96.

Boilot, D. J. (1960). 'al-Bīrūnī', in *EI*², 1: 1236–8.

Bosworth, C. E. (1967). *The Islamic Dynasties: A Chronological and Genealogical Handbook*. Edinburgh.

—— (1996). *The New Islamic Dynasties: A Chronological and Genealogical Mannual*. Edinburgh.

—— (1990). 'Bīrūnī, Abū Rayhān', in *EIr*, 4: 274–87.

Bosworth, C. E., S. S. Blair and J. M. Bloom (2002). 'Yas͟hm', in *EI*², 11: 296–8.

Bosworth, C. E., M. Hartmann and R. Israeli (1997). 'al-Sīn', in *EI*², 9: 616–25.

Bowie, T. (ed.) (1966). *East–West in Art: Patterns of Cultural and Aesthetic Relationships*. Bloomington.

Boyer, M. (1952). *Mongol Jewellery: Researches on the Silver Jewellery Collected by the First and Second Danish Central Asian Expeditions under the Leadership of Henning Haslund-Christensen 1936–37 and 1938–39*. Copenhagen.

Boyle, J. A. (ed.) (1968). *The Cambridge History of Iran, Volume 5: The Saljuq and Mongol Periods*. Cambridge.

—— (1971a). *The Successors of Genghis Khan*. New York.

—— (1971b). 'Rashīd al-Dīn: the first world historian', *Iran*, 4: 19–26.

—— (1977a). *The Mongol World Empire 1206–1370*. London.

—— (1977b). 'The capture of Isfahan by the Mongols', in Boyle (1977a), VIII.

—— (1977c). 'Bīrūnī and Rashīd al-Dīn', *CAJ*, 21: 4–12.

Brandenburg, D. (1982). *Islamic Miniature Painting in Medical Manuscripts*. Basel.

Brend, B. (1980). 'Rocks in Persian miniature painting', in Watson (ed.) (1980), 111–37.

—— (1989). 'The arts of the book', in Ferrier (ed.) (1989), 232–42.

—— (1991). *Islamic Art*. London.

—— (1994). 'A reconsideration of the Book of Constellations of 400/1009–10 in the Bodleian Library', in Hillenbrand (ed.) (1994), 89–93.

—— (1995). 'Rasm', in *EI*², 8: 451–3.

Brentjes, B. (1978). 'The fall of Baġdād and the Caliph al-Mustaʿsim in a Tabrīz miniature', *East and West*, 28: 151–4.

Bretschneider, E. (1910). *Mediaeval Researchers from Eastern Asiatic Sources: Fragments towards the Knowledge of the Geography and History of Central and Western Asia from the 13th to the 17th Century*, 2 vols. London; repr. 2000.

Bronstein, L. (1981). 'Decorative woodwork of the Islamic period', in *SPA*, 2607–27.

Brown, C. (2000). *Weaving China's Past: The Amy S. Clague Collection of Chinese Textiles*. Phoenix.

Browne, L. E. (1933). *The Eclipse of Christianity in Asia from the Time of Muhammad till the Fourteenth Century*. Cambridge.

Büchner, V. F. (1934). 'Sīmurg͟h', in *EI*¹, 4: 426–8.

Buchthal, H. (1939). 'The painting of the Syrian Jacobites in its relation to Byzantine and Islamic art', *Syria*, 20: 136–50.

—— (1940). '"Hellenistic" miniatures in early Islamic manuscripts', *AI*, 7: 125–33.

—— (1941). 'Indian fables in Islamic art', *Journal of the Royal Asiatic Society*, 317–24.

Buchthal, H., O. Kurz and R. Ettinghausen (1940). 'Supplementary notes to K. Holter's check list of Islamic illuminated manuscripts before *AD* 1350', *AI*, 7: 147–64.

Buckton, D. (ed.) (1994). *Byzantium: Treasures of Byzantine Art and Culture from British Collections*. London.
Bulliet, R. W. (1976). 'Naw Bahār and the survival of Iranian Buddhism', *Iran*, 14: 140–5.
Bush, S. (1965). '"Clearing after Snow in the Min Mountains" and Chin landscape painting', *OA*, NS 11, no. 3: 163–72.
Bush, S. and H. Shih (1985). *Early Chinese Texts on Painting*. Cambridge, MA.
Bussagli, M. (1963). *Central Asian Painting*. Geneva.
Cadonna, A. and L. Lanciotti (eds) (1996). *Cina e Iran: Da Alessandro Magno alla Dinastia Tang*. Florence.
Cahen, C. (1969). 'The Mongols and the Near East', in Wolff and Hazard (eds) (1969), 715–32.
Cahill, J. (1960). *Chinese Painting*. Geneva.
—— (1969). 'Some rocks in early Chinese painting', *Chinese Art Society of America*, 16: 77–87.
—— (1976). *Hills beyond a River: Chinese Painting of the Yüan Dynasty 1279–1368*. New York.
—— (1980). *An Index of Early Chinese Painters and Paintings: T'ang, Sung, and Yüan*. Berkeley.
Caiger-Smith, A. (1985). *Lustre Pottery: Technique, Tradition and Innovation in Islam and the Western World*. London.
—— (1995). 'A kind of alchemy: Persian ceramics of the twelfth & thirteenth centuries', in Tilden (ed.) (1995), 138–53.
Caldwell, J. R. (ed.) (1967). *Investigations at Tal-i-Iblis*. Springfield.
Cammann, S. (1944). 'Development of the Mandarin square', *Harvard Journal of Asiatic Studies*, 8: 71–130.
—— (1948). 'Notes on the origin of Chinese k'o-ssu tapestry', *AA*, 11: 90–110.
—— (1951). 'The symbolism of the cloud collar motif', *AB*, 33, no. 1: 1–9.
—— (1952). *China's Dragon Robes*. New York.
—— (1963). 'Mongol costume: historical and recent', in Sinor (ed.) (1963), 157–66.
Canby, S. (1993a). *Persian Painting*. London.
—— (1993b). 'Descriptions of Buddha Sakyamuni in the Jamiʿ al-Tawarikh and the Majmaʿ al-Tawarikh', *Muqarnas*, 10: 299–310.
Cao, W. et al. (1990). *Zhongguo gudai dituji Zhanguo–Yuan* [An Atlas of Ancient Maps in China: From the Warring States Period to the Yuan Dynasty (476 BC–AD 1368)]. Beijing.
Carboni, S. (1988–9). 'The London Qazwīnī: an early 14th-century copy of the ʿAjā'ib al-Makhlūqāt', *IA*, 3: 15–31.
—— (1992). 'The wonders of creation and the singularities of Ilkhanid painting: a study of the London Qazwīnī British Library MS. Or. 14140', unpublished Ph.D dissertation. School of Oriental and African Studies, University of London.
—— (1994). 'The illustrations in the Mu'nis al-ahrār', in Swietochowski and Carboni (1994), 9–47.
—— (1997). *Following the Stars: Images of the Zodiac in Islamic Art*. New York.
—— (2001) *Glass from Islamic Lands*. London.
—— (2006). 'Narcissism or catoptromancy? – mirrors from the medieval eastern Islamic world', in P. L. Baker and B. Brend (eds), *Sifting Sands, Reading Sings: Studies in Honour of Professor Géza Fehérvári*. London, 161–70.

Carboni, S. and A. Contadini (1990). 'An illustrated copy of al-Qazwīnī's the Wonders of Creation', *Sotheby's Art at Auction 1989–9*, 228–33.

Carboni, S. and D. Whitehouse (2001). *Glass of Sultans*. New York.

Carey, M. (2001). 'Painting the stars in a century: a thirteenth-century copy of al-Sufī's treatise on the fixed stars, British Library Or. 5323,' unpublished Ph.D. dissertation. University of London.

Carswell, J. (1966). 'An early Ming porcelain stand from Damascus', *OA*, NS 12, no. 1: 176–82.

—— (1967). 'A fourteenth century Chinese porcelain dish from Damascus', *American University of Beirut Festival Book*, 29–58.

—— (1972a). 'Six tiles', in Ettinghausen (ed.) (1972), 99–124.

—— (1972b). 'China and the Near East: the recent discovery of Chinese porcelain in Syria', in Watson (ed.) (1972b), 20–5.

—— (1976–7). 'China and Islam in the Maldive Islands', *TOCS*, 42: 121–98.

—— (1979). 'Sīn in Syria', *Iran*, 17: 15–24.

—— (1985). *Blue and White: Chinese Porcelain and its Impact on the Western World*. Chicago.

—— (1996). 'The excavation of Mantai', in J. Reade (ed.), *The Indian Ocean in Antiquity*. London, 501–15.

—— (1999). 'China and the Middle East', *OA*, NS 45, no. 1: 2–14.

—— (1999–2000). 'Kharakhoto and recent research in Inner Mongolia', *OA*, NS 45, no. 4: 19–32.

—— (2000). *Blue and White: Chinese Porcelain around the World*. London.

Caubet, A. and M. Bernus-Taylor (1991). *The Louvre: Near Eastern Antiquities*. Paris.

Chen, B. (2000). *Zhongguo huaniao zhuangshi* [Chinese Flower-and-Bird Patterns]. Nanning.

Chen, D. (ed.) (1984). *Quanzhou Yisilanjiao shike* [Islamic Inscriptions in Quanzhou (Zaitun)]. Fujian.

—— (1992a). 'Sources from Fujian on trade between China and Hurmuz in the fifteenth century', in Golombek and Subtelny (eds) (1992), 191–4.

—— (1992b). 'Chinese–Iranian relations: vii. Persian settlements in south-eastern China during the T'ang, Song and Yuan dynasties', in *EIr*, 5 (1992), 443–6.

Chʻen, J. (1965). 'Sung bronzes – an economic analysis', *BSOAS*, 28, no. 3: 613–26.

Chen, J. and W. Ma (2002). *SongYuang banke tushi* [Catalogue of Woodblock Prints of the Song and Yuan Perios], 4 vols. Beijing.

Chen, T., D. Wu and X. Yue (eds) (1999). *Zhongguo gudai jianzhu datudian* [Ancient Chinese Architecture], 2 vols. Beijing.

Chen, Y. (1963). *Shilin guangji* [Vast Record of Varied Matters], Chunzhuang Academy imprint of 1328–1332, Jianan. Beijing.

Chen, Y. (1966). *Yuan Xiyuren huahua kao* [Western and Central Asians in China under the Mongols: Their Transformation into Chinese]; trans. X. Qian and L. Carrington Goodrich. Los Angeles.

Cheng, T. (1969). *Jade Flowers and Floral Patterns in Chinese Decorative Arts*. Hong Kong.

Cheuk, Y. (1986). 'A study of Hu Chou mirrors in [*sic*] Southern Sung dynasty', *Journal of the Institute of Chinese Studies of the Chinese University of Hong Kong*, 17: 145–61.

Chü, C. (1972). 'Government artisans of the Yüan dynasty', in Sun and De Francis (eds) (1972), 234–46.

Chu, Q. (2000). *Zhongguo bihua shi* [History of Chinese Murals]. Beijing.

Cleaves, F. W. (1953). 'The Mongolian documents in the Musée de Téhéran', *Harvard Journal of Asiatic Studies*, 16: 1–107.
Colledge, M. (1976). *The Art of Palmyra*. London.
Contadini, A. (1988–9). 'The Kitab Manafiʿ al-Hayawan in the Escorial Library', *IA*, 3: 33–57.
—— (1992). 'The Kitāb Naʿt al-Hayawān (Book on the Characteristics of Animals, BL, Or. 2784) and the 'Ibn Bakhtīshūʿ' Illustrated Bestiaries', unpublished Ph.D. dissertation. University of London.
Corbin, H. et al. (1938). *Les Arts de l'Iran: L'Ancienne Perse et Baghdad*. Paris.
Cort, L. A. and J. Stuart (1993). *Joined Colors: Decoration and Meaning in Chinese Porcelain*. Washington, DC.
Corun, G. (1992). *Tissus Islamiques de la Collection Pfister*. Vatican.
Cowen, J. (1989a). *Kalila wa Dimna: An Animal Allegory of the Mongol Court*. Oxford.
—— (1989b). 'Drama and morality in two early Mongol illustrated sequences from the Kalila wa Dimna', *OA*, NS 30, no. 3: 167–77.
Crowe, Y. (1975–7). 'Early Islamic pottery and China', *TOCS*, 41: 263–78.
—— (1976). 'The Islamic potter and China', *Apollo*, 103: 296–301.
—— (1978). 'Khazaf', EI^2, 4: 1164–71.
—— (1985). 'Change in style of Persian ceramics in the late part of 7/13th c.', *Rivista degli Studi Orientali*, 59: 47–55.
—— (1991). 'Late thirteenth-century Persian tilework and Chinese textiles,' *BAI*, 5: 153–61.
—— (1996). 'The chiselled surface: Chinese lacquer and Islamic design', in Tilden (ed.) (1996), 60–9.
—— (2002). *Persia and China: Safavid Blue and White Ceramics in the Victoria & Albert Museum 1501–1738*. London.
Curatola, G. (1982), 'The Viar dragon', in *Soltāniye III, Quaderni del Seminario di Iranistica, Uralo-Altaistica e Caucasologia dell'Università degli Studi di Venezia*, 9, 71–88.
—— (1987). 'Some Ilkhanid woodwork from the area of Sultaniyya', *IA*, 2: 97–116.
—— (1989). *Draghi: la Tradizione Artistica Orientale e i Disegni del Tesoro del Topkapï*. Venice.
Curtis, E. B. (ed.) (2004). *Pure Brightness Shines Everywhere: The Glass of China*. London.
Daneshvari, A. (1986). *Animal Symbolism in Warqa wa Gulshāh, Oxford Studies in Islamic Art II*. Oxford.
Dang, B. (2003). 'The plait-line robe: a costume of ancient Mongolia', *CAJ*, 47, no. 2: 198–216.
Dawson, R. (1967). *The Chinese Chameleon: An Analysis of European Conceptions of Chinese Civilization*. London.
Day, S. (1989). ''*Chinoiserie*' in Islamic carpet design', *Hali*, 48: 38–45.
Degeorge, G. and Y. Porter (2002). *The Art of the Islamic Tile*. Paris.
Deng, G. (1997). *Chinese Maritime Activities and Socioeconomic Development, c. 2100 BC–1900 AD*. Westport.
Denny, W. (1974). 'Blue-and-white Islamic pottery on Chinese themes', *Boston Museum Bulletin*, 72, pt 368: 76–99.
Déroche, F. (ed.) (1989). *Les Manuscrits du moyen-orient: Essais de codicologie et de paléographie*. Paris.
Diba, L. (1989). 'Lacquerwork', in Ferrier (ed.) (1989), 243–53.
Diez, E. (1934). 'Sino-Mongolian temple painting and its influence on Persian illumination', *AI*, 1: 160–71.

Dimand, M. S. (1973). *Oriental Rugs in the Metropolitan Museum of Art*. New York.

Dodd, E. (1969). 'On the origins of medieval dinanderie: the equestrian statue in Islam', *AB*, 51: 220–32.

Dohrenwend, D. (1980–1). 'Glass in China: a review based on the collection of the Royal Ontario Museum', *OA*, NS 26, no. 4: 426–46.

Dold-Samplonius, Y. and S. L. Harmsen (2005). 'The muqarnas plate found at Takht-i Sulayman: a new interpretation', *Muqarnas*, 22: 85–94.

Donovan, D. (1988–9). 'The evolution of the throne in early Persian painting: the evidence of the Edinburgh Jāmiʿ al-Tawārīkh', *Persica*, 13: 1–79.

Dozy, R.P.A. (1845). *Dictionnaire détaillé des noms des vêtements chez les arabes: Ouvrage couronné et publié par la troisième classe de l'Institut royal des Pays-Bas*. Amsterdam.

Dubosc, J. (1948). 'A contribution to the study of Song tapestries', *AA*, 6: 73–89; repr. *Orientations*, 20, no. 8 (1989), 82–6.

Eilers, W., M. Bazin, C. Bromberger and D. Thompson (1985). 'Abrīšam', in *EIr*, 1: 229–47.

Ellis, M. (2001). *Embroideries and Samples from Islamic Egypt*. Oxford.

Emmerick, R. E. (1983). 'Buddhism among Iranian peoples', in Yarshater (ed.) (1983), 949–64.

—— (1990). 'Buddhism: i. in pre-Islamic times', in *EIr*, 4: 492–6.

Enderlein, V. (1973). 'Das Bildprogramm des Berliner Mosul-Beckens', *Forschungen und Berichte, Staatliche Museen zu Berlin*, 13: 7–40.

Esin, E. (1963). 'Two miniatures from the collections of Topkapi', *AO*, 5: 141–61.

—— (1970–1). 'Oldruğ-Turuğ: the hierarchy of sedent postures in Turkish iconography', *KdO*, 7: 1–29.

—— (1979). 'Turk-i māh chihrah (the Turkish norm of beauty in Iran)', in *Akten des VII. internationalen Kongresses für iranische Kunst und Archäologie, München 7.–10. September 1976*. Berlin, 449–60.

Ethé, H. (1903–37). *Catalogue of Persian Manuscripts in the Library of the India Office*, 2 vols. Oxford.

Ettinghausen, R. (1936). 'Evidence for the identification of Kā<u>sh</u>ān pottery', *AI*, 3: 44–75.

—— (1950). *Studies in Muslim Iconography: 1. The Unicorn*. Washington, DC.

—— (1954). 'The covers of the Morgan Manâfiʿ manuscript and other early Persian bookbindings', in D. Miner (ed.), *Studies in Art and Literature for Belle da Costa Greene*. Princeton, 459–73.

—— (1955). 'An illustrated manuscript of Hāfiz-i Abrū in Istanbul. Part 1', *KdO*, 2: 30–44.

—— (1957a), 'The "Wade cup" in the Cleveland Museum of Art: its origin and decorations', *AO*, 2: 327–66.

—— (1957b). 'Persian ascension miniatures of the fourteenth century', Accademia Nazionale dei Lincei, XII Convegno "Volta", promosso dalla classe di scienze morali, storiche e filologiche. Tema: Oriente e Occidente nel Medioevo. Rome, 360–83; repr. in Rosen-Ayalon (ed.) (1984), 244–67.

—— (1959a). 'New light on early animal carpets', in Ettinghausen (ed.) (1959), 93–116.

—— (1959b), 'On some Mongol miniatures', *KdO*, 5: 44–65.

—— (ed.) (1959). *Aus der Welt der islamischen Kunst: Festschrift für Ernst Kühnel zum 75. Geburtstag am 26.10.1957*. Berlin.

—— (1961). 'An early Ottoman textile', in *First International Congress of Turkish Arts, Ankara, 19th–24th October, 1959*. Ankara, 134–40.
—— (1962). *Arab Painting*. Geneva; repr. 1977.
—— (1963). 'Chinese representations of Central Asian Turks', in O. Aslanapa (ed.), *Beiträge zur Kunstgeschichte Asiens. In Memoriam Ernst Diez*. Istanbul, 208–22.
—— (1972). *From Byzantium to Sasanian Iran and the Islamic World*. Leiden.
—— (ed.) (1972). *Islamic Art in the Metropolitan Museum of Art*. New York.
—— (1977). 'Abrī painting', in M. Rosen-Ayalon (ed.), *Studies in Memory of Gaston Weit*. Jerusalem, 345–56.
—— (1979a). 'Bahram Gur's hunting feats or the problem of identification', *Iran*, 17: 25–31.
—— (1979b). 'The taming of the horror vacui in Islamic art', *Proceedings of the American Philosophical Society*, 123, no. 1: 15–28.
—— (1984). *Richard Ettinghausen. Islamic Art and Archaeology. Collected Papers*, ed. M. Rosen-Ayalon. Berlin.
Ettinghausen, R. and O. Grabar (1987). *The Art and Architecture of Islam 650–1250*. New Haven.
Ettinghausen, R., O. Grabar and M. Jenkins-Madina (2001). *The Art and Architecture of Islam 650–1250*. New Haven.
Ettinghausen, R., M. S. Dimand, L. W. Mackie and C. G. Ellis (1974). *Prayer Rugs*. Washington, DC.
Fahd, T., B. van Dalen and R. Milstein (1997). 'Shams', *EI*[2], 9: 291–5.
Falk, T. (ed.) (1985). *Treasures of Islam*. Secaucus.
Farès, B. (1953). *Le Livre de la Thériaque: Manuscrit arabe à peintures de la fin du XIIe siècle conservé à la Bibliothèque nationale de Paris*. Cairo.
—— (1959). 'Figures magiques', in Ettinghausen (ed.) (1959), 154–62.
Farquhar, D. M. (1990). *The Government of China under Mongolian Rule*. Stuttgart.
Fehérvári, G. (1963). 'Two early ʿAbbāsid lustre bowls and the influence of Central Asia', *OA*, NS 9: 79–88.
—— (1970). 'Near Eastern wares under Chinese influence', in Watson (ed.) (1970), 27–34.
—— (1973). *Islamic Pottery: A Comprehensive Study Based on the Barlow Collection*. London.
—— (1976). *Islamic Metalwork of the Eight to the Fifteenth Century in the Keir Collection*. London.
—— (1982). 'Near Eastern lacquerwork: history and early evidence', in Watson (ed.) (1982), 225–31.
—— (2000). *Ceramics of the Islamic World in the Tareq Rajab Museum*. London.
—— (2005). 'Islamic incense-burners and the influence of Buddhist art', in O'Kane (ed.) (2005), 127–41.
Fehérvári, G. and J. R. Caldwell (1967). 'Islamic sites outside the Bard Sir Valley: surveys of 1964 and 1966', in Caldwell (ed.) (1967), 41–64.
Feng, X. (1976). 'Persian and Korean ceramics unearthed in China', *Orientations*, 17, no. 15: 47–53.
—— (1981). 'Seika jiki no kigen ni kansuru shomondai [Problems of the origin of blue-and-white porcelain]', in Mikami (ed.) (1981), 261–9.
Ferrier, R. W. (ed.) (1989). *The Arts of Persia*. New Haven.

Fiey, J. M. (1975). *Chrétiens syriaques sous les Mongols (Il-Khanat de Perse, XIIIe–XIVe s.), Corpus Scriptorum Christianorum Orientalium, Vol. 362*. Louvain.

—— (1993). 'Nasārā', in *EI²*, 7: 970–3.

Firdausi, Abu al-Qasim Hasan (1905–25). *The Sháhnáma of Firdausi*, trans. A. G. Warner and E. Warner, 9 vols. London; repr. 2000.

Fitzgerald, C. P. (1965). *Barbarian Beds: The Origin of the Chair in China*. London.

Fitzherbert, T. (1991). 'Khwājū Kirmānī (688–753/1290–1352): an éminence grise of fourteenth century Persian painting', *Iran*, 29: 137–51.

—— (1996). 'Portrait of a lost leader: Jalal al-Din Khwarazmshah and Juvaini', in Raby and Fitzherbert (eds) (1996), 63–77.

—— (2001). '"Balʿami's Tabari": an illustrated manuscript of Balʿami's Tarjama-yi Tārīkh-i Tabarī in the Freer Gallery of Art, Washington (F.59.16, 47.19 and 30.21)', unpublished Ph.D. dissertation. University of Edinburgh.

FitzHugh, E. W. and W. M. Floor (1992). 'Cobalt', in *EIr*, 5: 873–5.

Folsach, K. von (1990). *Islamic Art: The David Collection*. Copenhagen.

—— (1994). 'Textiles and Society', in Marcuson (ed.) (1994), 8–23.

—— (1996). 'Pax Mongolica: an Ilkhanid tapestry-woven roundel', *Hali*, 85: 80–7.

—— (2001). *Art from the World of Islam in the David Collection*. Copenhagen.

Folsach, K. von and A. Bernsted (1993). *Woven Treasures: Textiles from the World of Islam*. Copenhagen.

Foltz, R. (1999). *Religions of the Silk Road: Overland Trade and Cultural Exchange from Antiquity to the Fifteenth Century*. New York.

Fong, W. C. (1973). *Sung and Yuan Paintings*. New York.

—— (1992). *Beyond Representation: Chinese Painting and Calligraphy 8th–14th Century*. New York.

Fong, W. C. and J. C. Y. Watt (1996). *Possessing the Past: Treasures from the National Palace Museum, Taipei*. New York.

Fong, W. C., A. Murck, S. Shih, P. Ch'en and J. Stuart (1984). *Images of the Mind: Selections from the Edward L. Elliott Family and John B. Elliott Collections of Chinese Calligraphy and Painting at the Art Museum, Princeton University*. Princeton.

Franke, H. (1951). 'Some sinological remarks on Rashid ad-Din's History of China', *Oriens*, 4: 21–6.

—— (1953). 'Could the Mongol emperors read and write Chinese?' *Asia Minor*, 3: 28–41.

—— (1966). 'Sino-Western contacts under the Mongol empire', *Journal of the Royal Asiatic Society (Hong Kong Branch)*, 6: 49–72.

—— (1978). 'A Sino-Uighur family portrait: notes on a woodcut from Turfan', *Canada–Mongolia Review*, 4: 33–40.

—— (1987). 'Tibetans in Yüan China', in Langlois (ed.) (1987), 296–328.

—— (1994). *China under Mongol Rule*. Aldershot.

Franke, H. and D. Twitchett (eds) (1994). *The Cambridge History of China, Volume 6: Alien Regimes and Border States 907–1368*. Cambridge.

Franses, M. (2007). 'The Khitan: their art and their textiles 907–1125', *Hali*, 150: 76–85.

Fraser, S. E. (1999). 'Formulas of creativity: artist's sketches and techniques of copying at Dunhuang', *AA*, 59: 189–224.

—— (2004). *Performing the Visual: The Practice of Buddhist Wall Painting in China and Central Asia, 618–960*. Stanford.

Frumkin, G. (1970). *Archaeology in Soviet Central Asia*. Leiden.
Frye, R. (1954). *The History of Bukhara*. Cambridge, MA.
—— (1975). *The Golden Age of Persia*. London.
Fujiansheng bowuguan (ed.) (1982). *Fuzhou Nansong Huang Sheng mu* [The Southern Song Tomb of Huang Sheng in Fuzhou]. Beijing.
Fukai, S., K. Horiuch, K. Tanabe and M. Domyo (1969–84). *Taq-i Bustan*, 4 vols. Tokyo.
—— (1973). *Perushia no garasu* [Persian Glass]. Tokyo and Kyoto.
Fux, H. (1969). 'Chinesische Medaillonformen in der islamischen Kunst', in Aslanapa and Nawmann (eds) (1969), 278–300.
Fyodorov-Davydov, G. A. (1984). *The Culture of the Golden Horde Cities*. Oxford.
—— (1991). *The Silk Road and the Cities of the Golden Horde*. Berkeley.
Garner, Sir H. (1979). *Chinese Lacquer*. London.
Garrett, V. (1990). *Mandarin Squares: Mandarins and their Insignia*. Hong Kong.
—— (1994). *Chinese Clothing: An Illustrated Guide*. Hong Kong.
Gernet, J. (1970). *Daily Life in China on the Eve of the Mongol Invasion 1250–1276*, trans. H. M. Wright. Stanford.
—— (1996). *A History of Chinese Civilization*, 2nd edn. Cambridge.
Ghirshman, R. (1956). 'Un Miroir T'ang de Suse', *AA*, 19: 230–3.
Ghouchani, A. (1364/1986). *Katibaha-yi sufal-i Nishabur* [Inscriptions on Nishabur Pottery]. Tehran.
—— (1371/1992). *Ash'ar-i farsi-i kashiha-yi Takht-i Sulayman* [Persian Poetry on the Tiles of Takht-i Sulayman (13th century)]. Tehran.
Gibbs, E. (1998–9). 'Mamluk ceramics 648–923 AH/AD 1250–1517', *TOCS*, 63: 19–44.
Gierlichs, J. (1993). *Drache·Phönix·Doppeladler: Fabelwesen in der islamischen Kunst*. Berlin.
—— (1996). *Mittelalterliche Tierreliefs in Anatolien und Nordmesopotamien: Untersuchungen zur figürlichen Baudekoration der Seldschuken, Artuqiden und ihrer Nachfolger bis ins 15. Jahrhundert*. Tübingen.
Giès, J. (ed.) (1994). *Les Arts de l'Asie centrale: La Collection Paul Pelliot du musée national des arts asiatiques – Guimet*, 2 vols. Paris.
Gladiss, A. von (1998). *Schmuck im Museum für Islamische Kunst*. Berlin.
Godard, A. (1937). 'Isfahān', *Athār-é Īrān*, 2: 6–176.
—— (1965). *The Art of Iran*. New York.
Godard, Y. A. (1937). 'Pièces datées de céramique de Kāshān à décor lustré', *Athār-é Īrān*, 2: 309–37.
Goldstein, S. M. (2005). *Glass: From Sasanian Antecedents to European Imitations*. London.
Golmohammadi, J. (1989). 'Wooden religious buildings and carved woodwork in central Iran', unpublished Ph.D. dissertation. University of London.
Golombek, L. (1972). 'Toward a classification of Islamic painting', in Ettinghausen (ed.) (1972), 23–34.
—— (1974). 'The cult of saints and shrine architecture in the fourteenth century', in D. K. Kouymjian (ed.), *Near Eastern Numismatics, Iconography, Epigraphy and History: Studies in Honor of George C. Miles*. Beirut, 419–30.
—— (1988). 'The draped universe of Islam', in Soucek (ed.) (1988), 25–38.
Golombek, L. and M. Subtelny (1992). *Timurid Art and Culture: Iran and Central Asia in the Fifteenth Century*. Leiden.

Golombek, L., R. Mason and G. Bailey (1996). *Tamerlane's Tableware: A New Approach to the Chinoiserie Ceramics of Fifteenth- and Sixteenth-Century Iran*. Toronto.

Gölpinarli, B. (1939). *Tanksuknamei Ilhan der Fünunu Ulûmu Hatai Mukaddimesi*. Istanbul.

Gorelik, M. (1979). 'Oriental armour of the Near and Middle East from the eighth to the fifteenth centuries as shown in works of art', in R. Elgood (ed.), *Islamic Arms and Armour*. London, 30–63.

Grabar, O., R. Holod, J. Knustad and W. Trousdale (1978). *City in the Desert: Qasr al-Hayr East*, 2 vols. Cambridge, MA.

—— (1987). *The Formation of Islamic Art*, rev. and enlarged edn. New Haven.

—— (1992). *The Mediation of Ornament*. Princeton.

—— (2000). *Mostly Miniatures: An Introduction to Persian Painting*. Princeton.

Grabar, O. and S. Blair (1980). *Epic Images and Contemporary History: The Illustrations of the Great Mongol Shahnama*. Chicago.

Grabar, O. and C. Robinson (eds) (2001). *Islamic Art and Literature*. Princeton.

Gray, B. (1940). 'Fourteenth-century illustrations of the Kalilah and Dimnah', *AI*, 7: 134–9.

—— (1940–1). 'The influence of Near Eastern metalwork on Chinese ceramics', *TOCS*, 18: 47–60.

—— (1948–9). 'Blue and white vessels in Persian miniatures of the 14th and 15th centuries re-examined', *TOCS*, 24: 23–30.

—— (1954). 'An unknown fragment of the "Jāmiʿ al-Tawārīkh" in the Asiatic Society of Bengal', *AO*, 1: 65–77.

—— (1955). 'Art under the Mongol dynasties of China and Persia', *OA*, NS 1: 159–67.

—— (1961). *Persian Painting*. Geneva; repr. 1995.

—— (1963). 'Persian influence on Chinese art form from the eighth to the fifteenth centuries', *Iran*, 1: 13–18.

—— (1964–6). 'The export of Chinese porcelain to India', *TOCS*, 36: 21–37.

—— (1969). 'Some *chinoiserie* drawings and their origin', in Aslanapa and Nawmann (eds) (1969), 159–71.

—— (1971–3). 'The development of taste in Chinese art in the West 1872 to 1972', *TOCS*, 39: 19–42.

—— (1972a). 'A Timurid copy of a Chinese Buddhist prince', in Ettinghausen (ed.) (1972), 35–8.

—— (1972b). 'Chinese influence in Persian painting: 14th and 15th centuries', in Watson (ed.) (1972b), 11–19.

—— (1975–7). 'The export of Chinese porcelain to the Islamic world: some reflections on its significance for Islamic art, before 1400', *TOCS*, 41: 231–61.

—— (1978). *The World History of Rashid al-Din: A Study of the Royal Asiatic Society Manuscript*. London.

—— (ed.) (1979). *The Arts of the Book in Central Asia 14th–16th Centuries*. London.

—— (1981). 'The *chinoiserie* elements in the paintings in the Istanbul albums', *IA*, 1: 85–9.

—— (1984). *Sung Porcelain and Stoneware*. London.

—— (1985). 'The monumental Qurʾans of the Il-Khanid and Mamluk ateliers of the first quarter of the fourteenth century (eighth century H.)', *Rivista degli Studi Orientali*, 59: 135–46.

—— (1987). *Studies in Chinese and Islamic Art*, 2 vols. London.

—— (1994). 'Shāhnāma illustration from Firdausī to the Mongol invasions', in Hillenbrand (ed.) (1994), 96–102.

Grohmann, A. (1934). 'Tirāz', in *EI*[1], 4: 785–93.

Grube, E. J. (1962). *Muslim Miniature Paintings from the XIII to XIX Century from Collections in the United States and Canada*. Venice.

—— (1962–3). 'Some lustre painted tiles from Kashan of the 13th and early 14th centuries', *OA*, NS 8, no. 4: 167–74.

—— (1966a). *The World of Islam*. London.

—— (1966b). 'Islamic sculpture: ceramic figurines', *OA*, NS 12, no. 3: 165–75.

—— (1968). *The Classical Style in Islamic Painting: The Early School of Herat and its Impact on Islamic Painting of the Later 15th, 16th and 17th Centuries. s.l.*

—— (1972). *Islamic Paintings from the 11th to the 18th Century in the Collection of Hans P. Kraus*. New York.

—— (1975). *Miniature Islamiche nella Collezione del Topkapi Sarayi Istanbul*. Padova.

—— (1976). *Islamic Pottery of the Eight to the Fifteenth Century in the Keir Collection*. London.

—— (1978a). 'Islamic pottery and the ceramic arts of the Far East', in *Atti del IX Convegno Internazionale della Ceramica, Albisola, 28–31 Maggio 1976*. Albisola, 395–422.

—— (1978b). 'Persian painting in the fourteenth century: a research report', *Supplemento n. 17 agli Annali dell' Instituto Orientale di Naples*, 38, no. 4; repr. in Grube 1995, 159–290.

—— (1979). 'The Kalilah wa Dimnah of the Istanbul University Library and the problem of early Jalairid painting', in *Akten des VII. internationalen Kongresses für iranische Kunst und Archäologie, München, 7.–10. September 1976*. Berlin, 491–507.

—— (1990–1). 'Prolegomena for a corpus publication of illustrated Kalīlah wa Dimnah manuscripts', *IA*, 4: 301–481.

—— (1991). 'The early illustrated Kalilah wa Dimnah manuscripts', in E. Grube (ed.), *A Mirror for Princes from India: Illustrated Versions of the Kalilah wa Dimnah, Anvar-i Suhayli, Iyar-i Danish, and Humayun Nameh*. Bombay, 32–51.

—— (1992). 'Ceramics: the Islamic period, 5th–9th/11th–15th centuries', in *EIr*, 5: 311–27.

—— (ed.) (1994). *Cobalt and Lustre: The First Centuries of Islamic Pottery*. London.

—— (1995). *Studies in Islamic Painting*. London.

Grube, E. J. and E. Sims (eds) (1985). *Between China and Iran: Paintings from Four Istanbul Albums*. London.

Gruber, C. J. (2005). 'The Prophet Muhammad's ascension (Miʿrāj) in Islamic art and literature, ca. 1300–1600', unpublished Ph.D. dissertation. University of Pennsylvania.

Guest, G. (1943). 'Notes on a thirteenth century beaker', *AI*, 10: 148–52.

Guest, G. and R. Ettinghausen (1961). 'The iconography of a Kāshān luster plate', *AO*, 4: 25–64.

Gunter, A., C. Jett and P. Jett (1992). *Ancient Iranian Metalwork in the Athur M. Sackler Gallery and the Freer Gallery of Art*. Washington, DC.

Guojia wenwu ju (ed.) (1989). *Zhongguo guqian pu* [Ancient Chinese Coinage]. Beijing.

Guy, J. (2001–2). 'Early Asian ceramic trade and the Belitung ("Tang") cargo', *TOCS*, 66: 13–27.

Gyllensvärd, B. (1971). *Chinese Gold, Silver and Porcelain: The Kempe Collection*. New York.

Haldane, D. (1978). *Mamluk Painting*. Warminster.

Halm, H. (1991). *Shiism*. Edinburgh.

Han shu (1962). [History of the Han Dynasty], 8 vols. Beijing.

Hansen, H. H. (1950). *Mongol Costumes: Researches on the Garments Collected by the First and Second Danish Central Asian Expeditions under the Leadership of Henning Haslund-Christensen 1936–37 and 1938–39*. Copenhagen; repr. London 1993.

Hansman, J. (1985). *Julfār, an Arabian Port: Its Settlement and Far Eastern Ceramic Trade from the 14th to the 18th Centuries*. London.

Harb, U. (1978). *Ilkhanidische Stalaktitengewölbe: Beiträge zu Entwurf und Bautechnik*. Berlin.

Hardie, P. (1998). 'Mamluk glass from China', in Ward (ed.) (1998), 85–90.

Harris, J. (ed.) (1993). *5000 Years of Textiles*. London.

Hartner, W. (1938). 'The pseudoplanetary nodes of the moon's orbit in Hindu and Islamic iconographies', *AI*, 5: 113–54.

—— (1965). 'al-Djawzahar', in *EI*[2], 2: 501–2.

Hasebe, G (ed.) (1996). *Chugoku no toji: jishu yo* [Chinese Ceramics: Cizhou Wares], vol. 7. Tokyo.

Hattstein, M. and P. Delius (eds) (2000). *Islam: Art and Architecture*. Cologne.

Hayashi, M. (1993). *Ryu no hanashi* [The Story of the Dragon]. Tokyo.

Hayashi, R. (1966). *Shirukurodo to Shosoin* [The Silk Road and the Shoso-in]. Tokyo; trans. R. Ricketts. New York, 1975.

—— (1992). *Toyo bijutsu no soushoku monyo: shokubutsumon hen* [The Study of Ornament in Eastern Art: Floral Patterns]. Kyoto.

Hearn, M. and W. Fong (1999). *Along the Riverbank: Chinese Paintings from the C. C. Wang Family Collection*. New York.

Hillenbrand, C. (ed.) (2000). *Studies in Honour of Clifford Edmund Bosworth, Volume II, The Sultan's Turret: Studies in Persian and Turkish Culture*. Leiden.

Hillenbrand, R. (1977). *Imperial Images in Persian Painting*. Edinburgh.

—— (1982). 'Problems in Islamic pottery', *Persica*, 10: 119–42.

—— (1990). 'Mamlūk and Īlkhānid bestiaries: convention and experiment', *AO*, 20: 150–87.

—— (1992). 'The uses of space in Timurid painting', in Golombek and Subtelny (eds) (1992), 76–102.

—— (1994a). *Islamic Architecture: Form, Function and Meaning*. Edinburgh.

—— (1994b). 'The relationship between book painting and luxury ceramics in 13th-century Iran', in Hillenbrand (ed.) (1994) 134–41.

—— (ed.) (1994). *The Art of the Saljūqs in Iran and Anatolia*. Costa Mesa.

—— (1999). *Islamic Art and Architecture*. London.

—— (2000a). 'Images of Muhammad in al-Biruni's Chronology of Ancient Nations', in Hillenbrand (ed.) (2000), 129–46.

—— (2000b). 'The Architecture of the Ghaznavids and Ghurids', in C. Hillenbrand (ed.) (2000), 124–206.

—— (ed.) (2000). *Persian Painting from the Mongols to the Qajars*. London.

—— (ed.) (2004). *Shahnama: The Visual Language of the Persian Book of Kings*. Aldershot.

—— (2006). 'Erudition exalted: the double frontispiece to the Epistles of the Sincere Brethren', in Komaroff (ed.) (2006), 183–212.
Hirth, F. and W. W. Rockhill (1911). *Chau Ju-Kua: His Work on the Chinese Arab Trade in the Twelfth and Thirteenth Centuries, Entitled Chu-Fan-Chï*. St Petersburg.
Hitchman, F. (1962–3). 'Buddhistic symbols on Chinese ceramics', *OA*, NS 8, no. 1: 15–20.
Holmberg, B. (1993). 'Nastūriyyūn', in *EI*², 7: 1030–3.
Holter, K. (1937). 'Die Islamischen Miniaturhandschriften vor 1350', *Zentralblatt für Bibliothekswesen*, 54: 1–35.
Honigmann, E. and P. Sluglett (1991). 'al-Mawsil', in *EI*², 6: 899–902.
Honour, H. (1961). *Chinoiserie*. London.
Houhan shu (1965). [History of the Later Han Dynasty], 6 vols. Beijing.
Howarth, H. H. (1876–1927). *The History of the Mongols from the 9th to the 19th Century*, 4 vols. London.
Huang, N. and J. Chen (eds) (2001). *Zhongguo fuzhuang shi* [History of Chinese Costumes], rev. edn. Beijing.
Huff, D. (2006). 'The Ilkhanid Palace at Takht-i Sulayman: excavation results', in Komaroff (ed.) (2006), 94–110.
Hukk, M. A., E. Ethé and E. Robertson (1925). *A Descriptive Catalogue of the Arabic and Persian Manuscripts in Edinburgh University Library*. Hertford.
Huxley, F. (1979). *The Dragon: Nature of Spirit, Spirit of Nature*. London.
Ibn Battuta (1958–2000). *The Travels of Ibn Battuta, AD 1325–1354*, 5 vols, trans. H. A. R. Gibb. Cambridge.
Impey, O. (1977). *Chinoiserie: The Impact of Oriental Styles on Western Art and Decoration*. New York.
İnal, G. (1963). 'Some miniatures of the Jamiʿ al-Tawarikh in Istanbul, Topkapi Museum, Hazine Library No. 1654', *AO*, 5: 163–75.
—— (1965). 'The fourteenth-century miniatures of the Jāmiʿ al-Tavārīkh in the Topkapı Museum in Istanbul, Hazine Library No. 1653', unpublished Ph.D. dissertation. University of Michigan.
—— (1975). 'Artistic relationship between the Far and the Middle East as reflected in the miniatures of the Gamiʾat-Tawarih', *KdO*, 10: 108–43.
—— (1992). 'Miniatures in historical manuscripts from the time of Shahrukh in the Topkapi Palace Museum', in Golombek and Subtelny (eds) (1992), 103–15.
İpşiroğlu, M. (1964). *Saray-Alben: Diez'sche Klebebände aus den Berliner Sammlungen*. Wiesbaden.
—— (1967). *Painting and Culture of the Mongols*, trans. E. D. Phillips. London.
—— (1971). *Das Bild im Islam: ein Verbot und seine Folgen*. Vienna.
—— (1980). *Masterpieces from the Topkapı Museum: Paintings and Miniatures*. London.
Irwin, R. (1997). *Islamic Art in Context*. New York.
Ismailova, E. M., E. A. Poliakova and G. A. Pugachenkova (1980). *Oriental Miniatures of Abu Raihon Beruni Institute of Orientology of the UzSSR Academy of Sciences*. Tashkent.
Ivanov, A. (2000). 'The name of a painter who illustrated the World History of Rashid al-Din', in Hillenbrand (ed.) (2000), 147–50.
Jackson, P. (1993). 'Muzaffarids', in *EI*², 7: 820–2.
Jacobson, D. (1999). *Chinoiserie*. London.

Jagchid, S. and V. Symons (1989). *Peace, War, and Trade along the Great Wall: Nomadic–Chinese Interaction through Two Millennia*. Bloomington and Indianapolis.
Jahn, K. (1956a). 'Kamālashrī – Rashīd al-Dīn's "Life and Teaching of Buddha": a source for the Buddhism of the Mongol period', *CAJ*, 2: 81–128.
—— (1956b). 'A note on Kashmīr and the Mongols', *CAJ*, 2: 176–80.
—— (1964). 'The still missing works of Rashid al-Din', *CAJ*, 9: 113–22.
—— (1965). *Rashīd al-Dīn's History of India*. Hague.
—— (1970a). 'Rashid al-Din and Chinese culture', *CAJ*, 14: 134–47.
—— (1970b). 'Paper currency in Iran: a contribution to the cultural and economic history of Iran in the Mongol period', *Journal of Asian History*, 7: 101–35.
—— (1971). *Die Chinageschichte des Rašīd ad-Dīn*. Vienna.
James, D. (1980). *Qur'ans and Bindings from the Chester Beatty Library*. London.
—— (1988). *Qur'āns of the Mamlūks*. London.
—— (1992). *The Master Scribes: Qur'ans of the 10th to 14th Centuries AD*. London.
Jenkins, M. (ed.) (1983). *Islamic Art in the Kuwait National Museum*. London.
Jenkins, M. and M. Keene (1982). *Islamic Jewelry in the Metropolitan Museum of Art*. New York.
Jenkins-Madina, M. (2006). *Raqqa Revisited: Ceramics of Ayyubid Syria*. New York.
Jenyns, R. S. (1954–5). 'The Chinese rhinoceros and Chinese carving in rhinoceros horn', *TOCS*, 29: 31–62.
Jenyns, R. S. and W. Watson (1963–5). *Chinese Art: The Minor Arts*. vol. 1. New York; vol. 2. London.
Jiayao, A. (1991). 'Dated Islamic glass in China', *BAI*, 5: 123–37.
Jin shi (1975). [History of the Jin Dynasty], 8 vols. Beijing.
Jing, A. (1994). 'The portraits of Khubilai Khan and Chabi by Anige (1245–1306), a Nepali artist at the Yuan court', *AA*, 54, pts 1–2: 40–86.
Jiu Tang shu (1975). [Old History of the Tang Dynasty], 16 vols. Beijing.
Johnson, L. C. (1983). 'The wedding ceremony for an imperial Liao princess', *AA*, 44. nos 2–3: 107–36.
Jones, D. and G. Michell (eds) (1976). *The Arts of Islam*. London.
Juliano, A. L. and J. A. Lerner (2001). *Monks and Merchants: Silk Road Treasures from Northwest China*. New York.
Juvaini, ʿA. (1958). *Tarikh-i Jahan-gusha* [The History of the World Conqueror], trans. J. A. Boyle, 2 vols. Manchester.
Kadoi, Y. (2000). 'The world history of Rashid al-Din: Chinese landscape elements re-examined', unpublished M.Sc. dissertation. University of Edinburgh.
—— (2002). 'Cloud patterns: the exchange of ideas between China and Iran under the Mongols', *OA*, NS 48, no. 2: 25–36.
—— (2005a). 'Beyond the Mandarin square: garment badges in Ilkhanid painting', *Hali*, 138: 41–50.
—— (2005b). 'Aspects of frescoes in 14th-century Iranian architecture: the case of Yazd', *Iran*, 43: 217–40.
—— (2008). 'The palmette and the lotus: the decorative interaction between Greece and China along the Silk Road', in C. Stavrakos (ed.), *Proceedings of the First International Congress for Sino-Greek Studies: Relations*

between the Greek and Chinese World, 2–4 October, 2004. Ioannina, 127–42.

—— (forthcoming a). 'Textiles in the Great Mongol *Shahnama*: a new approach to Ilkhanid costumes', in *Proceedings of the Second Shahnama Conference, 'Illustrating the Narrative', 8–9 March 2003, Edinburgh*. London.

—— (forthcoming b). 'Mirrors: with special reference to the Sino-Iranian relationship during the 12th and 14th centuries', in *Proceedings of the International Symposium on Iranian Metalwork: Metals and Metalworking in Islamic Iran, Chester Beatty Library, Dublin, 3–4 September, 2004*. Dublin.

—— (forthcoming c). 'Buddhism in Iran under the Mongols: an art-historical analysis', in *Proceedings of the European Society for Central Asian Studies Ninth Conference, Krakow, 12–14 September, 2005*. Newcastle-upon-Tyne.

Kahle, P. (1940–1). 'Chinese porcelain in the lands of Islam', *TOCS*, 18: 27–46.

Kalter, J. and M. Pavaloi (eds) (1997). *Uzbekistan: Heirs to the Silk Road*. London.

Kalus, L. (1986). *Catalogue of Islamic Seals and Talismans*. Oxford.

Karamağarali, B. (1966–8). 'Camiu't-tevarih'in bilinmeyen bir nüshasina âit dört minyatür', *Sanat Tarihi Yıllığı*, 2: 70–86.

Kauz, R. (2006). 'The maritime trade of Kish during the Mongol period', in Komaroff (ed.) (2006), 31–67.

Kawami, T. S. (1992). 'Archaeological evidence for textiles in pre-Islamic Iran', *Iranian Studies*, 25, nos 1–2: 7–18.

Keene, M. (2004). 'Old world jades outside China, from ancient times to the fifteenth century: section one', *Muqarnas*, 21: 193–214.

Keller, D. and R. Schorta (eds) (2001). *Fabulous Creatures from the Desert Sands: Central Asian Woolen Textiles from the Second Century BC to the Second Century AD*. Riggisberg.

Kennedy, A. (1997). 'A time of renewal: Liao luxury silks', *Hali*, 95: 74–7.

Kennedy, H. (2002). *Mongols, Huns and Vikings: Nomads at War*. London.

Kennet, D. (2004). *Sasanian and Islamic Pottery from Ras al-Khaimah: Classification, Chronology and Analysis of Trade in the Western Indian Ocean*. Oxford.

Kerr, R. (1982). 'The evolution of bronze style in the Jin, Yuan and early Ming dynasties', *OA*, NS 28, no. 2: 146–58.

—— (1986). 'Metalwork and Song design: a bronze vase inscribed in 1173', *OA*, NS 32, no. 2: 161–76.

—— (1990). *Later Chinese Bronzes*. London.

Kessler, A. T. (1993). *Empires beyond the Great Wall: The Heritage of Genghis Khan*. Los Angeles.

Khaleghi-Motlagh, D. (1992). 'Chinese–Iranian relations: x. China in medieval Persian literature', in *EIr*, 5: 454–5.

Khalili, N. D., B. W. Robinson and T. Stanley (1996–7). *Lacquer of the Islamic Lands*, 2 vols. London.

Kiani, M. Y. (1982). 'Early lacquer in Iran', in Watson (ed.) (1982), 211–24.

Klimburg-Salter, D. E. (1976–7). 'A Sufi theme in Persian painting: the Dīwān of Sultan Ahmad Ğalā'ir in the Freer Gallery of Art, Washington DC', *KdO*, 11: 43–84.

Knauer, E. R. (1998). *The Camel's Load in Life and Death: Iconography and Ideology of Chinese Pottery Figurines from Han to Tang and their Relevance to Trade along the Silk Routes*. Zurich.

Koechlin, R. (1928). 'Chinese influences in the Musulman pottery in Susa', *Eastern Art*, 1: 3–12.
Kolbas, J. (2006). *The Mongols in Iran: Chingiz Khan to Uljaitu 1220–1309*. London.
Komaroff, L. (1994). 'Paintings in silver and gold: the decoration of Persian metalwork and its relationship to manuscript illustration', *Studies in the Decorative Arts*, 2, no. 1: 2–34.
—— (ed.) (2006). *Beyond the Legacy of Genghis Khan*. Leiden.
Komaroff, L. and S. Carboni (eds) (2002). *The Legacy of Genghis Khan: Courtly Art and Culture in Western Asia, 1256–1353*. New York.
Kong, X. (1992). *Zhongguo tongjing tudian* [Illustrated Catalogue of Chinese Bronze Mirrors]. Beijing.
Kong, X. and Y. Liu (1991). *Zhongguo gudai tongjing* [Ancient Chinese Mirrors], trans. H. Takakura et al., Fukuoka; original publication, Beijing, 1984.
Kong, Y. (1966). *Kongshi zuting guangji* [Genealogy of Confucius], Qufu imprint of 1242, Sibu congkan, 2nd edn. Taipei.
Kotz, S. (ed.) (1989). *Imperial Taste: Chinese Ceramics from the Percival David Foundation*. Los Angeles.
Kouymjian, D. K. (1986). 'Chinese elements in Armenian miniature painting in the Mongol period', in D. K. Kouymjian (ed.), *Armenian Studies in Memoriam Haïg Berbérian*. Lisbon, 415–68.
—— (2006). 'Chinese motifs in thirteenth-century Armenian art: the Mongol connection', in Komaroff (ed.) (2006), 303–24.
Krahl, R. (1989). 'Designs on early Chinese textiles', *Orientations*, 20, no. 8: 62–73.
—— (1997). 'Mediaeval silks woven in gold: Khitan, Jürchen, Tangut, Chinese or Mongol?' *Orientations*, 28, no. 4: 45–51.
Krahl, R. and J. Ayers (1986). *Chinese Ceramics in the Topkapi Saray Museum Istanbul: A Complete Catalogue*, 3 vols. London.
Kramarovsky, M. (1996). 'Mongol horse trappings in the thirteenth and fourteenth centuries', in Alexander (ed.) (1996), vol. 1, 48–53.
—— (1998). 'The import and manufacture of glass in the territories of the Golden Horde', in Ward (ed.) (1998), 96–100.
—— (2004). 'The "sky of wine" of Abu Nuwas and three glazed bowls from the Golden Horde, Crimia', *Muqarnas*, 21: 231–38.
Kröger, J. (1995). *Nishapur: Glass of the Early Islamic Period*. New York.
Kühnel, E. (1923). *Miniaturmalerei im islamischen Orient*. Berlin.
—— (1937). 'A Bidpai manuscript of 1343/4 (744 H.) in Cairo', *Iranian Art and Archaeology*, 5: 137–41.
—— (1949). *The Arabesque*, trans. R. Ettinghausen. Graz.
—— (1959a). *Persische Miniaturmalerei*. Berlin.
—— (1959b). 'Malernamen in den Berliner "Saray"-Alben', *KdO*, 3: 66–77.
Kurz, O. (1972). 'Folding chairs and Koran stands', in Ettinghausen (ed.) (1972), 299–314.
Lach, D. F. (1970). *Asia in the Making of Europe, Vol. II, A Century of Wonder, Book One: The Visual Arts*. Chicago.
Laing, E. J. (1978). 'Patterns and problems in later Chinese tomb decoration', *Journal of Oriental Studies*, 16: 3–20.
—— (1988–9). 'Chin "Tartar" dynasty (1115–1234) material culture', *AA*, 49: 73–126.
—— (1991). 'A report on Western Asian glassware in the Far East', *BAI*, 5: 109–21.

—— (1995). 'Recent finds of Western-related glassware, textiles, and metalwork in Central Asia and China', *BAI*, 9: 1–18.
—— (1998). 'Daoist Qi: clouds and mist in later Chinese painting', *Orientations*, 29, no. 4: 32–9.
Lambton, A. K. S. (1988). *Continuity and Change in Medieval Persia: Aspects of Administrative, Economic, and Social History, 11th–14th Century*. New York.
Lambton, A. K. S. and J. Sourdel-Thomine (1978). 'Isfahān', in *EI*², 4: 97–107.
Lane, A. (1939). 'Glazed relief ware of the ninth century AD', *AI*, 6: 56–65.
—— (1946–7). 'Sung wares and the Saljuq pottery of Persia', *TOCS*, 22: 19–30.
—— (1947). *Early Islamic Pottery: Mesopotamia, Egypt and Persia*. London; rev. edn, 1965.
—— (1957). *Later Islamic Pottery: Persia, Syria, Turkey*. London.
Lane, G. (2003). *Early Mongol Rule in Thirteenth-Century Iran: A Persian Renaissance*. London.
Langlois, J. D. (ed.) (1981). *China under Mongol Rule*. Princeton.
Laufer, B. (1919). *Sino-Iranica: Chinese Contributions to the History of Civilization in Ancient Iran with Special Reference to the History of Cultivated Plants and Products*. Chicago.
Lawton, T. (1973). *Chinese Figure Painting*. Washington, DC.
Le Coq, A. von (1913). *Chotscho: Facsimile-Wiedergaben der wichtigeren Funde der Ersten Königlich-Preussischen Expedition nach Turfan in Ost-Turkistan*. Berlin.
—— (1925). *Bilderatlas zur Kunst und Kulturgeschichte Mittel-Asiens*. Berlin.
—— (1928). *Buried Treasures of Chinese Turkestan*, trans. A. Barwell. London.
Le Strange, G. (1903). *Mesopotamia and Persia under the Mongols in the Fourteenth Century AD*. London.
—— (1966). *The Lands of the Eastern Caliphate: Mesopotamia, Persia, and Central Asia from the Moslem Conquest to the Time of Timur*, 3rd edn. London.
Lee, S. (ed.) (1998). *China 5000 Years: Innovations and Transformation in the Arts*. New York.
Lee, S. and W. Ho (1968). *Chinese Art under the Mongols*. Cleveland.
Leiser, G. (2000). 'Tamgha', in *EI*², 10: 170.
Lentz, T. W. and G. D. Lowry (1989). *Timur and the Princely Vision: Persian Art and Culture in the Fifteenth Century*. Washington, DC.
Lerner, M. (1984). *The Flame and the Lotus: Indian and Southeast Asian Art from the Kronos Collections*. New York.
Leroy, J. (1964). *Les Manuscrits syriaques à peintures conservés dans les bibliothèques d'Europe et d'Orient*, 2 vols. Paris.
Li, C. (1968). 'The Freer Sheep and Goat and Cao Meng-fu's horse paintings', *AA*, 30, no. 4: 279–346.
—— (ed.) (1989). *Artists and Patrons: Some Social and Economic Aspects of Chinese Painting*. Kansas.
Li, C. and J. C. Y. Watt (eds) (1987). *The Chinese Scholar's Studio: Artistic Life in the Late Ming Period*. New York.
Li, H. (2001). '*Qinghua ciqi de chuxian ji qi fazhan* [The birth of blue-and-white porcelain and its development]', *Gugong wenwu*, 18, no. 10: 40–53.

Li, J. (1968). *Yingzao fashi* [Manual of Architecture], Guoxue jiben congshu edition, 8 vols. Taipei.
Liao shi (1974). [History of the Liao Dynasty], 5 vols. Beijing.
Lings, M. (1976). *The Quranic Art of Calligraphy and Illumination*. London.
Little, D. P. (2006). 'Diplomatic missions and gift exchanges by Mamluks and Ilkhans', in Komaroff (ed.) (2006), 30–42.
Liu, S. (1997). *Liaodai tongjing yanjiu* [A Study of Liao Mirrors]. Shenyang.
Liu, X. (1988). *Ancient India and Ancient China: Trade and Religious Exchanges AD 1–600*. New Delhi.
—— (1995). 'Silks and religions in Eurasia, c. AD 600–1200', *Journal of World History*, 6, no. 1: 25–48.
—— (1998). *Silk and Religion: An Exploration of Material Life and the Thought of People AD 600–1200*. Delhi.
Liu, Y. and P. Jackson (1992). 'Chinese–Iranian relations: iii. in the Mongol period', in *EIr*, 5: 434–6.
Lo, J. (1955). 'The emergence of China as a sea power during the late Sung and early Yüan periods', *Far Eastern Quarterly*, 14: 489–503.
Lopez, R. S. (1952). 'China silk in Europe in the Yuan period', *Journal of the American Oriental Society*, 72: 72–6.
Lorey, E. de (1935a). 'L'École de Tabriz: l'Islam aux prises avec la China', *Revue des arts asiatiques*, 9: 27–39.
—— (1935b). 'Le Bestiaire de l'Escurial', *Gazette des beaux-arts*, 6: 228–38.
Loubo-Lesnitchenko, E. (1973). 'Imported mirrors in the Minusinsk Basin', *AA*, 35: 25–61.
—— (1995). 'Concerning the chronology and ornamentation of Han period textiles', *Orientations*, 26, no. 5: 62–9.
Louis, F. (1999). *Die Goldschmiede der Tang- und Song-Zeit*. Bern.
—— (2003). 'Shaping symbols of privilege: precious metals and the early Liao aristocracy', *Journal of Sung-Yuan Studies*, 33: 71–109.
Loukonin, V. and A. Ivanov (1996). *Lost Treasures of Persia: Persian Art in the Hermitage Museum*. Washington, DC.
Lovell, H. (ed.) (1984). *Jingdezhen Wares: The Yuan Evolution*. Hong Kong.
Lowry, G. D. and S. Nemazee (1988). *A Jeweler's Eye: Islamic Arts of the Book from the Vever Collection*. Washington, DC.
Luo, F. (1981). *Guxiyin gailun* [The Survey of Ancient Seals]. Beijing.
Ma, W. (1994). 'Liaomu Liaota chutu de Yisilan boli [Islamic glass found in Liao tombs]', *Kaogu*, 8: 736–43.
—— (2002). 'Faku yemaotai zaoqi Liaomu chutu de Yishilan boli tiaowei fangpen [A study of the Islamic-type glass unearthed from the tomb of the Liao dynasty in Fakuyematai, Liaoning province]', *Zhongguo lishi wenwu*, 38, no. 3 (2002), 46–8.
—— (2003). 'Zhongguo qinghuaci yu Yisilan qingtao [A comparative study on Chinese and Islamic blue-and-white wares]', *Zhongguo lishi wenwu*, 42, no. 1: 62–71.
—— (2004). 'Islamic glasses unearthed from China', in Curtis (ed.) (2004), 29–36.
McDowell, J. A. (1989). 'Textiles', in Ferrier (ed.) (1989), 151–69.
McNeill, W. (1977). *Plagues and Peoples*. New York.
Maddison, F. and E. Savage-Smith (1997). *Science, Tools and Magic: Part One. Body and Spirit, Mapping the Universe*. Oxford.
Madelung, W. (1988). *Religious Trends in Early Islamic Iran*. New York.

Maenchen-Helfen, O. (1943). 'From China to Palmyra', *AB*, 25: 358–62.
Magagnato, L. (ed.) (1983). *Le stoffe di Cangrande: Ritrovamenti e ricerche sul 300 veronese*. Florence.
Mahler, J. G. (1966). 'The art of the Silk Road', in Bowie (ed.) (1966), 70–83.
Mailey, J. (1971). *Chinese Silk Tapestry: Ko-ssun from Private and Museum Collections*. New York.
Majeed. T. (2006). 'The phenomenon of the square Kufic script: the cases of Ilkhanid Isfahan and Bahri Mamluk Cairo', unpublished D.Phil. dissertation. University of Oxford.
Marcuson, A. (ed.) (1994). *The First Hali Annual: Carpets and Textile Art*. London.
Marshak, B. I. (2002). *Legends, Tales, and Fables in the Art of Sogdiana*. New York.
Marshak, B. I. and M. G. Kramarovsky (1993). 'A silver bowl in the Walters Art Gallery, Baltimore (thirteenth century silversmiths' work in Asia Minor)', *Iran*, 31: 119–26.
Martin, F. R. (1912). *The Miniature Painting and Painters of Persia, India and Turkey from the 8th to the 18th Century*, 2 vols. London.
Mason, R. B. and L. B. Golombek (1991). 'Differentiating early Chinese-influenced blue-and-white ceramics of Egypt, Syria, and Iran', in E. Pernicka and G. A. Wargner (eds), *Proceedings of the XXVIIth International Symposium on Archaeology Held in Heidelberg April 2–6 1990* (Basel, 1991), 465–74.
Mason, R. and E. J. Keall (1991). 'The ʿAbbāsid glazed wares of Sīrāf and the Basra connection: petrographic analysis', *Iran*, 29: 51–66.
Masuya, T. (1997). 'The Ilkhanid phase of Takht-i Sulayman', unpublished Ph.D. dissertation. Institute of Fine Arts, New York University.
Mathews, T. F. and A. K. Sanjian (1991). *Armenian Gospel Iconography: The Tradition of the Glajor Gospel*. Washington, DC.
Mayer, L. A. (1952). *Mamluk Costume*. Geneva.
—— (1958). *Islamic Woodcarvers and their Works*. Geneva.
—— (1971). *Mamluk Praying Cards*. Leiden.
Medley, M. (1970). 'T'ang gold and silver', in Watson (ed.) (1970), 19–26.
—— (1969–71). 'The early development of blue and white porcelain', *TOCS*, 38: 41–4.
—— (1972a). *Metalwork and Chinese Ceramics*, Monograph Series No. 2. London.
—— (1972b). 'Chinese ceramics and Islamic design', in Watson (ed.) (1972b), 1–10.
—— (1974). *Yüan Porcelain and Stoneware*. London.
—— (1975). 'Islam, Chinese porcelain and Ardabīl', *Iran*, 13: 31–7.
—— (1982). 'Lacquered furniture', in Watson (ed.) (1982), 70–84.
—— (1987–8). 'Patterns of Chinese taste in porcelain', *TOCS*, 52: 63–82.
—— (1989). *The Chinese Potter: A Practical History of Chinese Ceramics*, 3rd edn. London.
Meinecke, M. (1989). 'Islamische Drachentüren', *Museums-Journal: Berichte aus den Museen, Schlössern und Sammlungen im Land Berlin*, 3, no. 4: 54–8.
Meister, M. W. (1970). 'The pearl roundel in Chinese textile design', *AO*, 8: 255–67.
Melikian-Chirvani, A. S. (1966). 'The Sufi strain in the art of Kashân', *OA*, NS 12, no. 4: 251–8.

—— (1970a), 'Iranian silver and its influence in T'ang China', in Watson (ed.) (1970), 12–18.
—— (1970b). *Le Roman de Varqe et Golšāh: Essai sur les rapports de l'esthétique littéraire et de l'esthétique plastique dans l'Iran pré-mongol, suivi de la traduction du poéme*. Paris.
—— (1972). 'The Buddhist heritage in the art of Iran', in Watson (ed.) (1972a), 56–65.
—— (1973). *Le Bronze iranien*. Paris.
—— (1974a). 'L'Évocation littéraire du bouddhisme dans l'Iran musulman', *Le Monde iranien et l'Islam*, 2: 1–72.
—— (1974b). 'Les Bronzes du Khorassan I', *SI*, 3: 29–50.
—— (1975). 'Recherches sur l'architecture de l'Iran bouddhique 1: Essai sur les origines et le symbolisme du stūpa iranien', *Le Monde iranien et l'Islam*, 3: 1–61.
—— (1979). 'Conceptual art in Iranian painting and metalwork', in *Akten des VII. internationalen Kongresses für iranische Kunst und Archäologie, München, 7.–10. September 1976* (Berlin, 1979), 392–400.
—— (1982). *Islamic Metalwork from the Iranian World: 8th to 18th Centuries*. London.
—— (1984). 'Le Shāh-nāme, la gnose soufie et le pouvoir mongol', *Journal asiatique*, 272: 249–337.
—— (1986). 'Silver in Islamic Iran: the evidence from literature and epigraphy', in Vickers (ed.) (1986), 89–106.
—— (1987). 'The lights of Sufi shrines', *IA*, 2: 117–47.
—— (1990). 'Buddhism: ii. In Islamic times', in *EIr*, 4: 496–9.
—— (1991). 'Le Livre des Rois: miroir du destin. ii: Il-Takht-e Soleymān et la symbolique du Shāh-nāme', *SI*, 20: 33–148.
—— (1997a). 'Conscience du passé et résistance culturelle dans l'Iran mongol', in Aigle (ed.) (1997), 135–77.
—— (1997b), 'Precious and semi-precious stones in Iranian culture: chapter 1. Early Iranian jade', *BAI*, 11: 123–73.
Melville, C. (1990). 'Pādshāh-i Islām: the conversion of Sultan Mahmūd Ghāzān Khān', in C. Melville (ed.), *Persian and Islamic Studies in Honour of P. W. Avery*. Cambridge, 159–77.
—— (1997). 'Abū Saʿīd and the revolt of the amirs in 1319', in Aigle (ed.) (1997), 89–120.
—— (ed.) (1998). *History and Literature in Iran: Persian and Islamic Studies in Honour of P. W. Avery*. London.
Melville, C. and ʿA. Zaryāb (1992). 'Chobanids', in *EIr*, 5: 496–502.
Metropolitan Museum of Art (1987). *The Metropolitan Museum of Art: The Islamic World*. New York.
Michaelson, C. (1999). *Gilded Dragons: Buried Treasures from China's Golden Age*. London.
Mikami, T. (1965). 'Chugoku toji to isuramu toki no kankei ni kansuru nisan no mondai [A study of Chinese influence upon early Islamic polychrome pottery]', *Seinan Asia kenkyu*, 14, June, 1–12.
—— (1980 1). 'China and Egypt: Fustat', *TOCS*, 45: 67–89.
—— (ed.) (1981). *Sekai toji zenshu* [Ceramic Art of the World], vol. 13: Liao, Jin and Yuan dynasties. Tokyo.
Milstein, R. (1986). 'Light, fire and the sun in Islamic painting', in M. Sharon (ed.), *Studies in Islamic History and Civilization in Honour of Professor David Ayalon*. Jerusalem and Leiden. 533–52.
Ming shi (1974). [History of the Ming Dynasty], 14 vols. Beijing.

Minorsky, V. (1956). 'The older preface to the *Shāh-nāma*', in G. Levi (ed.), *Studi Orientalistici in Onore di Giorgio Levi Della Vida*, vol. 2. Rome, 159–79.
Minorsky, V. and S. S. Blair (1997). 'Sultāniyya', *EI*², 9: 859–61.
Moghadam, M. E. and Y. Armajani (1939). *Descriptive Catalog of the Garrett Collection of Persian, Turkish and Indic Manuscripts Including Some Miniatures in the Princeton University Library*. Princeton.
Moore, O. (1998). 'Islamic glass at Buddhist sites in medieval China', in Ward (ed.) (1998), 78–84.
Morgan, D. (1986). *The Mongols*. Oxford.
—— (1995). 'Rashīd al-Dīn Tabīb', *EI*², 8: 443–4.
—— (1997). 'Rašīd al-Dīn and Gazan Khan', in Aigle (ed.) (1997), 179–88.
—— (2000). 'Reflections on Mongol communications in the Ilkhanate', in C. Hillenbrand (ed.) (2000), 375–85.
Morgan, P. (1991). 'New thoughts on Old Hormuz: Chinese ceramics in the Hormuz region in the thirteenth and fourteenth centuries', *Iran*, 29: 67–83.
—— (1995). 'Some Far Eastern elements in coloured-ground Sultanabad wares', in Allan (ed.) (1995), 19–43.
Morgan, P. and J. Leatherby (1987). 'Excavated ceramics from Sīrjān', in Allan and Roberts (eds) (1987), 23–172.
Morley, W. H. (1854). *A Descriptive Catalogue of the Historical Manuscripts in the Arabic and Persian Languages Preserved in the Library of the Royal Asiatic Society of Great Britain and Ireland*. London.
Mostaert, A. and F. W. Cleaves (1952). 'Trois documents mongols des archives secrètes vaticanes', *Harvard Journal of Asiatic Studies*, 15: 419–506.
Mowry, R. D. (1993). *China's Renaissance in Bronze: The Robert H. Clague Collection of Later Chinese Bronzes 1100–1900*. Phoenix.
Munakata, K. (1991). *Sacred Mountains in Chinese Art*. Chicago.
Murray, J. K. and S. Cahill (1987). 'Recent advances in understanding the mystery of ancient Chinese "magic mirrors": a brief summary of Chinese analytical and experimental studies', *Chinese Science*, 8: 1–8.
Museum für Islamische Kunst (2001). *Museum für Islamische Kunst: Staatliche Museen zu Berlin Preußischer Kulturbesitz*. Mainz.
Muthesius, A. (1995). *Studies in Byzantine and Islamic Silk Weaving*. London.
Nakamura, G. and T. Hisano (eds) (2002). *Bukkyo bijutsu jiten* [Encyclopedia of Buddhist Art]. Tokyo.
Nakano, T. (1981). 'Ryo Kin Gen toji no monyou [Decorative patterns in Liao, Jin and Yuan ceramics]', in Mikami (ed.) (1981), 279–94.
Nassar, N. (1985). 'Saljuq or Byzantine: two related styles of Jazīran miniature painting', in Raby (ed.) (1985), 85–98.
Natural History (1958). 'The animal lore of the past two medieval bestiaries', *Natural History*, 67, no. 10: 558–67.
Naumann, E. and R. Naumann (1969). 'Ein Köşk im Sommerpalast des Abaqa Chan auf dem Tacht-i Sulaiman und seine Dekoration', in Aslanapa and Naumann (eds) (1969), 35–65.
Naumann, R. (1981).'Takht-i-Suleiman and Zindan-i-Suleiman', in *SPA*, 3050–60.
Nedashkovsky, L. F. (2004). *Ukek: The Golden Horde City and its Periphery*. Oxford.
Needham, J. (1954–). *Science and Civilisation in China*, 7 vols. Cambridge.

Nicolle, D. (1990). *The Mongol Warlords*. London.
Ogasawara, S. (1989). 'Chinese fabrics of the Song and Yuan dynasties preserved in Japan', *Orientations*, 20, no. 8: 32–44.
O'Kane, B. (1979). 'The Friday Mosques of Asnak and Sarāvar', *Archaeologische Mitteilungen aus Iran*, 12: 341–51.
—— (1990–1). 'Rock faces and rock figures in Persian Painting', *IA*, 4: 219–46.
—— (1996). 'Monumentality in Mamluk and Mongol art and architecture', *Art History*, 19, no. 4: 499–522.
—— (2003). *Early Persian Painting: Kalila and Dimna Manuscripts of the Late Fourteenth Century*. London.
—— (ed.) (2005). *Iconography of Islamic Art: Studies in Honour of Robert Hillenbrand*. Edinburgh.
—— (2006). 'The iconography of the *Shahnama*, Ms. Ta'rikh Farisi 73, Dar al-Kutub, Cairo (796/1393–4)', in C. Melville (ed.), *Shahnama Studies I*. Cambridge, 171–88.
—— (ed.) (2006). *The Treasures of Islamic Art in the Museums of Cairo*. Cairo.
Olschki, L. (1946). *Guillaume Boucher: A French Artist at the Court of the Khans*. Baltimore.
Öney, G. (1966–8). 'The fish motif in Anatolian Seljuk art', *Sanat Tarihi Yıllığı*, 2: 142–68.
—— (1969). 'Dragon figures in Anatolian Seljuk art', *Belleten*, 33: 191–216.
Oshima, R. (1983). 'The Chiang-hu in the Yuan', *Acta Asiatica*, 45: 69–95.
Otavsky, K. (ed.) (1998). *Entlang der Seidenstraße: Frühmittelalterliche Kunst zwischen Persien und China in der Abegg-Stiftung*. Riggisberg.
Otto-Dorn, K. (1978–9). 'Figural stones reliefs on Seljuk sacred architecture in Anatolia', *KdO*, 12: 103–49.
—— (1982). 'Das seldschukische Thronbild', *Persica*, 10: 149–94.
Paludan, A. (1994). *Chinese Tomb Figurines*. Hong Kong.
Pancaroğlu, O. (2001). 'Socializing medicine: illustrations of the Kitāb al-Diryāq', *Muqarnas*, 18: 155–72.
—— (2002). 'Serving wisdom: the contents of Samanid epigraphic pottery', in *Studies in Islamic and Later Indian Art from the Arthur M. Sackler Museum, Harvard University Art Museums*. Cambridge, MA, 59–75.
Pellat, C. (1960). ''Ankā', *EI*², 1: 509.
—— (1993). 'Mir'āt', *EI*², 7: 105–6.
Pelliot, P. (1928). 'Des Artisans chinois à la capitale abbasside en 751–762', *T'oung Pao*, 26: 110–12.
—— (1930). 'Notes sur le "Turkestan" de M. W. Barthold', *T'oung Pao*, 27: 12–56.
—— (1936). 'Les Documents mongols du Musée de Teherān', *Athār-é Īrān*, 1: 37–44.
—— (1959–63). *Notes on Marco Polo*, 2 vols. Paris.
Peng, X. (1988). *Zhongguo huobi shi* [A Monetary History of China], 3rd edn. Shanghai.
Petech, L. (1983). 'Tibetan relations with Sung China and with the Mongols', in Rossabi (ed.) (1983), 173–203.
Philon, H. (1980). *Early Islamic Ceramics: Ninth to Late Twelfth Centuries*. London.
Pickett, D. (1997). *Early Persian Tilework: The Medieval Flowering of Kāshī*. London.

Pierson, S. (2001). *Designs as Signs: Decoration and Chinese Ceramics*. London.
—— (ed.) (2002). *Qingbai Ware: Chinese Porcelain of the Song and Yuan Dynasties*. London.
Pinder-Wilson, R. (ed.) (1969). *Paintings from Islamic Lands*. Oxford.
—— (1991). 'The Islamic lands and China', in H. Tait (ed.), *Five Thousand Years of Glass*. London, 112–43.
Piotrovsky, M. B. (ed.) (1993). *Lost Empire of the Silk Road: Buddhist Art from Khara Khoto (X–XIIIth Century)*. Milan.
—— (ed.) (2000). *The Treasures of the Golden Horde*. St Petersburg.
Piotrovsky, M. B. and A. D. Pritula (eds) (2006). *Beyond the Palace Walls: Islamic Art from the State Hermitage Museum*. Edinburgh.
Piotrovsky, M. B. and J. M. Rogers (eds) (2004). *Heaven on Earth: Art from Islamic Lands, Works from the State Hermitage Museum and the Khalili Collection*. London.
Poliakova, E. A. and Z. I. Rakhimova (1987). *Miniatiura i literatura Vostoka: evoliutsiia obraza cheloveka*. Tashkent.
Polo, M. (1993). *The Travels of Marco Polo: The Complete Yule–Cordier Edition*, 2 vols. New York; original publication, *The Book of Ser Marco Polo the Venetian Concerning the Kingdoms and Marvels of the East*, trans. and ed. H. Yule, 2 vols. London, 1871.
Pope, A. U. and P. Ackerman (eds) (1981). *A Survey of Persian Art from Prehistoric Times to the Present*, 3rd edn, 16 vols. Ashiya.
—— (1981).'Furniture', in *SPA*, 2628–58.
Pope, J. A. (1952). *Fourteenth-Century Blue and White: A Group of Chinese Porcelains in the Topkapu Sarayi Müzesi, Istanbul*. Washington, DC; 2nd edn, 1970.
—— (1956). *Chinese Porcelain from the Ardebil Shrine*. Washington, DC.
—— (1959). 'An early Ming porcelain in Muslim style', in Ettinghausen (ed.) (1959), 357–75.
—— (1972). 'Chinese influences on Iznik pottery: a re-examination of an old problem', in Ettinghausen (ed.) (1972), 125–298.
Porter, V. (1995). *Islamic Tiles*. London.
Pourjavady, N. (ed.) (2001). *The Splendour of Iran*, 3 vols. London.
Pugačenkova, G. A. and Z. I. Usmanova (1995). 'Buddhist monuments in Merv', in A. Invernizzi (ed.), *In the Land of the Gryphons: Papers on Central Asian Archaeology in Antiquity*. Florence, 51–81.
Qin, D. (2000–1a), 'A study of the relationship between Cizhou and Ding wares', *TOCS*, 65: 1–18.
—— (2000–1b), 'The success of Cizhou wares during the Jin dynasty (AD 1115–1234)', *TOCS*, 65: 25–40.
Qixin, Z. (1990). 'Royal costumes of the Jin dynasty', *Orientations*, 21, no. 12: 59–64.
Raby, J. (ed.) (1985). *The Art of Syria and the Jazīra 1100–1250, Oxford Studies in Islamic Art I*. Oxford.
—— (1987–8). 'Between Sogdia and the Mamluks: a note on the earliest illustrations to Kalīla wa Dimna', *OA*, NS 33: 381–98.
Raby, J. and T. Fitzherbert (eds) (1996). *The Court of the Il-Khans 1290–1340, Oxford Studies in Islamic Art XII*. Oxford.
Rashid al-Din, Fadl-Allah (1940). *Tarikh-i Mubarak-i Gazani*, ed. K. Jahn, *Geschichte Ġāzān-ẖān's aus dem Ta'rīẖi-Mubārak-i- Ġāzānī des Rašīd al-Dīn Fadlallāh B. 'Imād al-Daula Abūl-Ḫair*. London.

—— (1971). *Jamiʿ al-Tawarikh*, trans. J. A. Boyle, *The Successors of Genghis Khan*. New York.
Rawson, J. (1982). *The Ornament on Chinese Silver of the Tang Dynasty (AD 618–906), British Museum Occasional Paper No. 40*. London.
—— (1984). *Chinese Ornament: The Lotus and the Dragon*. New York.
—— (1991). 'Central Asian silver and its influence on Chinese ceramics', *BAI*, 5: 139–51.
—— (ed.) (1992). *The British Museum Book of Chinese Art*. London.
—— (1995). *Chinese Jade from the Neolithic to the Qing*. London.
Rawson, J., M. Tite and M. J. Hughes (1987–8). 'The export of Tang *Sancai* wares: some recent research', *TOCS*, 52: 39–61.
Ray, H. P. and J. F. Salles (eds) (1996). *Tradition and Archaeology: Early Maritime Contacts in the Indian Ocean*. New Delhi.
Reitlinger, G. (1938). 'The interim period in Persian pottery: an essay in chronological revision', *AI*, 5: 155–78.
—— (1944–5). 'Sultanabad: classification and chronology', *TOCS*, 20: 25–34.
Rempel', L. I. (1961). *Arkhitekturnyi ornament Uzbekistana*. Tashkent.
Rhie, M. M. (2002). *Early Buddhist Art of China and Central Asia*, 2 vols. Leiden.
Riboud, K. (1995). 'A cultural continuum: a new group of Liao & Jin dynasty silks', *Hali*, 82: 92–105.
Rice, D. S. (1957). 'Inlaid brasses from the workshop of Ahmad al-Dhakī al-Mawsilī', *AO*, 2: 283–326.
—— (1961). 'A Saljuq mirror', in *First International Congress of Turkish Arts, Ankara, 19th–24th October, 1959*, Ankara: Türk Tarih Kurumu Basimevi, 288–90.
Rice, D. T. (1959). *The Art of Byzantium*. London.
—— (1970). 'Who were the painters of the Edinburgh Rashid al-Din?' *CAJ*, 14: 181–5.
—— (1971). *Islamic Painting: A Survey*. Edinburgh.
—— (1975). *Islamic Art*. London.
—— (1976). *The Illustrations to the 'World History' of Rashīd al-Dīn*. Edinburgh.
Rice, T. T. (1969). 'Some reflections on the subject of arm bands', in Aslanapa and Naumann (eds) (1969), 262–77.
Richard, F. (1997a). *Splendeurs persanes: Manuscrits du XIIe au XVIIe siècle*. Paris.
—— (1997b). 'Un des peintres du manuscrit supplément persan 1113 de l'histoire des mongols de Rashid al-Din identifié', in Aigle (ed.) (1997), 307–20.
Richards, D. S. (ed.) (1970). *Islam and the Trade of Asia: A Colloquium*. Oxford.
Riefstahl, R. M. (1931). 'Persian Islamic stucco sculptures', *AB*, 13: 438–63.
Robb, D. M. (1936). 'The iconography of the Annunciation in the fourteenth and fifteenth centuries', *AB*, 18: 480–526.
Robinson, B. W. (1958). *A Descriptive Catalogue of the Persian Paintings in the Bodleian Library*. Oxford.
—— (1967). *Persian Miniature Painting from Collections in the British Isles*. London.
—— (1976). *Persian Paintings in the Indian Office Library: A Descriptive Catalogue*. London.
____ (ed.) (1976). *The Keir Collection: Islamic Painting and the Arts of the Book*. London.

—— (1980). 'Rashid al-Din's World History: the significance of the miniatures', *Journal of the Royal Asiatic Society*, 212–22.
—— (1982). 'A survey of Persian painting (1350–1896)', in Adle (ed.) (1982), 13–82.
—— (1993). 'Murakka'', in *EI*², 7: 602–3.
Rogers, C. (ed.) (1983). *Early Islamic Textiles*. Brighton.
Rogers, J. M. (1969). 'On a figurine in the Cairo Museum of Islamic art', *Persica*, 4: 141–79.
—— (1970). 'China and Islam – the archaeological evidence in the Mashriq', in Richards (ed.) (1970), 67–80.
—— (1970–1). 'Seljuk influence on the monuments of Cairo', *KdO*, 7, 40–68.
—— (1972). 'Evidence for Mamlūk–Mongol relations, 1260–1360', in *Colloque international sur l'histoire du Caire*, Cairo: Ministry of Culture of the Arab Republic of Egypt, 385–403.
—— (1989). 'Ceramics', in Ferrier (ed.) (1989), 255–69.
—— (1992a). 'Chinese–Iranian relations: ii. Islamic period to the Mongols', in *EIr*, 5: 431–4.
—— (1992b). 'Chinese–Iranian relations: iv. the Safavid period, 907–1145/1501–1732', in *EIr*, 5: 436–8.
Rogers, J. M., F. Çağman and Z. Tanındı (1986). *The Topkapı Saray Museum: The Albums and Illustrated Manuscripts*. London.
Rorex, R. A. (1984). 'Some Liao tomb murals and images of nomads in Chinese paintings of the Wen-chi story', *AA*, 45, pts 2–3: 174–97.
Rosen-Ayalon, M. (1974). *La Poterie islamique*. Paris.
Rosenzweig, D. L. (1978–9). 'Stalking the Persian dragon: Chinese prototypes for the miniature representations', *KdO*, 7: 150–76.
Rossabi, M. (1981). 'The Muslims in the early Yüan dynasty', in Langlois (ed.) (1981), 257–95.
_____ (ed.) (1983). *China among Equals: The Middle Kingdom and its Neighbors 10th–14th Centuries*. Berkeley.
—— (1988). *Khubilai Khan: His Life and Times*. Berkeley.
Rougeulle, A. (1991a). 'Les Importations extrême-orientales trouvées sur les sites de la période addasside', unpublished Ph.D. dissertation, University of Paris.
—— (1991b). 'Les Importations de céramiques chinoises dans le Golfe arabo-persique (VIIIᵉ–XIᵉ siècles)', *Archéologie islamique*, 2: 5–46.
—— (1996). 'Medieval trade networks in the western Indian Ocean (8th–14th centuries): some reflections from the distribution pattern of Chinese imports in the Islamic world', in Ray and Salles (eds) (1996), 159–80.
Roux, J. (1982). *Études d'Iconographie islamique: Quelques objets numineux des turcs et des mongols*. Leuven.
Rowley, G. (1959). *Principles of Chinese Painting*, rev. edn. Princeton.
Roxburgh, D. J. (1995). 'Heinrich Friedrich von Diez and his eponymous albums: Mss. Diez A. Fols.70–74', *Muqarnas*, 12: 112–36.
_____ (ed.) (2005). *Turks: A Journey of a Thousand Years, 600–1600*. London.
Rubruck, W. (1990). *The Mission of Friar William Rubruck*, trans. P. Jackson and ed. D. Morgan. London.
Rührdanz, K. (1997). 'Illustrationen zu Rašhīd al-dīns Ta'rīḫ-i Mubārak-i Ġāzānī in den berliner Diez-Alben', in Aigle (ed.) (1997), 295–306.
Rupert, M. and O. J. Todd (1935). *Chinese Bronze Mirrors: A Study Based on the Todd Collection of 1,000 Bronze Mirrors Found in the Five Northern Provinces of Suiyuan, Shansi, Honan and Hopei, China*. Beijing.

Ryan, J. D. (1998). 'Christian wives of Mongol khans: Tartar queens and missionary expectations in Asia', *Journal of the Royal Asiatic Society*, series 3, 8, no. 3: 411–21.
Sachau, C. E. (1879). *The Chronology of Ancient Nations. An English Version of the Arabic Text of the Athâr-ul-Bâkiya of Albîrûnî, or 'Vestiges of the Past', Collected and Reduced to Writing by the Author in A.H. 390–1, A.D. 1000*. London.
Saeki, P. (1928). *The Nestorian Documents and Relics in China*. London.
Salim, M. et al. (1997). *Islamische Textilkunst des Mittelalters: Aktuelle Probleme*. Riggisberg.
Salmony, A. (1943). 'Daghestan sculptures', *AI*, 10: 153–63.
Santangelo, A. (1964).*The Development of Italian Textile Design from the 12th to the 18th Century*. London.
Sarre, F. (1925). *Die Ausgrabungen von Samarra: Band II, Die Keramik von Samarra*. Berlin.
Scanlon, G. T. (1970). 'Egypt and China: trade and imitation', in Richards (ed.) (1970), 81–95.
Scarcia, G. (1975). 'The "Vihār" of Qonqor-olong: preliminary report', *East and West*, NS 25: 99–104.
Schafer, E. (1963). *The Golden Peaches of Samarkand: A Study of T'ang Exotics*. Berkeley.
Schmidt, H. J., N. Steensgaard, H. İnalcık and A. K. Gharaibeh (1971). 'Harīr', *EI* ², 3: 209–21.
—— (1958). *Alte Seidenstoffe*. Brundwick.
Schmidt, H.-P. (1980). 'The sēnmurw: of birds and dogs and bats', *Persica*, 9: 1–85.
Schmidt-Colinet, A., A. Stauffer and K. al-Asʿad (2000). *Die Textilien aus Palmyra: Neue und alte Funde, Damaszener Forschungen 8*. Mainz.
Schmitz, B. (1994). 'A fragmentary mīnā'ī bowl with scenes from the Shāhnāma', in Hillenbrand (ed.) (1994), 156–64.
—— (1997). *Islamic and Indian Manuscripts and Paintings in the Pierpont Morgan Library*. New York.
Schnyder, R. (1994). 'In search of the substance of light', in Hillenbrand (ed.) (1994), 165–9.
Schorta, R. (2004). 'A Central Asian cloth-of-gold garment reconstructed', *Orientations*, 35, no. 4: 53–6.
—— (ed.) (2007). *Dragons of Silk, Flowers of Gold: A Group of Liao-Dynasty Textiles at the Abegg-Stiftung*. Riggisberg.
Schottenhammer, A. (2001). 'The role of metals and the impact of the introduction of Huizi paper notes in Quanzhou on the development of maritime trade in the Song period', in Schottenhammer (ed.) (2001), 95–176.
—— (ed.) (2001). *The Emporium of the World: Maritime Quanzhou, 1000–1400*. Leiden.
Schroeder, E. (1939). 'Ahmad Musa and Shames al-Dīn: a review of fourteenth century painting', *AI*, 6: 113–42.
—— (1942). *Persian Miniatures in the Fogg Museum of Art*. Cambridge, MA.
—— (1961). 'Mrs. Rockefeller's miniatures at the Fogg', *Connoisseur*, 148, no. 595: 70–5.
Schulz, P. (1914). *Die persisch-islamische Miniaturmalerei*, 2 vols. Leipzig.
Schurmann, H. F. (1956). 'Mongolian tributary practices of the thirteenth century', *Harvard Journal of Asiatic Studies*, 19: 304–89.
Scott, P. (1993). *The Book of Silk*. London.

Scott, R. (1989). *Percival David Foundation of Chinese Art: A Guide to the Collection*. London.
Scott, R. and J. Guy (eds) (1995). *South East Asia & China: Art, Interaction & Commerce, Colloquies on Art & Archaeology in Asia no. 17*. London.
Seherr-Thoss, S. P. (1968). *Design and Color in Islamic Architecture*. Washington, DC.
Serjeant, R. B. (1972). *Islamic Textiles: Material for a History up to the Mongol Conquest*. Beirut.
Shafiʿi, F. (1957). *Simple Calyx Ornament in Islamic Art (A Study in Arabesque)*. Cairo.
Shen, Y. (2001). 'Yuan mubihua zhong de yuandai fushi [Costumes in Yuan murals]', *Gugong wenwu*, 90, no. 8: 32–41.
Sheng, A. (1995). 'Chinese silk tapestry: a brief social historical perspective of its early development', *Orientations*, 26, no. 5: 70–5.
—— (1999a). 'Woven motifs in Turfan silks: Chinese or Iranian?' *Orientations*, 30, no. 4: 45–52.
—— (1999b). 'Why ancient silk is still gold: issues in Chinese textile history', *AO*, 29: 147–68.
Shepherd, D. (1966). 'Iran between East and West', in Bowie (ed.) (1966), 84–105.
—— (1974). 'Medieval Persian silks in fact and fancy', *Bulletin de liaison du centre international d'étude des textiles anciens*, 39–40: 1–239.
—— (1981a). 'Zandaniji revisited', in M. Flury-Lemberg (ed.), *Documenta textilia: Festschrift für Sigrid Müller-Christensen* (Munich, 1981), 105–22.
—— (1981b). 'Technical aspects of the Buyid silks', in *SPA*, 3090–9.
—— (1994). 'Saljūq textiles – a study in iconography', in Hillenbrand (ed.) (1994), 210–7.
Shepherd, D. and W. Henning (1959). 'Zandaniji identified?' in Ettinghausen (ed.) (1959), 15–40.
Shiba, Y. (1983). 'Sung foreign trade: its scope and organization', in Rossabi (ed.) (1983), 89–115.
Sickman, L. (1978). *Chinese Classic Furniture*. London.
Silbergeld, J. (1982). *Chinese Painting Style: Media, Methods, and Principles of Form*. Seattle.
Simcox, J. (1994). 'Tracing the dragon: the stylistic development of designs in early Chinese textiles', in Marcuson (ed.) (1994), 35–47.
Simpson, M. S. (1979). *The Illustration of an Epic: The Earliest Shahnama Manuscripts*. New York and London.
—— (1982a). 'The role of Baghdād in the formation of Persian painting', in Adle (ed.) (1982), 91–116.
—— (1982b). 'The pattern of early Shāhnāma illustration', *Studia atrium orientalis et occidentalis*, 1: 43–53.
—— (1985). 'Narrative allusion and metaphor in the decoration of medieval Islamic objects', in H. L. Kessler and M. S. Simpson (eds), *Pictorial Narrative in Antiquity and the Middle Ages* (Washington, DC, 1985), 131–49.
—— (2000). 'A reconstruction and preliminary account of the 1341 Shahnama: with some further thoughts on early Shahnama illustration', in Hillenbrand (ed.) (2000), 217–47.
Sims, E. (1982). 'The internal decoration of the Mausoleum of Öljeitü Khudābanda: a preliminary re-examination', in *Soltāniye III, Quaderni del Seminario di Iranistica, Uralo-Altaistica e Caucasologia dell'Università degli Studi di Venezia*, 9: 89–123.

—— (1988). 'The "iconography" of the internal decoration in the mausoleum of Ūljātū at Sultaniyya', in Soucek (ed.) (1988), 139–75.

—— (2002). *Peerless Images: Persian Painting and its Sources*. New Haven.

Sims-Williams, N. (1996). 'The Sogdian merchants in China and India', in Cadonna and Lanciotti (eds) (1996), 45–67.

Sinor, D. (ed.) (1963). *Aspects of Altaic Civilization: Proceedings of the Fifth Meeting of the Permanent International Altaistic Conference Held at Indiana University, June 4–9, 1962*. Bloomington.

—— (1998). 'The Kitan and the Kara Khitay', in Asimov and Bosworth (eds) (1998), 227–42.

Sirén, O. (1956–8). *Chinese Painting: Leading Masters and Principles*, 7 vols. London.

Skelton, R. (1972). 'The relations between the Chinese and Indian jade carving traditions', in Watson (ed.) (1972b), 98–108.

Smart, E. S. (1975–7). 'Fourteenth century Chinese porcelain from a Tughlaq Palace in Delhi', *TOCS*, 41: 199–230.

Smith, M. B. (1938). 'The wood minbar in the Masdjid–i Djamiʿ, Nāīn', *AI*, 5: 21–35.

Sokolovskaia, L. and A. Rougeulle (1992). 'Stratified finds of Chinese porcelains from pre-Mongol Samarkand (Afrasiab)', *BAI*, 6: 87–98.

Sonday, M. (1999–2000). 'A group of possibly thirteenth-century velvets with gold disks in offset rows', *Textile Museum Journals*, 38–9: 101–51.

Song shi (1985). [History of the Song Dynasty], 40 vols. Beijing.

Soucek, P. (1972). 'Nizāmī on painters and painting', in Ettinghausen (ed.) (1972), 9–21.

—— (1975). 'An illustrated manuscript of al-Bīrūnī's Chronology of Ancient Nations', in P. J. Chelkowski (ed.), *The Scholar and the Saint: Studies in Commemoration of Abu'l-Rayhan al-Bīrūnī and Jalal al-Din al-Rūmī*. New York, 103–68.

—— (1979). 'The arts of calligraphy', in Gray (ed.) (1979), 7–34.

—— (1980). 'The role of landscape in Iranian painting to the 15th century', in Watson (ed.) (1980), 86–110.

—— (ed.) (1988). *Content and Context of Visual Arts in the Islamic World. Papers from a Colloquium in Memory of Richard Ettinghausen. Institute of Fine Arts, New York University, 2–4 April 1980. Planned and Organised by Carol Manson Bier*. University Park.

—— (1999). 'Ceramic production as exemplar of Yuan-Ilkhanid relations', *Res*, 35: 125–41.

Soudavar, A. (1992). *Art of the Persian Courts: Selections from the Art and History Trust Collection*. New York.

—— (1996). 'The saga of Abu-Saʿid Bahādor Khān. The Abu-Saʿidnāmé', in Raby and Fitzherbert (eds) (1996), 95–218.

—— (1998) 'A Chinese dish from the lost endowment of Princess Sultānum (925–69/1519–62)', in K. Eslami (ed.), *Iran and Iranian Studies: Essays in Honor of Iraj Afshar*. Princeton, 125–36.

—— (1999). 'The concepts of "al-Aqdamo Asahh" and "Yaqin-e Sābeq", and the problem of semi-fakes', *SI*, 28: 255–73.

Soustiel, J. (1985). *La Céramique islamique*. Fribourg.

Soustiel J. and Y. Porter (2003). *Tombs of Paradise: The Shah-e Zende in Samarkand and Architectural Ceramics of Central Asia*. Saint-Rémy-en-l'Eau.

Soustiel, L. and J. Allan (1995). 'The problem of Saljuq monochrome wares', in Allan (ed.) (1995), 85–116.

Spuhler, F. (1978). *Islamic Carpets and Textiles in the Keir Collection*. London.
Spuler, B. (1955). *Die Mongolen in Iran: Politik, Verwaltung und Kultur der Ilchanzeit 1220–1350*. Berlin.
—— (1972). *History of the Mongols Based on Eastern and Western Accounts of the Thirteenth and Fourteenth Centuries*. London.
Spuler, B. and R. Ettinghausen (1971). 'Īlkhāns', in *EI*², 3: 1120–7.
Stauffer, A. (1996). 'Textiles from Palmyra: local production and the import and imitation of Chinese silk weavings', *Les Annals archéologiques arabes syriennes: revue d'archéologie et d'histoire*, 42: 425–30.
Stein, A. (1921). *Serindia: Detailed Report of Explorations in Central Asia and Westernmost China Carried out and Described under the Orders of HM Indian Government*, 5 vols. Oxford.
—— (1928). *Innermost Asia: Detailed Report of Explorations in Central Asia, Kan-su and Eastern Iran*, 4 vols. Oxford.
Steinhardt, N. S. (1983). 'The plan of Khubilai Khan's imperial city', *AA*, 44, nos 2–3: 137–58.
—— (1990–1). 'Yuan period tombs and their decoration: cases at Chifeng', *OA*, 36, no. 4: 198–221.
Steinhardt, N. S., X. Fu, D. Guo, X. Liu, G. Pan, Y. Qiao and D. Sun (2002). *Chinese Architecture*. New Haven.
Stern, S. M. (1969). 'A manuscript from the library of the Ghaznawid Amīr ʿAbd al-Rashīd', in Pinder-Wilson (ed.) (1969), 7–31.
Stewart, D. (1967). *Early Islam*. Amsterdam.
Stillman, N. A. (1986). 'Khilʿa', in *EI*², 5: 6–7.
Stillman, Y. K., N. A. Stillman and T. Majda (1986). 'Libās', in *EI*², 5: 732–53.
Stillman, Y. K., P. Sanders and N. Rabbat (2000). 'Tirāz', in *EI*², 10: 534–8.
Stockland, W. (1993–5). 'The Kitab-i Samak ʿAyyar', *Persica*, 15: 143–82.
Stuart, J. and E. S. Rawski (2001). *Worshiping the Ancestors: Chinese Commemorative Portraits*. Washington, DC.
Sugimura, T. (1981). 'The Chinese impact of certain fifteenth century Persian paintings from the Albums (Hazine Library Nos 2153, 2154, 2160) in the Topkapi Saray Museum, Istanbul', unpublished Ph.D. dissertation. University of Michigan.
—— (1986). *The Encounter of Persia with China: Research into Cultural Contacts Based on Fifteenth Century Persian Pictorial Materials*. Osaka.
—— (1992). 'Chinese–Iranian relations: xii. mutual influences in painting', in *EIr*, 5: 458–60.
Sui shu (1973). [History of the Sui Dynasty], 3 vols. Beijing.
Sullivan, M. (1962). *The Birth of Landscape Painting in China*. London.
Sun, E. and DeFrancis, L. (eds) (1966). *Chinese Social History: Translations of Selected Studies*. New York.
Sung, H. (2002). 'The symbolic language of Chinese horse painting', *National Palace Museum Bulletin*, 36, no. 2, July: 29–73.
Suriano, C. and S. Carboni (1999). *La seta islamica: temi ed influenze culturali*. Florence.
Suzuki, K. (1981–95). *Chugoku kaigashi* [History of Chinese Painting], 8 vols. Tokyo.
Swietochowski, M. L. (1994). 'The Metropolitan Museum of Art's small Shahnama', in Swietochowski and Carboni (1994), 67–127.
Swietochowski, M. L. and S. Carboni (1994). *Illustrated Poetry and Epic Images: Persian Painting of the 1330s and 1340s*. New York.

Świętosławski, W. (1999). *Arms and Armour of the Nomads of the Great Steppe in the Times of the Mongol Expansion (12th–14th Centuries)*. Łodź.

Tamari, V. (1995). 'Abbasid blue-on-white ware', in Allan (ed.) (1995), 117–45.

Tampoe, M. (1989). *Maritime Trade between China and the West: An Archaeological Study of the Ceramics from Siraf (Persian Gulf), 8th to 15th Centuries AD*. Oxford.

Tamura, J. and Y. Kobayashi (1953). *Keiryo: higashi Mongoria ni okeru ryodai teioryo to sono hekiga ni kansuru kokogakuteki chosahokoku* [Keiryo: Tombs and Mural Paintings of the Ch'ing-ling Liao Imperial Mausoleums of the Eleventh Century AD in Eastern Mongolia. Detailed Report of Archaeological Survey Carried out in 1935 and 1939], 2 vols. Kyoto.

Tang, S. (1982). *Chongxiu Zhenghe jingshi zhenglei beiji bencao* [The Revised Pharmacopoeia of the Zhenghe Era], Renmin weisheng chubanshe facsimile of the Huiming imprint of 1116. Beijing.

Tavakoli, F. (2002). *A Bibliography of Sultaniyeh*. Tehran.

Tha'alibi, 'A. (1968). *Lata'if al-ma'arif*, trans. C. E. Bosworth, *The Book of Curious and Entertaining Information*. Edinburgh.

Thackston, W. M. (1989). *A Century of Princes: Sources on Timurid History and Art*. Cambridge, MA.

Thompson, J. (2004). *Silk: 13th to 18th Centuries, Treasures from the Museum of Islamic Art*. Doha.

Thompson, N. (1967). 'The evolution of the T'ang lion and grapevine mirror', *AA*, 29: 25–40.

Tilden, J. (ed.) (1995). *Asian Art: The Second Hali Annual*. London.

—— (ed.) (1996). *Silk & Stone: The Third Hali Annual*. London.

—— (ed.) (1997). *First under Heaven: The Fourth Hali Annual*. London.

Titley, N. (1971). 'A fourteenth-century Khamsa of Nizami', *British Museum Quarterly*, 39: 8–11.

—— (1972). 'A 14th-century Nizāmī manuscript in Tehran', *KdO*, 8: 120–5.

—— (1981). *Dragons in Persian, Mughal and Turkish Art*. London.

—— (1983). *Persian Miniature Painting and its Influence on the Art of Turkey and India: The British Library Collections*. London.

Tonko bunbutsu kenkyusho (ed.) (1982). *Chugoku sekkutsu: tonko bakukokutsu* [Chinese Stone Caves: Dunhuang], 5 vols. Tokyo.

Toynbee, P. (1900). 'Tartar cloths', *Romania*, 29: 559–64.

Tung, W. and P. Leidy (1989). 'Recent archaeological contributions to the study of Chinese ceramics', in Kotz (ed.) (1989), 93–102.

Turner, G. L. (1966). 'A magic mirror of Buddhist significance', *OA*, NS 12, no. 2: 94–8.

Upton, J. M. (1932–3). 'A manuscript of "the Book of the Fixed Stars" by 'Abd ar-Rahmān as-Sūfī', *Metropolitan Museum Studies*, 4: 179–97.

Vainker, S. (1991). *Chinese Pottery and Porcelain: From Prehistory to the Present*. London.

—— (1996). 'Silk of the Northern Song', in Tilden (ed.) (1996), 160–75.

Valenstein, S. (1994). 'Concerning a reattribution of some Chinese ceramics', *Orientations*, 25, no. 12: 71–4.

Vardjavand, P. (1979). 'La Découverte archéologique du complexe scientifique de l'observatoire de Maraqé', *Akten des VII. internationalen Kongresses für iranische Kunst und Archäologie, München 7.–10. September 1976*. Berlin, 527–36.

Vernoit, S. (2000). 'Islamic art and architecture: an overview of scholarship and collecting, c. 1850–1950', in S. Vernoit (ed.), *Discovering Islamic Art: Scholars, Collectors and Collections, 1850–1950*. London.

Vickers, M. (ed.) (1986). *Pots & Pans: A Colloquium on Precious Metals and Ceramics in the Muslim, Chinese and Graeco-Roman Worlds, Oxford Studies in Islamic Art III*. Oxford.

Vickers, M., O. Impey and J. Allan (1986). *From Silver to Ceramics: The Potter's Debt to Metalwork in the Graeco-Roman, Oriental and Islamic Worlds*. Oxford.

Vinograd, R. (1992). *Boundaries of the Self: Chinese Portraits, 1600–1900*. Cambridge.

Vollmer, J. E. (1982). 'Chinese tapestry weaving: k'o-ssu', *Hali*, 5, no. 1: 36–48.

Vollmer, J. E., E. J. Keall and E. Nagai-Berthrong (1983). *Silk Roads, China Ships*. Toronto.

Volov, L. (1966). 'Plaited Kufic on Samanid epigraphic pottery', *AO*, 6: 107–33.

Waley, P. and N. Titley (1975). 'An illustrated Persian text of Kalīla wa Dimna dated 707/1307–8', *British Library Journal*, 1, no. 1: 42–61.

Walzer, S. (1959). 'The Mamluk illuminated manuscripts of Kalila wa Dimna', in Ettinghausen (ed.) (1959), 195–206.

Wan, Q. (2002). *Liaodai fushi* [Liao Costumes]. Shenyang.

Wang, Q. (2003). 'Guanding qinghua qiyuan de sikao [On the origins of blue-and-white porcelain]', *Gugong bowuyuan yuankan*, 190, no. 5: 58–64.

Wang, Y. (1995). *Looking at Chinese Painting*. Tokyo.

Ward, R. (1993). *Islamic Metalwork*. London.

—— (ed.) (1998). *Gilded and Enamelled Glass from the Middle East*. London.

Ward, W. E. (1952). 'The lotus symbol: its meaning in Buddhist art and philosophy', *Journal of Aesthetics and Art Criticism*, 11: 135–46.

Wardwell, A. E. (1987). 'Flight of the phoenix: crosscurrents in late thirteenth to fourteenth century silk patterns and motifs', *Bulletin of the Cleveland Museum of Art*, 74: 2–35.

—— (1988–9). 'Panni tartarici: eastern Islamic silks woven with gold and silver (13th and 14th centuries)', *IA*, 3: 95–173.

—— (1989). 'Recently discovered textiles woven in the western part of Central Asia before AD 1220', *Textile History*, 20, no. 2: 175–84.

—— (1992). 'Two silk and gold textiles of the early Mongol period', *Bulletin of the Cleveland Museum of Art*, 79, no. 10: 354–78.

—— (1992–3). 'Important Asian textiles acquired by the Cleveland Museum of Art', *OA*, NS 38, no. 4: 244–51.

—— (2000). 'Indigenous elements in Central Asian silk designs of the Mongol period, and their impact on Italian Gothic silks', *Bulletin de liaison du centre international d'étude des textiles anciens*, 77: 86–98.

Watson, O. (1973–5). 'Persian lustre-painted pottery: the Rayy and Kashan styles', *TOCS*, 40: 1–19.

—— (1975). 'The Masjid-i ʿAli, Quhrūd: an architectural and epigraphic survey', *Iran*, 13: 59–74.

—— (1977). 'Persian lustre tiles of the thirteenth and fourteenth centuries', unpublished Ph.D. dissertation. University of London.

—— (1982). 'An Islamic "lacquer" dish', in Watson (ed.) (1982), 232–46.

—— (1985). *Persian Lustre Ware*. London.

—— (1992). 'Chinese–Iranian relations: xi. mutual influence of Chinese and Persian ceramics', in *EIr*, 5: 455–7.

—— (2004). *Ceramics from Islamic Lands: Kuwait National Museum, The Al-Sabah Collection*. London.

Watson, W. (1962). *Ancient Chinese Bronzes*. London; 2nd edn, 1977.

—— (1970). 'On T'ang soft-glazed pottery', in Watson (ed.) (1970), 41–9.

—— (ed.) (1970). *Pottery & Metalwork in T'ang China: Their Chronology & External Relations, Colloquies on Art and Archaeology in Asia No. 1*. London.

—— (ed.) (1972a). *Mahayanist Art after* AD *900, Colloquies on Art and Archaeology in Asia No. 2*. London.

—— (ed.) (1972b). *The Westward Influence of the Chinese Arts from the 14th to the 18th Century, Colloquies on Art and Archaeology in Asia No. 3*. London.

—— (1973). 'On some categories of archaism in Chinese bronze', *AO*, 9: 1–13.

—— (ed.) (1974). *The Art of Iran and Anatolia from the 11th to the 13th Century AD, Colloquies on Art and Archaeology in Asia No. 4*. London.

—— (ed) (1980). *Landscape Style in Asia, Colloquies on Art and Archaeology in Asia No. 9*. London.

—— (ed.) (1982). *Lacquerware in Asia and Beyond, Colloquies on Art and Archaeology in Asia No. 11*. London.

—— (1984). *Tang and Liao Ceramics*. London.

—— (1986). 'Precious metal – its influence on Tang earthenware', in Vickers (ed.) (1986), 161–74.

—— (1995). *The Arts of China to AD 900*. New Haven.

—— (2000). *The Arts of China 900–1620*. New Haven.

Watt, J. C. Y. (1998). 'Textiles of the Mongol period in China', *Orientations*, 29, no. 3: 72–83.

Watt, J. C. Y. and A. E. Wardwell (1997). *When Silk Was Gold: Central Asian and Chinese Textiles*. New York.

Weibel, A. C. (1972). *Two Thousand Years of Textiles*. New York.

Weidner, M. (1989). 'Aspects of painting and patronage at the Mongol court, 1260–1368', in Li (ed.) (1989), 37–59.

____ (ed.) (1994). *Latter Days of the Law: Images of Chinese Buddhism 850–1850*. Honolulu.

Wellesz, E. (1959). 'An early al-Sūfī manuscript in the Bodleian Library in Oxford', *AO*, 3: 1–26.

—— (1965). *An Islamic Book of Censtellations*. Oxford.

Wenley, A. G. (1959). 'A parallel between Far Eastern and Persian painting', in Ettinghausen (ed.) (1959), 350–5.

Wenzel, M. (1990). 'Textiles and the Seljuks of Anatolia', *Hali*, 53: 136–43.

Wertime, J. T. and R. E. Wright (1995). 'The Tabriz hypothesis: the dragon & related floral carpets', in Tilden (ed.) (1995), 30–53.

Whitehouse, D. (1970). 'Some Chinese and Islamic pottery from Sīrāf', in Watson (ed.) (1970), 35–40.

—— (1972). 'Excavations at Sīrāf: fifth interim report', *Iran*, 10: 63–88.

—— (1973). 'Chinese stoneware from Siraf: the earliest finds', in N. Hammond (ed.), *South Asian Archaeology: Papers from the First International Conference of South Asian Archaeologists Held in the University of Cambridge*. London, 241–55.

—— (1976). 'Kīsh', *Iran*, 14: 146–7.

—— (1992). 'Ceramics: the early Islamic period, 1st–4th/7th–11th centuries', in *EIr*, 5: 308–11.

Whitfield, R. (1982–5). *The Art of Central Asia: The Stein Collection in the British Museum*, 3 vols. Tokyo.
—— (1995). *Dunhuang: Buddhist Art from the Silk Road*, 2 vols. London.
Whitfield, R., S. Whitfield and N. Agnew (2000). *Cave Temple of Mogao: Art and History on the Silk Road*. Los Angeles.
Whitfield, S. (ed.) (2004). *The Silk Road: Trade, Travel, War and Faith*. London.
Whitman, M. (1978). 'Persian blue-and-white ceramics: cycles of *chinoiserie*', unpublished Ph.D. dissertation. New York University.
Wilber, D. (1938). 'Notes on the Rabʿ-i-Rashidi', *Bulletin of the American Institute for Iranian Art and Archaeology*, 5, pt 3: 247–54.
—— (1955). *The Architecture of Islamic Iran: The Il Khānid Period*. Princeton; repr. New York, 1969.
Wilckens, L. von (1992). *Mittelalterliche Seidenstoffe*. Berlin.
Wilkinson, C. K. (1973). *Nishapur: Pottery of the Early Islamic Period*. New York.
Williams, C. A. S. (1974). *Chinese Symbolism and Art Motifs*, 3rd edn. Edison.
Wilson, E. (1994). *8000 Years of Ornament: An Illustrated Handbook of Motifs*. London.
Wilson, J. K. (1990). 'Powerful form and potent symbol: the dragon in Asia', *Bulletin of the Cleveland Museum of Art*, 77, no. 8: 286–323.
Wirgin, J. (1979). *Sung Ceramic Designs*. London.
Wolff, H. E. (1966). *The Traditional Crafts of Persia: Their Development, Technology, and Influence on Eastern and Western Civilizations*. Cambridge, MA.
Wolff, R. L. and H. W. Hazard (eds) (1969). *A History of the Crusades: Volume II. The Later Crusades, 1189–1311*. Madison.
Wu, H. (1996). *The Double Screen: Medium and Representation in Chinese Painting*. London.
Wu, T. (1997). *Tales from the Land of Dragons: 1000 Years of Chinese Painting*. Boston.
Wu, W. (2000). *Zhongguo yunwen zhuangshi* [Chinese Cloud Patterns]. Nanning.
Xin Tang shu (1975). [New History of the Tang Dynasty], 20 vols. Beijing.
Xu, X. (2001). 'Fojiao dui Liaodai gongyi de yingxiang [Buddhist influence on Liao decorative arts]', *Gugong bowuyuan yuankan*, 94, no. 2: 44–59.
Yaldiz, M., R. D. Gadebusch, R. Hickmann, F. Weis and R. Ghose (2000). *Magische Götterwelten: Werke aus dem Museum für Indische Kunst, Berlin*. Berlin.
Yang, B. (ed.) (1994). *Gugong wenwu dadian*, 4 vols. Fuzhou.
Yarshater, E. (ed.) (1983). *Cambridge History of Iran, Volume 3 (1)–(2): The Seleucid, Parthian and Sasanian Periods*. Cambridge.
Yohannan, A. (1917). 'A manuscript of the Manāfiʿ al-Haiawān in the library of Mr J. P. Morgan', *Journal of the American Oriental Society*, 36: 381–9.
Yongle dadian (1962). [Grand Compilation of Yongle]. Taipei.
Yu, F. (1988). *Chinese Painting Colors: Studies of their Preparation and Application in Traditional and Modern Times*, trans. J. Silbergeld and A. McNair. Hong Kong and Seattle.
Yuanchao mishi (1982). [Secret History of the Mongols], trans. F. W. Cleaves. Cambridge, MA; trans. I. de Rachewiltz, 2 vols. Leiden, 2004.
Yuan shi (1976). [History of the Yuan Dynasty], 15 vols. Beijing.

Zhang, P. and R. Whitfield (1991–2). 'New discoveries from recent research into Chinese blue and white porcelain', *TOCS*, 56: 37–46.

Zhao, F. (1999). *Treasures in Silk: An Illustrated History of Chinese Textiles*. Hong Kong.

—— (2004). *Liao Textiles and Costumes*. Hong Kong.

Zhao, F. and Z. Yu (2000). *Legacy of the Desert King: Textiles and Treasures Ecavated at Niya on the Silk Road*. Hong Kong.

Zhao, Q. (1991). 'Dragon: the symbol of China', *OA*, NS 37, no. 2: 72–80.

Zhou, X. (2000). *Zhongguo gubanhua tongshi* [History of Ancient Chinese Woodblock Prints]. Beiging.

Zhou, X. and C. Gao (1996). *Zhongguo yiguan fushi dacidian* [Encyclopaedia of Chinese Costumes]. Shanghai.

Zhu, H. (1991). *Guqian xindian* [Ancient Chinese Money], 2 vols. Xian.

Zhu, Q. (1990). 'Royal costumes of the Jin dynasty', *Orientations*, 21, no. 12: 59–64.

Zhu, T. (1998). *Liaodai jinyinqi* [Liao Metalwork]. Beijing.

Exhibition, museum and sales catalogues

Abu Dhabi (2008). *The Arts of Islam: Treasures from the Nasser D. Khalili Collection*, ed. J. M. Rogers, Emirates Palace Hotel.

Amsterdam (1999). *Earthy Beauty, Heavenly Art: Art of Islam*, ed. M. B. Piotrovsky and J. Vrieze, De Nieuwe Kerk.

Ann Arbor (1959). *Persian Art before and after the Mongol Conquest*, University of Michigan Museum of Art.

Beijing (2002). *Qidan wangchao: Neimenggu liaodai wenwu jinghua* [The Khitan Kingdom: Liao Dynasty Treasures from Inner Mongolia], China History Museum.

Berlin (2001). *Museum für Islamische Kunst: Staatliche Museen zu Berlin Preußischer Kulturbesitz*, Berlin.

Bonn/Munich (2005). *Dschingis Khan und seine Erben: Das Weltreich der Mongolen*, Kunst- und Ausstellungshalle der Bundesrepublik Deutschland, Bonn; Staatliches Museum für Völkerkunde, Munich.

Budapest (2007). *A Tatárjárás (1241–42)*, Hungarian National Museum.

Christie's (1995). *Christie's Sales Catalogue: Islamic Art and Indian Miniatures*, 17 October.

Christie's (1997). *Christie's Sales Catalogue: Islamic Art and Indian Miniatures*, 25 April.

Christie's (2000). *Christie's London Sales Catalogue: Islamic Art and Manuscripts*, 11 April.

Hong Kong (1995). *Heavens' Embroidered Cloths: One Thousand Years of Chinese Textiles*. Hong Kong Museum of Art.

Hong Kong (2004). *Noble Riders from Pines and Deserts: The Artistic Legacy of the Qidan*, ed. J. F. So, Art Museum, the Chinese University of Hong Kong.

Istanbul (2004). *Ben Mehmed Siyah Kalem, İnsanlar ve Cinlerin Ustası*, Yapı Kredi Kâzım Taşkent Art Gallery.

Kentucky (2000). *Imperial China: The Art of the Horse in Chinese History*, ed. B. Cooke, Kentucky House Park.

Kuwait (1990). *Masterpieces of Islamic Art in the Hermitage Museum*, Dar al-Athar al-Islamiyyah.

Los Angeles (1987). *The Quest for Eternity: Chinese Ceramic Sculptures from the People's Republic of China*, Los Angeles County Museum.

New York (1982). *Along the Ancient Silk Routes: Central Asian Art from the West Berlin State Museums*, Metropolitan Museum of Art.

New York (2006). *Gilded Splendor: Treasures of China's Liao Empire (907–1125)*, ed. H. Shen, Asia Society.

Paris (1992). *Terres secrètes de Samarcande: Céramiques du VIIIe au XIIIe siècle*, Institut du monde arabe.

Paris (2000). *L'Asie des steppes: D'Alexandre le Grand à Gengis Khan*, Musée national des arts asiatiques Guimet.

Paris (2001). *L'Etrange et le merveilleux en terres d'Islam*, Musée du Louvre.

Paris (2002). *Chevaux et cavaliers arabes dans les arts d'Orient et d'Occident*, Institut du monde arabe.

Paris (2004). *Lumières de soie: Soieries tissées d'or de la collection Riboud*, Musée national des arts asiatiques Guimet.

Paris (2007). *Chefs-d'œuvre islamiques de l'Aga Khan Museum*, Musée du Louvre.

Rouen (2000). *Miroirs – jeux et reflets depuis l'Antiquité*, Musée départemental des antiquités de Rouen.

Shanghai (2000). *Caoyuan kuaibao neiminggu wenwu kaogu jingpin* [Treasures on Grassland: Archaeological Finds from the Inner Mongolia Autonomous Region], Shanghai Museum.

Sotheby's (1981). *Sotheby's London Sales Catalogue: Fine Oriental Manuscripts and Miniatures* (The Hagop Kevorkian Fund), 27 April.

Sotheby's (1988), *Sotheby's London Sales Catalogue: Fine Oriental Manuscripts and Miniatures*, 29 April.

Sotheby's (1997). *Sotheby's London Sales Catalogue: Islamic Art*, 16 October.

Sotheby's (1998). *Sotheby's London Sales Catalogue: Oriental Manuscripts and Miniatures*, 29 April.

Spink (1999). *Threads of Imagination: Central Asian and Chinese Silks from the 12th to the 19th Century*, London.

Taipei (1986). *Gugong tongjing tezhan tulu* [Catalogue of Special Exhibition of Bronze Mirrors], National Palace Museum.

Taipei (1987). *Dingyao baici tezhan tulu* [Catalogue of Special Exhibition of Ding Ware White Porcelain], National Palace Museum.

Taipei (2000). *Qianxinian Songdai wenwu dazhan* [China at the Inception of the Second Millennium: Art and Culture of the Song Dynasty, 960–1279], National Palace Museum.

Taipei (2001). *Dahan de shiji: mengyuan shidai de duoyuan wenhua yu yishu* [Age of the Great Khan: Pluralism in Chinese Art and Culture under the Mongols], National Palace Museum.

Tokyo (1996). *Hoppo kibaminzoku no ogon masuku ten* [Treasures of Inner Mongolia], Orient Museum.

Washington, DC (2004). *Iraq and China: Ceramics, Trade, and Innovation* (www.asia.si.edu/exhibitions/online/iraqChina/defaultIC.htm#; accessed 10 June 2008), Freer and Sackler Galleries.

Illustration Acknowledgements

1.1 Cleveland Museum of Art, Cleveland. Andrew R. and Martha Holden Jennings Fund (1988.33)
1.2 Museo di Castelvecchio, Verona
1.3 Germanisches Nationalmuseum, Nuremberg (No. 394)
1.4 Cleveland Museum of Art, Cleveland. Purchase from J. H. Wade Fund (1991.4)
1.5 Drawing © Y. Kadoi
1.6 Kunstgewerbemuseum, Berlin (1875.258)
1.7 Kunstgewerbemuseum, Berlin (00.53)
1.8 Metropolitan Museum of Art, New York. Gift of Lisbet Holmes (1989.205) (photograph © Metropolitan Museum of Art, New York)
1.9 State Hermitage Museum, St Petersburg (LT-449)
1.10 Metropolitan Museum of Art, New York. Gift of John M. Crawford Jr (1983.105) (drawing © Y. Kadoi)
1.11 Cleveland Museum of Art, Cleveland. Purchase from the J. H. Wade Fund (1945.14)
1.12 Collection of Lloyd and Margit Cotsen, Los Angeles (T-0292)
1.13 David Collection, Copenhagen (30/1995)
1.14 David Collection, Copenhagen (40/1997)
1.15 Palace Museum, Beijing
2.1 Freer Gallery of Art, Washington, DC (F1956.2)
2.2 National Palace Museum, Taipei
2.3 Musée du Louvre, Paris (MAO 104) (drawing © Y. Kadoi)
2.4 Private collection (drawing © Y. Kadoi)
2.5 Nasser D. Khalili Collection of Islamic Art, London (POT 1310)
2.6 Victoria and Albert Museum, London (541-1900)
2.7 Victoria and Albert Museum, London (1893A–1897)
2.8 Inner Mongolia Institute of Archaeology, Huhhot (drawing © Y. Kadoi)
2.9 Musée national des arts asiatiques Guimet, Paris (AEDTA 3839/MA 11680) (photograph © RMN / Thierry Ollivier)
2.10 David Collection, Copenhagen (12/1962)

2.11 Ashmolean Museum, Oxford (EA1956.59) (drawing © Y. Kadoi)
2.12 Arthur M. Sackler Gallery, Smithsonian Institution, Washington, DC. Gift of Arthur M. Sackler (S1987.396)
2.13 David Collection, Copenhagen (22/1968)
2.14 Formerly Percival David Foundation of Chinese Art, London (PDF 265)
2.15 Victoria and Albert Museum, London (C.1955-1910)
2.16 Topkapı Saray Museum, Istanbul (TKS 15/235)
2.17 Shanghai Museum, Shanghai (drawing © Y. Kadoi)
2.18 Iran Bastan Museum, Tehran (No. 8678) (drawing © Y. Kadoi)
3.1 Metropolitan Museum of Art, New York. Rogers Fund, 1942 (1942.136) (photograph © Metropolitan Museum of Art, New York)
3.2 Victoria and Albert Museum, London (M.296-1956) (photograph © V&A Images/Victoria and Albert Museum, London)
3.3A Victoria and Albert Museum, London (546-1905)
3.3B After Melikian-Chirvani 1982, fig. 93D
3.4 Inner Mongolia Institute of Archaeology, Huhhot
3.5 Museum für Islamische Kunst, Staatsbibliothek zu Berlin – Stiftung Preussischer Kulturbesitz (I.C.1069) (after Enderlein 1973, Abb.1) (drawing © Y. Kadoi)
3.6 The Trustees of the National Museums of Scotland, Edinburgh (A.1909-547)
3.7 State Hermitage Museum, St Petersburg (BM-1132) (drawing © Y. Kadoi)
3.8 State Hermitage Museum, St Petersburg (SK-597)
3.9 David Collection, Copenhagen (7/1996)
3.10 National Palace Museum, Taipei
3.11 Art and History Trust, Courtesy of the Arthur M. Sackler Gallery, Smithsonian Institution, Washington, DC (LTS 1995.2.9)
3.12 National Palace Museum, Taipei
3.13 Freer Gallery of Art, Washington, DC (F. 1999.2)
3.14 After *SPA*, fig. 484 (drawing © Y. Kadoi)
3.15 Nasser D. Khalili Collection of Islamic Art, London (MTW 795)
3.16 Topkapı Saray Museum, Istanbul
3.17 Museum of Fine Arts, Boston. Gift of Mrs. Edward Jackson Holmes (55.106) (photograph © Museum of Fine Arts, Boston)
3.18 Metropolitan Museum of Art, New York. Rogers Fund, 1910 (10.218) (photograph © Metropolitan Museum of Art, New York)
3.19 Photograph © A. Anisi
3.20 Arthur M. Sackler Gallery, Smithsonian Institution, Washington, DC. Gift of Arthur M. Sackler (S1987.819)
4.1 MS Marsh 144, fo. 165. Bodleian Library, Oxford
4.2 Villa I Tatti, Settignano, Florence

5.12 MS Arab 20, fo. 121. University Library, Edinburgh
5.13 Inner Mongolia Museum, Hohhot
5.14 M 727, fo. 17. Nasser D. Khalili Collection of Islamic Art, London
5.15 National Palace Museum, Taipei
5.16 MS Arab 20, fo. 2v. University Library, Edinburgh
5.17 MS Arab 20, fo. 2. University Library, Edinburgh
5.18 MS Arab 20, fo. 1. University Library, Edinburgh (drawing © Y. Kadoi)
5.20 Hazine 1653, fo. 335. Topkapı Saray Museum, Istanbul
5.21 Diez A, Fol. 71.S.42.N.4 and N.6. Staatsbibliothek zu Berlin – Stiftung Preussischer Kulturbesitz, Orientabteilung, Berlin
5.23 Diez A, Fol. 71.S.53. Staatsbibliothek zu Berlin – Stiftung Preussischer Kulturbesitz, Orientabteilung, Berlin
5.24 Diez A, Fol. 71.S.54. Staatsbibliothek zu Berlin – Stiftung Preussischer Kulturbesitz, Orientabteilung, Berlin
5.25 Diez A, Fol. 71.S.51. Staatsbibliothek zu Berlin – Stiftung Preussischer Kulturbesitz, Orientabteilung, Berlin
5.26 Diez A, Fol. 71.S.62. Staatsbibliothek zu Berlin – Stiftung Preussischer Kulturbesitz, Orientabteilung, Berlin
5.27 Diez A, Fol. 70.S.20 and S.23. Staatsbibliothek zu Berlin – Stiftung Preussischer Kulturbesitz, Orientabteilung, Berlin
6.1 MS Pers.104.61. The Trustees of the Chester Beatty Library, Dublin
6.2 MS Pers.104.3. The Trustees of the Chester Beatty Library, Dublin
6.4 1974.290, fo. 28. Metropolitan Museum of Art, New York, Bequest of Monroe C. Gutman, 1974 (photography © Metropolitan Museum of Art, New York)
6.5 Museum für Asiatische Kunst, Staatliche Museen – Stiftung Preussischer Kulturbesitz, Berlin (MIK III- 8383)
6.6 LNS 9 MS, fos 1v–2. Al-Sabah Collection, Dar al-Athar al-Islamiyya, Kuwait
6.7 MS 3655, fo. 97. Bibliothèque royale, Rabat (drawing © Y. Kadoi)
6.8 LNS 59 MS. Al-Sabah Collection, Dar al-Athar al-Islamiyya, Kuwait
6.9 Diez A, Fol. 71.S43.N6. Staatsbibliothek zu Berlin – Stiftung Preussischer Kulturbesitz, Orientabteilung, Berlin
6.11 Diez A, Fol. 71.S10. Staatsbibliothek zu Berlin – Stiftung Preussischer Kulturbesitz, Orientabteilung, Berlin
6.12 Hazine 2153, fo. 68. Topkapı Saray Museum, Istanbul
6.13 Diez A, Fol. 71. S28. N1. Staatsbibliothek zu Berlin – Stiftung Preussischer Kulturbesitz, Orientabteilung, Berlin
6.14 Photograph © Y. Kadoi
6.15 541, fo. 9. Türk ve Islam Eserleri Müzesi, Istanbul
6.16 Is 1470, fos 1v–2. The Trustees of the Chester Beatty Library, Dublin

Index

Note: figure numbers are indicated in bold at the end of an entry